WHO MURDERED CHAUCER?

TERRY JONES is the author of several acclaimed works on the Middle Ages including *Chaucer's Knight*, *Crusades* and children's books such as *The Knight and the Squire*. A former member of Monty Python, he lives in London.

TERRY DOLAN is Professor of English at University College, Dublin, and a lexicographer and broadcaster.

JULIETTE DOR is Professor of Medieval English Literature at the University of Liège.

ALAN FLETCHER is a lecturer in Medieval English Literature at University College, Dublin.

ROBERT F. YEAGER teaches Old and Middle English Literature at the University of West Florida.

Who Murdered

Chaucer?

A MEDIEVAL MYSTERY

Terry Jones   Robert Yeager   Terry Dolan   Alan Fletcher   Juliette Dor

METHUEN

First published in hardback in Great Britain in 2003
by Methuen Publishing Ltd
215 Vauxhall Bridge Road
London SW1V 1EJ
www.methuen.co.uk

Paperback edition first published 2004

3 5 7 9 10 8 6 4 2

Copyright © Terry Jones, Terry Dolan, Juliette Dor,
Alan Fletcher and Robert F. Yeager, 2003, 2004

Terry Jones, Terry Dolan, Juliette Dor,
Alan Fletcher and Robert F. Yeager
have asserted their right to be identified
as the authors of this work

Hardback ISBN 0 413 75910 5

Paperback ISBN 0 413 75920 2

A CIP catalogue record for this book is available from the British Library

Methuen Publishing Limited Reg. No. 3543167

Acknowledgement for use of illustrations is given on pp. 407–8,
which constitute an extension of this copyright page

Design, setting, layout and reprographics
by Butler and Tanner Limited, Frome and London
www.butlerandtanner.com

Printed by New Era Printing Co. Ltd, Hong Kong

CONTENTS

How this book came about

The idea for *Who Murdered Chaucer?* had been floating around in my head for about thirty years, but I kept putting it off because I thought I'd never find the time to research and write it.

Then, in 1997, Helen Cooper invited me to do the closing session for the New Chaucer Society Congress in Paris. I happened to be visiting my old friend Terry Dolan at University College, Dublin, and when I told him of the invitation and that I had this vague idea of giving a talk on 'Who Murdered Chaucer?', Terry immediately suggested that instead of a talk we should stage a coroner's inquest on Chaucer's death.

Terry then proceeded to organize the event, bringing in Alan Fletcher and Juliette Dor as expert witnesses, while I brought in Bob Yeager with whom I'd already discussed some of the ideas. Terry took the role of coroner and I was Chief Accuser.

The Inquest took place at the Sorbonne at 6 p.m. on 20 July 1998.

It seemed obvious to all of us that we'd touched on a fascinating area, and that we needed to carry out more research and produce a book. We divided the research into areas of expertise or interest and produced individual essays, which I then worked into a whole.

I am much indebted to my co-authors for their indulgence towards me and the good-nature and tolerance they have shown throughout this project. Without their enthusiasm and expertise this book would never have come into being.

We hope the end result will provoke debate and stimulate further study that will shed more light on this rather shady corner of history.

TERRY JONES
1 August 2003

ACKNOWLEDGEMENTS

We would like to thank in particular Nigel Saul for being so generous and magnanimous with his time and advice, and for reading the manuscript so quickly and for his corrections and suggestions. Our thanks are also due to Andrew Prescott for checking the manuscript and for his advice and corrections. A very big thank you to Mary Robertson, Chief Librarian at the Huntington Library in California for all her help on the Ellesmere pictures. We are also indebted to Estelle Stubbs for all her help on the Hengwrt MS and to N.F. Blake for showing Terry round the Canterbury Tales Project at Sheffield. We would also like to thank Caroline Barron, Chris Given-Wilson, David Wallace, Paul Strohm, Gervase Rosser, Jill Mann and Christopher Starr for all their help, encouragement and debate. Thanks also to Lee and Annabel Patterson for pointing out the similarity in the three scallops motif in the Hawkwood portrait in the Duomo and the Ellesmere. Many thanks too to Christine Reynolds for her help on Richard II's epitaph, and finally to Helen Cooper, without whose invitation to the 1998 Chaucer Congress this book wouldn't have happened.

INTRODUCTION

The suspicious circumstances of Chaucer's death

This book is less of a Whodunnit? than a Wasitdunnatall?

Murderers – particularly political murderers – tend to be a reticent lot, and generally try not to commemorate their handiwork if they can possibly help it.

Besides, over a period of time evidence gets lost or tampered with, witnesses disappear or die, and the trail all too often goes cold. Many would consider it unsafe to try to convict someone for an offence committed more than fifty years ago, and the murder we are investigating here (if indeed it happened at all) took place 600 years ago.

Inevitably much of what follows is speculation. The evidence is mostly circumstantial, and we have to admit that we shall probably never really know the truth.

So why bother? Why ask an unanswerable question?

Well, as Douglas Adams pointed out some years ago in *The Hitch-Hikers' Guide to the Galaxy*, sometimes the questions can be more interesting than the answers. In the Adams example, the answer to Life, the Universe and Everything was 42. The trouble in *The Hitch-Hikers' Guide to the Galaxy* was that everyone had forgotten what the question was. In this book we are lucky enough to have the questions – plenty of them – even if we don't arrive at any conclusive answers. The questions we shall be asking will unlock a Pandora's box of historical detail and interpretation that challenges the way we perceive this moment in history.

In the first place, asking the question 'Who murdered Chaucer?' forces us to look at the year 1400 with a more critical eye. Forget the traditional image of a Happy England overjoyed to see the tyrannical Richard II gone and the throne occupied by the popular and pious Henry IV. That is the stuff of propaganda. That is what Henry and his coterie wanted us to believe. It is a long way from the truth.

The usurpation by Henry of Richard's throne in 1399 is probably one of the darkest moments in English history. Dark in both senses of the word. It is dark because it is hidden. Henry took great care to destroy the record and to leave behind only flattering accounts of his illegal seizure of the throne. It is also dark because it was a moment when the intellectual skies of England clouded over.

During the previous thirty years, England had enjoyed a period when almost anything could be thought and written, when almost any intellectual line could be pursued, when there were few limits to the questioning of fundamental issues: whether about civil society or religious belief. In 1399, almost overnight, the country passed into an age of iron control, of Thought Police and of intellectual straitjacketing on a level that has never been equalled before or since in this country. It was as if the nation had passed from the Permissive Sixties straight into Stalin's Russia.

In the second place, asking the question 'Who murdered Chaucer?' forces us to take a fresh look at one of our greatest poets. Geoffrey Chaucer – as possible victim – appears curiously different from Geoffrey Chaucer the Father of the English Language. His writing transmutes from 'Literature' into evidence – evidence of a man in a historical moment, when life-and-death considerations were daily bread. To speculate that he might have met with an untimely end, like so many of his friends and acquaintances, and to then ask: 'Who did it?' involves reassessing Chaucer's impact on his world and the enemies he might have made.

It helps us to see Chaucer as someone very different from the aloof, courtly poet, whose writing deftly skates across the current issues of his day with scarcely a trace or comment. He metamorphoses into a very much more political animal, whose work was inextricably bound into the political and social web of his age.

CHAUCER IS DEAD

The one incontrovertible fact we have is that Chaucer is dead. John Lydgate, a Monk of Bury St Edmunds, writing comparatively soon after the event, tells us so:

> Chaucer is dead that had such a name
> Of fair making [poetry] ...[1]

And so does Thomas Hoccleve, a minor civil servant in the court of Henry IV:

> Alas my father from the world is gone!
> My worthy master Chaucer ...[2]

But otherwise we know nothing at all about his death. Sometime in 1400 Chaucer's name disappears from the record, and that's it. We don't know how he died, where he died, or when he died. There is no official documentation of his death. No chronicle mentions it. There is no notice of his funeral or burial, and eighty years later, his publisher clearly thought the poet's grave was insufficient for so illustrious a man. Chaucer left no will and there is nothing to tell us what happened to his estate. Total silence. For such a famous man, isn't that a bit odd?

But perhaps the oddest thing of all is that no one ever seems to have asked the obvious question: what really happened to Chaucer? Why should we assume that he faded peacefully into eternity?

A FAMOUS MAN

Let's be quite clear just who it is we are talking about. We are not dealing with a serf or some petty merchant in a provincial town or even a minor poet living in obscurity. We are talking about Geoffrey Chaucer – *the* Geoffrey Chaucer!

Chaucer was a public man of affairs. He had held important offices: he had been a Justice of the Peace; a Knight of the Shire (another name for a member of the House of Commons). He had been Clerk of the Works at Westminster, the Tower of London and elsewhere. He had been Commissioner of Embankments and Ditches. And he had also been Controller of the Wool Custom and Wool Subsidy (one of the king's main sources of income) and he acted as spy and diplomat for both Edward III and Richard II. He was also extremely well connected: through his wife Philippa, he was brother-in-law to John of Gaunt – the most powerful man in the kingdom.

More importantly, however, he was one of the most prominent members of his society – one might even say the intellectual superstar of his time. He was certainly celebrated by his contemporaries as their greatest living poet, rhetorician and scholar.

Chaucer must have been in his late forties when Thomas Usk (who was beheaded in 1388) praised him as: 'the noble, learned poet in English ...' who 'in wisdom and in soundness of judgement ... passes all other poets'.[3] A few years earlier, the French poet Eustache Deschamps had gone into hyperbolic overdrive – calling Chaucer: 'Socrates, Ovid, god of earthly love in Albion, High poet, glory of the esquires and Great Translator!' By the 1390s John Gower tells us that 'the land is filled throughout' with Chaucer's songs and writings.[4] Even Chaucer himself refers to his own fame and prolific output, when he has the

Man of Law apologize for not being able to come up with a suitable tale that Chaucer has not already told, for, the Man of Law says, 'as knoweth many a man' if Chaucer has not told them in one book, 'he's told them in another'.[5]

It seems that Chaucer's work was famous and being widely read during his lifetime, and that Chaucer knew it was and wanted future readers to know it was.

In recent years, however, some scholars have cast doubt on just how widely Chaucer was, in fact, read. There is a consensus of opinion that he wrote primarily for a small coterie of professional men who, like himself, came from the lesser gentry. There is little evidence to connect him, it is claimed, with the aristocracy, the king, or even a wider reading public. There are, for example, no records of payments to the poet for works commissioned and little in the way of public dedication of his works to royal or aristocratic patrons.

The arguments are compelling and have won a substantial degree of agreement amongst scholars. We shall argue, none the less, that the poets of Richard's court aspired to be seen as members of the gentry rather than as professional performers, and direct payment for their literary endeavours was something that the 'gentlemen-poets' may therefore have wished to avoid.

The other main argument against Chaucer's popularity during his lifetime is based upon the lack of Chaucerian manuscripts recorded in wills and inventories and the lack of manuscripts dating from his lifetime. Again this argument is in many ways persuasive, but it fails to take into account one possibility which has never hitherto been considered, as far as we know. That is the possibility that Chaucer's manuscripts were deliberately destroyed by the usurping regime of Henry IV.

If Chaucer were a has-been when he died, that is not how his fellow poets remembered him a decade later. Of course the poets of Henry IV's and Henry V's time had their own political agenda to address (as we shall see), but their testimony is in no way invalidated by this. Indeed, the fact that a later regime felt the need to resuscitate Chaucer's reputation is in itself testimony to how important that reputation had once been.

Thomas Hoccleve noted that Chaucer's works were known and loved all over England:

> With books of his ornate writing
> That is to all this land illuminating.[6]

For Hoccleve, Chaucer was 'the flower of eloquence, universal father in science, the first finder of our fair language' and even the heir apparent 'to Aristotle in our tongue'.[7] This fame was not confined to a small coterie in London – it spread throughout the kingdom. Chaucer was, according to Lydgate: 'Flower of Poets throughout all Britain'.[8]

This was no mere poetic conceit. In another poem, Lydgate makes it clear that he expects Chaucer's *Troilus and Criseyde* to be available in borough, town, village and city and accessible both to lay people (who are free to move about the country) and to monks (shut up in their cloisters):

> And in this land if there be any
> In borough or town, village or city,
> That has enough learning to follow in his tracks
> Whether he can travel about or is shut in a cloister
> To him I give this piece of advice:
> Make an inspection of this book [*Troilus and Criseyde*].[9]
>   *Troy Book*, V, ll. 3531–6

Lydgate is insistent that it is Chaucer who has established the current reputation of the English language:

> Till Chaucer came and through his poetry
> First began to enlarge our language
> And adorn it with his eloquence
> To whom honour and praise and reverence
> Throughout this land be given and sung,
> So that the laurels of our English tongue
> Be given to him for his excellence.[10]
>   *Troy Book*, III, ll. 4541–7

How could the death of such a man have gone unrecorded? How could he have just disappeared from the record, without documentation, without notice – *unless a quiet disappearance was precisely what someone wanted?*

CHAUCER'S AGE

Chaucer certainly didn't seem to have been expecting to die in December 1399, for in that month he took out a 53-year lease on a house in the garden of the Lady Chapel of Westminster Abbey. Now, of course, he wasn't expecting to live for another 53 years either, but it is not the act of a man at death's door.

Chaucer's twentieth-century biographers picture him at the end of his life as an old man in declining health. Derek Pearsall writes simply: 'He was most probably in failing health ...', whilst John Gardner goes imaginatively over the top: 'Geoffrey Chaucer, his body wasted, his eyes half blind, his voice like an adder's, old Grim Death shaming him like an old smell of catshit in the house ...' Derek Brewer sees him as 'an old tired man' and goes on: 'I do not imagine a panic-stricken deathbed, but an open-eyed calmness, sincere repentance, religious meditation, and suffering patiently born.'[11]

But this is all pure speculation. There is no real evidence for Chaucer being either ailing or old. It is true that on one occasion he refers to himself as 'grey and chubby' and on another tells us that age has dulled his wits and bereft his writing of any subtlety, but these are conventional forms and written with the tongue in the cheek. The fact is that when he disappeared from the record, Chaucer was 59 or 60. We cannot simply assume he was old and infirm.[12]

It is a fallacy that people at that time didn't expect to live as long as we expect to today. *Average* life expectancy was lower than it is now (mainly because of infant mortality) but if you survived into mid-life, you could expect to see out your three score years and ten just as you could in biblical times. Many of Chaucer's fellow writers did exactly that: Gower lived to 83, Petrarch to 70, Guillaume de Machaut to 72, Deschamps to 68, Froissart to 67, Thomas Hoccleve probably to 70 and John Trevisa to 86. And these are just the writers!

In his last few months or weeks, Chaucer might well have been living in mortal fear (as we shall argue later), but he doesn't appear to be have been expecting to die from natural causes just then. On the contrary, according to *Chaucer Life-Records*, it is possible that Chaucer paid a visit to Calais early in 1400 – hardly the act of an ailing old man.[13]

Of course, he may have simply had a sudden heart attack or he may have fallen off a ladder, but both are mere assumptions – neither more nor less likely than the hypotheses that he was ill or that he was quietly put out of the way.

And when we look at his disappearance in the context of the political upheavals of the times, the suspicion that he might have met a sticky end begins to carry some weight. In 1387, thirteen years before his disappearance, he had barely survived the rebellion by the great magnates against Richard II. He survived then by keeping a low profile and staying away from the court. Other writers and recipients of court favours similar to Chaucer were less lucky and ended with their heads on the block, or worse. 'Worse' is exactly what happened to Chaucer's admirer Thomas Usk: in 1388, he was dragged from the Tower, hanged and then beheaded and his head stuck up on a pole above the gate of Newgate 'because his family lived in the part of the city'. Nice for them![14]

The coup of 1399 was even more dangerous to a man like Chaucer than the revolt of 1387–8 had been. We shouldn't be surprised if Chaucer didn't survive the events of 1399–1400. We should be surprised if he *did*!

FROM FRYING PAN TO FIRE

If Richard's reign had seemed like a very hot frying pan, with faction and revolt sizzling and spitting in all directions, the usurpation of Henry brought the fire – quite literally if you happened to be a heretic.

The dramatic events of 1399 changed for ever the social and intellectual landscape that would have been familiar to Geoffrey Chaucer. In those early months after Henry seized the throne, the very fabric of society changed, and Chaucer would have found himself suddenly caught up in an environment that was no longer friendly to his world-view nor to his literary output.

To understand what this would have meant to the poet, and to understand the implications for his life and safety, we need to go back to the period in which his literary genius had flourished. We need to start by reassessing the reign of Richard II, the character of the king, and the place of Chaucer himself within that court society.

CHAPTER I

The court that Chaucer lived in

≈

RICHARD AND PEACE

In 1401–2, a young Frenchman who had been a squire in the retinue of Richard II, and therefore well placed to observe matters of the court, recorded his opinion about Richard's downfall in 1399: 'In truth,' wrote Jean Creton, 'the only reason why he was deposed and betrayed, was because he loyally loved his father-in-law the king of France with a love as true and sincere as any man alive. That was the root of the problem, and the cause of the envy – although they charged him with having evilly caused the deaths of the dukes his uncles, and of being neither prudent nor wise enough to govern the realm.'[1]

What Richard actually thought about his French father-in-law is anybody's guess, but what is certain is that he had married the 7-year-old Isabel for the clear purpose of consolidating the peace between their two countries. It was a peace for which Richard had been working most of his reign.

In fact, the pursuit of peace is one of the most remarkable and yet least celebrated characteristics of Richard's rule. It may also have been, as the squire Jean Creton hinted, his undoing.

English and French arms united.

Richard's father, the Black Prince, had been a famous warrior, who from the day of his birth had 'cherished no thought but loyalty, nobleness, valour, and goodness, and was endued with prowess'.[2] He was 'the most valiant prince in all the world ... since the time of Charlemagne, Julius Caesar, or Arthur'.[3] The words are those of the Black Prince's chief eulogist: an anonymous herald in the retinue of Sir John Chandos, but they pretty much echoed the popular view of the prince. It was a daunting reputation for his son to live up to. It seems that

Richard didn't try. Like so many sons with a famous father, he chose – or was drawn to – an alternative lifestyle, and, as king, he tried to establish a different ethos at court.

The court of the Black Prince at Bordeaux had been permanently geared for war. So had the court of Richard's grandfather, Edward III. Both had been characterized by military games and chivalric culture. 'Prowess' (or military skill) seems to have been a determining factor in the status of their courtiers, and jousts were essential to the training of knights for war.[4]

Richard II, on the other hand, seems to have had no relish for war *per se*. He certainly encouraged the arts of chivalry and took an interest in tournaments and pageantry. Indeed, on the continent he was hailed as a representative of chivalry not only by Jean Creton, but as well by the chronicler of St Denys and that most impressive of medieval blue-stockings, Christine de Pisan, who even went so far as to call him 'a true Lancelot':

> A chevalier wearing a crown
> In a place near the sea ...
> Willingly he was praised
> For being valiant, a true Lancelot ...[5]

Of course, these may have been no more than conventional pieties; references to royal jousting in Richard's reign are far fewer than in his grandfather's, and it may be that he saw chivalry as a political tool, and not as an end in itself. Richard's interest in chivalric activities may well have been simply another aspect of his cultivation of the craft of kingship. Knights undoubtedly had to be encouraged in their knightly pursuits; to have done otherwise would have been folly for the prudent ruler. Chivalry was the fashion – it had become the standard mode of communication for the modern European court. 'Courts in every part of the continent became more formal, and more formally organized. Ambitious rulers presented themselves as patrons of letters and exemplars of chivalry and courtesy.'[6]

Besides, the pageantry and glamour of the tournament provided a ready-made opportunity for staging displays of power which could only help assert the central role of the crown.

But, when the chips were down, Richard's was a civilian court, and tournaments were seen as an *alternative* to war not a prelude.[7] As far as we know, Richard never jousted personally, and he appears to have had a genuine distaste for the spilling of Christian blood.[8] From the moment Richard took over personal control of the government in 1389, the pursuit of peace with France became a priority.

On a theoretical level, this shouldn't have come as a shock. Peace was seen by many influential thinkers of the day as an ideal of kingship and the desire for peace as the mark of a just ruler.

For example, the Italian theologian and philosopher Giles of Rome (1245–1316) taught that a true king desires peace and is not tempted to conquest. We know that Richard's education included the works of Giles – and Giles was not alone in his opinion. He was supported by Dante, and the writings of other Italian political theorists such

In 1396 a 28-year truce with France was announced.

as Marsilius of Padua, who was Rector of the University of Paris from 1312 to 1313. Chaucer, too, notes that it is the mark of a tyrant to delight in war and that it is always preferable to pursue policies of peace.[9]

The peace policy most probably expressed Richard's own inclination. It could, however, also have been the brainchild of his advisers, like Sir Simon Burley, or of John of Gaunt, who 'had the insight, rare among Englishmen of the time, to favor a realistic settlement with France'.[10] In any case, peace with France remained the objective of royal policy until the end of Richard's reign.

This was a quite extraordinary achievement, and it should not be surprising if it made Richard enemies.

HAWKS *VERSUS* DOVES

England had been at war with its neighbour almost continuously since 1337, and for many the habit was hard to break. As one historian writes: 'Gaunt and others close to Richard may well have shared his pacifist concerns but the country as a whole may have found it hard to abandon attitudes and expectations which had developed over two generations.'[11] The chronicler Froissart tells us that the king's policy of peace towards France did not make him popular at home.[12]

There were at least three members of the nobility who did not share Richard's 'pacifist concerns': his uncle Thomas of Woodstock, Duke of Gloucester, Thomas

Beauchamp, Earl of Warwick and Richard Fitzalan, Earl of Arundel. These three were the constant thorn in Richard's side throughout his minority and indeed throughout most of his rule. In 1398, writing to the Emperor Manuel Palaeologus, Richard complained of 'their rebellion and wantonness' and of the public humiliation he had been forced to endure at their hands for so long:

> You know, what I believe is notorious enough throughout all quarters of the world, how some of our subject magnates and nobles, while we were yet of tender age and afterwards also, have made many attempts on the prerogative and royal right of our regal state, and have wickedly directed their malevolence even against our person.[13]

Gloucester had many pressing reasons why he wished to remain at war with France, and none of them were to do with the good of the country as a whole. As the seventh and youngest son of Edward III, he suffered from that terrible, though familiar, debility – a lack of means. There he was: of royal blood and yet without the property or income to support himself in the manner in which he wished to become accustomed.

Thomas, Duke of Gloucester.

When his father died in 1377, Thomas, as Earl of Buckingham, was left no territorial endowment. The only lands he possessed were those of his wife. At his nephew's coronation, he had been raised to the estate of earl and granted an annuity of £1,000 per year, but this annuity was to prove a trifle elusive. 'To a degree exceptional for a royal duke, Gloucester was dependent for his income on exchequer goodwill; and when the exchequer was hard pressed for cash ... so too was the Duke.'[14]

In fact, the war with France was Gloucester's chief and brightest hope, not only for increasing his wealth but also for increasing his influence generally. As a military leader he could offer the gentry opportunities for fame, glory and profit in battle – but only while there was a war to be fought. Without war, his 'affinity' (or circle of influence) could not expand.[15]

His two confederates, the Earls of Warwick and Arundel, were also hawks opposed to the doves of Richard's court. As soon as these three seized power, in 1387, they threw out peace as a policy-objective, and reinstated the war. Arundel mobilized an expedition and public money was once again poured into the devastation of France.

There were also other magnates who would have
felt the pinch of peace. Peace with France brought
in its wake a truce with Scotland, and this meant a
reduction in the £3,000 a year that the Percy family
received for keeping watch over the East March.[16]
It is no wonder that the head of that family – the
Earl of Northumberland – spoke out in support of
the Lords Appellant (the name conveniently given
by historians to the revolting barons of 1387) when
they arrived in London.[17]

Gloucester, Arundel and Warwick's opposition to
Richard – or, rather, their antagonism to Richard –
was thus based upon a strong difference of policy.

*Thomas Beauchamp, Earl of
Warwick and his countess.*

But there was also something more to it – something
more personal. As with the hawks *versus* doves arguments of today, the differences
of policy went hand-in-hand with a hearty distaste for each other's lifestyles.

Gloucester, Arundel and Warwick were pretty rough customers – they were the
'embittered older generation of the nobility'.[18] Gloucester was highly literate but
he was also a 'rough, ruthless, and self-confident man' who 'had been a prominent enemy of the court from the first, and had brutally threatened his nephew,
the king, in 1386 with the fate of Edward II ... Richard, Earl of Arundel, was if
anything coarser and more ruthless. His life is punctuated with violent quar-
rels.'[19] Judging by his behaviour, as reported in the chronicles, Arundel had an
aggressive streak a mile wide. He was also someone who knew how to nurse a
hatred. Warwick seems to have been a rather tetchy, vigorous man, and perhaps
not overbright.

They were men who revelled in military society, and they must have been pretty
contemptuous of the new-style court of the 1380s. As Richard grew to maturity he
showed increasing signs of refinement and sensitivity and his court 'assumes a
rather precious, even effete, character'. It is the court of Venus rather than of Bellona,
comments the hawkish chronicler Thomas Walsingham, with evident disgust.[20]

The magnates were also ambitious and ruthless. 1387 was nothing less than an
armed rebellion. The triumvirate of Gloucester, Arundel and Warwick, joined
for the occasion by Henry of Derby (the future usurper) and others, imposed
their will on Richard and promoted their own relatives and friends. According
to one chronicle, it was only the fact that Gloucester and Henry of Derby squab-
bled amongst themselves about who was to take over as king that saved Richard
from being deposed in 1387.[21]

Of course the rebellious barons' complaints against the government of the realm, as recorded by the chroniclers, concentrate on the presence of evil counsellors surrounding the king, but this is scarcely surprising. To attack the king himself would have been treason. To attack the king's advisers was a convenient fiction – a way of side-stepping the main charge of treason whilst maintaining the pretence of loyalty to the crown: 'We're doing this for your own good, sire!'

And they showed no mercy.

In the aptly named Merciless Parliament of 1388, Gloucester, Arundel and Warwick ruthlessly eliminated Richard's associates. Perhaps most shameful – and hardest to understand – was the execution of the king's old tutor, Sir Simon Burley. Passions certainly ran high on the subject. The Westminster Chronicler describes how Gloucester nearly came to blows with his brother, the Duke of York, on the floor of parliament. York rose in full parliament offering to defend Sir Simon Burley in personal combat if need be, whereupon Gloucester retorted that he would prove Burley had been false in his allegiance 'with his own sword-arm and without multiplying arguments. At this the Duke of York turned white with anger and told his brother to his face that he was a liar, only to receive a prompt retort in kind from the Duke of Gloucester; and after this exchange they would have hurled themselves upon each other had not the king with characteristic mildness and good-will, been quick to calm them down.'[22]

Even when the king himself and the queen went down on their bended knees to beg for mercy for the old man, Gloucester showed his ultimate remorselessness and refused to listen.[23] Burley was beheaded despite all protest – perhaps an indication that he was seen as either the architect of the peace process or else as a disseminator of dangerous ideas.

It's scarcely surprising that Richard didn't get on with these bellicose barons. Their aims and tastes were poles apart. Richard simply 'was not "one of the lads" in a way that Edward I or Edward III had been, nor as Henry IV and Henry V were to be later ...'[24] He was trying to change the English court from a war culture to a peace culture. This was, according to the Westminster chronicler, one of the chief reasons for the barons' rebellion:

In common with his council the king ... thought it better to secure a short breathing-space from the tumult of strife in that quarter than to be harassed by the unending troubles of war. Although it came to nothing, it was nevertheless this project (with other matters ...) that formed a reason for the lords' rising.[25]

To offer men like Gloucester and Arundel tournaments with blunted weapons instead of real-life *chevauchées* into France was like asking Attila the Hun to settle down to a nice game of draughts and a cup of tea. Even the royal military expeditions that Richard did undertake had peace as their aim rather than the celebration of war.

THE ARGUMENT FOR PEACE

Richard (or whoever was directing court policy at this time) was determined to have peace, but his (or their) reasons were not necessarily idealistic or pacifist. Peace made economic sense.

The coffers of England had been emptied by the continual war against the French. What is more, the returns from that war had been diminishing. In the early days, Edward III had hit the jackpot with great victories like Crécy, Calais and Poitiers. But as the years went by the exorbitant expense and the lack of anything to show for it had taken some of the gilt off the whole enterprise.

Possibly the Peasants' Revolt of 1381 helped to concentrate people's minds on the fact that since 1377 a staggering £250,000 had disappeared into the military coffers with precious little to show for it. A lot of it had gone to finance the exploits of Gloucester and John of Gaunt in the name of chivalry. But the English crown had seen no conquests, no extension of territory and no guarantee of future safety. The shock of the Peasants' Revolt probably produced a more sensible attitude to relations with France. Quite simply, England could not afford to remain at war.

What is more, Charles V of France (1364–80) was achieving a greater success rate in challenging the English armies than had his predecessors, and he was ably backed up by his captains: du Guesclin, Olivier de Clisson and Jean de Vienne.[26]

And what if critics condemned the expense of the pageantry of peace? When Richard received his child-bride from the king of France, the rather over-the-top celebrations at Calais cost between £10,000 and £15,000 – a fortune! But this could be offset against the gains of peace – simply giving up the barbican towns of Cherbourg and Brest saved an outlay of that magnitude every year![27]

Part of the reasoning behind Richard's policy of peace with France may thus have been economic. As the Westminster Chronicler pointed out: the king, in order 'to maintain a ceaseless state of war against the king of the French, would

Richard II receives his 7-year-old bride, Isobel of France.

inevitably be compelled to be forever burdening his people with new imposts, with damaging results for himself'.[28]

Some scholars have imputed other motives to Richard. It has been suggested that, in seeking to establish an authoritarian monarchy free of all constraints, Richard was striving to be less dependent on parliament. Peace with France meant that his government would no longer be running to the Commons for ever-greater grants to finance the war. In other words, the argument goes, Richard's desire for peace went hand-in-glove with his absolutist ambitions.

But it is also possible that the main drive behind Richard's quest for peace came from his own character and his own particular range of interests, and there is no doubt that these interests revolved to a large degree around the court.

The 'peace dividend' would have been useful to any fourteenth-century monarch who wished to run an up-to-date court in the modern style, because the modern style was expensive. In the new international culture of the 1380s, war and militarism may have seemed a trifle *passé*.

THE INTERNATIONAL COURT CULTURE

The long-pointed shoes that became so fashionable in Richard II's court were called 'pykes' or sometimes 'cracowes'. The fashion had been imported from

Bohemia by Richard's Queen Anne and the name, of course, came from Cracow in Poland. Everywhere you looked in the court you would have seen and heard echoes of the other great courts throughout Europe, and the scale of this internationalism would perhaps be one of the most surprising things for a modern observer visiting the late fourteenth century.[29]

Indeed, it would have surprised observers from previous centuries just as much, or more. For the fact is that the courts of kings were undergoing a profound change throughout the fourteenth century. From extended family gatherings, the immediate households of rulers everywhere were taking on grander significance. In particular, the courts of Europe were becoming thoroughly cosmopolitan.

Opinion is divided as to where the new international court culture of Europe originated, but whether it was with Robert of Anjou's court in Naples (1309–43) or three-quarters of a century earlier with the Emperor Frederick II's court in Sicily, the fashion for internationalism spread through Europe like wildfire. One recent historian claims that the surprising amount of interchange between courts meant that fashions and styles spread with 'a near synchronism'. By the time Richard ascended the throne, no self-respecting monarch who wanted to cut a figure on the international scene could ignore the current mode.[30]

The new-style courts were larger than those of earlier monarchs and correspondingly more expensive to keep up. They revolved around fashion, and fashion – *A cracowe.*
just as it is now – was always changing. The great households of the country barons may have been sometimes tolerant of things *passé,* but the king's court demanded constant, up-to-the-minute chic in almost every walk of life.

A significant aspect of the fourteenth-century courts was the degree to which they were a reflection of the personal tastes of the king: 'It was perhaps a mark of the new courts that they centred not so much on the *power* as on the *preferences* of the monarch.'[31]

Both Robert of Anjou and Frederick II had been learned men. Frederick spoke six languages and fostered the activities of writers, scholars and lawmen. Robert was himself a great 'clerk' (a learned man), and he was the patron of Petrarch and Boccaccio. They established a culture of literature, science and the liberal arts as the mark of the modern, sophisticated ruler.

England may have been a trifle late in jumping onto this international band-wagon, but it enabled Chaucer to observe at first hand the conversion of the old-style military court of Edward III into the new, fashionable culture. Suddenly war games were out and literature, music, painting, jewel-work and all the other arts were in.

Perhaps the value placed on the attendance of women at the newly fashionable courts encouraged these sensibilities and modified the martial character of earlier royal milieux. Relationships between the sexes appear to have become more relaxed, and no doubt this accounts in some degree for the impor-tance attached to dress and music and dancing.

Ideal fourteenth-century courtiers were expected not only to be good listeners and critics of music and song but to be performers as well, as proficient in singing as in dancing. In fact, if they were dancing a 'carol' they would actually sing at the same time as they danced. It must have been a charming scene, with   *A 'carol' in a garden.*
courtiers moving about the hall in what we would nowadays think of as a 'country dance' – singing together, perhaps sometimes the men taking one part and sometimes the ladies. In the days before amplified music, the 'carol' must have been as rousing as it got.

One of the many fashions promoted by the international court culture of fourteenth-century Europe was the cultivation of literature written in the ver-nacular of that particular country. It was seen as part of the prestige of the prince to possess, in addition to his lands, his own literary territory.

This was the novel context in which Chaucer found himself at the very moment when he began to flex his muscles as a writer. It was an opportunity that Chaucer embraced with both hands.

CHAPTER 2

Chaucer and Richard II

∽

Chaucer would have witnessed a sea change in the culture of the court: from the military preoccupations of Edward III's court to the peace-motivated era of Richard II. The greater emphasis on artistic pursuits and intellectual speculation was to a certain extent the result of deliberate royal policy. Some of the change, however, was part of a general evolution that was taking place across Europe. In either event, the culture of the English court, in the last quarter of the fourteenth century, reinvented itself in a way that was to profoundly affect Chaucer's literary work.

THE SILENCING OF THE MINSTRELS

One change in fashion which was to have a tremendous effect on the intellectual landscape of the late fourteenth century was the decline of the professional minstrel. The all-round entertainers who combined singing, reciting, musicianship and sometimes even acrobatics enjoyed their heyday in the thirteenth century; by the fourteenth century, at court the term 'minstrel' had begun 'to lose its literary connotations and to take on the sense of a mere popular entertainer, generally a musician'.[1] Performers such as musicians, singers and acrobats became more spe-cialized and more down-market. At the same time, poets and authors – the 'makirs' of the medieval court – moved up-market.

The minstrel who recited or sang a well-known poem from memory became outmoded in the new court culture. The modern monarch wished to establish his own tastes and his own reputation as a man of letters. He needed to stake out his own intellectual territory as clearly as he did the boundaries of his state, and

this he did by commissioning new works from highly accomplished and intellectual writers whom he often retained in his circle.

When Robert of Anjou encouraged a young poet by the name of Boccaccio, he was displaying his own impeccable taste. Richard's Queen Anne of Bohemia had a father who had been a patron of the internationally acclaimed writer  Petrarch; her uncle was a poet himself and a patron of the French poet, Eustache Deschamps. Her grandfather had been 'the rather negligent patron of Dante'.[2] Meanwhile in France, King John II (1350–64) sought to project a new image of sophistication and culture by hiring writers and artists – like the poet-composer Guillaume de Machaut – who had already entertained the households of John of Luxembourg, Charles of Navarre and Pierre de Lusignan. Even the *nouveau-*

Minstrels were often acrobats and jugglers too.

riche princes of northern Italy – the 'tyrants of Lombardy', as Chaucer calls them – sought to raise their prestige through association with men of letters. Bernabò Visconti, for example, enticed Petrarch to reside in Milan in 1353, where he stayed (to his shame) for some years.

The travelling minstrels who rattled off traditional pieces that they had committed to memory long ago, must have begun to appear dog-eared and *passé*. Eustache Deschamps was very sniffy about them. The minstrels' performance, he tells us in his *Art du Dictier,* could be learnt by 'the most uncouth man in the world'.[3] And Chaucer himself mocks the popular romances memorized by the minstrels: in his persona as the pilgrim 'Geoffrey' in *The Canterbury Tales*, he confesses to Harry Bailey, the host, that he only knows one tale – *The Tale of Sir Thopas* – and it is a poem he has committed to memory a long time ago ('a ryme I lerned longe agoon'). But he gets no further than the beginning of the third 'fit' before Harry Bailey cuts him off, and delivers what may well be Chaucer's personal estimate of the professional minstrel's art – or, at least, the view that was then fashionable amongst the sophisticates of the court:

> 'Namoore of this, for Goddes dignitee,'
> Quod oure Hooste, 'for thou makest me
> So wery of they verray lewednesse
> That, also wisly God my soule blesse,
> Myne eres aken of thy drasty speche.

Now swich a rym the devel I biteche!
This may wel be rym dogerel,' quod he.
  The Canterbury Tales, VII, ll. 919–25
'No more of this, for God's dignity,'
Swore our Host, 'for you make me
So weary of your total unlearnedness
That, just as God will bless my soul,
My ears are aching with your dreadful speech.
Now such a rhyme I'll teach the devil!
This may well be doggerel rhyme,' said he.

The court poets of Chaucer's day saw themselves as much more sophisticated. They tried to distance themselves from the journeymen performers of the past – the *jongleurs* and the minstrels. 'Poetry is for delight,' as Petrarch put it, 'and not for necessity like cobbling and baking and the vile mechanic arts.'[4]

Perhaps the situation was a little like what happened in the mid-twentieth century, when the old vaudeville comedians, who had made a living out of a restricted repertoire of hand-me-down material, touring around the various music halls, found themselves displaced by the university-educated satirists of the television age, who wrote their own material – fresh every week.

It is worth noting that, having been 'stinted' of his old-fashioned *The Tale of Sir Thopas*, Chaucer-the-Pilgrim immediately swings to the other end of the spectrum. *The Tale of Melibee*, which he tells to atone for *Sir Thopas*, would probably have been regarded as the pinnacle of the modern 'makir's' art at the time. It is a highbrow example of the 'advice to princes' genre that would have established Chaucer as a serious heavyweight in court circles – not simply an entertaining poet, but an intellectual worthy of consultation by his monarch. You couldn't get much further away from the cheapjack trade of the wandering minstrel.

The contrast between the two tales graphically charts the decline of the old jobbing minstrel, and asserts the ascendancy of the new court poets with their claims to operate at the very centre of state affairs.

HOW BOOKS WERE READ

The new-style courts may have been bright and shining, but they could not stop the sun going down or the long winter nights from drawing in. All they could do was provide the entertainment. Dinner might be about midday, then the royal audience might be held until vespers – which might be as early as 3 o'clock. Dancing and storytelling would follow, and stretch into the hours of darkness until a supper of spiced cakes and wine sent everyone to bed.[5]

Not every court ran to this sort of schedule, however. The great fourteenth-century chronicler Jean Froissart recounts how he entertained the court of the Count of Foix. The count, he tells us, was a 'night person': 'the count's custom was that it was high noon before he arose out of his bed and he always took supper at midnight.'[6] Froissart's portrait of the Count of Foix's dining habits incidentally sheds some light on the question of illumination in the aristocratic household of the fourteenth century. 'At midnight,' Froissart tells us, 'when he came out of his chamber into the hall to supper, he always had before him

Froissart at the court of the Count of Foix.

twelve torches burning, carried by twelve varlets, standing in front of his table all through supper; they gave a great light, and the hall was always full of knights and squires, and many other tables laid out for whoever wished to dine.'[7] So it appears that having twelve torches was an exceptional extravagance, and most halls would have been more modestly lit. Probably to the modern eye they would have been pretty dark.

Froissart describes how he read from his book *Meliador* over a period of ten weeks. The count forbade anyone to talk during the reading, but occasionally would, himself, interrupt to ask questions. Sometimes, the earl would go off to bed during the reading. There are 31,000 lines to the poem which means that Froissart must have read something like 480 lines per night.[8]

Through the long hours of winter darkness, reading aloud was an integral part of court life. It was also the accompaniment to many a meal. In abbeys and monasteries, silence was often the rule at mealtimes, whilst one of the brethren read from some improving text. Christine de Pisan, writing in 1401, implies that it was the norm for aristocratic ladies to be read to during mealtimes.

Reading aloud also went on in the more private areas of the court. The household records of Edward IV, written around 1471, reminisce about the entertainment habits of the previous Edward: 'In the old days, these squires of the household, in winter and summer, in the afternoons and evenings, used to withdraw to the lord's chambers within the court, there to keep honest company according to their understanding, talking about the chronicles of kings or of other "polycyez" (arts of government), or playing the flute or harp or singing, or taking part in other martial sports, to help occupy the court and entertain strangers, until the time came for them to depart.'[9]

The Latin verb *legere,* which meant 'to read', could also be used as a synonym for *dicere,* 'to say': silent reading was the exception, rather than the norm, in Chaucer's time.[10]

In 1395 a huge scandal was caused when a bill was fixed to the doors of Westminster Hall setting out the demands and beliefs of the religious dissenters of the day – the Lollards. In it, under Item 7, the writers refer to 'a bok that the kyng herde'.[11] It was assumed that the king listened to books being read aloud rather than sat and read them silently.

Beata Umilita reading to the Poor Clares.

Even amongst ordinary folk, it seems to have been expected that there would be someone to read aloud to the others. In 1382, when William Courtenay, Archbishop of Canterbury, wanted to make quite sure that nobody in the country could plead ignorance about the beliefs he had condemned as heresies, he ordered his bishops to 'cause true copies of these letters ... to be affixed to the doors of the said Churches, and shall leave them affixed to the extirpation of the aforesaid heresies ... '[12]

In the court, the choice of reader was obviously a crucial matter. It appears to have crossed boundaries of class and vocation. Charles V's favourite reader was his valet, Gilles Malet. Charles the Bold's favourite reader was Guy de Brimeu, lord of Humbercourt – a nobleman-warrior. Sometimes the reader would be a beautiful damoiselle of the court or a handsome young man.[13] A dull book presumably seemed less dull when read aloud by someone of youth and beauty.

But in the fourteenth century, as far as in-court entertainment went, the author-performer was king. It's not hard to imagine the excitement that would be generated in a court where an author was about to read from his own work. For a start there would have been the interest of seeing a famous writer perform. In the Italian courts: Dante (1265–1321), or Boccaccio (1313–75), or Petrarch (1304–74). In France, Eustache Deschamps (1340–1407), Guillaume de Machaut (1305–77) or Froissart (1333–1400). Then again, an author-reading might well herald the 'première' of a new work – something entirely original that no one had ever heard before. The anticipation would have been on a different level from that generated by a well-worn romance recited, for the umpteenth time, by a professional minstrel.

This anticipation may have been all the keener for the fact that the four-teenth-century author-performers almost invariably wrote in the vernacular (Petrarch being the odd man out). In other words, the court would be gathered to hear brand-new works in their own language.

And here perhaps it is worth pointing out that reading aloud was a matter of both habit and choice. It was not a halfway stage between the oral tradition of remembered poetry and the modern habit of silent reading. Reading aloud in a group was seen as the natural and preferred medium for the book. People *chose* to listen in a group for the same reason that nowadays people may prefer to watch a film in the cinema rather than watch a video at home. It is a totally different experience – particularly with a performance that requires some audience participation, such as a comedy. The communal experience was seen as superior to the solitary one.

As one scholar puts it: 'the normal thing to do with a written literary text ... was to perform it ... Reading was a kind of performance. Even the solitary reader most often read aloud ... and most reading was not solitary.'[14]

It is hard to imagine nowadays the extent to which life in the Middle Ages was communal, and the degree to which solitary activity was not something to be aimed for but – on the contrary – something to be pitied. Reading to yourself in silence was probably regarded by most people as a bit odd – possibly something that you would only do for professional reasons.

In *The House of Fame* Chaucer makes fun of himself by having an eagle admonish him for his solitary reading habits. One can almost hear Philippa Chaucer scolding her husband: 'You come back from work! You sit down in front of yet another book! Dumb as any stone! What fun do I get? Eh? Geoffrey! Are you listening?'

For when thy labour doon al ys,
And hast mad alle thy rekenynges,
In stede of reste and newe thynges
Thou goost hom to thy hous anoon,
And, also domb as any stoon,
Thou sittest at another book
Tyl fully daswed ys thy look.
    The House of Fame, ll. 652–8

For when your labour is all done,
And you have finished your accounts,
Instead of rest and entertainment
You go home to your house anon,
And, just as dumb as any stone,
You sit before another book
Till fully dazed is your look!

Real reading – for the majority of people – meant the celebration of a book by its being read aloud in public.[15] In a way it was a simple question of good manners – at a time when books were scarce it would have seemed extraordinarily selfish to devour the contents of one all alone and by yourself.[16]

THE ROLE OF THE POET IN RICHARD II'S COURT

The court of Richard II, in which Chaucer reached his maturity as an artist, was styled in the height of fashion. It was oriented towards the pursuits of peacetime – to art and literature and the pursuit of knowledge. Chivalry was cultivated, but more as a fashion accessory than as a preparation for war. The court fostered music, entertainment, dancing, fashion and feasting, as it turned its back

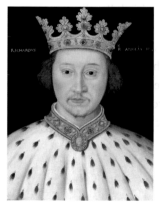

Richard II.

on the bad old days of constant war with France. To men like Gloucester and Arundel, it must have seemed trivial and effeminate. Their personal fortunes were hitched to war and all that arty-farty stuff ran directly counter to their own ambitions.

What was Richard II's contribution to the cultural make-up of his court? And how close were Chaucer's own ties to the King?

Recent historians and Chaucerians have been at pains to distance Richard from the patronage of literature. In a seminal essay, Derek Pearsall proposed that the role of Richard II as a patron of letters had been over-emphasized. Rather than concentrating on the person of the king, Pearsall suggested that we look beyond Richard and his noble entourage 'to the multitude of household knights and officials, career diplomats and civil servants, who constitute the "court" in its wider sense, that is, the national administration and its metropolitan milieu'.[17]

This suggestion has been taken up by a number of distinguished critics, who have suggested that neither Gower nor Chaucer were patronized by the aristocracy. They point out that no reward that Chaucer received can be directly connected with his literary activity. They also make out a case that there was a split between the literary preferences of the aristocracy and some knightly courtiers on one hand, and the tastes of the career diplomats, civil servants, officials and administrators who were attached to the court and government, on the other.[18] It is a hypothesis which has won over many weighty supporters. The historian Nigel Saul, for example, detects 'a division of taste between the middle-ranking officials at court and the higher aristocracy – the former preferring the newer lyric poetry and the latter the more traditional romances and chivalric works'.[19]

The argument, however, may be flawed.

To distinguish the literary tastes of the aristocracy and knightly courtiers, for example, V.J. Scattergood, one of the most influential critics, analyses the record of wills and forfeitures. To ascertain the reading preferences of the career diplomats and civil servants, on the other hand, he cites the anecdotal references contained within their own works. He is not comparing like with like.

Scattergood's conclusion was that: 'Gower and Chaucer were hardly essential reading among the aristocracy or among certain members of the knightly class who are known to have owned books.'[20] The career diplomats, civil servants and officials, however, were familiar with each other's works. Thus Chaucer and Gower read each other's works; Thomas Usk, under-sheriff for Middlesex, read *Troilus and Criseyde* and *Boece*; Sir John Clanvowe, soldier, diplomat and chamber-knight, knew *The Knight's Tale*; Ralph Strode, a lawyer, had probably read *Troilus and Criseyde* (because it is addressed to him); Hoccleve, a clerk in the London Office of the Privy Seal, read Chaucer's works, and so on.[21]

On the other hand, the comparison between what is recorded in the wills and forfeitures and what is recorded in anecdotal references might simply mean that there is a discrepancy between the books that someone might *own* and the current literature that everyone was listening to and talking about.

Books were valuable commodities – prime possessions to be passed down in wills. So the absence of secular English books in the library lists of the late fourteenth century is probably a testament to the rarity of such books. But rarity, at least initially, doesn't equate to unpopularity. Mass production takes a while to catch up with originality – especially in the fourteenth century, when copying manuscripts was slow going, even for the best professional scribes. Works which had only been written in the last few years had scarcely had the chance to have been copied out many times, and few had reached the stage of being handed on in wills. The library lists bear witness – in many ways – not to preferences but to what had been available to previous generations.

It is interesting to note that when V.J. Scattergood assesses the reading preferences of London merchants – as recorded in their wills – he comes up with a profile very similar to that of the aristocracy and knightly courtiers. In other words, they leave books in Latin in their wills not because that was their preferred reading but because books in Latin were more available to leave. The suggestion that their tastes did not seem to favour the new vernacular literature may be just another indicator that the books recorded in wills and forfeitures are not a reliable guide to people's literary tastes.

In fact the very idea that the ownership of books should give firm evidence for a work's popularity is based on the assumption that fourteenth-century reading habits were essentially similar to ours today. It assumes that people wanted to own books so that they could sit and read them privately and at their own convenience, which was not necessarily the case in an age when reading aloud was the preferred form of entertainment. One book, in such a culture, would go a long way.

As for the tastes of Richard II himself, there is precious little to go on. There is a list of fourteen books contained on a Memoranda Roll for 1384–5. Otherwise there are only eight which we can certainly identify with the king. It is scarcely surprising if neither Chaucer's nor Gower's work appears on the Memoranda Roll list, since a fair proportion of their work had not yet been written by 1384. In any case, the list is hardly evidence of the 17-year-old Richard's literary tastes. The books on the Memoranda Roll are all books bequeathed to Richard by his grandfather, Edward III. What is more, they were probably recorded on the Roll because they 'had been sold or pawned to raise cash for chamber expenses'.[22] So it is just as likely that these titles are the books that Richard wanted to get rid of.

Of the other eight books, four were presented to the king, and there is no evidence that Richard actually requested them. Of the remaining four, one is a book of recipes by his cook, two are books of statutes and only one – the *Libellus Geomancie,* a collection of fortune-telling techniques and advice – can be thought to have been actually commissioned by Richard.

So, once again, the examination of the wills and forfeitures tells us little about Richard II and his attitude to literature.

There is, however, plenty of evidence, within their texts, to suggest that Chaucer and Gower expected their books to be received by an aristocratic or courtly audience. Chaucer's first major poem, *The Book of the Duchess*, was clearly written to please his then patron, John of Gaunt, as an elegy on the death of Gaunt's beloved wife Blanche. It is a highly fashionable piece of writing that borrows from the French poet Guillaume de Machaut.[23] Another command performance is described by Gower at the start of his *Confessio Amantis*. He tells how he was rowing in a boat on the Thames when he chanced to come across the king. Richard II invited him onto his barge and encouraged him to write 'som newe thing'.[24] In *Troilus and Criseyde*, Chaucer addresses himself specifically to the aristocratic ladies – 'every gentil woman' – in his audience.

References to Richard are sprinkled throughout Chaucer's work. In the ballade *Lak of Steadfasteness* he actually addresses the king, who was, according to a fifteenth-century annotation in one manuscript, 'then being at his Castle of Windsor'.[25] This poem and its address to Richard has been convincingly linked with Chaucer's appointment as Clerk of the King's Works in 1389.[26] In the F Prologue to *The Legend of Good Women*, Chaucer describes the God of Love in terms which would have reminded his audience of the golden-haired Richard and his badge of the sun in splendour: 'His golden hair was crowned with a sun/ In place of gold ...' (ll. 230–1). And the god also sports one of the favourite badges of the Plantagents: the rose. In another passage that may have been redolent with references to Richard II and his Queen Anne, the mythical figure of Alceste commands the fictional Chaucer of the poem to:

'Goo now thy wey ...
And when this book ys maad, yive it the quene,
On my byhalf, at Eltham or at Sheene.'
   The Legend of Good Women, Prol. F, ll. 495–7
'Go now thy way ...
And when this book is made, give it to the queen,
On my behalf, at Eltham or at Sheen.'

Eltham and Sheen were Richard's and Anne's favourite residences. It has been observed that in the later revised version of the Prologue, Chaucer omitted mention of 'the queen' and the two royal residences. We are therefore warned that we cannot take the references seriously.[27] In fact, the later omission ties the poem even closer to the court, for Chaucer made the amendments after Anne's death. If Richard found the memory of his beloved queen so painful that he had the palace at Sheen burnt to the ground, the fact that Chaucer removed the painful references in his poem displays the close sympathy and connection between the poet and sovereign.

Similarly in *The Tale of Melibee*, the fact that Chaucer silently removes a reference to the ills attendant on a child-king – 'unfortunate is the land that has a child as lord' (which is what his French source says) – suggests that Chaucer expected the young Richard II to 'read' (or hear) the treatise.

CHAUCER – THE PRINCE'S COUNSELLOR

The *Melibee* itself is in the tradition of books of advice for princes, and it would have been seen in its day as a most topical and important volume – indeed crucial reading for the young Richard. The subjects covered include the most pressing concerns of the moment, such as vital information for the young king on how to select his advisers and how to deal with their advice. That it was a French treatise (although itself translated from a Latin original) would have also given urgency to the arguments it advanced against the use of war, at a time when an influential element at court was anxious to shift from a policy of war against France to one of peace.

In fact the arguments marshalled by Dame Prudence in the *Melibee* were tailor-made for the peace party – Richard II and his advisers who found themselves holding the reins of power in 1389. In the first place, says Dame Prudence, war is an expensive business and no matter how wealthy you might be you will never have enough, because the wealthier you are the more it will cost you.

'I counsel you not to begin a war, trusting in your riches, for riches alone are not enough to maintain wars. On this subject the philosopher Aristotle says: "The man who desires war and will have war by any means, will never have enough money, for the richer he is, the more costs he will incur, if he wants to be honoured and victorious." '[28]

In the second place, Dame Prudence warns, you can never be certain of the outcome: 'it is written in Kings II: "What happens in war is full of chance and in no way certain, for one man can be as easily wounded by a spear as another"; and because there is great peril in war, therefore a man should avoid and flee from war, as far as he is able to do so. For Solomon says: "He that loves peril shall fall in peril." '[29]

Prudence advises Melibee to make peace with his enemies – exactly as Richard's advisers were recommending in the teeth of the bitter opposition of the Gloucester–Arundel faction.

'For certain,' she said, 'I advise you to come to some agreement with your enemies and make peace with them. For St James says, in his Epistle, that "by agreement and peace small riches grow great, and by conflict and discord great riches fall down"' [30]

The reply that Melibee makes to his wife (lines 1680 onwards) must have been exactly the sort of argument that the hawks of Richard's court were making at the time.

The *Melibee* recounts how the young men of the council rise up and cry with loud voices: 'Werre! Werre!' against those that have done them wrong. But one of the wise old counsellors replies: 'Lords ... there is full many a man that cries out "War! War!" that knows full little what war means. War at his beginning has such a great entry and so wide that every man may enter when he wants and easily he can find war. But certainly what the end shall be is not easily known. For truly, when war is once begun, there is full many a child unborn of his mother that shall die young because of that war, or else live in sorrow and die in wretchedness. And therefore, before any war begins, men must take great council and great deliberation.' [31]

Those lines must have echoed the very debates that were going on in the royal council chamber at that very moment, with Richard and his closest counsellors urging peace against the warmongering of Gloucester and Arundel. And here it is worth considering why Chaucer chose to translate the *Melibee* in the first place. Was he commissioned by the 'court peace party' to translate it as part of the propaganda war against the hawks? Or did Chaucer choose to make the translation as his contribution towards a cause with which he agreed? Or, indeed, did Chaucer translate it in order to improve his own standing with the king and the court party? Whatever the truth, the fact that Chaucer chose this tale as his own contribution to *The Canterbury Tales* must have identified him indelibly as a member of the court peace party. He nailed his colours to the mast.

It has been said that *The Tale of Melibee*, *Lak of Steadfastness* and *Boece* all demonstrate that Chaucer conformed in some ways to the career of 'court poet'. [32] Further evidence that Chaucer anticipated a courtly audience for his work is found in *The Parliament of Fowls*, which seems to have been written with some allusion to the negotiations leading up to Richard's marriage to Anne of Bohemia, even though the poem itself is not allegorical.

And in the introduction to the *Treatise on the Astrolabe*, Chaucer appeals to Richard for protection against those who would attack him for translating such scholastic knowledge into the vernacular (see below p.35)[33].

Chaucer certainly addressed poems to those within the charmed circle of the royal affinity. *Lenvoy de Chaucer a Scogan* displays an easy familiarity with the man who would later become the tutor of Henry IV's children, and possibly contains a plea from Chaucer in Greenwich to have a word put in for him at the court at Windsor. Then there is the ballad *Truth*, addressed to Philip de la Vache, a member of the gentry and one of Richard's chamber knights.[34] And finally there is Chaucer's *Complaint to His Purse*, with its playful (though curiously impenetrable) envoy addressed to Henry IV – of which more later.

THE REVEALING NATURE OF CHAUCER'S STYLE

The content of some of Chaucer's poetry suggests that he was addressing a courtly audience. But perhaps one of the most compelling arguments that Chaucer aimed his literary production at his social superiors is found in the matter of his *style*.

Chaucer's voice as poet is shot through with self-effacement and deference to his audience. Of course, he is writing within the then current framework of politeness. He is adopting the fashionable courtesy and modesty of chivalry and courtly manners. But a strong case has recently been made that this style is also the result of 'the literary revolution which displaced the old minstrel performances'.[35]

The old-style minstrel would declaim his set pieces with that sense of authority – or bravado – that one expects from a professional performer. He would openly tout his wares:

Yet listen, lordes, to my tale
Merrier than the nightingale ...

So chirps the fictional *jongleur* of Chaucer's *Tale of Sir Thopas*. Or he might even call for a down-payment on his performance, as does the reciter of *Havelock the Dane*:

At the beginning of our tale,
Fill me a cup of full good ale;
And while I drink it, here I tell,
May Christ shield all of us from Hell![36]

Having made his pitch, the minstrel would proceed to declaim authoritatively on the subjects of battle, chivalry and courtly love, and the audience was quite willing to grant him that narrative authority – even when they knew he'd just walked off the street and had never been in a battle in his life – or, for that matter, been loved by a noblewoman. In her *Lai du Chevrefoil*, Marie de France (late twelfth century) tells of the knight Tristran's grief at being separated from his lady-love, and then she turns aside to her audience to explain about this love-longing:

This shouldn't cause anyone surprise –
Every lover grieves and broods that way
If he is true and far away
From the lady who has won his heart.[37]

In the court of Richard II such a direct explanation of the rules of love would have been unthinkable.

Chaucer and his fellow poets came from the lesser gentry. They gained access to the world of the aristocracy through their writing, but they still remained in their own social class, and as such they had to show due deference to those of higher estate. To expound the mysteries of courtly love would be to claim an unacceptable expertise. The capacity to love had long been regarded as an aristocratic prerogative,

Love was the prerogative of the aristocracy.

and no new-style court poet could set himself up as an authority on such a subject when his audience were his social superiors in such matters.[38] It is therefore unsurprising that when Chaucer deals with the question of Troilus' love-longing, in *Troilus and Criseyde*, he immediately defers to the superior judgement of his aristocratic audience:

Thow, redere, maist thiself ful wel devyne
That swuch a wo my wit kan nat diffyne
  Troilus and Criseyde, V. ll. 270–1
You, reader, may easily guess yourself
That such a woe my wit cannot define.

'Chaucer's self-deprecation here,' writes one scholar, 'for all its playful irony, reflects a quite genuine change that had come about in the relationship between the poet and his audience.'[39] The replacement of the professional minstrel by the gentleman-poet, addressing an audience of his social superiors, may account for the popularity of irony and allegory and all those other ways by which a writer could demonstrate a suitable degree of self-effacement.

Chaucer was able to let his hair down, however, in his own tale of *Sir Thopas*. It is quite remarkable that, as one of the new-style court authors, Chaucer chooses as his first contribution to *The Canterbury Tales* a parody of the old-style *jongleurs* whom he and his like were replacing – making fun of the idea that these minstrels could teach their social superiors to suck eggs. The opening of the third 'fit' (an archaic term for 'story' or 'song' even in Chaucer's day) of *Sir Thopas* replaces the customary deference and humility that a humble poet should show to his aristocratic listeners with an abrupt command to knights and ladies, all, to 'shut their mouths'! Its sheer rudeness must have been hilarious and shocking at the time:

Now holde youre mouth, *par charitee*,
Bothe knyght and lady free,
And herkneth to my spelle;
Of bataile and of chivalry,
And of ladyes love-drury
Anon I wol yow telle.
  Sir Thopas, ll. 889–95
Now hold your mouth, *par charitee*,
Both knight and lady free,
And listen to my story;
Of battle and of chivalry,
And of ladies' love-making
Anon I will you tell.

Chaucer's poetry, then, both implies a courtly audience and assumes – despite the conventions of deference and self-deprecation – that there was an easy-going familiarity between 'makers' and courtiers rather than a formal relationship of patron to patronized. The poems, as one critic puts it, bespeak a courtly ambience which 'reflects the ease of reference to the habits, aspirations and short-comings of polite society'.[40]

The same ambience runs through the work of Chaucer's contemporaries. John Gower begins the *Confessio Amantis*, his major poem in English, by describing how he bumps into Richard II while rowing on the Thames. The incident may or may not have happened – but even as a conventional flourish, it suggests that such casual meetings with the monarch might be expected. Sir John Clanvowe tells us in his *Boke of Cupide* that the birds desire to sing 'Before the chambre wyndow of the Quene At Wodestokke' (ll. 284–5).[41] He may be simply echoing Chaucer's similar lines in *The Legend of Good Women*, but the phrase demonstrates the same easy familiarity with the royals that Chaucer shows in his work.

For all this, however, there is little in the written record left by the aristocracy that actually acknowledges Chaucer's existence.

One of the few such references comes from Edward, the second Duke of York, while he was in prison sometime before 1413. He translated a French treatise on hunting, and in it he included a garbled version of some lines from the *Prologue* to *The Legend of Good Women*:

'For as Chaucer saith in this prologe of the XXV good wymmen. Be wryteng have men of ymages passed for writyng is the keye of alle good remembraunce.'[42]

As evidence of aristocratic interest in Chaucer, this one example may not seem much to go on, but the mention is revealing nevertheless. It demonstrates that Chaucer's poem was so familiar to the duke that he was prepared to quote from it even though he clearly did not have the text to hand. The way the duke refers to the poet without introduction or qualification but simply 'as Chaucer saith' also indicates how familiar he knew his audience would be with Chaucer and with his work. And since what the duke was translating was a treatise on hunting, his audience must have been aristocratic.

Besides there may have been another reason for the lack of aristocratic recognition of Chaucer – especially in the decade following his death – as we shall argue later (see Chapter 14).

To claim that Chaucer's work was not read by the aristocracy simply because they did not own copies of his writing is to underestimate the difference between owning books and the nature of reading at the time. Since 'reading' usually meant a public performance, the ownership of the books that were read was not an indicator of what people were listening to. It would be rather like judging what is popular in the cinema by who owns the prints of the films.

Even the fact that Chaucer wrote in the vernacular bound him inextricably into the international culture of Richard's court. 'The step taken by Chaucer when he wrote *The Book of the Duchess* in English', writes one eminent scholar, 'marks his clear understanding of himself as "nourished" by European traditions which had long been concerned to demonstrate the power of the vernacular languages for high and refined literary purposes ... His use of English is the triumph of internationalism.'[43] The use of the vernacular was not simply an expression of nationalism – on the contrary, it was also characteristic of the new internationalism of late fourteenth-century European courts, in which each country sought to assert its own individuality through its vernacular language.

DID RICHARD ENCOURAGE THE ENGLISH LANGUAGE?

There is no question that literature flourished under Richard II. It is also a fair assumption that the king was aware of what went on in his own court and that what went on reflected his own tastes. Likewise there is no doubt that Richard enjoyed the company and friendship of men of letters, such as Sir John Clanvowe and Sir John Montagu. 'If a man can be judged by the company that he keeps,' writes Richard's most recent biographer, 'Richard deserves to be seen as a patron of letters.'[44]

Furthermore, Richard is the first king of England to be hailed as the protector of the English language. In the preface to *Treatise on the Astrolabe* Chaucer writes: 'And pray God save the king, that is lord of this language ...' To us it sounds like a cliché, but it was far from that when Chaucer wrote it. It was a political statement, putting forward Richard as the protector of the English language against all those people (mostly in the church) who wished to suppress it.

'More than his Lancastrian supplanters', it has been said, 'Richard encouraged poets at court: Froissart, Chaucer, Sir John Clanvowe and Sir John Montagu; Gower wrote the *Confessio Amantis* at Richard's request. In 1390 Richard paid the clerks of London £10 to perform a play of *The Passion of Our*

Lord and *The Creation of the World* at Skinners' Well.' In 1396 he attended the mystery plays at York, and he may also have been to the plays at Chester or Coventry as well.[45]

What is more, a strong case has been made for Richard's being responsible for the encouragement of alliterative works such as *Sir Gawain and the Green Knight* and *Pearl*, written in the dialect spoken in Cheshire. Richard's increasing reliance on the men of Cheshire and his interest in the region in his later years makes it all the more probable that *Gawain* was 'given an airing at some level in the king's household as it moved around the west and north Midlands'.[46] Indeed, it may even have been a Christmas entertainment for Richard when his court was travelling through that area.[47]

The condemnation of the Oxford theologian and Bible translator John Wyclif's works in 1382 created a climate that was less favourable to works in English as far as the church was concerned – and yet it is precisely at this moment that Chaucer commences on *Troilus and Criseyde*, and John Gower (who previously had written only in French and Latin) starts upon his great work in English: the *Confessio Amantis*. The scale and brio of these works breathe with 'the sort of assurance that could only come from the highest sponsorship'.[48] And after all, why not? Richard II was the first king since the Norman Conquest of wholly English parentage and quite possibly the first to speak English as his first language – or at least to speak English naturally.[49]

There is no doubt that a lot of English was spoken at court. Richard, himself, certainly spoke it – otherwise, how would he have been able to converse with the

rebel leader Wat Tyler at Smithfield during the Peasants' Revolt? Or how else would he have become familiar enough with his Cheshire guards for them to call him 'Dicun'?

There is also an eyewitness account by the French chronicler, Jean Froissart, which seems to indicate that the language generally spoken at Richard's court was English. Froissart tells the story of how, while he was staying there, he was given the opportunity to present Richard with a book of his love poems. According to Froissart, the King 'dipped into several places, reading parts aloud, for he read and spoke French perfectly well' – which seems to imply

Froissart presents his book to Richard II.

that he was otherwise *not* speaking French. Since Richard is hardly likely to have been speaking Latin in this context, one can presume that the king and his court generally conversed in English or at least in a mix of French and English.[50]

Another French chronicler, Jean Creton, who was an eyewitness at the meeting of Richard II and Henry of Derby at Flint Castle, tells us pretty clearly that the two conversed in English rather than French. Creton swears to the truth of his report of the speech between king and usurper because, he says, 'I heard and understood them very well. And the Earl of Salisbury also rehearsed them to me in French.'[51]

So, in an age when reading aloud was the primary form of entertainment, it is unimaginable that the English-speaking king of an English-speaking court would not have fostered the production of works in English which he and his court could enjoy.

Moreover, since the cultivation of a vernacular literature was seen throughout Europe as crucial to the establishment of a prince's identity, Richard would not have dreamt of neglecting it – not if he wanted to be regarded as the fashionable and progressive monarch that he demonstrably aspired to be.

The vernacular was seen to be part and parcel of what a king ruled over. It was as much a part of his chattels as the physical land over which he ruled. When Chaucer addressed Richard as 'the king that is lord of this language' he was not only claiming protection, he was also adding to his sovereign's magnificence. This, after all, was what had been happening in France, where 'Although the expression "the King's French" did not exist, Charles V and his translators seem to have tried to promote the idea that the language of his people was part of the realm or domain of the king.'[52] As another scholar puts it: Chaucer's claims for English as heir to Latinity might be read within a European theatre of operations: if translations into French had done much to bolster the prestigious court of Charles V (1364–80), then perhaps the time had come for English translators to offer comparable service "to the king that is lord of this langage"...'[53]

We cannot, however, assume that the translation of material into English was necessarily seen as a method of bringing enlightenment to the masses. There is, on the contrary, evidence that it became a symbol of prestige for the nobility. At Berkeley Castle in Gloucestershire, for example, Thomas, the fourth Lord Berkeley, kept his chaplain, John Trevisa, hard at work translating into English texts that would have been of little interest to the lay population. It seems likely that Berkeley's aim was not the promotion of learning amongst his inferiors, but that, on the contrary, he was appropriating learning and the English language as a status symbol for the lay aristocracy.[54]

The European frame of reference in which Richard's English-speaking court was created makes it virtually certain that Richard would have promoted the literature of his own language, and the fact that there *was* such a flowering of literature in English during his reign seems to prove the point. And yet there is a mysterious absence of concrete evidence for Richard's involvement in any of this. We are faced with a remarkable gap in the archives: there is no record of any payment made on behalf of the king to any literary figure. How do we explain this?

It may be that the record has simply been lost. In all probability the order to write or present a piece of work would have been made orally, and if any money had been paid over after the work was executed, it would have come out of the chamber accounts, and these no longer survive. English kings jealously guarded their privilege of being unaccountable in their chamber accounts.[55]

Medieval account books may sound a dull subject, but they actually provide riveting glimpses into court life six or seven centuries ago. The chamber journals of Edward II, for example, inform us in all seriousness that the king paid his painter, Jack of Saint Albans, 50 shillings because 'he danced before the king on a table and made him laugh very greatly'. Seems a lot of money! On another occasion the accounts tell us that the king awarded the princely sum of 20 shillings to one of his cooks 'because he rode before the king there and often fell from his horse, at which the king laughed very greatly'. Henry VII, mysteriously, paid half a mark to a friend for eating some coal![56]

One wonders if Richard II's chamber accounts would have revealed a similar delight in low comedy. Somehow it seems doubtful.

An entry in one of the Exchequer account books for Easter 1399 offers a provocative glimpse of what Richard's entertainment bills might have been like had they been preserved. It shows large amounts of money (1,000 marks, £106 13s 4d and £113 6s 8d) given as gifts to chamber officials and it specifically mentions ten marks paid out to some minstrels – William Byngeley and his companions. There is also a gift of £20 paid to a certain 'Massy', and since some scholars now claim that the poet of *Sir Gawain and the Green Knight* was none other than a certain John Massy, the entry holds out the tantalizing possibility that it records an actual performance of the poem for the benefit of Richard II.[57]

It would be wrong to make too much of Richard's missing chamber records, but since they are indeed missing, and since these records are where one would naturally look to find payments to poets and entertainers, it seems equally wrong to draw the conclusion that the lack of any records meant that Richard did not reward his entertainers at all.

It may be significant that there is no record of any gift from Richard to Froissart following Froissart's presentation of that copy of his poems in 1395. 'The manuscript is not extant, and no record of any gift from the king to Froissart has survived. There is no good reason to doubt Froissart's account, however, and the loss of this valuable book demonstrates the danger of assuming that our records of Richard's manuscripts, even of elaborate presentation copies, are at all complete.'[58]

Another possibility, however, is that patronage, in Richard's reign, operated under more elusive rules. Perhaps patronage was as oblique as the references to it within the works themselves.

CHAUCER AS A COURTIER

Being employed in the king's *familia* in the fourteenth century was not at all the same as being employed by ICI or General Motors in the twenty-first. Relations between king and retainer were not based on a bare cash nexus; they invoked an intimate relationship involving loyalty and duty on the part of the retainer, and a reciprocal benevolence on the part of the monarch. The king was not simply intent on screwing out as much work from his employees as he possibly could under the terms of a contract.

Chaucer.

It would be difficult to say, even, where to draw the line between the king's retainers and the king's friends. He would rely on those around him for political advice, for the execution of his business, for undertaking secret commissions and also for his domestic service, pleasures and entertainment. To this end, Richard II seems to have brought men with literary tastes like Clanvowe and Montagu into his personal circle.

Chaucer too, though apparently not necessarily a regular intimate, is linked closely to the king in the records. As early as 1368 he is referred to as one of 'the valets of the king's chamber'. In 1373 he is down as one of the squires of Edward III's chamber, and in 1385 he appears in a catalogue of Richard II's household servants as one of the valets 'of both the chamber and various offices of the lord king's household'.[59]

At about this same time, Chaucer's reputation as a courtly poet seems to have spread abroad, and the French poet, Eustache Deschamps, sends a poem addressing him as: 'High poet, *glory of the esquires*'.[60]

It was around the king's chamber that the social life of the court revolved, 'and since it was in his chamber and amongst his chamber servants that the king sought private diversion, it was here that aristocratic taste was formed, and here that the court poet, if he was to have a hearing or to win any recognition for his efforts, had to seek his audience.'[61]

But, whatever his relationship with the king's chamber itself, Chaucer must have been a familiar and trusted figure in royal circles. Edward III trusted him enough to send him on secret business to Genoa and Florence in 1372, and Richard (or, more probably, his counsellors) sent him on another secret mission in 1378, this time to Lombardy. Any reader of *The Tale of Melibee* would know that a prudent ruler should send only his most loyal and well-tried retainers on such missions. Chaucer was certainly familiar with those closest to the young Richard. In 1376, he travelled on secret business – possibly abroad – with Sir Simon Burley, the prince's beloved and trusted tutor. The next year, Froissart tells us, Chaucer was to be found in the company of Guichard d'Angle (who had been Richard's tutor until 1372) and Sir Richard Stury – as one of the three English envoys charged with carrying out the delicate proposals for a marriage between Prince Richard and the daughter of the French king. And being an envoy to foreign parts must have been a plum job – despite the dangers and arduousness of the journey – for the competitiveness of international court culture demanded that embassies and envoys be treated one station above their actual rank. So it is worth bearing in mind that on these visits to foreign courts, Chaucer, as a squire, would have been entertained as a knight.[62]

For all these undertakings, Chaucer was financially rewarded – but what about his literary endeavours? Chaucer's grant of £10 a year from John of Gaunt may not have been specifically linked to his poem *The Book of the Duchess*, but it was made within a year or two of his writing it, and whether the grant was dependent on the poem or not, it certainly didn't discourage Chaucer from continuing to write.

Perhaps we cannot tie any of Chaucer's appointments to any particular works of literature, yet it is possible to say that those works of literature wouldn't have existed without those appointments. In 1374, for example, Edward III appointed him to the customs, thereby enabling his move to London. In addition the king granted him a daily pitcher of wine, a free house in Aldgate and the continuation of his life annuity – not a bad situation for an aspiring author.

Richard II, of course, inherited Chaucer from his grandfather's regime, and Chaucer was to become equally dependent on Richard's good will. During

Richard's eclipse under the Lords Appellant, Chaucer disappears from public life, but surfaces once again when the king resumes power. In fact 'Chaucer was one of the very first of the "old courtiers" to be given preferment after Richard's reassertion of control ...' Almost as soon as Richard regained office, he appointed Chaucer his Clerk of the King's Works.[63]

Chaucer's biographer, Derek Pearsall, warns us that 'the job was in no sense a sinecure, and we should put out of our minds any idea that it was a reward for a favoured poet. On the contrary, if any appointment could have been contrived to ensure a writer's silence, this was it. It was an arduous post.'[64] However, although Pearsall lists all the responsibilities of the office, he does not produce any evidence as to how much time Chaucer spent at his desk. The fact that none of the records are in Chaucer's own hand might provide a clue. It may also be significant that the only other layman to hold the post, one Roger Elmham, seems to have had more responsibilities than Chaucer did. Certainly Chaucer was rewarded with a very handsome salary: £36 per year – twice as much as the great architect Henry Yevele.[65]

Henry Yevele the architect. A boss in Canterbury Cathedral.

Chaucer was a well-paid servant of the court who received his monies with a regularity far about the average. It has been suggested that he was able to secure such regular salaries either because his experience as a civil servant had taught him how to get what he wanted or else because he was by nature a shrewd business man. Another possibility, of course, is that he was valued, beyond his immediate employments, as a celebrated adornment to the court circle.

On the other hand we have no reason to suppose that Chaucer did not take his responsibilities seriously. He tells himself, in that passage from *The House of Fame* (already quoted on pp. 24–5), that he had to do his reading after a full day's work.

Maybe he found his duties too onerous, and incompatible with his poetic activities, for after two years he appears to have asked to be relieved of his post as Clerk of the King's Works. It may even be that he found this sort of work too dangerous, for he was robbed no less than three times during his career and, quite possibly, wounded in the process.[66]

It is possible that Chaucer wrote the poem *Fortune* at this time, for it apparently contains a reference to the ordinance passed by the Privy Council in March 1390, decreeing that all Richard II's grants or gifts should be endorsed by the dukes of Lancaster, York and Gloucester, or any two of them.[67] If this interpretation is correct, then Chaucer refers to Richard as his 'beste frend', and one refrain in the poem would seem to celebrate the fact that Richard has survived the assault on the throne by the barons in 1387–8: 'And eek thou hast thye beste frend alyve.'

On this reading, the poem is nothing less than a petition to Richard for another appointment:

> And but you list releve him of his peyne,
> Preyeth his beste frend of his noblesse
> That to som beter estat he may atteyne.
>   *Fortune*, ll. 77–9
> And if you don't relieve his pain,
> [Then] pray his best friend [to do so] out of his nobility
> So that he may attain some better condition.

HOW WERE POETS PAID IN RICHARD II'S COURT?

To say that royal patronage had nothing to do with Chaucer's abilities and reputation as a poet simply because no payments are related to specific poems, is to ignore the complex interrelationships of the royal court. Thomas Wimbledon, who preached a famous sermon at St Paul's Cross in 1388, had no doubt that writers thought they could use their talents to advance themselves at court. He complains that educated men renounce the study of philosophy or divinity and join 'the king's court to write official documents and records' in the hope 'that these occupation will be a means to make them great in the world'.[68]

As we have already seen, the social life of the court revolved around the king's chamber and it was there that the court poet had to seek his audience.[69] The literary historian, Richard Green, writes: 'Literature in the court occupied some kind of ill-defined no man's land somewhere between a job and a hobby ...' and while poets frequently found positions in the *familia regis* 'there seems to have been no obvious connection between the nature of their professional employment and the fact that they were men of letters.'[70] Indeed, if it was the case that they were not directly remunerated for their poetry perhaps this is precisely what distinguished the court poets of Richard's day, in their own eyes, from the despised *jongleurs* of the previous era. It may have been their position as amateurs that gave them a status on a par with their social superiors. As Green remarks, the opposition of 'household poets *versus* minstrels' was the same as the old sporting category of 'gentlemen *versus* players'. It was a class distinction between those who were socially exalted enough to possess independent means, and could therefore practise without the need for remuneration against those who were socially inferior and dependent on payment for their participation.

The practice of poetry raised a middle-ranking bureaucrat like Chaucer onto the level of a 'gentleman' and the 'indirect advantages in terms of household advancement which he might gain by showing himself a gentleman would far outweigh any occasional rewards he could hope to command as a professional player'.[71] Chaucer clearly saw himself as a courtier and gentleman and one of the last documents we have relating to him describes him definitively as *Galfrido Chaucers armigero* (Geoffrey Chaucer, esquire).[72]

In other words, the patronage was there, but it was invisible and indirect – almost as if actual payment for a literary work was seen as *infra dig*.

The patronage was certainly assumed to have been there by later writers. Thirty years after Chaucer's death, the poet Lydgate tells us that Chaucer, like Virgil, Dante and Petrarch before him, was able to practise his art because he received the patronage of princes:

Dante in Italy, Virgil in Rome town,
Petrarch in Florence had all his pleasure,
And wise Chaucer in Brutus's Albion
Found as good a livelihood as he desired,
The generosity of Lords weighed in their favour,
Because they flowered in wisdom and knowledge,
The support of princes found them their livelihood.
    Lydgate, *The Fall of Princes*, Book III, ll. 3858–64[73]

We may not know just how the patronage of literature functioned in Richard's court, but it clearly functioned in some indirect way. 'Though there is little evidence of widespread patronage,' we are told, 'the circumstances for the production and dissemination of literature were obviously not unfavourable.[74] And those circumstances must mean financial provision for authors to pursue their time-consuming vocation. There was 'a great range of household officers, who often appear to have had a variety of duties and occupations; poets and chroniclers whose professional designation may be that of chaplain or "clerc de chambre": "knights and esquires of the chamber" who may also be poets.' In other words the court 'provided a framework within which that culture could develop'.[75]

DIRECT *VERSUS* INDIRECT PATRONAGE

Chaucer himself actually provides us with a description of this sort of patronage. In the Prologue to *The Legend of Good Women*, the poet encounters the God of Love and Queen Alceste. Both figures are often identified with Richard II and Anne of Bohemia. When Queen Alceste commands Chaucer the poet to write *The Legend of Good Women*, she tells him that he is not to think of it as some hobby for his spare time. He must devote most of his time to his work of writing:

> Thow shalt, while that thou lyvest, yer by yere,
> The moste partye of thy tyme spende
> In makyng of a glorious legende
> Of goode wymmen ...
> > *The Legend of Good Women*, Prol. F, ll. 481–4
> You will, while that you live, year by year,
> Spend the most part of your time
> In composing a glorious legend
> Of good women ...

In order to make this possible, however, she tells Chaucer that she will ask the God of Love (possibly identified with Richard II) to ensure that his servants assist the poet in any way they can, to guarantee that he has an income.

> And to the god of Love I shal so preye
> That he shal charge his servantz by any weye
> To forthren thee, and wel thy labour quyte.
> > *The Legend of Good Women*, Prol. F, ll. 492–4
> And to the god of Love I shall so pray,
> That he shall charge his servants by any way
> To help you and to quit your labour well.

So it is not to be a direct commission, with the God of Love himself (i.e. Richard) paying the poet for his work, but an indirect affair in which he instructs his servants to provide for the poet 'by any weye'. That this system of patronage is to be associated with Richard is made quite clear from the lines that follow (quoted above, see p.28), in which Alceste instructs Chaucer to deliver the completed book to Queen Anne at either of their favourite residences: 'at Eltham or at Shene'.[76]

On the Continent, Charles V and Philip the Good were *direct* patrons of literature – particularly translation and history – publicly commissioning and paying for works, which were, of course, inevitably designed to exalt their own authority. In England the definition and role of the author seems to have been less precise. 'All too easily the service which the author performed might be interpreted as falling within the general terms of his agreement as a household servant, in other words, as a service warranting no special consideration or remuneration.'[77] In this context it might be well to point out the lack of any official history, commissioned by the king. 'Why medieval England failed to produce official history on the lines of the *Grandes Chroniques* in France is a question not easily answered,' writes one historian.[78] Perhaps it simply wasn't the English style of doing things.

Rather than looking for evidence of direct payment from Richard to the poets of his court, then, perhaps we need to be looking at the environment that he created as king in which literature could, and *did*, flourish.

Increasingly the argument that Richard had no role in the elevation of literature during his reign seems somewhat perverse. The tastes of the court were the tastes of the king. If Richard had not been interested in literature, how could there have been a flowering of literature within his court? Surely it cannot be a simple coincidence that the breakthrough in the writing of English comes in the mid-1380s at 'the very time when it becomes meaningful to talk about the impact of the king's personality and the role of the court'?[79]

And here it might be as well to bear in mind how extraordinarily tiny the society we are talking about would seem in comparison to the present day. The whole of London numbered around 40,000 souls – less than half the size of the present-day town of Sittingbourne (on the road to Canterbury).[80] Richard's court itself was probably smaller than most modern schools; perhaps 450 with a staff of 400 to 700.[81] In such a society it seems rather pointless to talk about 'who knew who?' Clearly everyone knew everyone else. 'Who was *friends* with who?' is a different question.

Certainly two of Chaucer's friends, Sir John Clanvowe and Sir Lewis Clifford, were chamber knights of Richard II and – what's more – in daily attendance upon the king. Are we really to suppose they never talked about Chaucer's poetry, or discussed his latest production? Besides, Chaucer was already famous by the

1380s. Is it conceivable that when the literary star of Richard's court performed one of his new works the king would not be there to listen? And if he was, what meaning do we attach to the question, 'What did he read?' If he listened to Chaucer reading aloud, that is what Richard 'read'. Or are we to suppose that while the rest of the court were enjoying the very latest up-to-the-minute works of art, King Richard locked himself away, silently reading out-of-date authors?

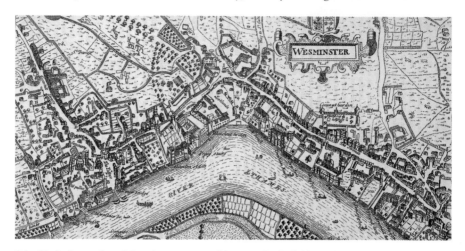

John Norden's map shows Westminster separated from London by fields. London was smaller than present-day Sittingbourne.

CHAPTER 3

The nature of Richard's rule

~

The evidence from within the poems indicates an easy-going familiarity between poet and sovereign. This is something quite different from the formal, officially sanctioned relationships between prince and poet that we find in the European courts.[1] Such ease and familiarity, however, are strangely at odds with the portrait of Richard that emerges from the pages of most modern historians. Is it possible to reconcile the two?

RICHARD THE MEGALOMANIAC

The *Oxford History of England* paints a colourful picture of Richard's 'megalomania'.[2] It quotes the evidence of the chronicle known as the *Continuation of the Eulogium* which records Richard sitting enthroned after dinner conversing with nobody but watching everyone:

> he would order a throne to be prepared for him in his chamber on which he liked to sit ostentatiously from after dinner until vespers, talking to no one but watching everyone; and when his eye fell on anyone, regardless of rank, that person had to bend his knee towards the king ...[3]

But can we really take this account at face value? The chronicle was compiled by either a monk of Christchurch, Canterbury, or a friar resident in one of the several friars' houses in the city. The passage refers to the king's behaviour shortly after Richard exiled the Archbishop of

Richard II – all had to bend the knee to him.

Canterbury, Thomas Arundel, and was written *after* Arundel's return to power, under Henry IV, and as such should most probably be regarded as a later interpolation deliberately designed to blacken Richard's character. Nor should it come as any surprise that hostile chroniclers should go out of their way to create an image of Richard behaving as a despot and tyrant. That was the image they were at pains to project.[4]

But, it might be objected, even the writer of the *Westminster Chronicle*, a relatively sympathetic chronicler, depicts Richard as a king who demanded excessive formality and deference from his court. Under the year 1385, the Westminster Chronicler comments on Richard's 'lust for glory and eagerness to have from everyone the deference properly due to his kingship'.[5]

Once again the context provides an explanation, for this passage of the *Chronicle* was written at a time when relations between Richard II and Westminster Abbey were at a particularly low ebb. In 1383 the crown had confiscated the abbey's temporalities (worldly possessions and revenues) as a reprisal for ignoring a royal prohibition against appealing to the pope in a certain matter. And in 1385 the crown petitioned the pope to remove the church of Westminster's 'privilege in the matter of debt'. So perhaps it is no wonder that the Monk of Westminster, writing within three years of the events he describes, should have been hostile to Richard.[6]

In any case, the passage quoted should be read in context. The Monk of Westminster is complaining that the young king has forced the Archbishop of Canterbury to kneel before him to beg his pardon over a quarrel. He criticizes not just the king but the archbishop, too, for not being made of the stuff of Thomas the Martyr who would 'never have bent head or knee in that fashion to anybody'. The monk continues: 'it is rather the necks of kings and princes which should be bowed in submission at the feet of pontiffs.'[7]

By the time he comes to describe the events of 1388, however, matters had entirely changed and the Monk of Westminster is hailing Richard II as the great defender of the church.[8]

According to the Introduction to the *Westminster Chronicle*, the Monk of Westminster starts out generally hostile to Richard and supportive of his opponents: the Duke of Gloucester and the Earl of Arundel. The editor suggests that the Duke of Gloucester was close to the abbey during this part of the reign and was, indeed, the monk's chief informant for the first part of the rebellion organized by himself and the Earl of Arundel in 1387. In 1388, however, Gloucester and his cronies invaded the sanctuary of Westminster to seize the Lord Chief Justice,

Robert Tresilian, whom they subsequently executed. Both Thomas Arundel, then Bishop of Ely and Chancellor of the Realm, and William Wykeham, Bishop of Winchester, defended the violation of sanctuary – much to the Monk of Westminster's disgust. Richard, however, supported the abbey's privileges, and this, whether or not it was the direct cause, proved to be the turning point in Richard's relationship with the abbey. From 1388 onwards, the abbey and the king grew closer and closer, and the monk's assessment of Richard's character grew appropriately warmer.[9]

RICHARD AND THE CULT OF RITUAL

It may well be that Richard did indeed foster 'a more elaborate and ceremonial style of monarchy', as his recent biographer puts it, but rather than seeing this as the product of a personality defect, it could equally be seen as deliberate policy adopted for specific ends.[10] Richard was doing no more than adopting the fashion that was then current in the courts of Europe. There was nothing peculiar to the English court in this cult of deference. In France, the kings had enjoyed the titles of 'princes' and had been addressed as 'your majesty' for over a century. In the court of the Holy Roman Emperor, where Richard's Queen Anne had grown up, the way in which important persons were addressed was more elevated than it had been in England. Even Richard's grandfather, Edward III, had begun to

encourage the 'lengthening of the hierarchy of degree'.[11] Richard, who had expressed ambitions towards the imperial throne, could not be left behind in this status race.

Charles of France.

But it was not simply a question of fashion. There were also practical reasons for adopting the cult of ritual. King Charles of France did it because he 'believed that a policy of exalting the monarchy would contribute to the rebirth of French power, and he was almost certainly justified in this view'.[12] In England, a similarly pragmatic purpose probably lay behind the increased ceremonial. Richard and his advisers were concerned to minimize the adverse effects of their peace policy. War had the happy effect of rallying loyalty to the crown, whereas peace allowed faction to proliferate. Emphasizing the ceremonial of royalty was an attempt to counter this unfortunate tendency.

The concept of a strong personal monarchy was not just an aberrant idea that emanated from Richard II's slightly crazed and overblown vision of his own importance. That is what the Lancastrian propagandists would have us believe. In fact, a strong personal monarchy was seen by many people as an ideal in the late fourteenth century. After all what was the alternative? It certainly wasn't democracy. For the people in the fourteenth century, democracy was not the universal panacea it has become in the twentieth and twenty-first centuries.

Indeed, Dante claimed it was a perverted form of government on a par with despotism: 'It is only when a monarch is reigning that the human race exists for its own sake, and not for the sake of something else. For it is only then that perverted forms of government are made straight, to wit, democracies, oligarchies, and tyrannies, which force the human race into slavery (as is obvious to whosoever runs through them all) ...'[13]

Dante was, admittedly, writing for the benefit of the Holy Roman Emperor, but the same arguments against 'democracy' are echoed in Chaucer's translation of the *Melibee*: 'For the truth of things and the benefit thereof are better found by a few folk who are wise and full of reason, rather than by a great multitude of people in which every man shouts out and prattles on about whatever he wants.'[14]

Dante: the portrait in the Duomo, Florence.

One of the most influential books of political instruction was an eighth-century volume written in Arabic and claiming to be advice from Aristotle to Alexander the Great. The *Secretum Secretorum* was translated in the twelfth century, and by the fourteenth was *de rigueur* on any thinking person's reading list. The book is a compendium of pronouncements on political and ethical matters and 'assumes a strong personal monarchy is the most desirable form of government and offers advice on a variety of means by which a king can maintain and extend his power'.[15]

A strong central monarchy was seen as the only way to control the warring barons who, for their own advancement, might otherwise tear the country to pieces. The fear of factionalism and internecine war was particularly strong where the ruler was a child. In England in 1377, the barons were circling like vultures around the 10-year-old Richard, from the moment the crown touched his head.

But the political theorists were careful to point out a difference between the strong, all-powerful monarch and a tyrant. The difference lay in his motivation. If he ruled in the interests of his people, he was a rightful ruler. If he ruled in his own interests, however, he was a tyrant. Marsilius of Padua, the one-time rector of the University of Paris, wrote: 'A kingly monarchy, then, is a temperate government wherein the ruler is a single man who rules for the common benefit, and in accordance with the will or consent of the subjects. *Tyranny*, its opposite, is a diseased government wherein the ruler is a single man who rules for his own private benefit apart from the will of his subjects.'[16] So, too, Bartolus of Sassoferrato, professor of law at Pisa (1339–43): 'The test of a tyrant by defect of conduct is that his actions "are not directed toward the common good but to his own advantage, and that means to rule unjustly – as is the case *de facto* in Italy".'[17]

Dante, too, considers that the legitimate ruler must exist for the sake of the people, not the people for the ruler. The debate on the nature of monarchy and tyranny was one which would have been raging in Italy when Chaucer went on his missions on behalf of the English crown.[18]

According to then current fourteenth-century political theory, Richard would not necessarily be displaying tyrannical tendencies if he wanted to concentrate power in the hands of the crown. He was simply bringing peace to the country. Nor was he acting as a tyrant when he tried to augment the authority of the throne.

The idea of a strong, centralized monarchy would have been familiar to the young king through his tutor, Sir Simon Burley, whom we know possessed a copy of Giles of Rome's *De Regimine Principium*. Giles stresses the duty of subjects to obey their ruler. Obedience is the source of all peace, honour, and prosperity in the realm. Obedience to the ruler brings rewards to the dutiful citizenry. These were ideas that powerfully attracted the Black Prince and Michael de la Pole – who was to become Richard's chancellor (1383–6).[19]

As long as Richard acted in the interests of his people and not his own, he was ruling in accord with the best political ideas of his time – ideas that were endorsed by the major thinkers of his day: Dante, Petrarch, William of Ockham, Marsilius of Padua, Giles of Rome, Coluccio Salutati and so on. Richard was simply putting into effect the lessons on kingship he had learnt as a boy.

A CONTRADICTION IN RICHARD'S BEHAVIOUR

It may be that this duty to act the part of the strong ruler conflicted with Richard's own personal inclinations, and it is possible that this produced a fundamental contradiction in his behaviour. The historian Nigel Saul sums it up thus: 'This is the king who at one moment could be so distant that those approaching him had to bend the knee and address him in exalted terms of majesty – and who, at another, could be spoken to in familiar terms by his Cheshire archers: "Dycun, sleep quietly while we guard you" ... a tension is to be felt between the alternating behavioural styles of distance and intimacy; or to put it another way, between the king being raised above his subjects and the king intermingling with them.'[20]

In other words, Richard was playing a part. He knew he had to appear as a strong and distant ruler, but he was not always able to pull it off. And some of his court circle knew it. Perhaps it even provided them with a bit of fun.

In the Prologue to *The Legend of Good Women,* Chaucer, as we have already mentioned, probably identifies the God of Love with Richard and Alceste with Queen Anne. So imagine the excitement that first reading of the poem must have generated, if the king and queen were mingling in the audience – as they are in the frontispiece to the Corpus Christi College manuscript of *Troilus and Criseyde.*[21] We might picture Chaucer, at a lectern, adopting a deadpan delivery, as he describes the God of Love looking so severe that it makes the poet's blood run cold.

Chaucer reads or recites Troilus and Criseyde to Richard II and his court – who all look suitably enraptured by this new kind of story-telling.

> For sternly on me he gan byholde,
> So that his loking dooth myn herte colde.[22]

Surely there must have been an outbreak of nudging and whispering, as the court began stealing glances at the king at this point. How would he react to this gentle bit of fun at his expense?

Chaucer's work must have generated tremendous excitement amongst his immediate contemporaries. At the very least, this playful allusion to the king's official 'stern countenance' – if it is indeed that – demonstrates the ease and familiarity of Richard's court as a literary forum – whatever its outward allegiance to the increased formality of majesty in other fields.

Despite the cultivation of outward formality at court, and despite his increasingly aggressive pursuit of the principles of centralized monarchy, Richard's actions consistently suggest that he himself set unusually little store by the distinctions of birth.

He didn't really get on with the blue-blooded bishops like William Courtenay and Thomas Arundel, for instance; he 'preferred more clerkly bishops such as Edmund Stafford whom he raised to the See of Exeter in 1391 or Thomas Merks, once a monk at Westminster who was made Bishop of Carlisle.'[23] Instead of surrounding himself with men of high blood and noble family, he chose instead men of ability and intelligence regardless of their social origins. This is precisely what got up the noses of his enemies.

A nobleman like Thomas of Woodstock, Duke of Gloucester, whose only fortune was his title, regarded high birth as his meal-ticket, and yet here he was being virtually ignored by the young king. Instead of showering favours and money in his direction, Richard seemed intent on elevating mere nobodies to high office and – what's worse – high status. Richard's tutor, Sir Simon Burley was a man of obscure origins, and yet the king wanted to make him Earl of Huntingdon! Sir William Bagot – one of the counsellors to whom Richard entrusted the governance of England when he left for Ireland in 1399 – was no more than 'a knight of low birth who had been raised by the King to high places'.[24] Michael de la Pole was the son of a Hull wool merchant and yet here he was now, not only Chancellor of the Realm but Earl of Suffolk as well, and enjoying lavish grants of land into the bargain! It was enough to make a baron's blood boil blue!

Then there was John Beauchamp – or 'Jankyn' as Richard liked to call him – a chamber knight whom Richard had raised to the peerage as Baron Kidderminster. No wonder the rebellious magnates of 1387, when they put him on trial, contemptuously threw away the baronage and referred to him as plain 'John Beauchamp of Holt'. And of course it went without saying that the king's intimacy with that dreadful Sir Nicholas Brembre (Mayor of London, but a mere merchant) was a stain on the honour of the crown.

Most of these men got their comeuppance at the hands of the rebel lords in 1387. Brembre, Burley, Beauchamp and two other chamber knights were executed, while Michael de la Pole was sentenced to death in his absence and died in exile.

Adam of Usk, in his chronicle, sums up the Lancastrian contempt for Richard's disregard of social status: 'It was in this King Richard's nature to debase the noble and to exalt the ignoble – as he did with this Sir William [Bagot], for example, and with other such low-born men whom he elevated to great positions ...'[25] These were the famous 'duketti' or 'dukettes' so despised by the fiercely partisan Lancastrian chronicler Walsingham.

Perhaps it would be wrong to read too much egalitarianism into Richard's creation of nobility from commoners. To a large extent he simply wanted to create his own nobility – a nobility that was entirely beholden to himself and thus a check to the potentially dangerous aristocratic factions already established. In this he was merely carrying on the policy of his grandfather, Edward III.

But there was also a philosophical aspect to it. In surrounding himself with those whom he adjudged the wisest in counsel – regardless of age or birth – Richard was once again simply following the prevailing political theory of the time. The *Secretum Secretorum,* with which Richard would almost certainly have been familiar, advised that the king should not despise the counsel of those who were young or low-born. 'And if it so be that a young man of low degree give you good counsel, do not underestimate him.' The rather curious reason the book gives for this extraordinarily liberal attitude to status is that you never know what star sign someone has been born under. It might be one that has conferred wisdom: 'For it is possible that a man shall be born under such a constellation that he shall have wisdom.'[26]

There was one creation, however, which might even indicate a spirit of sexual egalitarianism in Richard's policy of ennoblement – for in 1397 he created Margaret Marshal a duchess – making her the first woman to hold the title of duchess in her own right.[27]

To judge men by their merit rather than by their birth was clearly anathema to the great magnates of the realm – and well it might be, for such a policy gave them no advantage. But nevertheless it seems to have been the practice (for whatever reasons) of King Richard II.

CHAUCER AND NOBILITY

These same ideas of meritocracy appear throughout Chaucer's works. Indeed, one of the most important questions which thread their way in and out of the poems is: 'What is the true nature of *gentilesse*' – that is, 'nobility'? What makes a person noble?

The Wife of Bath is particularly scornful of the idea that nobility of character is something that just anyone can inherit:

'But, for ye speken of swich gentillesse
As is descended out of old richesse,
That therefore sholden ye be gentil men,
Swich arrogance is not worth an hen.
Looke who that is moost virtuous always,
Pryvee and apert and moost entendeth ay
To do the gentil dedes that he kan;
Taak hym for the grettest gentil man.'
       The Wife of Bath's Tale, III, ll. 1109–16

'But, because you speak about gentility
As if it is inherited like old money,
And so by line of descent you are gentlemen,
Such arrogance is not worth a hen.
See who is always the most virtuous,
In private and in public, and always most intends
To do the gentle deeds that he is able:
Take him for the greatest gentleman.'

Here the Wife of Bath is almost echoing the famous verse attributed to John Ball, one of the leaders of the Peasants' Revolt of 1381: 'When Adam delved [dug] and Eve span [spun]/ Who was then the Gentleman?' Of course, it might be argued that the Wife is a character, and no character speaks for Chaucer himself. But the same point occurs in the tales of the Franklin and the Clerk and in Chaucer's short poem *Gentilesse*. It is also there in *The Tale of Melibee*, which is told by Chaucer the pilgrim-narrator. Besides, just look at who are the only two absolutely praiseworthy characters in *The Canterbury Tales*: the salt-of-the-earth brothers, the Parson and the Plowman. Chaucer himself, it seems, gave no weight to nobility of birth as a guarantee of nobility of character.

The whole question of personal nobility and social advancement must have turned over more than once in the private depths of Chaucer's mind, as the fortunate son of a humble vintner made his way among the great and powerful at court. But it

The Wife of Bath.

is also possible that, as the chief poet of Richard's affinity, he was expressing a major aspect of royal policy – and an aspect which we see operating throughout Richard's reign and one which sorely vexed his enemies. Chaucer put thoughts on parchment that the rebels cheered in 1381 – and they weren't notions that barons like Warwick, Arundel and Gloucester would have liked one little bit ...

RICHARD'S INFORMAL ENTERTAINMENT

Perhaps we should distinguish between the official policies which Richard adopted and his private preferences. Elaborate ceremonial and exaggerated deference to princes were all the fashion in the modern European court. Richard could not but maintain such things – and perhaps, too, they suited his concept of kingship. But it may be that he also sought to escape such formality in his entertainment. He was certainly capable of dropping the trappings of formality when he chose. The Monk of Evesham describes how in 1389 Richard caused a *frisson* by suddenly turning up at the Great Council and sitting down casually and without the usual ceremony.[28] In that instance he was clearly doing it for effect, but on the other hand he does seem to have fostered an easy-going atmosphere during public readings at court. Social ranks were allowed to mingle and a relaxed atmosphere apparently was encouraged.

A recent study of late medieval reading habits contrasts the public readings of the continental courts with those of Britain. In France, we are told, a public reading 'was isolated as an event and carried on with a certain self-consciousness and intensity. It featured the ruler in his official capacity as patron, supporter, and exemplar of officially approved values, and channelled attention towards texts designed specifically to augment the prestige of the political establishment.'

The British courts were, on the other hand, characterized by a certain 'status-suspension'. 'The records that preserve the secular reading behaviour of James I of Scotland and Richard II attribute no great moral or political virtue to their activity, beyond the simple pleasure it brought them. Although, no doubt, due respect was observed, the king or lord as reader [*i.e.* as listener-cum-reader] is generally subsumed into the background, part of the happy group ... Unlike France and the Burgundian court, therefore ... British reading almost invokes a sense of festival, or ritual inversion and status relaxation.'[29]

THE ART OF KEEPING A LOW PROFILE

But even if Richard liked his court to be easy-going in its entertainment, the political reality was anything but relaxed.

The country was riven by faction, with the royal court pitted against the magnates. These were a loose and variable coalition, generally headed by Thomas of Woodstock, Duke of Gloucester; Thomas Beauchamp, Earl of Warwick; Richard, Earl of Arundel; and Thomas Mowbray, Earl of Nottingham.

Literary scholars have been rather reluctant to see Chaucer as a participant in factional politics, and yet in such an atmosphere it was not possible to sit on the sidelines. You could not be unaligned. And whatever the mechanics of patronage, there is little doubt that Chaucer was a king's man. In his book *Social Chaucer*, Paul Strohm writes: 'As a person of his time and as a professional courtier and civil servant, he had no choice but to participate in factional politics.'[30]

Strohm painstakingly builds up a picture of Chaucer's circle of friends and acquaintances. The vast majority of them were members of the royal faction; and the records indicate that Chaucer had very little contact with anyone of the opposite faction: 'the "aristocratic" group is very sparsely represented in Chaucer's circle of acquaintance.'[31]

Strohm also demonstrates how dangerous any such political affiliation could be. In 1387, the 'aristocratic' faction – the so-called 'Lords Appellant' – rebelled and took control of the government. In 1388, eleven royal retainers were condemned by the rebels. Of these Chaucer had verifiable contact with no less than eight.

Chaucer, more than many, in those last years of the fourteenth century, was vulnerable to being tarred by the brush of his acquaintance. It was precisely Chaucer's class of upwardly mobile professional courtiers that was most at risk from the vengeance of the great lords. All those who died under the rule of Gloucester, Arundel, Warwick and Co. came from this middle stratum – what Paul Strohm calls 'that particularly volatile segment of non-aristocratic gentlepersons *en service* ...' Strohm adds: 'All were king's men, but Chaucer and his associates managed to be king's men in a less rushed, less greedy, more circumspect, and more thoughtful way.'[32]

In other words, they were more canny, and therefore managed to survive the vengeance of the rebel lords. It was probably only by skilful playing of the political cards that Chaucer avoided the fate suffered by his fellow bureaucrat, Thomas Usk, who was beheaded in 1388.

For example, in 1385, the magnates proposed a bill to take the power to appoint customs officers away from the king and restrict such appointments to the advice of the King's Council. Chaucer was a customs officer at the time this bill was presented, and it may be that he read the warning signs. By December of 1386 he had voluntarily handed over his controllerships of the wool and petty customs. He also started to make a base for himself in Kent, and, although remaining a king's man, he established an increasing distance between himself and the

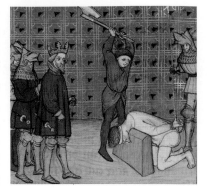

Executions followed the seizures of power by the rebel barons of 1386.

court. It is even possible that he spent some time in hiding abroad.

In May 1388, when things began to get really dangerous, the rebel magnates demanded a wholesale cancellation of certain royal annuities of which Chaucer was again a beneficiary. There is no doubt that Chaucer must have felt extremely exposed at this point.[33] However, some time after the presentation of the rebel lords' petition and before the close of parliament, Chaucer deftly transferred his questionable annuity to one John Scalby. Once again he proved himself an astute player in dangerous times.

Strohm writes: 'Those chamber knights who perished in 1388 ... Burley, Beauchamp, Berners and Salisbury – harvested patronage throughout the decade and with accelerating intensity in those critical years when Richard sought to confirm old supporters and reward new ones ... In contrast, the active chamber knights who survived – Clanvowe, Neville, Stury, and Vache, together with household knight Clifford – appear to have distanced themselves from Richard by strategies very similar to Chaucer's. They kept a low profile in terms of patronage.'[34]

One chamber knight who kept a very low profile may have done so because of advice from Chaucer. Philip de la Vache was a friend of the poet and probably around this time Chaucer addressed a poem to him (*Truth – Balade de Bon Conseyl*). In it he advises Vache to flee from the crowd, to live off his own resources, because of the hatred directed at those who have made money and to remember that social climbing is a dangerous business ... In other words, all the things that Chaucer put into practice himself at this time he recommended as appropriate action for his friend. And it looks as if Vache took the advice. He resigned as Keeper of the King's Park in October 1386 and didn't surface again until Richard was back in power.

And it seems likely that it was at this moment, when Richard had taken back the reins of power, that Chaucer addressed what is, perhaps, his most overtly political poem to him. *Lak of Stedfastnesse* is the one poem Chaucer left us which has an expressly political message. Although the poem has been traditionally dated to the late 1390s, Paul Strohm has convincingly placed the poem in the years 1389–90.[35] Strohm notes that it is 'highly conventional' and an example of the standard advice-to-princes poetry of the period. Times are parlous, Chaucer says; the world is not what it was when honest folk were protected by neighbour and nation. In an envoy, which in one manuscript is explicitly addressed to Richard, Chaucer exhorts the king to be honourable, to look after his people, to hate abusing power in order to gain money, to allow nothing that is shameful to his position as prince, and to punish those who have done wrong.

Now on the surface this sounds as if Chaucer is being highly critical of Richard and advising him to reform himself. Perhaps this is why critics have generally placed it at the end of Richard's reign. But if, as seems more likely, Chaucer wrote this in 1389–90, the stern advice would actually have been highly congenial to Richard. For this was the moment when the king was reasserting his royal authority. He had turned the tables on the baronial opposition who had so nearly ousted him but a few years before, and who had since been running the country for their own extortionate ends. The 'advice' that Chaucer 'offers' in the envoy is, in fact, little more than a policy statement on behalf of the king. The poem demonstrates both Chaucer's closeness to Richard, and his role as mouthpiece for the court party.

It is also worth noting that once the danger of baronial vengeance against Richard's party had passed, Chaucer felt himself able to accept from the king a new lucrative appointment – this time as Clerk of the King's Works. There seems little doubt that Chaucer was a skilful player of the political game – or maybe a lucky one – in the 1387–8 crisis. Perhaps this canniness extended to his acceptance of literary patronage.

CHAPTER 4

A time of intellectual ferment

~

St Dunstan writing. The church had long been the torch-bearer for literacy.

The last quarter of the fourteenth century was a period of intense intellectual ferment and – oddly enough – intellectual freedom. And in a way it was all the church's own fault.

Of course, the church had had no intention of inciting *hoi polloi* to inappropriate activities such as reading the Bible and then discussing it, and it certainly never intended the masses to start debating the tenets of the Christian faith or to begin demanding radical changes to the social fabric of the country. It was all the unfortunate result of circumstances spiralling out of ecclesiastical control. But, none the less, the church had started it.

A century and a half earlier, in 1215, Pope Innocent III and his advisers had gathered in the Lateran Palace in Rome, and ingenuously laid down some provisions for the universal instruction of ordinary folk. It seemed to be a reasonable enough proposition that those people who thought of themselves as Christian should have at least some glimmering as to what being a Christian meant. In a world in which the practice of religion was carried out almost exclusively in Latin, this required, in practical terms, providing the uneducated mass of the people with some form of instruction in a language they could understand.

Roll the clock forward 64 years to 1281, and change the scene to England. That staunch defender of the rights of the church, the eminent Archbishop of Canterbury, John Peckham, tries to put Innocent's ideas into effect with a systematic programme of instruction for the laity. Alas! Had he known that his seemingly innocuous proposals would result in one of the most serious challenges to the authority of the church in the nation's history, he would probably have kept his mouth shut. Had he realized the strife and violence that would ensue precisely one hundred years after he signed the edict, he might never have let the ink dry on the parchment.

But how could Archbishop Peckham have foreseen that, in the second half of the fourteenth century, ordinary English men and women would become increasingly interested in what we might nowadays refer to as 'leisure pursuits'? Even if he were clairvoyant, he could never have guessed the terrible consequences of such self-indulgence ...

The problem for the church began, unforeseeably enough, in the mid-fourteenth century when a plague reduced the population of Europe by a third. Terrible as the Black Death was, it had this happy effect for those who lived through it: since there were fewer people to do the work, the survivors could charge almost what they liked for their services. And they could pick and choose. More money and choice meant more leisure time.

Of course in those days that didn't mean surf-boarding and D-I-Y. The 'leisure pursuits' enjoyed by our fourteenth-century forebears were, some of them, slightly more cerebral than ours today, and (especially after the horrors of the plague made them pay fresh attention to heaven and hell) they revolved a great deal around the discussion of religion. That was the trouble.

Since Peckham's day, the church had been happily encouraging the production of religious texts in the English language, with the admirable objective of spreading the knowledge of Christianity around amongst its believers. Even as late as 1357, the Archbishop of York, John Thoresbey, had his instructions to parish priests distributed in English. Naturally, such a publication was not designed to turn the laity into religious adepts – 'rather they were given a moral agenda and told to believe'.[1]

It was unfortunate that this initiative on the part of the church coincided with the rise to eminence of the church establishment's most formidable critic to date, John Wyclif.

THE CHURCH'S WEALTH UNDER ATTACK

The date of Wyclif's birth is unknown, but he was a Yorkshireman from the North Riding. He became Warden of Merton College, Oxford, in 1356, Master of Balliol College in 1361 and the Warden of Canterbury Hall in 1365. He graduated as a Doctor of Theology in 1372. Even on the evidence of an implacable enemy like the chronicler Henry Knighton, Wyclif was a formidable figure. 'He was', said Knighton, 'the most eminent theologian of that time. He was reckoned second to none in philosophy, and incomparable in scholastic learning. He strove to outshine the ability of others in the subtlety of learning, and the profundity of his reasoning, and to change their opinions.'[2] Knighton, in fact, seems to have held him somewhat in awe. Wyclif's talents were certainly recognized in royal circles. Edward III employed him to

John Wyclif.

negotiate with the Pope in 1374, and in the same year Wyclif was rewarded with the living (that is a church position with an annual income) of Lutterworth in Leicestershire. As Wyclif's star rose in royal circles and at Oxford, his criticisms of the church establishment increased. For the most part, however, his criticisms were not new, nor were they all that extraordinary.

Over the centuries there had been a healthy tradition of criticism from within the church itself. The monastic orders, the mendicants and the parish priests were all in competition with each other for the support and resources of the faithful. Monks would criticize friars, who would in their turn criticize the parish priests and the monks. Gerald of Wales (*c.* 1146–*c.* 1220) and Walter Map (*c.* 1200), for instance, attacked the monastic orders for the extravagance and hypocrisy of their behaviour. And Richard FitzRalph, Archbishop of Armagh (*d.* 1360), spent the last ten years of his life attacking the validity and delinquency of the mendicant orders. The Dominican Catherine of Siena (1347–80) lambasted the bishops as 'those incarnate demons, who think of nothing but of good cheer and of having magnificent palaces and fine carriages' – and yet she was employed on papal missions and eventually canonized![3]

The fact was that the church had grown over time into the richest and most powerful institution in Europe. In England, it rivalled and sometimes threatened the royal power and dominated much of the cultural life of the country. It collected vast amounts of money in taxes and enjoyed privileges and exemptions that the lay magnates could only dream about. The huge sums that passed through its coffers every year had turned the church into a gigantic commercial operation on a par with today's global corporations. No wonder if accusations of corruption were rife. It was only to be expected. The ecclesiastics lived like lords in their abbeys and monasteries, where, instead of the plain diet and austerity enjoined on them by their founders, they ate and drank the best that money could buy. They lived in fantastical palaces of soaring spires, dressed in fine cloth, and taxed the poor: everyone was expected to pay his tithes – or a yearly 'tenth' of their worldly possessions. Those who failed could suffer the worst penalty that the church could provide: excommunication, which would shut them off not simply from the right to participate in religious services but also from the love of God *in aeternitate*. It would also, of course, shut them off from the rest of the community.

The medieval church created wealth in a variety of ingenious ways. It took money and goods in lieu of sins committed; this was the business of Pardons and Indulgences. It also encouraged folk to get away from it all and go on pilgrimage, or at least promise to go, and if they failed to fulfil their promise, they could make up for it by donating the money they would have spent on the pilgrimage to the church. If they *did* go on pilgrimage, they'd give the money to the church anyway. The church couldn't lose either way.

The church also ran a very interesting insurance scheme. You paid money to a group of priests who would promise to sing a daily mass for you after you died, thereby ensuring that God provided you with a better quality service in the after-life. And of course any money or goods offered up to dead saints and inanimate images had to be taken care of by the living and the mobile. All in all, it added up to a huge industry – conjuring money out of thin air – or rather, according to the critics, out of the credulity and superstition of simple folk.

Avignon: the Palace of Paranoia.

John Wyclif contrasted the image of the destitute Christ walking 'in painful poverty' with the church he saw all around him, 'whose dark recesses hid away wealth that, liberated, could set the public world to rights'.⁴ The pope's palace in Avignon, built in the earlier part of the century, symbolized what the church had become.

It was a paranoid's palace – a fortress turned in on itself with its back set against the rest of humanity. There was only one entrance, ensuring that ingress and egress could be tightly controlled. In the inner courtyard, the window at which the pope would appear to give his blessings was tucked into the corner to minimize his exposure to any malevolence in the carefully selected crowd. In the 'Grand Tinnel', or refectory, the meat was cut up by specially licensed carvers, because no one was allowed to carry a knife in the presence of the pope – so fearful was he of assassination. And deep in the inner recesses of the palace lay the Great

The window from which the Pope would bless the crowd – safely tucked into a corner

Treasury – complete with a stone-flagged floor that was entirely false. Should any robber pierce through the multi-layered guards of this most tightly controlled of palaces, the riches he would see in this treasure house were not the whole story. The real wealth, provided by the rich and poor from all over Christendom, lay beneath the pope's false floor. This was the grubby secret that lay at the heart of the Catholic church six hundred years ago.⁵

Wyclif argued that the church should give up its vast wealth and property, and return to the simplicity and poverty that Christ had maintained whilst he lived upon the earth. Most dangerous of all, Wyclif argued that the church should have no monopoly of teaching the Word of God and that, in fact, it had forfeited the right to do so by its very pursuit of wealth and power. The ultimate authority was not the church, Wyclif claimed, but the Bible.

Such arguments were, of course, music to the ears of the lay aristocracy who stood to benefit from any redistribution of the church's wealth. If the monasteries and abbeys were to be broken up, and the church reduced to Biblical poverty, new owners for all that vast wealth and those huge estates would have to be found, and the upper gentry were generously prepared to fulfil the role.

Wyclif's arguments were also useful ammunition against the church for its chief rival, the crown, in the continual struggle for political and financial supremacy. That wily old power-broker, Chaucer's one-time patron and brother-in-law, John of Gaunt recognized Wyclif's potential and encouraged him in his denunciations of the church.

THE CHURCH FINALLY CONDEMNS WYCLIF

By 1377, however, the ecclesiastical hierarchy had caught on to the frightening implications of the eminent doctor's discourse. The Bishop of London, William Courtenay, summoned Wyclif to St Paul's to answer charges of heresy and error. Wyclif arrived with an armed guard including Gaunt and others. Heated words ensued in the cathedral between the bishop and the lords. John of Gaunt threatened to drag Courtenay out by his hair, and a riot broke out, during which Wyclif made a prudent retreat.[6] Pope Gregory XI then condemned a selection of Wyclif's ideas, and the next year there was an attempt to put Wyclif on trial again. The doctor presented himself at Lambeth before the bishops, but, before the trial could begin, Chaucer's old friend Sir Lewis Clifford stood up and announced himself as an emissary from the Princess of Wales on whose behalf he was instructed to prohibit any formal sentence on the doctor of theology from Oxford. The trial collapsed.

There had always been critics of the church, and the church could be cheerfully tolerant of them – indeed it may well have welcomed them. Healthy self-criticism – even radical reappraisal – was not something that the ecclesiastics necessarily shrank from, but (and here is the big 'but') such criticism was tolerable only as long as it was carried on within the church. It was perfectly acceptable to discuss fundamental issues of faith in low voices in the cloisters or across the polished floorboards of the bishop's study, but it was not at all desirable to have any old shoemaker or weaver raising such questions in the local tavern or in a Bible study group over the shop. The church had no desire to see its dirty linen washed in public by any Tom, Dick or Harriet. And in all practical terms that meant confining the discussion of religious reform to the language of the church – Latin. So long as the debate took place in Latin, the church could control who participated in it.

ATTACKING THE CHURCH IN ENGLISH!

It was thus unfortunate that Wyclif's discomposing analysis of the church coincided with the blossoming of the English language. The church itself, under the generalship of Archbishop Peckham, had been in the vanguard of the march towards the vernacular and now, in the 1380s, the royal court was rallying to the same flag.

The recognition of English as a language as capable as any other of conveying complex ideas also fitted in with Wyclif's theology. Since Wyclif claimed that the ultimate authority was not the church but the Bible, and since the church had forfeited the right to be the Good Book's sole interpreter, every man had the right – indeed, the *duty* – to examine it for himself. Religion was to be handed back to the ordinary Christian, and that meant that not only the texts but also the *discussion* of the texts had to be in English.

The danger of this (from the church's point of view) was that men would not simply read the Gospels for themselves, but that before long they would learn 'how to formulate arguments themselves and how to evaluate critically arguments presented to them'.[7] This was more than the church was prepared to accommodate.

There was Wyclif, provoking a whole generation of translators and writers to produce an avalanche of religious discussion and criticism in the vernacular. His followers had already launched a vast programme to translate the Bible itself. And suddenly biblical translation itself no longer seemed so attractive to the average monk in the scriptorium. Tucked away in the Abbey of St Mary's, Leicester, the chronicler Henry Knighton complained that the Bible had been entrusted to the clergy and the doctors of the church so that they could administer it as, and when, they deemed necessary. It was their precious 'talent' to use as they saw fit. The Gospels were their 'jewels', their personal treasure. By making them available to just *anyone* (including 'women who could read'), Wyclif had 'spread the Evangelists' Pearls to be trampled by swine'.[8]

The pages of Knighton give a vivid impression of the fear and hatred that Wyclif aroused in the comfortable monastic world. Trying to convey something of the horror of those dark days, the huge popular support for Wyclif's ideas and the power of the arguments (which Knighton clearly felt himself) the poor chronicler flails in all directions, trips over his own accusations and contradicts himself on page after page. At one point he claims that the people only flock to hear these radical preachers because they were forced to do so at sword point by the gentry. At another he says it was the power of the ideas that won folk over: 'They so far prevailed with their laborious dogmas that a half or even the greater part of the populace supported their sect: for some they persuaded in their hearts, but others they compelled to join them from fear and shame.' Elsewhere again he accuses them of barking like dogs: 'they filled the land', he says, 'and peopled it as though they were begotten in a single day, and they became so bold that they blushed at nothing, and shamelessly barked in public as well as in private places, with the voices of tireless dogs'. In another place he ascribes their success to their 'eloquent and mellifluous charm', then again, he tells us: 'almost everywhere the greater number of them were vicious, and few others adhered to them', and a few pages later that the 'sect was highly regarded in those days, and it grew so rapidly that you might hardly see two people in the street, but one of them would be a follower of Wyclif'.[9]

Criticism of the worldly church was coming from all quarters. Even an orthodox and conservative writer like John Gower was mumbling into his Latin text gobbets of censure that would later carry an embarrassingly Wycliffite ring to them:

> What is Holy Church except a faithful band of men? Hence it is evident that the layman whom faith itself protects is a part of the Church, and that a priest is not his better unless he lives better. Who would deny this to me? ... Why then does the clergy want to keep the name of Holy Church for itself, as if it were another God?[10]

Recent historians have shown that it was not necessarily Wyclif himself who sparked all this off, and that lay criticism of the church had been mounting for some time.[11] But as far as the late fourteenth-century church establishment was concerned, there was no doubt at all. The blame could be laid firmly at Wyclif's door. And yet by 1380, although the church hierarchy was growing uneasy, no one still had any idea just how dangerous the situation really was.

This ferment of radical ideas was a heady brew for a population unused to having any access to learning. The disputes over religious matters were bound to spill over into political discussion, for the two were inextricably linked. With their new-found independence of means and their new exposure to ideas, the English population of the late fourteenth century must have been one of the most politicized in the history of Britain.

People must have known they were living in exciting times, and they must have felt a tremendous sense of empowerment. For the first time since anyone could remember, the fate of ordinary people appeared to be in their own hands. Maybe.

The taverns and corner shops of old England must have been buzzing – not with the latest news of how England was doing in the World Cup or of celebrity divorces – but with the latest sermon preached in the town or the latest religious scandal.

These were extraordinary times to be living in. And in 1381 it was all to boil over. The times were to get even more exciting and extraordinary ... perhaps *too* exciting and *too* extraordinary ...

THE PEASANTS' REVOLT OF 1381

Nobody saw it coming. And when it did come, it all happened so fast that no one had time to organize any real resistance. It was quite astonishing.

In mid-May there were rumours about some people in Essex refusing to pay their taxes. Never mind! The commissioners ought to be able to deal with them. But then towards the end of the month a group of commissioners were violently attacked at Brentwood – north-east of London on the Colchester road. Within two or three days, rebels had attacked the Abbey of Lesnes, near what is now Woolwich. Within another three days the small town of Dartford was up in arms, and by the 10th of June – just eleven or twelve days after the first outbreak of violence – the town of Canterbury was under rebel control. Two days later, tens of thousands of rebels were encamped on Blackheath, on London's doorstep, and the boy-king Richard II and his court had taken shelter in the Tower and the Archbishop had been murdered.

John Ball addresses the peasants during the revolt of 1381.

How could all this have happened? How could so many people have congregated so suddenly and so unexpectedly from so many shires of England, without anyone in authority having had the slightest suspicion that something was brewing?

For many years, following the cue of the medieval monastic chroniclers, the rebels were written off as a brutal rabble, without a programme and without organization, but historians have now begun to realize that to make something like that happen on that sort of scale, with that sort of speed, requires tremendous organization. Even back then, the chronicler Thomas Walsingham was vaguely aware that it was an amazing feat of logistics: 'All these evils befell the various regions of England at about the same time and almost on the same days ...' he wrote, 'despite the long distances that separated them.'[12] It could not have been a spontaneous outburst of anger. The distances were too great and the timing too precise, as anyone who has tried to organize a demonstration in today's world could testify.

'The revolt happened', writes one historian, 'because a newly powerful class of "peasant leaders" had emerged who could lead and articulate economic and social grievances which grinding poverty had previously kept suppressed.' These leaders were men of standing in their local communities – bailiffs, jurymen and stewards. The same prosperity that had brought the religion of ordinary people to life had enabled literacy, and literacy in its turn had enabled 'informed protest and the rejection of authoritative pronouncements'. [13]

Far from being the 'slavish band possessed by utter lunacy' that John Gower saw, the rebels were intelligently organized and intellectually motivated. They tended towards the better-off of the rural population, with perhaps as little as a tenth being actual serfs. They attacked political targets and made great efforts to attack the records of the fiscal and judicial administration. They demonstrated a lively awareness of the written word and of its power. [14]

One claim which the rebels made, however, might not seem very clever to us. It was a claim that sounds so like total moonshine that for many years it has helped to reinforce the impression of the rebels as an ignorant, simple-minded rabble. They appeared to be convinced that the king was on their side.

From the start, the rebel watchword had been 'With King Richard and the true commons'. And especially in East Anglia the rumour was that the movement had the king's blessing. When the rebels took over Canterbury almost the first thing they did was to summon the mayor, bailiffs and commons of the town and examine them 'as to whether they would swear in good will to be faithful and loyal to King Richard and the loyal commons of England or not'. [15]

One of the secret messages that were circulated during the revolt ran: 'Look you shape you to one head and no more ... The king's son of heaven shall pay for all.' An allusion to Christ, 'the king's son of heaven', certainly; but the dark message could also have resonated on another level: as a reference to the 14-year-old Richard – the young, bright and beautiful son of the Black Prince and grandson of Edward III, whose badge was the sun in splendour in the heavens.

Of course, a delusion of royal complicity would be exactly the sort of thing one might expect rebels to employ to encourage each other. But is it possible that there was a grain of truth in it? The closer we look at the demands made by the rebels, the more they seem to fit with the ambitions and philosophy of those closest to the young king. And if we are right to give the rebel leadership more credit for literacy and cogent political thought, then we ought also to place their ideas in the context of fourteenth-century internationalism. We cannot simply assume these newly educated people were ignorant of political developments and thought on the Continent. The internationalism of fourteenth-century culture may have permeated down to the roots of English society.

THE CONCEPT OF DIRECT KINGLY RULE

One of the most authoritative records of the revolt tells us that the rebels 'said among themselves that there were more kings than one and that they would neither suffer nor have any king except King Richard'.[16]

As everyone knew, the danger of having a child ascend the throne was that the great barons might take advantage of the subsequent weakness at the centre of power, in order to take over and run the country in their own interests. And indeed that is exactly what had been happening. Since 1377 the astronomical sum of £250,000 had been thrown away on the magnates' military ambitions in France, with not a single victory or gain of territory to show for it. The hawkish barons, like Arundel and Gloucester (then the Earl of Buckingham), saw the war with France as their main chance – and one which they could happily pursue at the expense of the English tax-payer. And the boy-king and his party, even if they wanted to stop the war, were powerless to hold back these mighty warlords. The reins of power were in too many hands. The crown party must have agreed with the peasants, that there were indeed 'more kings than one'.[17]

A strong centralized monarchy, able to dominate and subdue rival magnates, was not, as we have seen, a wild idea conjured up by Wat Tyler to sugar the pill of revolt. It was a much-discussed political ideal. Dante wrote: 'There must be one king to rule and govern otherwise not only do they in the kingdom fail to reach the goal [peace and tranquillity] but the kingdom itself lapses into ruin.'[18] Marsilius of Padua suggested an Aristotelian formula for ensuring the dominance of one ruler: 'The ruler must have a force which is so great that it is larger than that of a single individual or of several taken together, but smaller than that of the multitude.'[19]

Clearly this was not the case in Richard's reign. The Duke of Lancaster's retinue could outnumber and outshine the King's, and the Duke of Gloucester and the Earl of Arundel were forever scheming together to achieve their own ends. Richard and certain of his advisers may have had a sneaking sympathy with the rebels' determination 'not to give way until all the nobles and magnates of the realm had been completely destroyed'.[20]

Of course, the court party would not have imagined a land without any dukes and earls at all. The monarchists simply wanted to get rid of the current lot of barons, who claimed their lordship by right of birth handed down since the time of William the Conqueror. In their place, the young king and his advisers sought to establish a 'service aristocracy' appointed by Richard in the royal interest. And, curiously enough, this is exactly what the rebels were demanding.

When the 14-year-old Richard finally confronted the rebel leader, Wat Tyler, at Smithfield, the young king might not have been particularly shocked to hear the rebel leader state that 'No lord should have lordship in future, but it should be divided among all men, except for the king's own lordship.'[21] After all, Richard must have heard the same ideas in the poem that was on everybody lips and in everybody's consciousness in the 1380s, *Piers Plowman*:

> The King and the Commons . and Commonsense the third
> Shape law and honesty . each man to know his own.[22]

The idea of the king directly ruling his people, without the hostility of a self-seeking magnate class, was not a crazy anarchist proposal; it was an ideal of monarchy recognized by political thinkers all over Europe and traceable back to Aristotle. What the rebels of 1381 were demanding was little more than a social system already in place in some Italian city republics – a free citizenry under a strong ruler. Of course, there were differences: the strong rulers of the Italian states tended to be self-made despots, whilst the rebel leaders would have agreed with Dante, Marsilius and other political thinkers of the time that the strong ruler should be a hereditary monarch.

Philippe de Mézières presents his extraordinary book to Richard II.

Fourteen years later, the ex-Chancellor of Cyprus, Philippe de Mézières, presented the 28-year-old Richard with an even more radical proposal than that of the rebels of 1381. He proposed the abolition of all personal property on the grounds that the king serves as a 'father' to his people and has complete responsibility for their welfare.[23] Philippe de Mézières describes the Delectable Garden in which the ideal monarchy could flourish. It's actually an extraordinary socialist vision ('to each according to his need') and not necessarily something you'd expect from a man who was one of the last great propagandists of the crusades:

> All fruits were held in common by the inhabitants, to each according to his need, and the words 'my own' were never heard. These people lived so happily together, that they seemed never to grow old. All tyranny and harsh rule was banished from the garden, though there was a king, who stood for authority and the common good, and he was so loved and looked up to that he might have been the father of each and all. And no wonder, for he had such concern for the welfare of his subjects, dwellers in the garden, that neither he nor his children owned anything in person.[24]

The Italian jurists may not have gone this far, but Marsilius of Padua stressed the need for unity of government: 'Let us say that in a single city or state there must be only a single government; or if there is more than one ... there must be among them one in number which is supreme, to which all other governments are reduced, by which they are regulated, and which corrects any errors arising in them.'[25]

Of course, we are not suggesting that the Peasants' Revolt was necessarily instigated by the court party. But once it got under way, it would have presented the royal faction with a tempting opportunity to eliminate the baronial opposition. For the court party to encourage the uprising in this way would not have been an act of idealism – it would simply have been a piece of political opportunism by which the old troublesome aristocracy could be replaced with a service nobility totally within the king's gift.

In such a scenario, it would have been no surprise that the boy-king responded to Wat Tyler's demands as he did. When Tyler asked that 'no lord should have lordship in future, but it should be divided among all men, except for the king's own lordship' and 'that all men should be free and of one condition' he wasn't suggesting anything very different from what Philippe de Mézières was to propose in his *Letter to King Richard II*. And we should not be amazed that the boy king should have agreed to something in 1381 which he was to accept from the hand of the confidant of the King of France in 1395.

'To this the king gave an easy answer, and said that Wat should have all that he could fairly grant, reserving only for himself the regality of his crown.'[26]

If that is what the 14-year-old boy said, it sounds suspiciously like a well-rehearsed reply. Perhaps it was not mere youthful bravado, as the chroniclers would have us believe, that made Richard strike his spurs into his horse and cry out: 'Follow me, for I am your leader now!' Perhaps it had all been carefully rehearsed.

THE SAVAGE DEATH OF SIR SIMON BURLEY

The poll tax, which sparked off the 1381 revolt, had been pushed through Parliament to fund the ambitions of Gloucester, Arundel and John of Gaunt. Is it possible that the royal advisers saw the violent hostility the tax provoked as an opportunity to neutralize the baronage? The court was certainly prepared to allow itself to be thought friendly towards the rebels, despite the fact that the rebels were demanding the destruction of the baronial class. Perhaps it was not just a stance for the sake of deception.[27]

We are entering into the realms of speculation here, but it's a speculation that might help to explain a mystery that has puzzled observers of the reign over the centuries. What if the leading exponent of the idea of neutralizing the baronage were the boy-king's tutor, Sir Simon Burley? Burley's influence over Richard's household had increased after the resignation of the effective head of the administration, the chancellor, Richard, Lord Scrope in 1380; he was more than a mere ex-tutor.[28] Six years after the revolt, the Duke of Gloucester and the Earl of Arundel finally made their play for power. They directly challenged Richard's rule and, according to one chronicler, they even deposed him for a few days but failed to agree on which of them should take the crown. They executed Richard's key supporters and friends. But why were they so adamant that the elderly Sir Simon Burley must go to the executioner's block?

Despite desperate pleas from Queen Anne, from King Richard, and even from one of the rebel lords, Henry of Derby (the future Henry IV), the old man simply had to die. Why? What fuelled this extraordinary and unyielding hatred? Could it really be, as some scholars have suggested, just because they were jealous of the money Burley had made from his position at the king's right hand? Or could the reason for Gloucester's particularly bitter enmity have lain in Burley's role as political architect back during those dark days of 1381? Did the barons blame Burley for urging the young Richard to embrace the rebels' cause as a means of gutting the magnates' power?

Writing sometime around 1386 – possibly within a few months of the barons' uprising – John Gower conveys something of the hatred that was directed at the boy-king's advisers: 'The boy is free of blame, but those who have instrumented this boyish reign shall not endure without a fall. So not the king but his council is the cause of our sorrow, for which the land grieves as with a general murmur.'[29]

We may not know the precise extent – if any – of Burley's involvement in the revolt of 1381, but one thing seems certain. The revolt itself was not simply an unpremeditated outburst of anger. It was meticulously planned and executed and it came out of the dissemination of knowledge and ideas that marked the 1370s. The revolt was the physical expression of the extraordinary and unprecedented ferment of intellectual activity that made the latter fourteenth century such an exciting and exceptional time to be alive. A time when you could dare to think the unthinkable. A time when – to the horror of many powerful interests – you could even *do* the unthinkable.

THE BLOODY REPRESSION

The revolt of 1381 must have polarized attitudes towards the intellectual emancipation of ordinary men and women. The spread of ideas through the increasing
availability of texts in the vernacular was bound to be seen as yet another
contributing factor to the discontent of the peasant in the street. 'From 1380 on
the various ideas about the use of English came into violent collision.'[30] But the
intellectual ferment of the times did not diminish. Far from it. As we have seen,
the 1380s and 1390s were to witness the flowering of the English language as a
vehicle for intellectual and cultural communication, even as the church grew
more and more implacably opposed to it.

After that fateful confrontation at Smithfield, the boy-king led the rebels
away to Clerkenwell Fields, where the peasants then dispersed. One assumes
they felt they'd got what they'd come for. Richard had announced himself as
their leader, he'd already signed their pardons and granted their requests – so
what was the point of hanging around? Everyone presumably heaved a sigh of
relief. A short time passed, and then came the days of revenge.

The ax was sharpe, the stokke was harde
In the xiiij yere of kyng Richarde

went the rhyme (Richard was fourteen years old in 1381).[31] The king and the
lords pursued the rebels and 'had some of them dragged behind horses, some
put to the sword, some hanged on gallows, and some dismembered; and thus',
notes Adam Usk with a touching absence of Christian charity, 'did they slaughter them in their thousands'.[32] Seven thousand, according to the Monk of
Evesham.

According to one chronicler, the whole thing got quite out of hand. The
Monk of Westminster tells us that 'the populace shuddered at the spectacle of so
many gibbeted bodies exposed to the light of day ...' It reached the point when
many people thought it ought to stop: 'Despite all the retribution thus visited on
the guilty the severity of the royal displeasure seemed to be in no way mitigated
but rather to be directed with increased harshness towards the punishment of
offenders, so that it was widely thought that in the circumstances the king's generous nature ought to exercise leniency rather than vindictiveness ...'. On the
other hand there were some who maintained that the scale of the slaughter was

poetic justice – equalling the havoc that the rebels themselves had caused in the first place. [33]

By now the numbers of executions had grown so great that the Mayor of London had set up a wooden block and axe in the middle of Cheap – the medieval equivalent of Oxford Street – so that they could get through the day's quota of killings. The friends of Flemings who had been killed during the revolt were handed the axe to carry out the punishment themselves, and even wives were given permission to execute their husbands' murderers. Some 'were hanged, some beheaded, some drawn, and some punished by a combination of these sufferings'. It was all spiralling out of control. Those with grudges began to inform on their enemies, whilst others found they could get rich quick by denouncing their neighbours and then taking money to drop the charges. It was saddening, said the Westminster Monk, 'to see the servant accusing his master, the citizen rising up against his neighbour, the wife convicting her husband, the maid threatening her mistress; and subordinates ... making monstrous charges against their superiors ... the ingenuities of greed threatened the overthrow of the entire body politic ...'[34]

And here we come to one of those curious omissions of history. Pick up almost any history book written in the second half of the twentieth century and you won't read much about the blood-letting after the revolt. Perhaps such unedifying behaviour struck historians as somehow inherently un-English, for they came to the general opinion that the chroniclers (despite their unusual degree of agreement) had got it wrong.

The *Oxford History of England*, for example, tells us: 'In Hertfordshire and Essex the severity shown moved even the monastic chroniclers to shocked protest, but, on the whole, the judicial proceedings reflect credit on the government. No mass reprisals were allowed; there were no tortures and very few attempts to convict without trial; and a surprisingly large number of persons whose guilt seems to have been clear, were either acquitted or punished with moderation.'[35]

The historians' generous assessment of the revenge wreaked on the peasants is based on an examination of the judicial record, which shows that relatively few executions took place after the revolt – perhaps as few as one hundred and ten. It is gratifying to reflect on the restraint shown by our forebears in such trying circumstances.

However, a recent study has swung the burden of evidence back in favour of the chroniclers. The historian, Andrew Prescott, has argued that the judicial records that have survived would not, in general, have recorded executions. However, the lists of forfeitures – that is, of lands and property seized by the crown in the wake of the revolt – give an entirely different picture. The number of forfeitures of property arising from those rebels executed or put to flight after the revolt was so huge that the officials could not cope, and emergency deputies had to be drafted in. The fact that the civil servants, who were supposed to record the reversion of forfeited lands to the Crown, were so overwhelmed is suggestive of a brutal persecution. A thousand killed in armed encounters and three hundred executed would probably be an underestimate. 'It is clear that, by any reckoning, 1381 is in the same league as the "Bloody Assizes", and that it ranks with the bloodiest reprisals in English history.'[36]

Upwards of thirteen hundred people is a sizeable proportion of a population of two and a half million, but the mass killings don't seem to have dampened the enthusiasm for reform – at least in one major area.

WYCLIF GETS THE BLAME

No matter where present-day historians place the origins of the Peasants' Revolt, those in power who lived through it, particularly the clerics, had no doubt how it came about: it was all the fault of that arch troublemaker, John Wyclif. If he hadn't encouraged all those people to start challenging the authority of the church establishment, none of this would have happened. At least as far as the church leaders were concerned, the responsibility for creating a climate of insubordination, disobedience and outright defiance, rested firmly with the Demon Doctor of Divinity from Oxford.

Neither the cataclysmic events of the revolt nor the savage repression, however, seem to have had much effect on either Wyclif's own activites or on the popular demand for changes within the church.

The country was buzzing. Radical reform was on many people's lips. When, in 1382, a certain William Smith boiled his cabbage soup over a fire he'd made from a painted statue of St Catherine, the frisson must have fanned the flames of many a market-square discussion and chilled the cosy recesses of many an abbey. 'If her head bleeds when we chop her up,' William is reported to have said, 'then we shall worship her as a saint.' Whoever heard of such sacrilege flaunted so brazenly?[37]

In the same year, when William Swinderby stood in front of a couple of millstones that had been propped up for sale outside a chapel in Leicester, crowds of people flocked to listen to him fulminate against the corruption of the clergy and the wickedness of the rich and powerful prelates. He had been banned from preaching in either church or churchyard, and yet people came in even greater numbers to listen to him now than before, complained the chronicler, Henry Knighton. They came from the town and they came from the country. It was living politics on their own doorstep. For, as always behind the statement of faith, there lay the implied struggle between the church and the state. Swinderby may have been banned from preaching in the church, but, he claimed, he 'could and would preach in the *king's highway*, in spite of the bishop'.[38] If the bishop's churches would not give him a platform, then the king's highway would.

At the same time, John Wyclif showed no sign of being chastened, neither by the violence of the previous year nor by the bloodiness of the subsequent repression.

The cloisters up and down England were probably quietly reverberating with the whispered words 'I told you so'. The dangers of letting *hoi polloi* dabble in the world of ideas could not have been more clearly demonstrated than by the horrors of the revolt. Hadn't the rebels' ideological leader, John Ball himself, confessed to being a follower of John Wyclif? That was the story that was going round. Wyclif must have been aware that many bejewelled ecclesiastical fingers were already pointing in his direction. No matter how much he abhorred and condemned the uprising, he was tarred by it.

Wyclif, however, was not the sort of man to lie low until the storm blew over. He went on the offensive. As soon as parliament met, in early May of 1382, Wyclif was there presenting a document to the Commons outlining his programme for the immediate dismantling of the church. The government of England, he advised, should break away from obedience to the pope at once; it should relieve the church of its property and forbid the employment of churchmen in secular offices. These were all demands, incidentally, that were on the wish-list that Wat Tyler presented to the king at Smithfield. Wyclif was hardly looking to ingratiate himself with the ecclesiastical powers that be.

Parliament, however, was in no mood for more radicalism no matter how heroic.

What happened next is worth covering in some detail because it illustrates the passions aroused by what can easily seem to us an arcane and arid theological debate. The intellectual ferment of the late fourteenth century was not just a question of scholastic penpushing.

Oxford was suddenly engulfed in an action-packed sequence of events more suited to the streets of New York during Prohibition than the quiet groves of academe. The philosophical wounds of the previous decade were re-opened, sore and still bleeding, and the knives were out – literally. If they'd had machine guns, they'd have been ready in the violin cases.

POWER-STRUGGLE:

THE CHURCH *VERSUS* THE OXFORD INTELLECTUALS, 1382

Of all the events of 1381, the most unfortunate from Wyclif's point of view was probably the murder by the rebels of the Archbishop of Canterbury, Simon Sudbury. He had been a nice man and no match for the Thundering Doctor of Divinity. Sudbury's replacement, however, was a different character altogether.

William Courtenay was a high-born aristocrat with a zero-tolerance programme in mind for anyone who tried to diminish his power as archbishop – and that included the pope.[39] Courtenay had long been one of Wyclif's bitterest opponents within the church, and he was probably the architect of the strategy of bloody repression after the revolt. He had no interest whatsoever in reconciliation. And he blamed the revolt on Wyclif.[40]

Archbishop Courtenay.

While Wyclif was cheerfully canvassing parliament in May 1382 to destroy the church as a power base, Courtenay was regrouping his nervous colleagues for a pre-emptive strike against the Evil Rector of Lutterworth. He summoned the bishops to a council at Blackfriars and laid before them his proposals to condemn Wyclif's ideas as heretical and to outlaw their circulation. This time there were going to be no interruptions by John of Gaunt or by the Princess of Wales.

There was, instead, an even more dramatic interruption. Some time around two or three o'clock in the afternoon, the whole place shook. The whole of London shook. The whole countryside for miles around shook. It was one of those rarest of phenomena – an English earthquake ... and in the Home Counties, what's more!

The weaker brethren amongst the bishops must have wobbled a trifle in their resolve to prosecute the eminent Oxford theologian. Perhaps they thought for one ghastly moment that God was telling them they were wrong and the Dreadful Doctor was right.[41] William Courtenay, however, was not a man who tolerated any sort of superstitious nonsense – not, that is, if got in the way of his plans. He told the bishops to pull themselves together and that the earthquake was simply a signal that they should root out heresy from the depths of the earth. By that evening, he had the satisfaction of seeing Wyclif's fate as a heretic signed and sealed by his bishops.

In the meantime, matters in Oxford were going from bad to worse. On Ascension Day, the most important sermon of the year was entrusted to one of Wyclif's most ardent supporters, Nicholas Hereford, and it was a sensation. It was reported that Hereford not only supported the Evil Rector in everything he said, but he also incited the people to insurrection and claimed that the murder of Archbishop Sudbury was totally justified – and what was worse, he said it all in plain English! To countenance these wretched ideas in the first place was bad enough, but to announce them to all and sundry, in broad daylight, in the common tongue, so that every yokel who packed the cemetery at St Frideswide, could hear and understand them – that was not only lunacy, it was treachery against his fellow clerks.

What on earth was going on at Oxford? The chancellor of the university, Robert Rigg, was not known as a follower of Wyclif. So why did he entrust such an important sermon to such a man at such a time? It may be that Robert Rigg, like the church leaders whom he was confronting, was more concerned with the power-play than he was with the theology. For him the important thing to establish was the university's independence of the archbishop. Whatever was said, however it was said, it was the business of the university and not the business of some churchman in London or Canterbury.

To make his point a little clearer, Rigg gave the next important sermon – for the festival of Corpus Christi – to another radical critic of the church establishment, Philip Repingdon – a man who had not even yet qualified as a doctor.

Courtenay went into action. He dispatched a letter to a certain Carmelite friar at Oxford, by the name of Peter Stokes. He enclosed a copy of the resolution passed by the council condemning Wyclif and ordering the arrest of anyone supporting his ideas, and instructed the friar to read it out to the congregation before Repingdon's up-coming sermon.

Peter Stokes must have regarded the missive from the primate as a mixed blessing. Of course it was all very nice to get communications from the spiritual leader of the country – especially a man with royal blood flowing his veins like William Courtenay. Yet did the great man really know what he was asking him to do?

Stokes had already bravely come out as an opponent of Hereford and had even appointed notaries to follow the fellow round and jot down everything he said, but it was one thing to have paid for a bit of innocent snooping and quite another to be expected to stand up in public and brave the wrath of the whole university.

Come Corpus Christi, Peter Stokes made his way to the church to find that Chancellor Rigg had taken unusually thorough precautions to protect freedom of speech within the university. He had gathered a hundred men armed with hauberks and swords and had got the mayor to provide another hundred. We don't quite know what happened, but we can imagine the scene: presumably Peter Stokes got up to speak, but before he could open his mouth the sound of a hundred swords sliding out of their scabbards caused him to sit down again rather quickly. Or perhaps he never even stood up. Perhaps when all eyes turned to him, he simply shrugged and nodded to Philip to carry on. Whatever happened, Peter Stokes didn't dare to read out Archbishop Courtenay's message of condemnation. In fact, after the sermon was over, he had to sit tight, amidst the bitter ashes of a mission unaccomplished, and watch as Philip Repingdon was escorted from the church by twenty armed men. Stokes reported sourly to his boss that he saw Repingdon wait for Chancellor Rigg at the church door, and then the two of them went off together in high spirits. The poor friar, meanwhile, didn't even dare leave the church for fear of his life.[42]

A week or so later, Stokes actually attempted to deliver a sermon rebutting Hereford's arguments, but again his courage failed him. He spotted that at least twelve members of his audience were carrying weapons badly concealed under their cloaks. The sight of the cold steel quite reasonably brought Stoke's oration to a halt, and he climbed ignominiously down from his chair. To his immense relief, that same day he received orders from Courtenay to abandon Oxford and report to Lambeth.[43]

Stokes wasn't the only one whose courage failed him. Chancellor Rigg had already presented himself before the Archbishop of Canterbury, but Courtenay refused to listen to him until he had heard Stokes's side of the story. When he finally summoned the Chancellor of Oxford before the convocation, he knew exactly what had been going on and was, as always, in no mood to compromise. Although Rigg tried to defend the privileges of his university, he was no match for the formidable Courtenay, and before the end of the session, the chancellor was on his knees begging forgiveness and promising to publish the condemnation of Wyclif's views all over Oxford. It was a humiliating climb-down.

Courtenay was now free to make his mark on the university. He demanded that the errant clerics be brought into line. Repingdon and another radical, John Aston, promptly disappeared from the scene. Nicholas Hereford, meanwhile, rushed off to appeal to the pope. Considering Hereford's previous blistering attacks on papal jurisdiction in England, this was, perhaps, a rather surprising plan of action. The result, however, was less surprising. As one historian puts it: Hereford 'with a disregard for the logic of his stance which boded ill for his commitment to the cause, left the country for Rome to put his case before the Pope, who showed somewhat greater consistency by committing him to prison'.[44]

CHAPTER 5

The church strikes back

⁓

The events of 1382 set the scene for the rest of the century. From now on the radical critics of the church were on the defensive. Wyclif's thoughts and ideas were now officially beyond the pale, and anyone who sympathized with them would have to reconcile themselves to the possibility that they could be condemned as heretics. It was an entirely novel situation in England.[1]

Many of those who had most vociferously voiced criticisms of the church either disappeared from the scene for a bit or else recanted, sometimes after a short spell of R&R in the Archbishop Courtenay's prison. Some, like Philip Repingdon (and later Nicholas Hereford) went on to achieve high office in the church establishment and became themselves champion persecutors of the unorthodox. There was no middle way. Either you were with the church or against it. If you were with the church you could not stand idly by while others attacked her.

But although Archbishop Courtenay had succeeded in putting the lid on the pot, it was still boiling away. He hadn't actually put out the fire. The critics of the church had to tread more carefully perhaps, but they were still at it – writing and preaching. What is more, the same issues were still being debated around the family fireside, in the alehouses and under village oaks up and down the country – and debated now with even greater fierceness and bitterness. The delight of new ideas and the hopes of changing society were now tinged with the resentment of wrongs suffered and blood spilt.

The church must also have been aware that its prohibitions against preaching were but a holding operation. Unless it could control the dissemination of ideas, the pot would continue to boil. To control the ideas, the church needed to put a stop to the use of the English language – at least on its own turf. The church establishment performed a spectacular U-turn on the emancipation of English.

THE CHURCH TURNS AGAINST THE ENGLISH LANGUAGE

The last twenty years of the fourteenth century witnessed the church and state becoming ever more sharply divided on the issue of language. The court still saw the expansion of English as essential to its integration into the international community. The church watched on anxiously, afraid that the spread of vernacular literacy would foment disaffection with its own authority. English became its *bête noire*. But – even so – few people in the 1380s could have guessed that, in a couple of decades, the mother tongue would become the litmus test for heresy.

When Archbishop Courtenay interrogated John Aston (an associate of Hereford and Repingdon) at Blackfriars in 1382, Aston insisted on replying in English – to the horror of the scribe recording the trial. The most significant moment came when the archbishop ordered Aston to reply in Latin 'on account of the laymen who were present'.[2] The great prelate had spilled the beans: he hated the idea of the secular people hearing or, even worse, *understanding* the arguments. The wheel had turned full circle from the days when Archbishop Peckham was so concerned to make the Word of God accessible to lesser mortals.

The aristocratic Courtenay saw the church as a power-base. As far as he was concerned, the church's role as mediator between the common people and their religion was what gave the church its power over them. He had no intention of surrendering any part of that power by allowing just anybody to understand sacred texts and theological debate. The language barrier was not a problem for Courtenay. On the contrary, it was all part of his meal-ticket. As long as the scriptures remained in Latin, the church remained the interpreter and the controller of Holy Writ.

But the church was not just Archbishop Courtenay. There were within it other men of a very different frame of mind – after all, the reform movement had found its origins within the church itself. And the church was becoming increasingly polarized between the conservatives, who were anxious to maintain all her privileges and wealth, and the liberal intellectuals, who acknowledged that there was some room for reform.

Consequently it was not a simple matter to whip the entire ecclesiastical establishment into line and to present a united front against the spread of English. That said, however, the more conservative elements in the church were already rounding to Courtenay's side. In 1384, for example, there was a brief inquiry held at Cambridge into the orthodoxy of a book called the *Speculum*

Vitae. Now this was an entirely mainstream, orthodox text. Everyone knew that. The only possible reason for questioning its orthodoxy was the fact that it had been translated into English.[3]

Of course, the church was not particularly keen to advertise its new-found aversion to the vernacular – perhaps because it was too much of a U-turn, perhaps because it simply wasn't good public relations – so we have little evidence for all the behind-the-scenes efforts to control the use of English that must have been going on, though the fact that most of the anti-reformist writing was in Latin is a pretty clear indicator of where the authorities stood on the matter. It was not until 1395, however, that Archbishop Arundel came out of the closet and presented a bill to parliament to ban outright the translation of the Bible into English. He met with no success, but that didn't mean he'd given up.

The church's growing hostility to the language spoken by the man in the street as a vehicle for learning gave a certain *frisson* to the whole question of translation. As one recent scholar puts it: 'Transferring the terms, modes, and topics of academic argumentation to English carried a special charge, and claims to write clergially [i.e. in a learned way] for a wider audience had a kind of untried excitement.' The years between 1370 and 1390 witnessed 'a phase of experimental ferment ... gradually superseded by increasing repression or prevention of the possibilities that first phase had envisaged'[4]

William Langland's poem, *Piers Plowman*, caused the excitement it did because it explored this very tension. It picked at the pros and cons of circulating religious ideas and texts in the vernacular, and it did so in English – thereby becoming itself a part of the very phenomenon it was examining.[5]

The conservative elements in the church might have been alarmed by the spread of the vernacular, but they could do little about it. For a start, the church and the state were pulling in different directions on the issue. The translation of learned material into English continued to gain momentum. And the instigation came from the lay lords.

THE LAY LORDS PROMOTE ENGLISH

One of the chief centres for the translating industry was a castle in Gloucestershire whose main claim to fame was the fact that Edward II had been brutally murdered in one of its dungeons. Thomas, the Fourth Lord Berkeley, kept John Trevisa, one of the great translators of his time, working away at his castle, from

around 1387 to 1412, producing volume
after volume of philosophical, political and
theological treatises – including a translation of work by the Irish primate, Richard
FitzRalph, some of whose radical ideas
influenced Wyclif. Although it is doubtful
that Lord Berkeley ever envisaged anyone
but his fellow aristocrats setting eyes upon
his books, his was none the less a potentially

Berkeley Castle.

dangerous pastime. The innovative – and possibly revolutionary – thing about
Trevisa's work was not that he was the first to translate scientific or philosophical
material into English (he was not) but that he was the first to translate 'highly
learned argumentative Latin material to a new lay audience'.[6]

Meanwhile, on the other side of England, at Braybrooke in Northampton-
shire, Thomas Latimer, a knight with royal connections, seems to have funded a
large scriptorium, on a par with those of the great religious houses, which was
engaged in churning out sermons in English, and related material of a radical
nature.[7]

Elsewhere, Wyclif's ex-secretary at Lutterworth, John Purvey, was busy
translating the Bible into English.[8] It's hard to imagine today the intense excitement
having the Bible in English must have caused our ancestors six hundred years
ago. Perhaps the nearest equivalent would be the arrival of television. The Bible
dominated people's lives – quotation from it and reference to it accompanied
their deeds and thoughts every day of their lives, and yet they could not read it
for themselves. It was an enigma in a magical tongue whose mysteries were only
revealed to the common man as and when the priesthood saw fit to lift the veil.
To have the Bible in their own tongue not only satisfied a deep curiosity on the
part of ordinary men and women, it empowered them.

Purvey presented a copy of his English version of the Gospels to Richard's
Queen Anne.[9] For, of course, it was at court that the encouragement of English
found its chief proponents – whether in the figure of the king himself or in the lesser
gentry and bureaucrats who thronged the halls of the king's presence. And of the
court writers, it was Chaucer who was pre-eminent in the art of translation. He
was saluted as such by the French poet Eustache Deschamps, and he himself
regarded a great proportion of his work effectively as translation.[10]

Whether all this translating was aimed at the man in the street is a moot
point. It has been suggested that translation was a good way to win royal

favour: turning into English such books as Boethius's *De Consolatione* or the *Melibee* was a way of gaining recognition as a heavyweight intellectual, worthy of a king's counsel.[11] On the other hand, Chaucer may well have been charged with the spirit of the earlier churchmen, and he may have seen the instruction and amusement of his fellow Englishmen – whether high or low – as a worthwhile aim in itself. Perhaps both motives came into play.

But it wasn't just the church that was opposed to the spread of learning amongst the lower orders. There were also plenty of secular conservatives who saw it as a destabilizing factor in society. By the time he came to revise his great poem *Piers Plowman* for the last time, even Langland had begun to complain that the lower orders were getting ideas above their station through all this learning, and that clerics should only be appointed from the sons of franklins and free-men. He even criticized members of the gentry who got into learned arguments which were really the business of the clerics.[12]

In 1391, the Commons petitioned the king to forbid serfs (*neif*) or low-born commoners (*villeins*) from putting their children into school 'to advance them by clergy [learning], and this in maintenance and saving of the honour of all freemen of the realm'. Of course, the Commons were, themselves, prosperous burgesses and gentry with a vested interest in keeping the lower orders in their place. Interestingly, however, Richard returned a non-committal answer – which might give us some indication that the court in which Chaucer produced his translations was not opposed to the information explosion amongst ordinary people.[13]

DID RICHARD II CRUSH THE HERETICS?

And this brings us to the question of Richard II's attitude to the intellectual ferment in which his kingdom was embroiled. On which side did he come down? Did he stand four-square behind the church conservatives, or did he sympathize with their critics?

Most modern historians credit Richard with totally orthodox religious attitudes. It is claimed that although Richard gave the church no support in the first ten years of his reign, by 1389 he had become a vigorous defender of orthodoxy. In support of this, we have letters from the king to the Archbishop of Canterbury during the 1390s, and one to the Bishop of Chichester, urging him to arrest all heretics.[14]

By his own account, too, Richard appears to have seen himself as a hammer of the heretics. The Latin epitaph on his tombstone, which he commissioned in 1395, reads: 'He favoured the Church, he overthrew the proud and threw down whoever violated the royal prerogative. He crushed heretics and laid low their friends.'[15] And yet as so often the case with Richard's pronouncements, his words don't really seem to tie in with his deeds. What is more, the famous epitaph may not be at all what it claims to be.

In fact, far from crushing the heretics and laying low their friends, Richard numbered heretics amongst his closest companions. William Neville, Lewis Clifford, John Clanvowe, Richard Stury, Thomas Latimer and John Montagu, for instance, were all branded as heretics by the chroniclers. And although it might seem unlikely to us that a king in the Middle Ages would have associated himself with anything so subversive as heresy, it isn't at all. The crown often thought the church to be as much of a rival as the magnates. Both Richard's father, the Black Prince, and his grandfather, Edward III, had had little sympathy with the ecclesiastical establishment. Doubtless both would have liked to have got their hands on at least a part of the wealth that the church represented. John of Gaunt, Richard's uncle, was notorious as the protector and defender of the arch-heretic Wyclif. Perhaps Gaunt's enthusiasm had waned somewhat since the dreadful business of 1381, but it was still only a few years since he had threatened to have the Bishop of London dragged out of St Paul's by his hair.

The king's mother, Joan of Kent, had also defended Wyclif. She was, moreover, a long-time benefactor of Montagu, who had left her service to join Richard's circle, and who stayed a close and valued companion of the king's until the very end of his reign. Richard was not by his nature two-faced. If he had indeed been the hammer of the heretics, he would scarcely have remained close to men like Neville, Clifford, Clanvowe, Stury, Latimer and Montagu – men whose orthodoxy was openly questioned by the church.[16]

Richard's Queen Anne also showed a friendly face to the reformers. When she was presented with the Gospels in English by Wyclif's former secretary, John Purvey, she

John of Gaunt.

had accepted them graciously.[17] It was not an action that Courtenay would have considered helpful to his campaign against vernacularization. The archbishop would probably have gone around muttering that it was 'sending out the wrong signals' – or the fourteenth-century equivalent of such a phrase.

All in all, the record shows that as long as Richard had his hands on the levers of power, comparatively little action was taken against the heretics – despite the rhetoric of government. When Richard's enemies took control, however, vigorous persecution of the church's critics delighted the ecclesiastics. Take, for example, the events of 1386–9.

There was certainly no love lost between the young King Richard and William Courtenay – then the chief scourge of the heretics. In 1385, during a council held at Westminster, the archbishop had accused Richard and his ministers of having plotted the death of John of Gaunt, and of intending to murder others to whom they bore ill will. Richard leapt to his feet and delivered a volley of threats at Courtenay. That evening, after dining with the mayor, Richard happened to come across the archbishop on the Thames, whereupon Courtenay renewed his attack. Richard totally lost control, drew his sword and would have leapt into the prelate's boat had he not been restrained.[18] The next year, however, when the baronial opposition to Richard gained control in parliament, Archbishop Courtenay was given responsibility for overseeing Richard's household – meaning that Richard's erstwhile enemy was given *carte blanche* to pry into every corner of his private affairs.

The barons knew how to humiliate Richard and they spared no effort to do so. In 1387, Gloucester, Arundel and Warwick led an armed insurrection against the king and defeated the royal army at Radcot Bridge, some fifteen miles west of Oxford. They then arrived at London 'in a splendid and amazing array, drawn up in three shining battalions, the day bright with the blaze of their arms' and demanded the keys to the city. Once in power they decimated Richard's affinity – that is his immediate circle of associates and friends. Richard's men were either dragged off for torture and execution or condemned as outlaws in their absence.[19] It was a brutal and bloody blow to the king and the court party which involved the 'ruthless and wholesale elimination of Richard's household'.[20]

Now the barons gave the ecclesiastics their head in running their critics to ground. In 1387 Wyclif's heir and the current leader of the reformers, Nicholas Hereford, who had escaped from the pope's prison, was seized and thrown back into jail. The next spring, a search was ordered for Wycliffite writings – whether in English or Latin, and investigators were given full power to imprison those dealing in forbidden literature.

To cause maximum embarrassment to Richard, one of his chamber knights, Sir Thomas Latimer, was ordered to bring certain books in his possession to be examined for heresy by the prelates in London. Heresy 'was to be found in the inner circle of royal power, and those who made it their business to know the power at court knew, or felt they knew, that it was there'. Whatever organization Wyclif's followers had set up lay in ruins before the end of the year, and the point had been made, publicly, that the king's closest circle of associates was suspect.[21]

The period of the Appellants' control was the only time during the reign that new legislation was introduced to combat criticism of the church. Once Richard himself regained power, the impetus seems to have slackened – existing legislation may have been strengthened somewhat, but nothing new was allowed – despite considerable pressure from the prelates.

In 1395, for example, after the reformers brazenly nailed a declaration of rights and beliefs to the doors of Westminster Hall, Archbishop Arundel pleaded for English translation of the Bible to be banned forthwith. He also demanded that England should follow the excellent example of the Continent, and burn unrepentent heretics. But Richard did nothing. And as long as he remained in power no such legislation was passed. Only when Richard was dead and buried was the burning of heretics introduced.

Thomas Walsingham insists that when Richard returned from Ireland in 1395, he rounded furiously on his knights for attacking the church and supporting the ideas of Wyclif – activities which, by this time, had all been conveniently branded as 'Lollardy'. In particular, says Walsingham, the king threatened Sir Richard Stury with the 'most shameful death' unless he swore an oath to abandon his heretical opinions.[22] However, one historian comments: 'Whatever gestures Richard may have made towards orthodox susceptibilities, his supposed surprise does not ring true. In addition to being a long-serving member of Richard's household, Stury was one of the king's most regular councillors during the early 1390s, and it seems unlikely that anyone in such an exposed position could have been totally successful in concealing active Lollard affiliations.'[23] Moreover, Richard still kept other suspected Lollards close to him, for example Clifford and Montagu, who succeeded to the title of Earl of Salisbury two years later, and was entrusted with diplomatic missions right up to the end.[24]

This is not to say that Richard II was, himself, a favourer of Wyclif's ideas, but just that whatever the rhetoric he adopted in public, in private he showed himself at the very least neutral towards those whom the prelates condemned.

Though he made no public gestures of tolerance, his actions against unorthodoxy seem reluctant, and until the end of his life he remained the associate and friend of men who were regarded as heretics. Indeed, it is possible that the fact that the magnates – Richard's enemies – took a stronger line on heresy may indicate that they felt this was an issue on which they could embarrass the king.[25]

John Gower certainly seems to throw the accusation of heresy at Richard in his later reworking of the ending of his poem *Confessio Amantis*:

> For if a kyng wol justifie
> His lond and hem that beth withynne,
> First at hym self he mot begynne,
> To kepe and reule his owne astat,
> That in hym self be no debat
> Towards his god: for othre wise
> Ther may non erthly kyng suffise
> Of his kyngdom the folk to lede,
> But he the kyng of hevene drede ...
> 　*Confessio Amantis*, viii, ll. 3080–8
> For if a king wants to administer
> His land and those in it
> First at himself he must begin,
> To keep and rule his own estate,
> That in himself there should be no debate
> Towards his god: for otherwise
> There may no earthly king suffice
> To lead the folk of his kingdom
> Unless he honours the king of heaven ...

How then to explain the epitaph that Richard wrote, or had written, for his own tombstone in which he claimed to have 'crushed the heretics'? The answer to this may be that Richard did not, in fact, write his own epitaph but that its inscription was instead part of the propaganda exercise that Henry V undertook in 1413, when he transferred Richard's remains from Kings Langley (where Henry IV had unceremoniously hidden them away) to Westminster.

RICHARD'S EXTRAORDINARY EPITAPH

The proposition that Richard was the author of the epitaph on his tomb is an assumption rather than a fact. We know he commissioned the memorial in 1395. We also know that he intended there to be an inscription, but no evidence exists that he actually wrote the epitaph that finally went on it.[26] The effigies of Richard and Anne seem not to have been completed until 1398–9 when the two coppersmiths who made them were paid another £300 for gilding them. We have no record of their being positioned on the tomb before Richard left for Ireland in 1399, the year of the usurpation. If they were not on the tomb by then, it is most unlikely that Henry IV would have bothered to install them in their rightful place; he didn't even put Richard's decaying corpse in its rightful place.

Richard lies side by side with his Queen Anne in Westminster Abbey.

And when Henry's son atoned for his father's shameful treatment of Richard, by bringing the body back from Kings Langley to the tomb that was waiting for it in Westminster, it is hard to imagine that he would not have taken full advantage of the occasion to promote both himself and his own political agenda. Henry V's main purpose in moving Richard was to legitimize his own rule by separating himself from his usurper father and hitching his star to the deposed – but legitimate – Richard. It was a propaganda exercise, and it would be surprising if the young Henry didn't maximize every possible advantage. Any inscription on the monument would have represented an opportunity to get his message across, and whatever epitaph Richard had intended, we might expect Henry to have introduced one that suited his purposes.

This was certainly the view of the first commentator on the memorial, John Weever, in 1631, who said he considered it most unlikely that Richard had written the epitaph, and thought it must have been the work of Henry V.[27] This view is supported by the fact that there are at least three or four details about the epitaph that do not sit comfortably with the idea of Richard as its author.

Here is the text in a translation supplied by Westminster Abbey Library:

Sage and elegant, lawfully Richard the Second, conquered by fate he lies here depicted beneath this marble. He was truthful in discourse and full of reason: Tall in body, he was prudent in mind as Homer. He showed favour to the Church, he overthrew the proud and threw down anybody who violated the royal prerogative. He crushed heretics, and laid low their friends. O merciful Christ, to whom he was devoted, may you save, through the prayers of the Baptist, whom he esteemed.[28]

The most obvious anomaly comes in the very first sentence: 'conquered by fate' (*per fatum victus*). Why would the 28-year-old Richard II, at the height of his power in 1395, and with every prospect of another twenty or thirty years on the throne, have commissioned the words: 'conquered by fate'? For a general reference to the inevitable fate of man, it is very oddly phrased. 'Conquered by death' one might just understand, but 'conquered by *fate*' implies an untimely end. It sounds like hindsight – something written by someone who knew of Richard's ultimate downfall.

Another unlikely phrase for Richard to have used is: 'lawfully Richard the Second'. There was no question of the legality of Richard's title to the throne; why would he have brought the subject up? And thirdly, as we have already noticed, it is odd for Richard to claim that he 'crushed heretics and laid low their friends' when his record shows he did no such thing. One might, in addition, note that it is also strange that Richard should have made no mention in his epitaph of his own personal favourite saint, Edward the Confessor.

But of all the enigmas presented by the epitaph, it is the last sentence which is the most perplexing and yet which, at the same time, may furnish us with a clue as to who actually wrote it.

In Latin the line, ringing with rhyme, runs: '*O clemens Christe: cui deuotus fuit iste: Votis Baptiste: salues quem pretulit iste.*' We are told that the repeated word *iste* or 'this man' in both cases refers to Richard. The sentence is thus very difficult to translate if you assume that it is Richard who wrote the epitaph. In fact the Latin doesn't quite make sense. Dr James Binns, who provided the Abbey with the above translation, notes that a better translation would be 'O merciful Christ, to whom he [Richard] was devoted, may you save, through the prayers of the Baptist, the man whom he [Richard] esteemed'. This translation however has been rejected by scholars, because of the assumption that it was Richard who wrote the epitaph and that an appeal on behalf of a third party would be nonsense. It has seemed better to assume the Latin is flawed.

However, the moment one assumes that Henry V was the author of the epitaph, as John Weever reckoned many centuries ago, then everything falls into place. Henry was indeed esteemed and promoted by Richard when he was a young man. The childless Richard may even have been grooming Henry for the throne. What could be more natural than for Henry to add a prayer on his own behalf? – especially a prayer that drew attention to his close relationship with the last legitimate king.

Henry was all too aware that his illustrious forebear had been 'conquered by fate'. The phrase 'lawfully Richard the Second' also sounds very like Henry's composition. It was his preoccupation, not Richard's, to establish the legitimacy of his own right to the throne. He had every reason to emphasize that the man from whom he claimed his regal inheritance was indeed 'lawfully Richard the Second'. Furthermore, it would also have been in Henry's interests to establish Richard as a thoroughly orthodox ruler who 'crushed heretics and laid low their friends', since that was Henry's own political agenda.

In short, it seems most unlikely that Richard wrote the epitaph that appears on his tomb, even though he did indeed commission the monument itself. It is much more probable that Henry V took the opportunity of the reburial to add his own epitaph – one that suited his own political needs.

But what are the practicalities? Could Henry have done it?

The epitaph is inscribed around the perimeter of the metal base plate on which the two effigies rest. Since the figures are separate from the base plate and merely bolted to it, there is nothing to tell us whether this is the original base, designed by Richard, or a later one introduced by Henry. The lettering has been dated as pre-1400, but there could be many reasons for using lettering that would have looked old-fashioned in 1413.[29] It may be that Henry wanted to increase the look of authenticity about the memorial, at the same time that he wanted to use it for his own purposes. There again the monument was deliberately styled on Edward III's tomb, and the lettering is copied from that. Henry would have had no reason for changing it. A third possibility is that the epitaph to Anne had already been engraved on the south and east sides of the base plate, but Richard's had not. It would therefore have been natural to continue in the same lettering.

To sum up, there is no evidence that the epitaph on Richard's tomb was written by Richard himself. The content and phrasing of the inscription make it more likely that it was written by Henry V as part of his propaganda exercise when he acceded to the throne and symbolically had the rightful King Richard's body reburied in its rightful place in Westminster.

The epitaph is therefore no guide as to Richard's orthodoxy nor to his attitude to the question of heresy.

RICHARD'S INCONCLUSIVE RECORD *RE* HERESY

Whatever Richard's attitude to heresy, the turmoil of ideas continued throughout his reign right up to the usurpation. The radical attack on the church became less visible at times, but at others, such as in 1395, it would break out and rock the ecclesiastical establishment. And all the while the translation of works of science, philosophy, politics, medicine, and literature spread learning beyond the cloister, beyond the court and even beyond the great households of the barons. For even if much of the work was undertaken with no intention of informing *hoi polloi*, once material had been translated into English, there was no way to put a stop on who had access to it.

Richard II: detail of tomb.

English men and women in the reign of King Richard II must have felt they were living in exciting and unprecedented times. New ideas were encountered and encouraged, new ways of looking at the world were allowed to spread, new words were introduced and an intellectual and cultural revolution was the order of the day.

Standard histories of the 1380s and 1390s often give the impression that England was being strangled in a noose of tyranny, imposed upon it by a wilful and foolish king who was clearly heading for disaster. Modern accounts of the period all too often switch on the headlamps of hindsight to peer through the fog of deliberate obfuscation, lies, and propaganda that Henry IV and his team instigated with such extraordinary success.

Perhaps the greatest achievement of Henry's propaganda machine was precisely the construction of this myth: that Richard was an unpopular king who was deservedly deposed by the common will of a disgruntled people. It wasn't necessarily like that at all.

CHAPTER 6

Was Richard really unpopular?

∽

In the eyes of many twentieth-century historians Richard was, most probably, mad.

On 10 July 1397, Richard invited his three old adversaries, Gloucester, Arundel and Warwick to a banquet in London. The Duke of Gloucester and the Earl of Arundel declined the invitation and only Warwick attended. After what seems to have been a pleasant meal with the king he was arrested. The other two, however, were no better off, for they too were arrested and before September was out Gloucester had been murdered, Arundel executed and Warwick was in exile. Arundel's brother, Thomas, the Archbishop of Canterbury, was also sent into exile for his part in the rebellion of 1386–8.

The *Oxford History of England* tells us that Richard's actions after he eliminated his enemies 'suggest a sudden loss of control, the onset of a mental malaise. If Richard was sane from 1397 onwards, it was with the sanity of a man who pulls his own house about his ears.' Others have argued that Richard was the victim of a clinical neurosis.[1] At the very least there is a consensus that he was an unpopular tyrant who was rightly deposed and met a deservedly sticky end. Even the most thorough and thoughtful studies, while revising these assessments, still see Richard as very much the architect of his own downfall.[2] But is there any evidence for all this? Or are we all still being deluded by the propaganda generated by Richard's usurper and still being beguiled by

Richard II: Westminster Abbey portrait.

the persuasive genius of Richard's most famous interpreter – William Shakespeare?

Was Richard really unpopular during his lifetime, and if so, when did that unpopularity set in? Nigel Saul, in his magisterial biography of Richard, tells us: 'the process of disillusion appears to have set in at the beginning of the 1380s'.[3] But, as he says, there is very little to go on when it comes to measuring public opinion in the late fourteenth century. And, in fact, the more we examine the sparse evidence the more it seems to melt away like snow in our hands.

JOHN GOWER'S EARLY CRITICISM OF RICHARD

The *only* concrete testimony offered for dating the start of Richard's unpopularity back as far as the early 1380s is a Latin poem by Chaucer's contemporary John Gower called *Vox Clamantis* or *The Voice of One Crying*. The title is a reference to Matthew 3.3, where St John the Baptist is described as fulfilling the prophecy of

'the voice of one crying in the wilderness'. The poem is one of the longest in Anglo-Latin and takes the form of a jeremiad lamenting the failures of the three estates: knights, clergy and peasantry. Books II to VIII were probably written in the 1370s, but Book I was added after the Peasants' Revolt of 1381, and lays the blame for all society's ills at the door of the rebels. It is clear that Gower kept adding bits and pieces over the years.

John Gower: detail of tomb in Southwark Cathedral.

Book VIII includes a letter addressed to Richard II, in which he blames the state of the nation on the young king's advisers but exonerates the boy-king himself: 'The boy is free of blame,' Gower writes, and then goes on to deliver an address to Richard cloying enough to turn the stomach of even the most seasoned sycophant:

May the day be near on which you, most handsome of kings, will go forth in aureate splendour behind four snow-white horses. And may the shoutings of praise such as Augustus once had at Rome be yours anew. Let the empire of our leader increase, let him increase his years, and let him protect our doors with his mighty crown. O good king, may you stand sublime in a vanquished world, and may no lesser things be on your shoulders. May the Supreme One from on high give to your right hand shining sceptres of gold which are of eternal glory ... Receive these writings, which I have composed with humble heart for you, good king ...[4]

Now, according to at least one present-day historian, sometime between 1381 and 1386 Gower changed this piece of embarrassing sycophancy to a peremptory ticking-off: 'the king, an undisciplined boy, neglects the moral behaviour by which a man might grow up from a boy ...'[5] Had Gower truly written this in the early 1380s, one could only have admired his forthrightness – even recklessness – in addressing his monarch with so little concern for any possible repercussions. In fact, the more one reads Gower's epistle to Richard, the more one is forced to wonder at the extraordinary tolerance he must have anticipated from his prince in 1381–6: '... the king's court contains whatever vice exists. Sin springs up on every side of the boy, and he, who is quite easily led, takes to every evil ...' (I hope you're enjoying this, my liege!) And what's this? Gower even knows what's going to happen to the doomed monarch – and what's more he takes exactly the same line as most modern historians: 'his destiny does arise out of this wrongdoing,' writes the outspoken and moral Mr Gower.[6]

But, in fact, Gower didn't write this in 1386. According to John Fisher, Gower's only biographer, 1386 was when he inserted the eulogistic purple passage. The schoolmasterly ticking off wasn't substituted until 1391 at the very earliest, and much more probably after 1399. Indeed, since 1391 was the year Richard took control away from the rebel barons, it would have been a foolhardy time to start criticizing him in such outspoken terms. Furthermore the degree of foresight required by the passage in making him author of his own downfall makes the later date seem almost certain.[7]

In other words, the *Vox Clamantis* tells us nothing specific about when Gower's attitude to Richard changed. What it does tell us is that in the 1380s Gower was effusive in his praise of the young king – and we have no reason to doubt that he meant it.

'The question as to whether Gower's view of Richard altered before the cataclysm of 1399 must ... turn upon the textual history of the *Confessio Amantis* rather than of the *Vox Clamantis*,' writes Fisher.[8] And here all is uncertainty and speculation.

The problem is that there is more than one version – in fact, there are three – of the *Confessio Amantis*. They are usually referred to as 'recensions' but let's just call them 'versions' to keep it simple. In the first version, Gower kicks the poem off with a casual, easy-going Prologue describing how he meets King

Richard on a barge on the Thames and is commanded by the king to write something new for his sake. At the end of the poem in this first version, Gower alludes to Chaucer as the pre-eminent love poet with whose writings and songs the land is filled, and concludes with a panegyric to Richard.

At some point Gower omitted both the reference to Chaucer and the panegyric to Richard in Book VIII – making version two. At the same time or at some other time, he excised the meeting with Richard on the Thames and instead, dedicated the book to Henry of Lancaster – making version three.

Now, the first version of the *Confessio* is usually assigned to 1390 because the manuscripts of this version include a Latin rubric (a heading or side-note) which dates Gower's criticism of the Great Schism – the years during which there were rival claimants to the papacy – as 1390.

Other rubrics also indicate that the revisions to Book VIII were made in 1390–1 – the fourteenth year of Richard's reign. The changes in the third version – the removal of the meeting with Richard and the re-dedication to Henry – are dated as 1392–3 – the sixteenth year of Richard's reign.

However, this timing presents a problem for those who would chalk up the re-dedication to Gower's growing disillusionment with Richard. As his biographer puts it: 'This is the period when Gower would have had least cause to change his opinion of the king.'[9] John Fisher suggests that the dedication is really referring to the *next* year – 1392 – when Richard fell out with the citizens of London, and hence Gower, as a Londoner, might have had some reason to become disillusioned with him. The only trouble with this theory, as Fisher himself admits rather engagingly, is 'that it conflicts with the date attached to the revision'. That seems a pretty big problem. Either we accept the date in the rubric as the date of the re-dedication or we don't. We can't just make it whatever date we like. If it isn't the date of the re-dedication, then it must be a later interpolation and of no use in dating the revision whatsoever.

Besides there's another problem with Fisher's theory. It's doubtful that Gower saw himself as a Londoner. His family were originally from Yorkshire and he grew up amongst the gentry in Kent.[10] With his means taking a house in London would have been simple, had he fancied it. Obviously he spent time across the river (what little we know of his business affairs come from Chancery and law court records) but nothing exists to connect Gower to the City – no professional, royal court or guild affiliations, no parish memberships, no record of noble patronage save Henry Bolingbroke in 1393, and again in 1399, of the kind we have for Geoffrey and Philippa Chaucer.[11] In Gower's poems, London figures almost mythically, as 'Troy novant' ('New Troy'), not as a sight-, smell- and sound-world of commerce and characters. In fact, the most famous association of Gower and London – his meeting with Richard II and the commissioning of the *Confessio Amantis* – takes place not in London, but on a barge on the Thames river, in what amounts to a no-man's land, near – but not *of* – the City. It is difficult to argue that Gower's ties or sympathies were with other than the gentry in the shires. He would not necessarily have been troubled by the king's quarrel with the City. So the 1392 dating falls to the ground.

Another recent critic suggests that Richard was already demonstrating absolutist tendencies in 1390 and would have alienated Gower by issuing badges to be worn by his affinity at the tournament in Smithfield. Gower, so the argument goes, would have been dismayed by Richard's attempts to centralize power and by his obvious intention to promote the royal party and transform it into a military force loyal only to him. Gower, it is suggested, would have found this contrary to his own notions of law and justice.[12] Now it is true that Gower has a lot to say about the villainy of tyrants – but a strong monarchy was not the same thing as a tyranny. In fact the whole argument could be quite easily turned on its head. A medieval king had no chance of administering law and justice *unless* he was able to centralize power. Without a strong military presence in the country, no monarch could hope to keep the warmongering barons in check and curb their propensity to fight each other and oppress the population.

And there is much evidence that Gower approved of a strong monarchy. Indeed, if he disapproved, why didn't he object to Henry's seizure of power in 1399? Gower seems to have had no problem with Henry's centralization of power. Why then should we assume he would have been opposed to Richard's? Gower also had no difficulty with accepting Henry's badge in the form of an 'S' collar – in fact, he was so proud of it that he had himself portrayed wearing it on his tomb. Why should Richard's badges have kindled so much ire in 1390?

Actually, the rubrics themselves may *all* be red herrings. As far as the re-dedication is concerned, the rubric may date the change of allegiance to 1392–3, but the text does not. What the *text* actually says is that the sixteenth year of King Richard's reign (1393) was when Gower had the first idea of making the poem:

> And for that fewe men endite
> In our englissh, I thenke make
> A boke for Engelondes sake,
> The yer sextenthe of kyng Richard.
>   *Confessio Amantis*, Prol. ll. 22–5

And because few men write
In our English, I thought to make
A book for England's sake,
In the sixteenth year of King Richard.

Some sixty lines later, he says he intends to send the book to Henry of Lancaster:

This bok, upon amendment
To stonde at his commandement,
With whom myn herte is of accord,
I sende unto myn oghne lord,
Which of Lancastre is Henri named:
The hyhe god him hath proclamed
Ful of knyhthode and alle grace.
    Confessio Amantis, Prol. ll. 83–9
This book, to be corrected
According to his commands,
I send to my own lord,
With whom my heart is in accord,
Who is named Henry of Lancaster:
The high god has proclaimed him
Full of knighthood and all grace.

Dating the re-dedication to Henry as 1392–3 is to assume that the Latin rubric goes without question. But the rubrics – and the revised dedication – actually beg a very big question.

In the early 1390s Henry's only proper title was Earl of Derby. He would not have dared to call himself (or let anyone else call him) 'Lancaster', because that was his father, John of Gaunt's title – and Gaunt was quite alive and still Duke, thank you very much. Only when Gaunt died in 1399 could Henry legitimately start calling himself 'Lancaster'.

Gower would have been perfectly aware of that, of course. And yet here he is, calling him Henry of Lancaster. The Latin rubric seems to recognize the problem and tries to deal with it: 'First it is declared how in the sixteenth year of King Richard the Second, John Gower composed this book and finally completed it, and how he then dedicated it with special reverence to his noblest lord, his lord

Henry of Lancaster, then Earl of Derby.'[13]

In other words the Latin acknowledges the impossibility of the dedication and tries – rather cack-handedly – to explain it away by saying that Henry of Lancaster was then Earl of Derby.

It can't be that Gower didn't know how to address Henry of Derby in the 1390s, for he addresses one copy of the *Confessio Amantis* to Henry sometime before June 1392 with the words: 'Go, dear book, to the Earl of Derby, well considered by those versed in praise; upon him rest your future.'[14] To have addressed Henry as Henry of Lancaster, rather than of Derby, in 1392–3, while John of Gaunt was still alive, would have been an insult to Gaunt.

It is therefore possible to say with some certainty that the re-dedication to Henry 'of Lancaster', must have been written after 1399 and most probably after the coup that deposed Richard. The Latin rubric is a fabrication designed to make it appear that the change had been made much earlier. The deception is actually comically transparent – and yet it seems to have fooled people for six hundred years!

One of the few commentators not to have been deceived by Gower's desperate reworking tells us that 'the years immediately following 1399 are the period of his [Gower's] greatest public activity as a poet, largely as a result of the change of dynasty … His most important new composition was the *Cronica Tripertita*, an attempt to justify Henry's usurpation by a rereading of the historical events that preceded it. He also revised his earlier advice to King Richard in the *Vox Clamantis* in order to make it more consistent with the presentation of Richard's character in the *Cronica*, and he dedicated a copy of the new composite work to the newly restored Archbishop Thomas Arundel …'[15]

Gower also made changes to the *Confessio Amantis* – especially to the prologue and epilogue – removing the dedications to Richard *and* – perhaps significantly – to Chaucer: 'the result is the version of the poem that we are now familiar with, in which the patronage of Henry's predecessor has been not just obliterated but denied'.[16]

Gower also wrote three new poems for Henry. In one of them, *Rex Celi Deus*, he brazenly takes words he'd previously used to praise Richard (in a cancelled passage in the *Vox Clamantis*), and transfers them, lock, stock and barrel, to Henry IV.[17]

There is thus no reason to credit Gower with mystical powers of prognostication for writing dire warnings of future disaster as early as 1391:

What schal befalle hierafterward
God wot, for now upon this tyde
Men se the world on every syde
In sondry wyse so diversed,
That it welnyth stant al reversed,
As forto speke of tyme ago.
   Confessio Amantis, Prol. ll. 26–31
What shall befall hereafterward
God knows, for now upon this tide
Men see the world on every side
In sundry wise so fragmented
That it well nigh stands reversed,
As for to speak of time past.

Gower was simply writing with hindsight sometime after the momentous events of 1399. In fact he was probably doing no more than what every writer in every scriptorium in the land was doing after Henry's usurpation and the terrifying cultural upheaval that followed.

The physical distribution of the manuscripts lends further support to the idea that Gower's change of attitude to Richard happened after the monarch's fall. There are thirty-two manuscripts of the first version of *Confessio Amantis*, containing the praise of Richard and the acknowledgement of Chaucer. By contrast there are only seven of the second version, and nine of the third. It seems clear that the first version of the *Confessio Amantis* 'continued to be the official version throughout Richard's reign'.[18]

The 'onset of disillusion, so evident in Gower's work' during Richard's lifetime proves to be a chimera.[19]

DISENCHANTMENT WITH RICHARD IN THE CHRONICLES

In the same way, the popular hostility to Richard that bursts with such certitude from the pages of the chronicles, and which has inspired so many historians with a similar antipathy, turns out to be no less illusory.

The major chroniclers depict a morally flawed and foolish Richard who is first and foremost the architect of his own downfall, and whose deserved fate is celebrated by his oppressed people. 'So now, Richard, farewell!' exults Adam of Usk, 'at the height of your glory, cast down by the wheel of fortune, to fall miserably into the hands of Duke Henry, amid the silent curses of your people.'[20] The destruction of his lifelong enemies in 1397, the execution of the Earl of Arundel, murder of the Duke of Gloucester and the exiling of the Earl of Warwick and of Archbishop Thomas Arundel were recorded by Henry IV's chronicles as the actions of a despot, and this verdict has haunted assessments of the reign right down to the present day. 'The king is often seen as an isolated and unpopular monarch, achieving what he did in 1397 only through force, fear, and the compliance of a narrow and self-interested cabal of favourites, while the overwhelming drift of noble and popular sympathy lay with his enemies.'[21]

The main trouble with this view is that the majority of the chronicles were written – or rewritten – after Henry's usurpation in 1399. They are therefore tarred by the brush of the Lancastrian propaganda machine.

Henry didn't even wait for Richard to abdicate before he started putting pressure on the chronicle-writers. In September of 1399 he sent letters to all the abbeys and major churches 'instructing the heads of these religious houses to make available for examination all of their chronicles which touched upon the state and governance of the kingdom of England from the time of William the Conqueror up until the present day ...'[22] The ostensible purpose for the search was to provide supporting evidence for Henry's claim to the throne, but the subtext must have been as clear as the gallows on the hill. The letters may have been sent in the name of King Richard, but no abbot could have missed the inference that he should beware of submitting any chronicle that presented the outgoing monarch in too favourable a light, or that failed to hail the incoming usurper as the saviour of the realm.

'Writing in the shadow of the Lancastrian revolution almost all chroniclers in England after 1399 cast Richard in an unfavourable light,' notes a recent review of Richard's treatment in the chronicles. 'The type of libel produced against deposed monarchs in later ages was also used against Richard.'[23] Nothing was too salacious or below the belt, so long as it blackened the character of the fallen king.

Adam of Usk, for example, cheerfully plays the illegitimacy card: 'this Richard, concerning whose birth many unsavoury things were commonly said, namely that he was not born of a father of the royal line, but of a mother given to slippery ways – to say nothing of many other things I have heard'.[24] It was the sort of gossip that must have been music to Henry's ears and which doubtless he encouraged – and perhaps even instigated.

When we turn to the chronicles that were actually written during Richard's reign, by writers who were, of course, uninfluenced by Henry's seizure of power, the evidence that Richard was disliked by the populace at large, proves non-existent.

There are just over half a dozen chronicles that survive from Richard's lifetime. Of these all apart from one are generally sympathetic to Richard.

Henry Knighton, a canon of St Mary's Abbey, Leicester, for example, was writing between 1378 and 1396. He conveys an impression of Richard that 'is unambiguously one of a king, resolute and resourceful in 1381, eloquent, intelligent, and redoubtable as he grows into maturity'.[25] It is true that he describes the events of the *coup d'état* of 1386–8 from the point of view of Richard's opponents – but that was probably the wise thing to do at the time. Once Richard takes control again in 1389, Knighton once again becomes the king's man: 'And there was none who sought to oppose the king's will', he writes, 'but all praised God that He had provided them with so wise a king to watch over them in future.'[26] Perhaps Knighton was a perfect Vicar of Bray.[27]

Another history that was compiled more or less contemporaneously with the events it describes, is the *Westminster Chronicle*. Richard emerges from its pages as 'a model of orthodoxy, and essentially as a man of innate dignity, impetuous by nature but impressively patient in adversity'.[28] Given Richard's generous patronage of Westminster one might have expected the abbey's chronicle to have been an out-and-out apologia for the young king, but it is suprisingly independent. There is one passage criticizing Richard for autocratic behaviour in the year 1385, but this is in a narrative which also criticizes the Archbishop of Canterbury and, moreover – as we have seen – coincides with a hiccough in the relations between the king and Westminster Abbey. It therefore cannot be said to represent any general disenchantment with Richard.

Two northern Cistercian chronicles, written during Richard's reign, bear witness that Richard was by no means without friends. The *Kirkstall Abbey Chronicle* pulls out all the stops when Richard seizes power in 1397. Far from championing the barons who had humiliated Richard ten years before, the *Kirkstall* praises Richard for his tolerance:

How admirable and longsuffering is the king's forbearance! Previously the sun was hidden behind a cloud – in other words, the royal majesty was obscured by a hostile force – but now, soaring in arms above the mountains, and bounding over the hills with his might, he has dispersed the clouds with his sun, whose light shines ever more brightly.[29]

These two chronicles, incidentally, both chart, in different ways, the malign influence that Henry's seizure of power had over the chronicle-writers. In the case of the *Kirkstall*, the writer begins writing in 1397–8 with unbounded admiration of Richard, but promptly modifies his tone in the early months of 1400. In the case of the other, *The Dieulacres Chronicle*, the section written before 1399 is compiled by a monk who is sympathetic to Richard. At some time during the usurpation another monk takes over the task, and the new compiler tut-tuts at the previous account of events, declaring that he finds much of it to be untrue.

WALSINGHAM'S DISILLUSIONMENT WITH RICHARD

The proposition that Richard became progressively more unpopular during his reign must rest on the evidence of only one text: the chronicle of Thomas Walsingham, Monk of St Albans. Walsingham was writing within a few years of the events he described, and the usual view is that his account shows disenchantment with Richard setting in many years before the usurpation. But does it?

The whole issue is made problematical by the fact that Walsingham wrote not just one chronicle but several – or, at least, he wrote several versions of the same chronicle. Over a period of about forty years he seems to have worked simultaneously on a brief annalistic history and at the same time a fuller history. What is more he produced various versions of each. It is certainly true that Walsingham's attitude to Richard II varies considerably from one to the other, but although his attitude

St Alban's Abbey, where Thomas Walsingham wrote his chronicles over many years.

towards Richard may change from one manuscript to another, there is no consistent change apparent within any given manuscript. Our sense of the degree to which Walsingham 'became increasingly disillusioned with Richard'[30] as the reign progressed therefore depends on the order in which we date the manuscripts.

The first comprehensive survey of Walsingham's manuscripts was made by V.H. Galbraith in 1932.[31] His dating and ordering were convincingly revised in 1984 by G.B. Stow.[32] Stow pointed out some errors in Galbraith's analysis and arrived at a slightly amended order of writing.

According to Stow, the earliest of Walsingham's manuscripts – the manuscript known as MS Bodley 316 – appears to have been written around 1388, when Richard had already been on the throne for eleven years.[33] It was completed, therefore, around the time of the attempted *coup* by Gloucester, Arundel and Warwick, who seized power from the young king and his party in 1387. The manuscript boasts the inscription: 'Pray for Thomas of Gloucester who gave me to this chantry or college of the Holy Trinity within the stronghold of Plecy.'[34] Whether it was actually commissioned by Gloucester or whether he simply acquired it, the work clearly must have been a compilation which fitted in with the duke's point of view. Yet despite this association with one of the king's sworn enemies – a man who probably tried to actually dethrone the king in the previous year – Walsingham, according to Stow, was not critical of Richard himself in this particular work.[35]

Even by 1394, when Walsingham compiled his second work, now known as manuscript Harley 3634, in only one instance does he alter his text in a way that is at all derogatory of Richard. 'Here', writes G.B. Stow, 'Walsingham injects for the first time a somewhat disparaging description of the young king, highlighting both the admirable qualities of Scrope (who had the courage, we learn, to criticize Richard's predilection for favourites), and the youthful ignorance of Richard.'[36]

It is not until we get to the third of Walsingham's manuscripts, known as MS Royal 13.E.ix, do we see a wholesale onslaught on the king's character. This manuscript, according to Stow, 'was probably written just before 1399'.[37] Suddenly Richard becomes 'a youthful, degenerate, and feckless tyrant'.[38] Thus, as one might have guessed, Walsingham's vitriolic attacks on Richard only start to appear in a manuscript written after the murder of the Duke of Gloucester, who had close ties to the abbey in which the chronicle was produced.

In the past, says Stow, scholars have failed to distinguish between the different manuscripts. They 'have cited the different texts indiscriminately, disregarding altogether the dates of their composition'.[39] A typical – and influential – instance is the view of one historian that: 'Walsingham became critical of Richard II even during his minority, in the 1380s.' But all the examples adduced to prove this are from the *Historia Anglicana* and from MS Royal 13.E.ix – both compiled after Henry's usurpation. They prove nothing about Walsingham's opinion of Richard in the 1380s.[40]

Judged by Stow's assessment of the manuscripts, Walsingham's works do not demonstrate a gradual disillusionment with Richard starting early in the reign. His first disparaging comments only appear in a manuscript written *after*

Richard's seizure of power from his uncles in 1389, when he dismisses the Duke of Gloucester, a man with whom Walsingham clearly identified.[41] And, as we have seen, Walsingham's harshest invective does not appear until at least after the murder of Gloucester, and possibly even after or during Henry's seizure of power.

That Walsingham was alive to the political implications of his writings is certain, as we shall see later in the cancellations and changes he made to one of his manuscripts at the time of Henry's usurpation (see below, p.166).

We know too from the inscription of the earliest manuscript, Bodley 316, that Walsingham was associated with the Duke of Gloucester. And it is quite clear from his writings after 1397 that Walsingham's sympathies lay with the barons against the court party. To take but one example: his account of Richard's *coup* in 1397 makes uncritical use of the propaganda circulated by the Lancastrians, and constructs a perfect fairy tale about the popularity of the barons whom Richard put under arrest.[42] Walsingham writes:

> When the news of the arrest and imprisonment of these lords got around, there was such public grief among all the people of the realm that one would have thought that the kingdom had been destroyed by enemies; for such hope had been placed in them, and especially in the Duke of Gloucester, by all the people that it was impossible to believe that with him alive and well the kingdom might not be not only governed well internally but also saved from its enemies abroad.[43]

This is fantasy-time. Gloucester and Arundel were not at all popular figures by this point. They had disappeared into the woodwork of the provinces, and their removal caused very little concern.[44]

It is possible that antipathy to the king was endemic in the abbey of St Albans, where Walsingham wrote for most of his life. St Albans, may have resented Richard's favouring of the rival house at Westminster. There was also the little matter of a horse that Richard had 'borrowed' in 1383 on one of his rare visits, and failed to return.[45] And there is some suggestion that the Abbot of St Albans until 1396, Thomas de la Mare, was associated with the baronial opposition to the king.[46]

None the less, according to Stow's dating, Walsingham's chronicles do not show antipathy to Richard personally before 1394, nor do they demonstrate a gradual disillusionment with Richard. Certainly they provide not a single shred of evidence of widespread public disquiet with Richard as king through the major portion of his reign. Rather the wholesale and 'deliberate revisionism' by which they cast Richard in a thoroughly evil light occurs towards its very end, quite possibly after Henry's usurpation itself.

RICHARD'S UNPOPULARITY: A LANCASTRIAN FABRICATION

Of course, it was in Henry's interests, after the events of 1399, to make Richard out to have been unpopular and to represent the usurpation as universally welcomed, but there are several indicators that this is a fabrication.

In the first place, had Henry been as popular as he claimed, and had this popularity been universal across the kingdom, when he took to the Channel in later June 1399 there would have been no reason for him not to land on the south coast, thence to march straight to London to claim the throne. Instead he seems to have hesitated 'taking his ships back and forth along the coastline, approaching different parts of the kingdom in turn'.[47] The fact that he finally chose to land as far north as Yorkshire, in his home territory, suggests he was less than secure about his reception in the south.

Nor does it seem as if the citizens of London were as hostile to Richard and as eager to befriend Henry as has often been supposed. Although Richard's relations with the City were not particularly good in his latter years, the mayor and aldermen of London did not rally to Henry's support the moment he landed at Ravenspur. It took them six weeks to make up their minds to desert Richard's allegiance. They did so only when the king had been taken prisoner and the die seemed cast in Henry's favour, and it seems likely that they gave their support to the usurper only after driving a hard bargain.[48]

On the other hand, one has to say that one of the pro-Ricardian chronicles, the *Dieulacres Chronicle*, suggests popular unease at Richard's money-raising measures in his last years. The *Chronicle* reports 'evil rumours' spreading through the community associated with Richard's demands for so-called 'blank charters' from the seventeen counties around London. Perhaps 'blank charters' is the wrong expression. They actually gave the king *carte blanche* over the lives and possessions of his subjects.[49] There also seems to have been some hostility to Richard's bodyguard of Cheshiremen who were accused of being unruly and violent, and there may as well have been resentment in gentry circles about Richard's attitude to property rights and a hostility towards his appointments to county offices.[50] But there are no grounds for supposing that the general unpopularity ascribed to him by his Lancastrian usurper had any reality for more than the last year or two of his lifetime.[51]

It may even have been quite the opposite. It may be that Richard was actually a popular king and *that* was Henry's problem.

RICHARD AS A POPULAR KING

In 1399, there was a young squire from Gascony in Richard's entourage by the name of Jenico. His compatriot, Jean Creton, records that this young man was so devoted to Richard that he simply refused to stop wearing Richard's device of the white hart, even after the king's arrest and the triumph of Henry – which was presumably an extremely dangerous thing to do. Jenico, reports Creton, 'was the last to wear the insignia of the white hart in England'.[52] Henry was so enraged by Jenico's refusal to lay aside the cognizance of King Richard, that he had him imprisoned in Chester castle.[53] It was an act of bravado, but one that indicates a good deal of devotion to the king.

In fact, once we prise ourselves free from the all-pervasive slanders of Richard's Lancastrian detractors, it becomes possible to detect a strong current of passionate devotion and loyalty amongst Richard's supporters. For Henry, this intense loyalty must have been a real bugbear.

For example, there was an abortive rising in favour of Richard after the Christmas of 1399 – that is, when he was already deposed and imprisoned. The leaders of the revolt had been treated leniently by Henry in hopes of weaning their loyalty away from the former king. They had everything to lose and little to gain by revolting against the usurper. It seems that their only motive must have been their loyalty to Richard – loyalty for which they were willing to risk their lives.[54] Indeed had Richard not commanded such loyalty, there would have been no need for Henry to put him to death (as he surely must have done). An unloved and unsupported Richard, as the Lancastrians portrayed him, would have represented no danger to Henry and could have been allowed to live.[55]

Perhaps Richard's vigorous and continual travelling around England laid the foundations for popularity – it certainly made him 'better known to the townsmen of England than any of his predecessors and they may have found the appearance and cost of his royal court to their liking'.[56]

But for Henry IV, perhaps the most worrying example of devotion to Richard was that shown by his own son.

When Richard II exiled Henry Bolingbroke, the newly created Duke of

The future Henry V is knighted by Richard II during his campaign in Ireland.

Hereford, in 1398, he kept Bolingbroke's young son, Henry, in his own house-hold as surety for the Duke (according to Walsingham).[57] One could quite imagine that the young Henry of Monmouth would have resented the man who had sent his father into exile, but quite the contrary. Richard seems to have won the youngster's wholehearted devotion. He took the young Henry with him to Ireland and there knighted him, even though the boy was only twelve.

When Bolingbroke invaded, and finally got the king in his clutches, the three of them confronted each other at Chester in August 1399. Young Henry greeted his father as was his due, says the chronicle, and then Bolingbroke commanded him to leave Richard's service and wait upon him instead. 'Then,' continues the chronicle,

> this young knight Henry brought the king to his chamber with a sorrowful heart, for cause he should depart from his godfather and his sovereign king, for he loved him entirely. And when he came into the king's chamber he told the king how he must the next day after, wait upon his father by straight and hard commandment. And then the king said to him these words: 'Good son Henry, I

give thee leave to do thy father's commandment, but I know well there is one Henry shall do me much harm and I suppose it is not thou. Wherefore I pray thee be my friend, for I wot [know] not how it will go.' And so on the next day after Henry took his leave of the king his godfather with a heavy heart and went to his father.[58]

Now it's true that this comes from a fifteenth-century chronicle that may have been written partly to justify Henry V's devotion to Richard, but it has a ring of truth about it. And indeed one could put it the other way round – that the young Henry's devotion to Richard is ultimately proven by his treatment of Richard when he, himself, became king. Almost his first act was to order Richard's body to be removed from its shameful burial at Kings Langley in Hertfordshire to its proper place in Westminster. He did this, according to one chronicler 'for the grete and tendre loue that he hadde to King Richard'.[59] There is no reason to suppose that Henry V's devotion to Richard did not begin while he was a youth in the king's household.

However much loyalty and affection Richard inspired, it was certainly not in Henry IV's interest to allow that loyalty to be recorded.

It's no surprise, therefore, that as soon as we turn to the texts written beyond the reach of Henry's heavy hand of censorship, we discover a very different Richard from the man portrayed in the Lancastrian chronicles. Writers across the Channel such as Christine de Pisan and Eustache Deschamps record their clear admiration for him, and in the pages of Jean Creton's *Histoire du Roy d'Angleterre Richart II,* the *Chronicque de la Traison et Mort de Richart Deux,* and the *Chronique de Saint-Denys,* we discover an admired and in many ways a much-loved monarch.[60]

Creton is by no means totally uncritical of Richard; he records sayings and deeds not always to Richard's credit. But he still thought highly of 'good king Richard'. 'For, in my opinion,' says Creton, 'he hated all kinds of sin, and every sort of vice. I never saw him deviate in the least from catholic faith and justice.'[61]

Now, of course, these chronicles only survived because they were written in France, and so it is easy to dismiss them as nothing but anti-English propaganda. But it is worth bearing in mind that Richard's popularity rating in France had dipped considerably by the end of the century. In 1399 he had dismissed his young queen's governess, Lady De Courcy, shortly before he himself left for Ireland, and whatever the reason for the dismissal, it was regarded in the French court as insensitive and unfair on his young wife. Richard had also broken his

promises to support the French in proposed joint military action against Milan
and there were constant disagreements over enforcing the truce in Gascony.[62] So
there is no reason to suppose that the French accounts of the usurpation should
have been particularly pro-Richard. Besides, some of the *Traison* and much of
the *Metrical History* is substantiated by the Cistercian chronicles – the
Dieulacres and the *Short Kirkstall* and the *Whalley Chronicle*.[63]

What is more, unlike any of the Lancastrian chroniclers, two of the French
writers had actually been members of Richard's court and were therefore eye-
witnesses to many of the events they described. Jean Creton, for instance, was a
French squire who had travelled in Richard's suite to Ireland and who remained
with him during the early days of his captivity in North Wales, while the author
of the (admittedly less reliable) *Traison* was probably in the entourage of Queen
Isabelle.

Creton writes with a compelling immediacy. He describes, for example, how
the persecuted Richard climbs on a rock to view Northumberland's army and is
absolutely astonished at the size of it. Creton continues with a personal slant that
sounds all too authentic: 'Then were we all in great fear. I could have wished myself
in France at that time, for I saw them almost in despair ... we were forced either
to die or to pass on into the midst of the earl's forces. He could be seen, armed in
mail. The king was so humbled and miserable that it was a pity to behold; he
kept saying, "O true God, what shame and trouble must I undergo!"...'[64]

Jean Creton is the kind of witness one cannot choose to ignore. He may have
been partial but at least he knew Richard more intimately than any of the
Lancastrian chroniclers. Walsingham, for example, may have glimpsed Richard
on the few occasions that the king visited St Albans, but otherwise had no first-
hand knowledge of him. Why should we give more weight to his opinion than
to Creton's?

In summary, then, as one historian writes: 'There is little contemporary evidence
for Richard's unpopularity in the mid-1390s, indeed quite the opposite ... Perhaps
what we see in 1397 is a relatively popular king taking measures which were
widely supported, in an attempt to reassert the traditional authority of the crown
against a group of public nuisances who had, through a succession of political
own goals, failed entirely to capitalize on the advantage they had gained in
1387–8. The later lionizing of Richard's victims in 1397 is largely propaganda.'[65]

Similarly, another scholar has recently challenged the three long-established
positions: that Richard's government in the late 1390s was unpopular; that
Richard had few supporters and that few rallied to his cause in 1399; and that

there was widespread support for Henry.[66] 'These three views,' writes Caroline Barron, 'none of them very well grounded, have served as a mutual support group in which each has been used to prop up the others.'[67]

It may well be that the *Chronicque de la Traison et Mort de Richart Deux Roy Dengleterre* – not usually noted for its historical accuracy – has the balance about right when it says that the citizens of London were split over their opinion of Richard's rule.

> And, as he rode through London on a little horse on his way to prison, they kept an open space round him, that every one might see him; and there was a boy behind him, who pointed him out with his finger, saying, 'Behold King Richard, who has done so much good to the kingdom of England!' It is true that some pitied him much, and others were exceedingly glad, cursing him loudly in their language, and saying, 'Now are we well revenged of this wicked bastard who has governed us so ill.'[68]

But, despite it all, affection for and loyalty to Richard continued to be Henry's major nemesis in the years that followed the usurpation. The new king was long plagued by persistent rumours that Richard was still alive. It's the kind of rumour that would only gather round a figure who enjoyed strong support and even affection. And it certainly didn't help Henry. As one commentator writes: 'There was no early closing of the political ranks. Richard's former courtiers, despite their generous treatment by the new king, continued to grieve over his loss and hankered after his restoration.'[69]

THE REBELLION AND DEPOSITION

One thing we can say for certain about Henry's revolt is that it was a surprise. It certainly took Richard II by surprise. Otherwise he wouldn't have packed up all his military resources and taken them over the sea to Ireland. Indeed the fact that he did has itself consistently surprised commentators down the years.

For a start Richard and Henry had been childhood companions. They had grown up together and together had been admitted into the Order of the Garter in 1377. Henry was more interested in military prowess, and had been on crusade to Prussia and to the Holy Land. The two young men may have been different in outlook and temperament, but there really didn't seem to be any particular bad blood between them. On the contrary, during the rebellion of 1386–7, Henry, although one of the Appellants, had acted as a moderating influence upon the others. He had also taken the king's part in pleading for the life of his old tutor Sir Simon Burley. And once Richard was back in power their relationship became once more warmer and more intimate.[70]

Furthermore, Henry was widely regarded as an honourable man and an exemplar of chivalry. As one historian reminds us: 'We are so influenced by our impression of Henry IV as a scheming usurper and care-worn ruler that we are apt to forget that in the 1390s he was worshipped as the conventional hero of chivalry. He is said to have conquered all hearts by his good looks, his liberality, his knightly skill and horsemanship, and by his reckless love of adventure ... Not in a single respect did he fall short of the ideal of knightly accomplishment.'[71] For

Thomas Mowbray, Duke of Norfolk, throws down the gauntlet to Henry Bolingbroke, Duke of Hereford.

such a hero to lead a rebellion against his rightful liege lord was extraordinary. Henry's treachery was probably as unthinkable for most people at the beginning of 1399 as it was a fact of life by the end of the year. The apparent inevitability of Henry's actions is a result of hindsight and of Lancastrian propaganda.

Of course, Richard had acted in a surprising way too. Early in 1398, a mysterious quarrel sprang up between Henry of Derby and Thomas Mowbray. The two of them came before Richard accusing each other of treason. Richard sensibly tried to get them both to cool down and drop their allegations, but neither would. Little could Richard have realised, as he acted the wise elder statesman to his two hot-headed contemporaries, that he was participating in the first steps to his own downfall.

Eventually gloves were thrown down, and the matter could not be resolved except by a legal battle – that is by a duel to the death between the two great barons.

The day was set for 16 September. Lists were constructed on a green outside Coventry with a handsome wooden pavilion for the Duke of Hereford.[72] Tents were pitched for the reception of the nobility and royalty. Everyone organized their calendar to be there or be square.

But when the great day arrived, sensation followed sensation. The contestants were already facing each other upon their chargers. Hereford signed himself with the cross, placed his lance upon his thigh and took the first few steps towards his adversary, when Richard suddenly rose in his seat and stopped the contest. The two contestants were sent back to their pavilions, and the crowd waited restlessly for two hours. Richard was within his rights to make this dramatic last-minute cancellation (according to a treatise on judicial duels, written by none other than Richard's old enemy, the late Duke of Gloucester) but one can't imagine it was a decision that would have been popular with the crowd.

The second sensation came later in the afternoon. A herald mounted the steps of the raised platform or 'tribune' and announced the king's judgement: Henry was to be banished for ten years and if he returned before he would be hanged and beheaded. There was instant uproar and the herald couldn't continue for some while. When he did, he further announced that Mowbray was to be exiled for life.[73]

Richard's motives for this double judgement have been much discussed. Perhaps he couldn't let either man win. They were both safer abroad. Henry's father, old John of Gaunt, agreed to the judgement, and it is likely that the banishment of Henry was seen simply as a cooling-off period.[74]

Once the excitement had died down, Richard would be able to allow Henry back and to effect a reconciliation between monarch and liege. Unfortunately, a spanner was thrown into the works by the death of Gaunt in February 1399. Richard, uncertain about allowing Henry back so soon, revoked the letters of attorney by which Henry would have been able to take possession of his inheritance *in absentia*. But he did not actually confiscate the Lancastrian estates. Unlike those estates forfeited by his enemies of 1397, Richard left the Lancastrian inheritance intact. He did not, as we shall see, divide it up or subsume it into other royal estates or distribute it amongst his favourites, and this leaves the real possibility that he was keeping it intact either for Henry or for Henry's son.[75]

It may even be that Richard, from the start, had a secret understanding with Henry that he would allow him back to claim his rights within a year or two of the banishment. The Monk of St-Denys, recounts how Henry complains bitterly about his punishment, but that 'the king quieted him by kind words, and promised him with an oath, to recall him before the end of the year'.[76] Such an understanding would explain what otherwise seems to have been an act of political folly on Richard's part, in taking ship to Ireland so soon after with his entire army and leaving the realm undefended.

Whether or not there was an understanding between them, Henry's return the following year caught everybody by surprise. So too did its consequences, for afterwards everything was utterly different in the kingdom that had once been Richard's.

CHAPTER 7

Chaucer's world changes

~

The world in which Chaucer found himself at the end of 1399 was profoundly altered from the world in which the year had begun. Everything had changed and – from the poet's point of view – for the worse. To understand how alarming – even terrifying – the world would have suddenly become to someone like Chaucer, it is necessary to peel back some layers of Lancastrian propaganda.

We need to consider the reasons behind Henry's surprise move against his cousin and liege lord, Richard. We need to look at who was supporting Henry's coup. And we need to consider the myth that Henry seized the throne easily and without undue loss of life and to universal acclaim. It is the same myth that all violent usurpers through all time have sought to establish. And it was, as such stories always are, totally bogus.

HENRY BOLINGBROKE IN EXILE

For the young Henry Bolingbroke, in 1398, things weren't really that bad. He was, admittedly, on an enforced holiday in Europe, but he'd been granted a cool £2,000 a year for the period of his exile, and he had plenty of places to go and plenty of people to visit. 'The Earl of Derby may readily go two or three years and amuse himself in foreign parts, for he is young enough,' said the lords amongst themselves, according to Froissart.

> He has two sisters, queens of Castile and of Portugal, and may cheerfully pass his time with them. The lords, knights and squires of those countries will make him welcome ... he may put them in motion, and lead them against the infidels of Granada, which will employ his time better than remaining idle in England. Or he may go to Hainault, where his cousin, and brother-in-arms, the Count d'Ostrevant, will be happy to see him ... He therefore cannot fail of doing well, whithersoever he goes ...[1]

Henry was warmly received in Paris, and he'd had his sovereign's assurance that, should anything happen to his father while he was away, he'd be able to benefit from Gaunt's estates through his lawyers 'until it shall please the king that he return ...'[2] Return was not only promised – it was down there on the record – albeit at the king's behest. Froissart tells us the expectation was that he'd be recalled sooner rather than later: 'the king may speedily recall him ... for he is the finest feather in his cap; and he must not therefore suffer him to be too long absent, if he wish to gain the love of his subjects'. Froissart is notoriously unreliable at this particular period, but even so it is hard to imagine that the two cousins, Richard and Henry, did not establish an understanding about when Henry's return would be.

Henry Bolingbroke.

The situation changed, however, at the start of the following year. Gaunt unexpectedly died in February. Richard spent a month and a half deciding whether to recall Henry or not before finally deciding that it was more convenient, or at least safer, to keep him out of the country for the moment. He therefore cancelled the letters of attorney by which Henry could have claimed the Lancaster estate in his absence. It looked as if Richard had gone back on his word and was determined to disinherit his cousin.

But things weren't actually *that* black for Henry, because Richard stipulated that the forfeited lands could only be held by others 'until Henry of Lancaster, duke of Hereford, or his heir, shall have sued the same out of the king's hands according to the law of the land'.[3] If Richard had really wanted to disinherit Henry, why would he have made such a provision?

By demanding Henry's total submission – that he put himself in his power before being forgiven – Richard was doing no more than acting out the advice to princes contained in the *Melibee* (ll. 1805–15). Perhaps Richard was simply demonstrating, once and for all, his dearly held tenet of kingship – that everything came from the royal hand – even for the highest-born noble in the land, *everything* was in the gift of the king.

Or then again, he might have been holding the estate on behalf of Henry's son – the young prince, then living in his household, whom he was soon to knight in Ireland and whom, perhaps, he was grooming as his successor.

Whatever the reason, the duchy of Lancaster was not divided up and distributed amongst favourites, as the estates of the rebel barons had been in 1397, but was kept intact ready to be handed over when Richard saw fit.[4] At least one chronicle mentions that there was secret diplomatic traffic between Henry and Richard, and it seems reasonable to assume that Richard would have carried on reassuring Henry about his ultimate return. Whether Henry believed it or not by this time, we don't know. But, according to one account, he seemed surprisingly unperturbed by the news of the forfeiture of his estate.

The Chronicle of Saint Denys (our main source of information for Henry's time in Paris) describes how, after an initial outburst of outrage (perhaps for the benefit of the French king) and after accusing Richard of perjury, Henry allows himself to be calmed down by the Duke of Berry. 'Henry thanked the Duke of Berry for his words of consolation; he feigned indifference, and pretended to be cheerful.' The French chronicler goes on to ascribe this to typical English hypocrisy: 'This, however, was but one of those ruses which are familiar to the English, a way of concealing more effectively the plan which he had to avenge his injuries, as will be seen later ...'[5] Another possibility, however, is that Henry was genuinely less troubled by Richard's revocation of the letters of attorney than he might have been, precisely because he knew that his inheritance was really not at risk.

AN ALTERNATIVE VIEW OF HENRY

The story of Henry's attack on the throne of England has, traditionally, placed Henry at the centre of energy. He is the prime mover in everything that happens over the next few months. But *The Chronicle of Saint Denys* also hints at another Henry: one who is altogether less dynamic. After his initial accusations and complaint, the chronicle informs us, Henry told the king of France 'that he knew not what to do, nor what course of action to take'. Maybe this was a figure of speech. Maybe it was the truth. Maybe Henry didn't really *want* to do anything – he was just cutting a figure of injured innocence.

In the first place, to return to England before he was recalled would be an act of treason, according to the terms of his exile.[6] Henry was under threat of hanging and beheading should he return before he was sent for. In the second place, Henry's French hosts clearly disapproved strongly of any treasonable action against Richard. When Henry showed the Duke of Berry letters from his sympathizers in England, urging him to return, the Duke told him to remember his father and 'advised him to eschew any dishonourable action which might sully the reputation bequeathed to him by so great a prince'.[7]

The Duke of Orleans, with whom Henry concluded a pact in 1399, later claimed that his trust had been betrayed by Henry's deposition of Richard. Henry's attack on Richard was a betrayal not just of the Duke of Orleans, it was a betrayal of everybody. He was betraying his sovereign lord. He was betraying his French hosts. He was betraying his own hard-won reputation as a chivalrous knight.

Why should he have risked so much opprobrium, if there were any chance whatsoever of reclaiming his inheritance by other means?

HENRY'S CHANGE OF PERSONALITY

Historians have long noted that it seemed as if Henry underwent a character change in 1399 – a change so profound as to be quite baffling. Before the usurpation Henry was 'the adventurous, chivalrous crusader; prompt, energetic, laborious; the man of impulse rather than of judgement'. But afterwards he became: 'suspicious, cold-blooded and politic, undecided in action, cautious and jealous in private and public relations, and if not personally cruel, willing to sanction and profit by the cruelty of others'.[8] What happened to change his personality so completely and utterly?

The famous joust in Calais.

In the 1390s Henry was admired as a chivalric hero, a heart-throb, a man of action and a reckless adventurer.[9] He jousted in the famous tournament held outside Calais in 1390, and he and his ten companions were recognized as 'the bravest of the opponents'.[10] He was liberal with his riches. He went off to fight with the Knights of the Teutonic Order in Prussia, and he went on pilgrimage to Jerusalem. On the way he seems to have dazzled and charmed almost everybody – he certainly charmed the young Lucia Visconti while he was in Milan. Six years later, she refused to marry the man her parents wanted her to marry because, she said, she had promised herself to Henry of Derby.[11]

Something of this chivalric, forthright character seems to show itself in the usurpation. For all his treachery and deviousness in returning to England,

Henry himself, according to Thomas Walsingham, appears to have favoured the idea of claiming the throne by right of conquest. This, at least, was straightforward, honest, and perhaps more honourable.[12] But it did not suit the scheming and political men who surrounded him and who made his usurpation possible. A committee was appointed in late August 1399, charged with working out how to effect the transfer of power from Richard to Henry. Sir William Thirning, the chief justice of the king's Bench, and the other doctors and bishops were looking for ways of clothing this bare-faced seizure in the fancy dress of legality, and they persuaded Henry not simply to drop the claim to the throne by 'right of conquest' but even to disavow it altogether (see below p.176). Henry's original instinct may have been in line with his persona of the chivalric hero, but he seems to have succumbed to the pressure to behave more deviously.

There was even something chivalrous in the way Henry treated many of Richard's former supporters. In the chivalric code, loyalty – even to an enemy – was always highly valued. Henry may have been following his chivalrous instincts when he took the young Gascon squire Jenico into his service – the same Jenico whom he had briefly imprisoned in Chester castle for his refusal to stop wearing Richard's badge even after Richard's arrest. Possibly, Henry's chivalric side could now reward the young squire for his act of bravado. Indeed, he seemed to have complete trust in the Gascon's loyalty, now it was sworn to himself, for he made him one of the three Special Commissioners charged with negotiating with the Scottish King Robert in January 1400.[13]

So maybe it wasn't a change in personality that Henry underwent, so much as a change of influence.

Although Henry liked to give the impression of independence of action, he had always had someone else to rely on. In the past he had been 'led sometimes by his uncle Gloucester, sometimes by his father'.[14] Both were now dead, and in exile Henry had no one else to turn to, apart from the French dukes, who counselled maintaining honour and patience. But in 1399 Henry came under the spell of someone else – someone who was full of intrigue – someone ruthless – someone who was hard-headed, pragmatic, and an extremely skilful politician. Someone who harboured a deep resentment against the man who then sat upon the throne of England. Someone who desperately needed Henry to be king.

In short, he fell in with ex-Archbishop Thomas Arundel.

And from that moment Henry would never be the same carefree chivalrous hero he'd been before. If to many he didn't seem himself, perhaps it was because he was no longer calling the shots. He had made a pact with his own peculiar devil …

HENRY MEETS ARUNDEL

Sometime in late 1398 or early 1399, in a Paris 'hôtel' (the sumptuous residence of an important man), Henry Bolingbroke met with Thomas Arundel, one-time archbishop of Canterbury and ex-Chancellor of England – now an exile – banished as a traitor for his part in the barons' revolt of 1386–8. This once-powerful man now found himself without a position and without an income. We don't know whether they sat and drank a glass of wine by the window, or whether they huddled away in a corner and talked nineteen to the dozen about the old days back in Blighty. But we *do* know that by meeting Arundel, Henry was committing a first act of treason. His terms of exile expressly forbade him from having anything to do with the ex-archbishop.

Richard II had 'ordained by the authority of Parliament ... that the said Duke of Hereford, should not in any way come into the company of the said Thomas Duke of Norfolk [Mowbray],

Henry meets Arundel in Paris.

nor of Thomas Arundel, and that he should not send nor cause to be sent, nor receive nor cause to be received, either message or any other communication, nor should he mix in any manner with either of them; and this under the penalty above [*treason*].'[15]

The exiled Mowbray was also forbidden, under pain of death, from meeting up with ex-Archbishop Arundel. Clearly Richard feared Arundel's influence and vengeance – probably with good reason.

Thomas Arundel, despite his priestly robes, was the ablest politician of his time. He came from a powerful and ancient Norman family, but, as the youngest of three sons, he could look forward to no fortune himself.[16] He was therefore turned out to the rich pastures of the church – the traditional form of Social Security for the younger sons of the fourteenth-century nobility. By the age of 17 he was given special dispensation by the pope to draw a salary from various ecclesiastical appointments without having to do anything, or even go through all the rigmarole of qualifying as a priest. A year later he was living like the young lord he was from the profits of at least six different benefices from as far apart as Exeter and York. When he reached 21, his high-placed connections persuaded the pope to stump up a bishopric for him, and the lad was hurried through the ecclesiastical ranks, being ordained a deacon and then a priest on the same day that he was finally consecrated Bishop of Ely. Arundel's career is a case study in almost everything Wyclif hated most about the Church Commercial. He also, as we shall see, represented the antithesis of Chaucer's idealized Parson.

Thomas may have been young when he was elevated to such lofty ecclesiastical appointments, but he was by no means inadequate for them. On the contrary he was a lot more than adequate. He seems to have taken his duties as bishop very seriously, and applied his considerable abilities to the benefit of his diocese. But, from the moment of his first elevation, he began to use the church as a power base for his political advancement. By 1386 he was Chancellor of the Realm, and ten years later he was Archbishop of Canterbury. He had always been part of the baronial opposition to Richard, but he was so skilled a politician that he managed to make himself acceptable to both sides. He was a ruthless, intelligent, and powerful man. Above all, though, he was an autocrat: a man for whom the exercise of power was second nature, and who would brook no opposition.

It is little wonder, then, that Richard tried to keep the exiled Henry Bolingbroke apart from the exiled Thomas Arundel. Henry possessed popularity, social position and a loyal band of armed followers, while ex-Archbishop Arundel possessed *brains* – brains and ravenous ambition. On their own perhaps, neither Henry nor Arundel presented too great a threat, but together they were a real danger.

Henry could look forward to a reasonably comfortable life in exile, and, as we have seen, it was even possible that he was anticipating an early return to England. Ex-Archbishop Arundel, on the other hand, must have viewed the future rather bleakly.

For many years he'd been one of the most important men in England. He'd been a bishop for a quarter of a century. He'd been Chancellor of England for practically ten years. He'd reached the top of his profession as Archbishop of Canterbury. And yet now, here he was aged only 46 – an exile with nothing to look forward to – not even a pension. He had been 'translated to the See of St Andrew' – which was a euphemism for not having a see at all (St Andrew's being outside papal jurisdiction) and – to Arundel's chagrin – the pope had confirmed Roger Walden as the new Archbishop of Canterbury. In January 1398 all Arundel's estates, churches, manors, farms, and other property were signed over to the new archbishop. He'd lost his top job and all the wealth and perks that went with it.[17]

Of course he wasn't exactly slumming it on the Continent. Even as an ex-archbishop, Arundel was not the sort of man to stint himself when it came to lifestyle choices. He'd left England with an entourage of twenty, plus all the appropriate horses and baggage. He was also lucky in that King Richard wasn't in the business of humiliating him – in contrast to Henry and Arundel's treatment of Richard two years later. The ex-archbishop appears to have enjoyed a decent reception in Ghent, to which town Richard had written requesting that his person and baggage be respected: 'For, although the said archbishop, owing to his crimes and according to law, has been exiled, the king does not want his person nor his belongings to be molested.'[18] In April Richard gave permission for a certain Nicholas Oterbourne to join Arundel on his travels. In Rome Arundel managed to win the pope's favour (so he claimed in a letter home) and he was now living in 'an Earthly paradise near Florence', where he found himself in the good company of the chancellor of Florence – the famous

Florence, where ex-Archbishop Arundel stayed with Coluccio Salutati.

humanist philosopher, Coluccio Salutati. Arundel clearly possessed charm and charisma, for he seems to have formed quite a friendship with the venerable chancellor, who wrote at least three letters to him on his return to England.[19]

But Arundel must have known that without income or office his pleasant lifestyle couldn't last forever. He would have foreseen grim times over the horizon, unless he managed to pull something out of the bag. A stiff letter from Richard to Pope Boniface hadn't helped; it damned Arundel's 'seditious and intriguing character' and requested the pope to refrain from helping him.[20] The Roman pope, still locked in battle with the pope in Avignon, needed King Richard's support more than he needed ex-Archbishop Arundel's gratitude.

By the summer of 1398, Thomas Arundel must have been getting pretty desperate. He still had no prospects and diminishing resources. The fifteenth-century chronicler John Hardyng records Arundel's poverty on his return:

At which time so the Duke Henry took land
At Ravenspur in Yorkshire, as it was known,
The archbishop Thomas, I understand,

Of Canterbury, Arundel, that was low
Both of riches and gold, as men saw,
For the king had him out of the land exiled
From Canterbury, never more to be reconciled.[21]

However, it's hard to imagine that a man of Thomas Arundel's temperament would have been depressed. Arundel was not one of life's victims. It's a fair guess that he would have been scheming to get back into power from the moment he stepped on the boat for France. In the same letter that he wrote from Florence to his colleagues in Canterbury he puts a brave face on his circumstances: 'Concerning my own affairs, things are far better disposed than the malicious people believe', implying that the general gossip was that the ex-archbishop was on his uppers.

A side-note in the printed text claims that Arundel 'seems to hint that his return from exile under the patronage of a new dynasty is not improbable', but it is difficult to see how this is derived from the admittedly obscure text. On the other hand, it would be no surprise if Arundel were already contemplating Richard's deposition in January 1398. Why not? He had been a party to the previous attempt to depose Richard, only a decade before. What had he to lose now by attempting to finish off the job he and his brother, Richard Earl of Arundel, and the other barons had started ten years earlier?[22]

Whether his plans already encompassed Henry Bolingbroke at this stage, we can only guess. Henry was not to be exiled for another seven months, but, on the other hand, the court was already buzzing with talk of who was to succeed the childless Richard. John of Gaunt may even have put his son Henry forward as a candidate to parliament. The Earl of March was the legitimate heir, but Henry's name was on some people's lips. At the same time powerful forces in the king's favour were eyeing the vast Lancastrian estates: in other words, an embryonic power struggle was already focussing on the question of the succession. This was the background to the quarrel between Henry (newly created Duke of Hereford) and Thomas Mowbray, the Duke of Norfolk, in January 1398 – the quarrel that culminated in Henry's banishment.[23]

The exiled Arundel was bound to have been following these matters with interest from abroad. The fifteenth-century chronicler Giovanni Sercambi tells us that this was one of the reasons the ex-archbishop chose to reside in Florence – where he could get news of goings-on in England and try everything he could to restore his fallen faction.[24] Clearly Arundel would never be able to return to England as long as Richard was on the throne. But who was there now to challenge him? The barons' opposition had been routed the previous year; the only remaining lord who had challenged Richard in 1386–8 and who might still pose a threat was Henry Bolingbroke. It does not seem far-fetched to suppose that Arundel already realized that a Lancastrian challenge to the throne would be the most likely vehicle for his own return to power. Although, of course, at the start of 1398 he would have had no idea how the story would play out – indeed, how it would play right into his hands.

A letter from Coluccio Salutati confirms that he must have been mulling over these plans while he was in Florence. The letter was written in the summer of 1399, when Arundel was already embarked on his rebellion in support of Henry. In it, the Florentine chancellor expresses the hope that Arundel's return to England will be successful. He clearly understands the dangerous business that Arundel is engaged in, and since it seems unlikely that the ex-archbishop would have broached such a sensitive subject as his proposed act of treason in writing, Salutati must be referring back to private conversations conducted while Arundel was in his 'earthly paradise' – sometime, that is, during his sojourn in Florence in 1398.

Whatever plans Arundel was actually envisaging at that stage, we can be sure that news of the exiling of the young Henry Bolingbroke, in September 1398, would have made up the ex-archbishop's mind for him. Henry's banishment presented Arundel with a golden opportunity. The news of the death of Henry's father, John of Gaunt, early in the next year, followed by Richard's repudiation of Henry's attorneys, was the icing on the cake.

We don't know whether Arundel and Henry started their forbidden collusion before or after the news of Gaunt's death. We also don't know exactly when they met up in Paris, but whenever it was, Arundel must have been aware that this was a make-or-break moment in his life. If he could persuade the young Henry to make an attempt on the throne of England, he would be back in business. If he failed, nothing awaited him but a slow and ignominious decline in bitter exile. Thomas Arundel would have had no wish to share the fate of Archbishop Neville, who was exiled in 1388, and had ended his days in exile in the obscurity of Louvain.[25]

When Arundel finally sat down with Henry, he must have had the whole plan worked out. That was his nature. He was a politician: someone who thought ahead; someone with plans and schemes. Henry – for all his reputation as a chivalric hero – had always relied on the direction of an older man. Most importantly, Henry did not have as much need of the throne of England as Arundel had need for Henry to seize it.

The two were not known as intimates. They'd been on the same side in the Appellants' *coup* of 1387 but there is no evidence that they were particular friends. Indeed, thirteen years earlier, Henry had accused the ex-archbishop's brother Richard, the Earl of Arundel, of plotting against the king. But in 1398–9, Thomas Arundel needed Henry Bolingbroke. He needed him badly.[26]

The ex-archbishop had old scores to settle with King Richard. In 1397, Richard had not only ruined him by sending him into exile, he had also inflicted a mortal wound on his pride. What is worse, some months beforehand he had made Thomas Arundel complicit in the death of his own brother. Richard had persuaded Thomas to act as his intermediary in persuading the haughty Earl of Arundel that if he quit his castle of Reigate no harm would come to him. Thomas duly persuaded his brother, and Richard duly had the earl executed.[27] Thomas Arundel must have been very keen to even the score with a king for whom he had long felt little but contempt, and for whom he now must also have entertained feelings of hatred.

Given Arundel's 'seditious and intriguing character', his wounded pride, his enmity to the king and his undoubted abilities, Richard was right to be afraid of him and doubly right to be afraid of his collusion with Henry. And since their collusion is inextricably bound up with the fate of Geoffrey Chaucer, it is worth exploring in more detail what exactly they had in mind, when they set out upon their return. In the first place what was Henry's motive for returning? Was he merely asserting his rights or was he going for the crown from the start?

Did he mean to depose Richard from the moment he left Paris?

HENRY'S MOTIVE FOR RETURNING TO ENGLAND

Historians have very generously tended to give Henry the benefit of the doubt. Generally they have followed the story as it is presented by the Lancastrian chroniclers. This is that Henry set out from Paris with nothing else on his mind other than to reclaim his rightful inheritance, which Richard had deprived him of – honest, guv! Once home, however, he found to his surprise the whole country rising to his banner and urging him to depose Richard, so he had no choice but to do as everyone wanted by deposing the wicked tyrant and taking the crown himself. Put like that it sounds like a pretty far-fetched tale, and yet this is what the chroniclers would have us believe.

'God', wrote Thomas Walsingham, '... implanted into the heart of Lord Henry, Duke of Hereford – and now, since the death of his father, Duke of Lancaster –

who had firstly been exiled for ten years and then most unjustly disinherited, the idea that he should return to his native land and demand the restoration of his ancestral rights, namely the duchy of Lancaster and all that pertained to it ...'[28] According to Walsingham, everyone was thoroughly behind Henry in his pursuit of his rightful due. The French encouraged him, and even the Duke of York, who was acting as regent while Richard was in Ireland, 'stated publicly that the Duke of Lancaster had been wrongfully disinherited, and that he had no intention of attacking someone who came in a just cause and to ask for the restoration of his rightful inheritance.'[29]

Henry IV.

It sounds pretty reasonable ... except for the fact that we know the French certainly did not encourage Henry to reclaim his inheritance – on the contrary, Henry had to dissemble his purpose for leaving Paris and he lied about his destination. Most of the French chronicles regard Henry's return to England as a dishonourable act.

What is more, the idea that Henry's sole declared objective was his inheritance is contradicted by the best account we have of Henry's meeting with Richard at Chester.

Creton's *Metrical History* seems to be a particularly reliable source for this meeting, for not only was Creton an eyewitness to the events he described, he goes out of his way to emphasize how accurate he is trying to be in this particular part of his story. He suddenly stops writing in verse and resorts to prose, saying: 'Now I shall tell you of the capture of the king, without attempting any more rhymes, so that I can relate better the whole conversation that passed between these two at their meeting; for I remember it well. So I will set it down in prose ...'[30]

In *The Metrical History*, Richard himself has no doubt that Henry is after the throne. From the moment the king hears of Henry's return from exile – which in itself was an act of treason – he is convinced that Henry means to topple him:

'Good Lord,' he says, pale with anger, 'this man plans to deprive me of my country.'[31] And when Richard later holds a council in Conway, his brother the Duke of Exeter says: 'It would be best to send immediately to the Duke ... to find out what he means to do, and what he hopes to gain, and why it is that he is trying to seize your kingdom, your person and your goods; and whether he wants to be king and sovereign lord of England ...'[32]

Creton was there when Henry's emissary, the Earl of Northumberland, arrived to tempt Richard out of his castle-keep at Conway. Instead of telling Richard that Henry has come to claim his inheritance, as one might expect,

Northumberland treacherously persuades Richard to leave Conway castle.

Northumberland claims that all Henry wants is for Richard to deliver up those who advised him to put his uncle, the Duke of Gloucester, to death, and for Richard to restore Henry to the office of 'chief justice of England, which the Duke his father, and all his ancestors have held for more than a hundred years'.

Now it is true that Northumberland also says that he knows Henry just wants his own lands back, but he does so only to emphasize that Henry is not trying to take anything that is Richard's.

He does not mention it as Henry's motive for returning to England. 'This I know well,' says the Earl of Northumberland, 'he wants nothing but his land, and whatever belongs to him. He desires nothing that is yours, for you are his immediate and rightful king; and he truly regrets the great mischief and wrong that he has committed against you ... and will come before you most humbly on his knees and sue for mercy.'[33]

If Henry had really come to claim his inheritance, then why didn't Northumberland say so? Why not state the obvious reason for the invasion?

To find the answer, we need to go back to the council that Henry held in Chester to plan for Richard's capture. Creton's account is necessarily less reliable at this juncture, because he was not there, but nevertheless it seems highly plausible. According to Creton, Henry was already reliant on Archbishop Arundel's political skills. Arundel gave the following summary of the situation: Richard was holed up in Conway castle and there was no point in a frontal assault, because the king would be able to slip away by sea. The archbishop therefore recommended that they winkle Richard out of the castle by deception. But in order to deceive him, they had to come up with a story that would convince Richard, and yet at the same time reassure him that his own person was not in danger.

Arundel advised Henry to pretend that he had come to avenge the murder of the Earl of Arundel and his uncle, the Duke of Gloucester. He further advised that Henry should claim that all he wanted was for a parliament to be summoned in order to punish 'those evil men by whom his uncles were put to death'. Everyone agreed it was the best advice they'd ever heard. It carried the ring of truth and at the same time it would reassure Richard of his own safety. Henry declared: 'It is a good plan and will suit our purposes well.'

But wait a minute!

It would have suited the conspirators' purposes just as well to say that Henry had come to claim the inheritance that Richard had deprived him of. That too would have carried the ring of truth and have implied no danger to Richard's person. So why didn't Arundel suggest the obvious motive for Henry's invasion – the motive which Henry was later to claim publicly?

The answer must be that it wouldn't have washed with Richard. In other words, Richard had *not* deprived Henry of his inheritance, didn't *intend* to deprive him of it, and he *knew* that Henry knew that this was the case. If Richard and Henry both understood that the exile was temporary and that the revocation of the attorneys' powers was a holding operation, Henry couldn't pretend to Richard's face that he had returned to recover his inheritance.

Even when Henry had Richard in his power and could drop his pretences, he still didn't try to pretend that he'd come to claim his estate. He openly insults Richard by saying he has come to help him govern better, but he doesn't touch on the Lancastrian lands.

'I have come sooner than you sent for me,' Henry begins – implying that there was indeed some sort of understanding about when he was to be sent for. 'And I will tell you why,' he continues. 'It is commonly said among your people that you have, for the last twenty or twenty-two years, governed them very badly and far too harshly, with the result that they are most discontented. If it please our Lord, however, I shall help you to govern them better than they have been governed in the past.'[34]

Again Jean Creton goes out of his way to emphasize the accuracy of his reporting: 'These, I assure you, are the very words that they exchanged,' Creton writes, 'no more and no less; for I heard them, and understood them perfectly.'

And there aren't many historians who could claim such credentials as that.

It is true, of course, that Henry actually took a formal oath that he would not take the crown from Richard. The Earls of Northumberland and Westmoreland made him swear it on the host. 'Even in those perjured days,' we are told, 'it was not believed that so perfect a knight as Henry of Lancaster would disregard so sacred an oath.'[35] But equally, it may have been no more than Northumberland and Westmoreland taking out an insurance policy on behalf of themselves and those who joined Henry: if the coup went wrong, they could always claim *they* had no intention of deposing Richard – in fact, they had Henry's sworn word for it.

Northumberland was certainly perjuring himself in Conway when he assured Richard that he would remain king, for when he made that promise, he had already accepted the appointment as Warden of the West March of Scotland from Henry – an appointment that was solely in the gift of the king.[36]

ARUNDEL'S EXTRAORDINARY RESUMPTION OF POWER

It seems unlikely that Henry would have set out on his audacious return without having fully decided to take the throne. For a start, to return without permission was an act of treason, punishable by death. In the second place, what on earth was Thomas Arundel doing in his entourage? Arundel was an exile, the same as Henry, with the doom of death against his return. If Henry's motive was merely to reclaim his estates, that would have been no protection for the ex-archbishop. Henry had been under specific instructions not to collude with Arundel while he was in exile. If returning was a treasonable act, returning with Arundel in tow was double treason. And as far as Arundel was concerned, the treason of returning from exile would not have been mitigated by helping restore Henry to his inheritance. Arundel's presence back in England would still have been an open provocation to the king. In returning to England, Arundel *must* have been relying on Richard's replacement by Henry.[37]

Surely, when Arundel and Henry met in that *hôtel* in Paris, Arundel would have stiffened Henry's resolve by offering him all the support of the holy church, should he make a bid for the crown. The two of them must have discussed a power-brokering deal, in which Henry's attempt on the throne would be given full ecclesiastical support provided Henry would, in return, promise certain concessions to the church. Exemption from taxes would have been placed on the bargaining table. So too would an old favourite of Arundel's, the introduction of the death penalty for heresy.

What is absolutely certain from the records is that, from the moment Henry's rebels set foot in England, Thomas Arundel reassumed the mantle of power without even attempting to sanction his actions with royal authority. There is no record of his official reinstatement; he simply ignored the Act of Parliament by which he had been declared a traitor and stripped of office, reassumed his role as archbishop, and nobody dared say a word against it. Arundel's self-reappointment to the archbishopric of Canterbury was as clear a signal as anyone could have asked for that, as long as the rebellion was successful, King Richard was doomed. His cavalier re-assumption of office displayed his open contempt not only for the king but also for the pope. Arundel had no papal authority for it – quite the contrary, but he was quite prepared to perjure himself on this as on so many matters. In for a penny, in for a pound.

According to Jean Creton 'the proud Archbishop of Canterbury' immediately preached a crusade against Richard: 'My good people,' says Arundel, 'hearken all of you here: you well know how the king most wrongfully and without reason banished your lord Henry; I have therefore, obtained of the Holy Father, who is our patron, that those who shall forthwith bring aid this day, shall, every one of them, have remission of all sins, whereby from the hour of their baptism they have been defiled. Behold the sealed bull that the pope of renowned Rome hath

Arundel reads a forged Papal Bull announcing a crusade against Richard II to a clearly sceptical audience.

sent me, my good friends, in behalf of you all. Agree then to help him to subdue his enemies, and you shall for this be placed, after death, with those who are in Paradise.' According to Creton, Arundel 'invented this device, because no one dared to stir through dread' of Richard's wrath.[38]

We have to take Creton's account of Arundel's speech with a pinch of salt, since we have no other record of his making such an appeal, and, in any case, Creton must have been relying on hearsay at this point. On the other hand, the Lancastrian chroniclers would scarcely have recorded for posterity such a gross piece of deception. At all events such a strategy would have been an eminently sensible way to kick-start Henry's campaign, and Arundel was an eminently sensible man.

The ploy certainly seems to have paid off, in Creton's words: 'Then might you have beheld young and old, the feeble and the strong, make a clamour, and regarding neither right nor wrong, stir themselves up with one accord; thinking that what was told them was true; they all, indeed, believed it, for such as they have little sense.'[39]

The fact that the Lancastrian chroniclers remain silent about Arundel's barefaced mendacity in claiming to have the pope's bull is scarcely surprising. Jean Creton felt confident enough in the story to represent it visually, and he included one of his most famous illustrations to make the point. And here it's worth pointing out that Creton's illuminations were not merely manuscript decorations; rather they were integral to his text and he used them to reinforce key points in his narrative.[40]

One thing we can say with certainty, however, is that on arriving back in England Arundel slipped seamlessly – and with consummate arrogance – into his old role as Archbishop of Canterbury. He didn't even give poor Roger Walden time to take his mitre off. We know that by 4 August 1399, Arundel was granting pardons and doling out church promotions, just as if the pope had never deprived him of his office. Adam of Usk, another eyewitness, had joined the party of Henry and Arundel, for whom he uses the revealing phrase 'my lord of Canterbury late returned'. He describes how they stayed in the royal castle at Ludlow, where apparently, they all hit the bottle: 'not sparing the wine which was therein stored'.

Perhaps they were all in their cups when Adam felt free enough to approach his superiors with a personal request. Henry and Arundel certainly responded with a generosity that might well have been engendered by good food and wine, and they certainly felt free enough to hand out favours as if they were already in power: 'I, who am now writing', says Adam of Usk, 'obtained from the Duke and from my lord of Canterbury the release of brother Thomas Prestbury, master in theology, who was kept in prison by King Richard ... I also got him promotion to the abbacy of his house.'[41]

Whether Arundel was on his third bottle or not when he made these magnanimous gestures we'll never know, but even stone cold sober he was not the sort of man to waste his time with legal niceties – any more than he was to footle around obtaining papal authority for his resumption of office. He was acting, as he always did, with breathtaking arrogance.

Indeed, Arundel's confidence in his own authority seems to have made itself felt through the centuries to the present day. Even modern historians continue to refer to him as 'the archbishop' through the period of his exile and after he'd ceased to be archbishop for two years! [42]

By September of 1399, Thomas Arundel was firmly back in the saddle. Adam of Usk reports how he dined with him at Lambeth, and notes that Roger Walden had torn down all Arundel's coats of arms – but that Arundel had already returned the compliment. Adam describes how he saw Walden's insignia 'stuffed ignominiously under benches or hurled from windows by menials'.

At the same time, Adam can't help but remark on the oddity of the situation, with Walden the official archbishop, but everyone acknowledging the powerful and dominating Arundel. His comments also give the lie to Arundel's claim (as reported by Creton) that the pope was a supporter of the *coup*:

> Thus might it be said that Thomas and Roger, these two archbishops in one church, were like two heads on one body, with Roger at that time in lawful possession according to the pope, but Thomas, although he had not yet been restored by the pope, in actual possession by dint of the secular power, which prevails in all things ...[43]

The more we look, then, at the circumstances of Henry's return, the harder it is to believe that his objective from the outset was anything other than the throne. Merely to have returned to English soil, unbidden, left him liable to beheading. To have returned with an armed escort (no matter how small) was open rebellion. And to return with a chief counsellor so detested by Richard would have left no doubt whatsoever that he cared nothing for his sovereign's forgiveness.

A year or two later, when the Duke of Orleans complained that Henry had betrayed his trust by deposing Richard, Henry wrote to Orleans: 'We apprised you openly and fully of [our plans] before our departure from overseas, at which time you approved our plans and promised aid against our dear lord and cousin King Richard ...'[44] So, on Henry's own admission in 1402, he was plotting to depose Richard even before he left the shores of France. Of course, he might have been just trying to embarrass the Duke of Orleans, but there again he might have been telling the truth.

All this is relevant to the fate of Chaucer, because it paints a picture of the usurpation very different from the sanitized official version. And there was worse to come. To understand what Chaucer was living through in his final months, we need to understand the bloody nature of Henry's rebellion and the culture of violence it brought in its wake.

CHAPTER 8

Chaucer's last bloody year

Henry 'raised his hands high and gave thanks to God ... for setting him up in the kingdom without bloodshed'. This is the official 'Thomas Walsingham Fantasy Version' of Henry IV's accession to power – 'Just the facts, ma'am,' the way all good Lancastrians would like to believe it.[1]

According to Walsingham, Henry's takeover of England is an endearing tale of the welcome hero rescuing the suffering nation from the hands of a vile and evil persecutor:

> When rumours began to circulate through England that the Duke of Lancaster had put to sea and was getting ready to return, there was great joy amongst the people, who now truly believed that God had sent him in order to release them from their dreadful yoke of servitude ... soon so many of those who had served his father, and of his own retainers, had flocked to join him, that within a short time he was in command of an almost invincible army ...

The only people to oppose the duke were the Bishop of Norwich and one William Elmham, 'a knight who seemed unaware that the whole world was now supporting the duke of Lancaster ...'[2]

When the good duke takes Bristol and beheads those miscreants, William le Scrope, John Bussy and Henry Green (Richard's close councillors who had helped convict Gloucester, Arundel and Warwick of treason), there is, of course, universal rejoicing: 'it was a judgement which was greeted with great joy by all the ordinary people of the kingdom, since it seemed to them that they had thus swiftly and opportunely been delivered from the enemies whom they most dreaded'.

Richard II arrested.

Similarly, Richard quickly gives up any hope of opposing Henry, because he is convinced that 'the common people, who had sworn to oppose him, hated him so much that they would rather die than give in to him'.

The whole enterprise is more like a carnival procession than a military exercise. Henry in essence floats around the country to universal applause and without opposition: 'It was a remarkable feat, in so short a time, to have brought such peace and stability to the whole realm, so much so, indeed, that the sole and universal desire of the inhabitants was now that King Richard should be set aside and Henry Duke of Lancaster become their king ...'[3]

WAS IT REALLY A BLOODLESS REVOLUTION?

It's a ludicrous account, of course, written not as history but as propaganda. It is even contradicted by one of Walsingham's fellow Lancastrian chroniclers, the Monk of Evesham – himself no apologist for Richard. The Monk of Evesham makes it clear that Henry's army proceeded not simply by popular acclaim, but by a mixture of bribery and threats. 'Those who refused to join him, or were too slow to do so, were despoiled of all or a large part of their goods, which, for the most part, were never subsequently restored to them. Thus, in order to protect both themselves and their goods, great numbers of men joined the Duke each day from this time onwards.'[4] The suggestion that Henry used intimidation to augment his support as he progressed across England is further borne out by the *Short Kirkstall Chronicle* which says: 'Crowds of gentlemen, knights and esquires from Yorkshire and Lancashire flocked to join him with their retinues, some of whom came willingly and others out of fear of what the future might hold.'[5]

As for making an example of the men of Cheshire, Henry did not confine himself to seeking out those who were Richard's bodyguards. He had one of the leaders, Piers de Leigh, beheaded and his head set up above the highest of the city gates. His revenge, however, was on the whole of Cheshire.

He proclaimed 'Havok!' on the entire county. The *Dieulacres Chronicle* tells us: 'Because nearly everyone hated the Cheshiremen, Henry IV took counsel against Chester to proclaim "Havok" upon the city and the entire county.'[6] Crying 'Havok!' was of course the signal for general despoliation and pillaging. In other words, it was the sign for the army to do their worst – without mercy or quarter, and with no fear of subsequent retribution from their commanders.

Adam of Usk, who was with the usurper at this time, says that when Henry announced that his army was to march on Chester, he took the line that it should 'spare the people and the country ... But little good did the proclamation do ...'. Usk continues:

> On the ninth day of August, the Duke with his host entered the county of Chester, and there, in the parish of Coddington and other neighbouring parishes, taking up his camping ground and pitching his tents, nor sparing meadow nor cornfield, pillaging all the country round, and keeping strict watch against the wiles of the men of Chester, he passed the night.

Usk concludes, rather ingenuously: 'And I, the writer of this chronicle, spent a not uncheerful night in the tent of the lord of Powis.'

Usk also lets the cat out of the bag when he boasts how he manages to reconcile Henry to the lordship of Usk, 'the place of my birth, which he had determined to harry, on account of the resistance of the lady of that place, the king's niece, there ordered'. Intimidation, it appears, was to be expected if anyone – even a high-born lady – put up resistance to Henry's triumphal progress.

The writer of the *Short Kirkstall Chronicle* is slightly more forthright about what 'Havok' involved:

> The Duke of Lancaster and his army marched towards and against the county of Chester, trampling down with their horses' hooves the corn and the meadows throughout most of the county; thus having captured the town of Chester and other castles, and having killed many of the local inhabitants and confiscated numerous goods from them, the Duke accomplished what he set out to do.[7]

So much for the idea of a bloodless revolution.

FEAR OF WHAT THE FUTURE MIGHT HOLD

Nor did the bloodshed stop once Henry was safely seated on the throne. The fact is that Henry was *never* safely seated on the throne. Or that is certainly what Henry himself thought. His reign was beset with scares and alarms, attempts on his life and abortive uprisings. Henry occupied his throne, a suspicious, paranoid figure riddled with guilt and surrounded by potential revolt.

The opening months of Henry IV's reign – the last of Chaucer's life – were not placid times. They were chaotic and dangerous. Those who had been fearful of what the future might hold were right to be fearful.

The first Parliament in October–November of 1399 was conducted in 'an atmosphere of near-hysteria generated by the accusation and counter-accusation which the bitterly divided nobles hurled at each other'.[8] More than forty

pledges were thrown down onto the floor of the chamber, as lord accused lord of treachery. Everyone was jittery. In the end, however, the only blood that was spilt was that of the unfortunate John Hall, who had been a possibly unwilling witness to the murder of the Duke of Gloucester. He was duly executed with a macabre ferocity that was to become only too familiar in the years to follow. Otherwise, Henry seems to have treated his enemies with a surprisingly wise leniency ... to begin with, at least.

Westminster Hall where parliament often met.

Within a short time, however, the blood started to flow. A plot to assassinate Henry shortly after Christmas was apparently hatched around the dinner table of the Abbot of Westminster. The plot was betrayed to Henry, possibly by the Earl of Rutland, and Henry dispersed the plotters. By a *remarkable* stroke of good fortune for the usurper, the non-clerical ringleaders were lynched by furious mobs in various cities, leaving Henry able to carry on with the appearance of clemency.

Whether the convenient dispatch of his enemies was orchestrated by Henry's agents, we'll never know, but certainly Archbishop Arundel seems to have been uncharacteristically supportive of this particular instance of mob rule. In a letter he sent back to the convent in Canterbury he turns *lynch mob* into 'the virtuous common people'. He writes:

> The authors of this crime [i.e. the 'January Plot' against Henry] – whom we can identify as the Earls of Kent and Salisbury, and Lords Ralph Lumley, Thomas Blount and Benedict Sely – were seized, along with some others, at Cirencester, by the virtuous common people of the neighbourhood who have made all

these facts publicly known; nor indeed did they simply capture them, but, lest others might arrive and succeed in snatching them from their grasp, they also beheaded the aforesaid Earls and Ralph Lumley, leaving the rest to our lord king's judgment.[9]

The 28-year-old Duke of Gloucester, Sir Thomas Despenser, managed to escape in a ship but was betrayed by the captain and brought to Bristol where, once again, the mob generously *insisted* on doing the beheading on behalf of the king.[10] The Earl of Huntington also managed to escape, but after a period of hiding eventually fell into the hands of the Countess of Hereford – Archbishop Arundel's sister. She kept him for a time in her castle at Pleshey, but finally … surprise! surprise! … felt she had *no* choice but to hand him over to the mob, who once again undertook the chore of beheading the miscreant – thus keeping the new king's hands unstained.

The Lancastrian chronicler Walsingham waxes lyrical at this point in his story: Henry, on his way to Oxford,

had heard news of the capture and well-deserved punishment of those who had committed treason against him, that is, that without any effort on the part of him or his army, they had been swiftly overcome, not through his ingenuity but through God's. When this news was confirmed, he raised his hands high and gave thanks to God for so favouring him not only for setting him up in the kingdom without bloodshed, but also for now delivering him from the clutches of his enemies without putting either himself or his followers in any serious danger; for he knew all these things had happened not through human agency but miraculously, through divine intervention.[11]

At least one chronicler, however, felt bold enough to question the wisdom of allowing mob rule. Adam of Usk wrote: 'Seeing that all these acts were perpetrated solely by the violence of the common people, I fear that possession of the sword, which, although contrary to the natural order, was allowed to them in such circumstances, might at some future time embolden them to rise up in arms against the lords.' The phrase which '*was allowed to them* in such circumstances' suggests that the mob may have been actually encouraged in their murderous activities – possibly by agents of the crown handing out swords. Such a scenario is supported by the fact that the leader of the townspeople at Cirencester was the usurper's own esquire, John Cosyn.[12]

HENRY'S SADISTIC SIDE

The Lancastrian accounts do their best to absolve Henry from the charge of shedding blood, but in reality there was bloodshed a-plenty. And – more importantly – it was a different *kind* of bloodshed from anything perpetrated by Richard. For although Richard is often accused of vindictiveness, he actually seems to have shown unaccountably little interest in that favourite hobby of medieval rulers: 'cruel and unusual punishments'.

The usual penalty for treason at this time was to 'draw' the victim by dragging them behind a horse, to the place of execution, then to half-strangle them by hanging, then to rip out their intestines (an optional extra, this), behead them, and finally cut them up into convenient, parcel-sized quarters. While Richard was in control, this punishment was frequently commuted. Even when Richard finally took revenge on his bitterest opponent and arch-enemy, the Earl of Arundel, he still would not allow the full sentence to be administered and personally reduced it to beheading.[13]

Hanging, drawing and quartering is back in vogue with the accession of Henry IV.

Indeed, the contrast between Richard's treatment of his opponents in 1397 and the bloodthirsty vengeance meted out by them ten years previously speaks for itself.

On one occasion, Richard was displeased with the Mayor of Dartmouth, who had (perhaps over-enthusiastically) burnt a woman for poisoning her husband. Although the mayor pleaded that he firmly believed that having a live bonfire was within 'the town's privileges and liberties', he was required to purchase a pardon from Richard because he had acted 'without express commission of the king'.[14]

And this was not a case of the king making a little pocket money on the side by the judicious sale of pardons. Richard really didn't seem to want people burnt at the stake. In 1395, for example, he came under tremendous pressure from the prelates to bring English law into line with continental practice and start burning heretics. Even the pope added his weight to the pro-immolation lobby. 'So long, however, as Richard II was king no such statute was made and no heretic was committed to the flames.'[15] Richard, it seems, had little relish for the refinements of torture or unusual and cruel deaths, and was generally moved by 'a genuine abhorrence of the shedding of blood'.[16]

Henry, on the other hand, was not such a spoilsport. With his arrival, the executioners and torturers could sharpen their knives with the cheery prospect of putting them to good use.

Besides the mob-lynchings of the ringleaders of the January 1400 assassination plot, there were plenty of other executions and tortures.

For example, thirty of the lesser rebels were bound and then made to march from Cirencester to Oxford – walking such a distance with your hands tied would, in itself, constitute a form of torture. A brief examination in front of the king concluded with the summary executions of nearly all of them. Henry seems to have had no qualms about carrying out the full sentence for treason with all the seasonal trimmings. Sir Thomas Blount and Sir Benedict Sely were drawn from Oxford to the place of execution, 'a long league or more', and there they were hanged. Then Blount was cut down and placed before a large fire and forced to speak. The executioner who arrived next 'had with him a small basin and a razor, and, kneeling between the fire and the lords, unbuttoned Sir Thomas Blount, and ripped open his stomach, and tied the bowels with a piece of whip-cord that the breath of the heart might not escape, and cast the bowels into the fire'. There then followed an exchange of pleasantries between Sir Thomas Blount and Sir Thomas Erpingham, while 'Sir Thomas was thus seated before the fire, his bowels burning before him'. The executioner then asked him if he would drink. 'No,' he replied, 'you have taken away wherein to put it, thank God!' and then 'he begged the executioner to deliver him from this world, for it did him harm to see the traitors. The executioner kneeled down, and, Sir Thomas having kissed him, the executioner cut off his head and quartered him; and he did the same to the other lords, and parboiled the quarters ...'[17]

Whether the other conspirators got the same treatment, we don't know, but we do know that their mangled remains were carried to London in triumph, as if they had been so much slaughtered game. Adam of Usk was an eyewitness: 'I saw their bodies chopped up like the carcasses of beasts killed in the chase, being carried to London, partly in sacks and partly on poles slung across pairs of men's shoulders, where they were later salted to preserve them.'[18]

Back in London, more executions followed – all with the full brutality of the law. Sir Bernard Brocas, Sir Thomas Shelley and two clerics, Richard Maudelyn and William Ferriby, amongst others, were 'drawn, hanged and eventually beheaded'.[19]

Finally the heads of the ringleaders were stuck up above London Bridge as a warning to all that Henry's clemency had its limits.[20] Henry was also notably lacking in a sense of humour about anything that touched the legitimacy of his occupation of the throne – as the unfortunate John Sparrowhawk found out. The story ran that one Sunday morning after breakfast Sparrowhawk had gone around the village of Morden in the county of Cambridge, claiming that it hadn't stopped raining since Henry IV had come to the throne. When Henry heard of this he was *not* amused and the wretched Sparrowhawk was drawn, hanged and beheaded. He actually made legal history as the first victim of treason by the spoken word.[21]

And if anyone had any further doubts about Henry's 'clemency', 1401 made it quite clear that the usurper and his colleagues had no intention of being mistaken for pussycats; for the first time in England a heretic was burnt alive in public for his beliefs.

The accession of Henry may have been hailed by the chroniclers who supported him as a bloodless revolution, but, in fact, his usurpation was not only bloody but heralded an escalation of violence in the public exhibition of death. Henry seems to have been unusual in this respect for, contrary to their popular image, the kings of the later Middle Ages seem to have inclined away from the barbarity of both their predecessors and successors. 'Judged against the Norman and Tudor periods, the English later middle ages was a time when penal brutality was uncommon ... The king also, whatever his personal opinions, hardly ever in act, ordinance, or writ showed that it was the purpose of punishment to terrify.'[22]

But this is not true of Henry IV. One of the very first Acts he puts into practice has as its acknowledged aim the purpose of terrifying the population into submission (see below p.167).

Violence and torture are not usually the sign of a popular regime. They usually indicate insecurity and unpopularity, and Henry was nothing if not insecure.

In January 1400, a plot to assassinate Henry was uncovered, and Richard's own murder followed as surely as the night the day. Yet scarcely a year passed in which rumours were not rife that Richard was still alive. A friar was arrested in Norwich and disciplined by his seniors for spreading such stories. Another was hauled before Henry himself and interrogated before being executed. In May 1401 commissions were issued to investigate the spread of sedition and rumours and for the arrest of those responsible. There were trials and executions throughout the spring of 1402. At one point a group of Franciscan friars spread the word that Richard was alive and living in Scotland. As a result, about twenty friars from different houses were executed.[23]

And as if the real threats were not sufficient, the Lancastrian usurper saw mysterious and supernatural dangers all around his precarious throne. Towards the end of 1400 he narrowly managed to escape when a magical potion was smeared on his saddle. It was apparently guaranteed to make him swell up and drop down dead before he'd ridden ten miles.[24] Walsingham tells the tale of a cunning instrument of iron with three teeth, placed in the usurper's bed straw, 'but, by the will of God, the king unexpectedly perceived the death-dealing instrument, and avoided this peril'.[25]

Henry seems to have been so worried about the treachery he had committed, and his likely reward – either in this world or the next – that he literally made himself ill. This, at least, was the opinion of some of his contemporaries. He developed leprosy, a disease commonly believed at the time to be caused by the sufferer's own sins. One observer surmised that it was because the pope had ordered Henry to expiate his guilt over Richard's deposition through certain penances which Henry failed to do 'during his life, whom as it is said, God touched and was a leper ere he died'.[26]

So, Henry IV's reign did not start in the warm glow of cheerful optimism that the Lancastrian chroniclers would like us to believe. His seizure of the throne was greeted with a 'somewhat stunned acquiescence' followed by a time of intimidation and fear, an 'atmosphere of betrayal, animosity, and aggressive intrigue engendered by the Lancastrian usurpation …'[27]

In other words, Geoffrey Chaucer did not meet his end – whatever that end was – in a world that had been saved from a tyrannical oppressor and that was now relaxing in the balmy security of a new and popular regime. On the contrary, Chaucer would have lived out his final months under constant stress in a turbulent world filled with danger, paranoia, uncertainty and alarm.

CHAPTER 9

Chaucer's enemies gain power

～

Nobody could have felt secure in that first year of Henry's rule – not even the man who had been the mainstay of the usurpation and who may even have master-minded it. Thomas Arundel may have acted with his usual arrogance and aplomb throughout the extraordinary events of 1399, but he was faced with considerable problems. There was significant resistance to himself within the church as well as widespread unease about the new regime. He was, however, not the man to let a few problems get him down.

In the year that Chaucer disappeared, Arundel was, probably, the most powerful man in England. His ruthless pursuit of those who wished to reform the church would have dominated the last few months of Chaucer's life, and, doubtless, would have alarmed the poet considerably. Chaucer's major work, which he was still in the middle of compiling, was not shy in its criticisms of the contemporary church establishment and of worldly prelates like the archbishop.

ARCHBISHOP ARUNDEL

Archbishop Arundel is the only Archbishop of Canterbury ever to have been sacked and sent into exile, only to return and reinvent himself as the head of the English church. He was a remarkable man.

Thomas Arundel is seldom celebrated as a particularly religious man. He is seen as an autocrat, a worldly politician, the embodiment of what Wyclif called the 'Caesarian clergy'. But 'pious'? 'devout'? 'ascetic'? No. Arundel was a man from the very same mould as his predecessor Archbishop Courtenay – though ten years his junior. Arundel was an aristocratic king-maker, 'a secular politician and official whose religious obligation took a very definite second place'. Even his admiring biographer Margaret Aston concedes that he was 'very far from being a visionary or an extremist'.[1]

He was above all a pragmatist. He was not a stickler for religious rules when he knew they would not help him get what he wanted. This is the man who, shortly before his death, wrote a letter to the barbers of London ordering them to close their shops on Sunday 'under penalty of a fine to the Chamber – the payment of such a fine being likely to have a greater effect upon them than the penalty of excommunication'.[2]

Arundel seems to have been an efficient administrator as Bishop of Ely, but the moment the opportunity arose to follow his brother into politics 'his work in his diocese was responsibly but emphatically delegated'. His move to the archbishopric of York was 'an unequivocally partisan act designed to enhance his political status rather than his ecclesiastical prestige, and he paid little attention to his new See for the whole of his tenure'. It is hard to think of him, writes Peter McNiven, as a man of the

The autocratic Archbishop Thomas Arundel. The book is open at John I, iii–iv: 'All things were made by him and without him was not anything made that was made.' The monk on the right is pointing at the formidable Arundel himself.

church. 'How was it, then, that he came to acquire the reputation of the vigorous upholder of the orthodox rites and traditional privileges of the church and the zealous persecutor of the Lollards?'[3] This is the key question.

For Thomas Arundel, former Chancellor of England, and now in 1400, despite the odds, once more Archbishop of Canterbury, the all too prevalent public criticism of the wealth and power of the church was not just a theological matter to be discussed in muted tones whilst strolling round the cloister. It was something he took very personally – very personally indeed.

As the youngest son of a noble family, the church had been his livelihood from the age of seventeen. It had been his security. It had been his *modus vivendi*. Without the church, goodness knows what he'd have done! Many a youngest son, in a family without the right connections, had had to make his way in the military, to become a soldier of fortune with all the uncertainty, discomfort and danger that that would entail. Thank God the Earls of Arundel were well connected within the ecclesiastical hierarchy. When Thomas Arundel's own nephew reached the grand old age of ten, Thomas obtained for him the right to hold benefices (i.e. to get the money from ecclesiastical offices that he had nothing to do with) and, what's more, the right to be ordained at fourteen![4]

Kind old Uncle Thomas knew the importance of a secure income at an early age. All his own material wealth had flowed from the generous teat of Mother Church. To deprive her of her huge estates, vast earthly treasures and regular income from tithes and penances, would have been to cut off the archbishop's life-support machine. Of course, I don't suppose Archbishop Arundel gave the impression that he owed anyone anything – any more than Henry Kissinger ever did.

But from his first elevation to a bishopric at the age of 20, Thomas Arundel must have watched in horror as a rising tide of opposition to ecclesiastical wealth and privilege threatened to deprive him of his birthright. As the young Thomas entered into the Episcopacy Business he would have seen all around him danger signs that the church was no longer the secure haven of wealth and easy living that it ought to have been.

The renewal of the war with France, coupled with the fact that the pope was a Frenchman living in France, made many Englishmen – clergy as well as seculars – reluctant to hand over money due to the church. To transfer cash willingly from English coffers to French coffers, when the two countries were at war, seemed to many nonsensical. Anti-papal feeling was growing within the church as well as outside it. And perhaps this meant that the eccelesiastics' guard was lower than it should have been.

Many powerful laymen were also beginning to wonder whether the church's vast resources could not be put at the disposal of some more deserving cause – such as their own.

John of Gaunt, for one, had begun to show a surprisingly lively interest in the theological concept of 'apostolic poverty' – that is, the notion that monks, friars, priests, bishops and so forth should give up their aristocratic lifestyles and live simple lives in the manner of Jesus. Gaunt began to promote John Wyclif enthusiastically, his imagination fired, no doubt, by the Oxford doctor's novel ideas about forcibly transferring the church's wealth to the secular nobility.

Thomas Arundel, at that time Bishop of Ely, probably thought the world was going mad: if the most powerful lay lord in the land started throwing his weight behind the likes of John Wyclif, then there was – unbelievably! incredibly! – a remote but real possibility that the crown might actually seize the worldly possessions of the church. End of career for T. Arundel, Esq. Apostolic poverty was decidedly *not* a career move that Arundel had in mind – if he could possibly help it.

It might not be too far-fetched to imagine that the young Bishop Arundel would have shared the pope's irritation with the English prelates' failure to deal decisively with the would-be reformers. And yet you can see the prelates' problem: it was difficult to pin the opposition down. To attack the arguments against clerical corruption and materialism was both difficult and risky. The arguments were well founded and any defence could backfire, and the last thing the church wanted was to wash its dirty linen in public.

Besides, the critics of the Church Commercial were a disparate lot, and their attacks had many different guises; they were a moving target and moving targets are always more difficult to hit. What Arundel and his fellow ecclesiasts needed to do was to get them all to stand still in a coherent group, as it were, in order to take a proper aim at them.

What was needed was a stalking horse – a topic on which the church establishment could attack the religious radicals without dragging in the inconvenient questions of ecclesiastical opulence or priestly veniality. The trouble was finding one. And then, in 1379, John Wyclif played straight into their hands. He presented them with a gift: a book called *De Eucharistia*.

THE DEADLY QUESTION OF THE EUCHARIST

The publication of Wyclif's work gave the bishops the fixed target they needed. It enabled them to change the ground rules by placing the sacrament of the Eucharist centre-stage as the litmus test of religious orthodoxy. Henceforth, the exact way in which you believed the wine and bread of the Eucharist became the body and blood of Christ was to determine whether you were a true believer or not –

rather like the question 'Are you or have you ever been a member of the Communist party?' during US Senator Joseph McCarthy's investigations in the 1950s. From 1382 onwards, it increasingly became a subject on which everyone would have been expected to have an opinion, and anyone who had the wrong opinion would have been in deep trouble. Indeed, by the time of Chaucer's disappearance, belief in the Eucharist was about to become a matter of life and death.

Archbishop Arundel did not invent the Eucharist as a test of orthodoxy, but he was a most vigorous and successful advocate of its use. To understand

The Eucharist became a life-or-death matter under Archbishop Arundel.

why he appeared to be so obsessed with it, and to understand why this would have been relevant to Chaucer's final moments on this earth, we need to understand something of the background to the debate about the sacrament of the Eucharist and the Mass in which it takes place.

The Mass is a celebration of Christ's words at the Last Supper, when he took the bread and wine and gave them to his disciples to eat and drink saying: 'Do this in memory of me.' The name 'Mass' really means 'the Dismissal'. It derives from the closing words of the ceremony: *ite, missa est* – 'Go, it is the dismissal', which, presumably, was the only bit of the service that most of the congregation understood and looked forward to! The Eucharist (which comes from the Greek *eukharistos*, meaning 'thankful') can be applied to the whole service, especially that part in which the bread and wine are administered, but it also refers to the elements of the bread and wine themselves.

The priest blesses the bread and wine by invoking the Holy Spirit:

Which oblation [offering] do thou, O God Almighty, vouchsafe ... that it may be made unto us the Body and Blood of thy most beloved Son, our Lord Jesus Christ.

The priest also recounts the story of the Last Supper:

Who on the day before he suffered took bread into his holy and most honoured hands ... he brake and gave to his disciples, saying, 'Take and eat ye all of this, for this is my Body.'

and:

'Take and drink ye all of this, for this is the cup of my Blood ...'[5]

Once they are blessed, the bread and the wine have become the body and the blood of Christ. They are given to the congregation to eat and drink and by this 'communion', the ordinary Christian is actually in touch with God – with the material body of Christ: 'We share communion with the Body and Blood of Christ.'[6]

Now there had always been a degree of debate within the church about the exact relationship of the bread and wine to the body and blood of Christ. But in the Fourth Lateran Council of 1215, the Roman church rejected any symbolic interpretation of the Eucharist and established the doctrine of 'transubstantiation', which was refined by the great scholastic theologian and philosopher St Thomas Aquinas a few years later.

Thus by the late fourteenth century, the official position was this: as the priest said the words of consecration, a miracle occurred, and the bread and the wine literally turned into the body and blood of Christ. They may not look any different from the wine and bread that had been there before, but – believe it or not (and in the fifteenth century your life would depend on believing it!) – they had turned into Christ's blood and flesh in the priest's hands.

The priest was thus acting in a quasi-magical capacity and the congregation were witnesses to a miracle. The priest 'made God' before their very eyes.

The idea that the bread and wine were 'annihilated' during the consecration (that is, they disappeared entirely, to be replaced by Christ's actual flesh and blood) was a departure from the early traditions of the church, and especially from the teaching of St Augustine. Even the rudiments of transubstantiation do not seem to have existed before the eleventh century.[7]

Understandably, some simple-minded medieval Christians found it a little difficult to come to terms with this – let's face it – slightly unimpressive miracle. I mean, any magician who says: 'Now I'm going to turn this rabbit into the Eiffel Tower ... Of course it will still *look* like a rabbit, but *actually* it will have changed completely and totally into the Eiffel Tower and not a trace of rabbit will remain!' isn't going to get top billing at the London Palladium.

On a popular level, then, this was a problem which the Catholic church had faced since the Fourth Lateran Council edict in 1215. Until the 1380s, English ecclesiastics chose to tread lightly on the subject and to keep it rather in the background. They certainly didn't see any advantage in throwing it into the spotlight.[8]

During Chaucer's lifetime, the orthodox Augustinian canon Walter Hilton warned the readers of his *Scale of Perfection* that although all Christians were obliged to accept the church's doctrine, there were doubts about the sacraments and not everyone found the official teaching to their liking. Around 1350, a Cornish priest by the name of Ralph de Tremur had outlined a position very close to Wyclif's without any undue harm coming to him. In other words, before the 1380s it was possible to speculate about the nature of the Eucharist without incurring the church's odium, and the miraculous nature of the Eucharist was not used as a litmus test of faith.[9] That was to change for reasons that were wholly political.

Until 1382 there was room within the orthodox fold for men to tolerate many ideas with which Wyclif and his colleagues would have felt comfortable. Even the then Archbishop of Canterbury himself, Simon Sudbury, seems have shared Wyclif's scepticism about pilgrimages and indulgences. Sudbury is supposed to have stopped a band of pilgrims on the road to Canterbury and to have told them that the plenary indulgence they were seeking from St Thomas would do them no good whatsoever.[10]

In 1379, however, Wyclif published *De Eucharista*. In fact, he published two books in which he questioned the doctrine of transubstantiation – or rather he questioned the 'annihilation' part. He took the position that the bread and the wine did indeed become the body and the blood of Christ, but that they were still in the form of bread and wine. 'The truth and faith of the church', he wrote, 'is that as Christ is at once God and man, so the Sacrament is at once the body of Christ and bread – bread and wine naturally, the body and blood sacramentally.'[11]

It seems, on the face of it, a pretty unexceptional position to adopt. Hardly a nuance of meaning that it would be worth putting people to death over. Nevertheless, the chorus of outrage and indignation that greeted the publication of his views on the Eucharist seemed to take even Wyclif by surprise. He wrote in his *Trialogus*: 'There's a real brawl going on about the Eucharist right now.'[12]

Why was the reaction so vitriolic? What had happened between the 1350s and the 1380s to make the 'annihilation' of the bread and wine such an emotive and damnable theological touchstone? The answer is that it wasn't really the theologians who got upset. The howl of protest came from churchmen all right, but not from the theologically trained churchmen. The hysterical campaign against Wyclif's eucharistic beliefs was spearheaded by the worldly bishops – many of whom were comparatively innocent of theological study.

For example, at the Council of Blackfriars, which condemned Wyclif's views in 1382, only two of the nine bishops present could claim doctorates in theology.[13] The rest were 'Caesarian Clergy' – like Archbishop Courtenay himself – actively engaged in the political scene of the day. Courtenay did not summon all the bishops of England as he might have done. He seems to have selected only those whom he knew he could rely on to condemn Wyclif's views. They were almost all politically motivated prelates and many were, like Thomas Arundel, 'aristocratic bishops'.

A glance at the biographies of some of those who were summoned to Blackfriars in 1382 gives us a good clue to their motives in prosecuting the war against heresy, which Arundel would later escalate with such dramatic effect in the last months of Chaucer's life.

THE WORLDLY BISHOPS OF 1382

Arundel was by no means the first aristocratic bishop to wield both ecclesiastical and secular power or to become a significant player in the politics of his day. In fact he was part of a phenomenon of the second half of the fourteenth century. Powerful families had for many years sought ecclesiastical appointments for their youngest sons. There was nothing new in that. The crown too had been in the habit of rewarding loyal servants with a church appointment. What changed after 1350 was the extent to which these 'aristocratic bishops' and politically appointed bishops became a powerful influence in political life. Theological qualifications were not a part of their background, and yet these were the very prelates who voiced the greatest outrage at Wyclif's views on the Eucharist.[14]

William Courtenay, the man who summoned the Blackfriars Council, was himself 'a prime example of the aristocratic bishop'.[15] He could boast earls on either side of his family and was a great-grandson of Edward I. He had been foisted on the University of Oxford as chancellor at the age of 25 or 26, despite opposition from the Bishop of Lincoln. Two years later his sponsors secured for him the bishopric of Hereford, for which he had had to get special papal dispensation, as he was under the legal age for such high office. At the time of the Blackfriars Council he had been Archbishop of Canterbury for less than a year. He was, according to his biographer, 'neither unusually brilliant nor unusually pious ... an ambitious, paternalistic prelate'.[16]

The bishops he summoned to anathematize Wyclif's views on the Eucharist were his brothers-in-arms – politically minded prelates rather than men of religion. William Wykeham, for example, had undergone no ecclesiastical training and went to neither Oxford nor Cambridge. His entire career had been in royal service, and he was rewarded with many benefices to become 'a mighty pluralist' – that is, he lived off the income from a variety of church appointments for which he did no work. He was eventually made Bishop of Winchester at the insistence of the doddering Edward III and in the teeth of papal opposition.

Thomas Brantingham had also been appointed a bishop as a reward for his long years of service to the crown in various offices such as Treasurer of Calais,

Keeper of the Wardrobe, Treasurer of the Exchequer. In 1381, Brantingham came to Blackfriars as Bishop of Exeter.

John Ergum had been John of Gaunt's chancellor and had represented Gaunt's interests on the committee of lords appointed to advise the Commons in the last parliament of Edward III. His reward was to be made Bishop of Salisbury.

But of all the bishops whom Courtenay gathered together at Blackfriars to put the seal of doom on Wyclif's radicalism, none had reached his ecclesiastical status via a more incongruous route than Henry le Despenser. Henry had sacrificed himself from an early age on the altar of war. Much of his youth had been spent fighting in Italy under the banner of Pope Urban V against the Visconti of Milan. The bishopric of Norwich was presented to him, at the ripe old age of 20, purely as a reward for his military services!

Even the orthodox chroniclers had trouble explaining Henry le Despenser's presence in the ecclesiastic hierarchy. Walsingham described him as: 'a man endowed with neither learning nor discernment, a youth unrestrained and arrogant, experienced in neither keeping nor forming friendships'. Another monkish chronicler calls him: 'more profligate in military frivolity than firm in pontifical development'.[17]

It is hard to believe that these ambitious and materialistic men were genuinely outraged by Wyclif's equivocations about the Eucharist. Why should cynical politicians-turned-bishops feel so much more passionate about such an arcane subject than learned clerks like the Franciscan William Woodford and the Carmelite John Cunningham with whom Wyclif seems to have engaged in debate at Oxford without any particular ill-feeling?[18] Can we really believe that the unschooled, arrogant warmonger, Henry le Despenser, thought poor William Sawtre's Wycliffite vision of the Eucharist miracle so evil that he should be burnt alive?

Isn't it more likely that these political prelates – Despenser, Courtenay, Wykeham, Arundel and the rest – saw the Eucharist as a convenient block on which to lay the heads of their critics? It was a clear-cut case: accept the church's ruling that the miracle takes place and that no atom of bread or wine remains in the Host – despite what your senses tell you – or be prepared to take the consequences as a heretic. As Paul Strohm puts it: 'The question of the Eucharist had been deliberately installed as the litmus test of orthodoxy, precisely because its internal paradoxes and contradictions were so pronounced, and its own understanding among different camps of the orthodox so fissured, as to constitute a ground so uneven that no one meant to stumble could fail to stumble.'[19]

For the worldly bishops, the *real* miracle of the Eucharist was that it transformed their critics into heretics.

ARUNDEL: THE POWER BEHIND THE THRONE

At the time of the Blackfriars Council of 1382, Thomas Arundel was only 29, but within four years he was Chancellor of England and two years later he was archbishop of York. He was fast becoming one of the most powerful figures in the land. He was no less astute a politician than Courtenay, and he was ruthless. As early as 1395 he had called for the death penalty for heresy, but with little response from Richard. Under Henry IV, he was able to define heresy as he liked and at last had the freedom to exterminate with fire those whom he wished to exterminate.

By the time Chaucer died, Thomas Arundel was the dominant force in the kingdom. That is certainly how he saw himself – well, all *right*, if you insist, the *second* most important person in the realm. Even Thomas Arundel magnanimously agreed that the king came first – if only by a whisker. A few years after the *coup*, he is supposed to have told Henry IV: 'Lord, I am your spiritual father and second person after you in the realm, and if you were to accept the advice of no one else before me, it would be a good thing.'[20]

Arundel had been one of the chief architects of the usurpation and he 'occupied a position of unique importance throughout the reign'.[21] He was at Henry's side at every stage of the rebellion, advising, planning and, when necessary, perjuring himself. As one historian puts it, Arundel brilliantly engineered 'the rather tricky ideological adjustments that were needed to legitimate Henry Bolingbroke's accession to a throne to which he had no right'.[22]

From the moment Arundel stepped back on English soil he became, by his own *fiat*, Archbishop of Canterbury once more. There was no debate. He simply ignored the current incumbent, Roger Walden, and carried on from where he had left off. He crowned Henry, he opened parliament on Henry's behalf (even though that was normally the prerogative of the chancellor), he most probably overruled the parliament's election of a Speaker, and almost certainly he dictated what matters should be put before the Great Council of 1400.[23]

Yet, none the less, his position in that first dangerous year of Henry's usurpation was anything but secure.

ARUNDEL DISPATCHES THE OPPOSITION

In particular, Arundel's triumphal return to his 'rightful' position as Archbishop of Canterbury was somewhat clouded by the fact that there were many powerful figures within the church hierarchy who were hostile to him. He could not count on the support of William Colchester, the Abbot of Westminster, Richard Scrope, the Archbishop of York, Thomas Merks, the ex-Bishop of Carlisle nor, naturally, on Roger Walden, now the ex-Archbishop of Canterbury. He couldn't even count on the notorious Henry le Despenser, Bishop of Norwich.

There was also significant hostility amongst the lesser clergy. Back in 1381, according to Knighton, Wyclif had estimated that a third of the clergy would defend his propositions with their lives. That estimate would doubtless have had to be scaled down by 1400, but there remained a substantial body of opinion within the church still sympathetic to at least some of the Dreadful Doctor's ideas. It was absolutely essential that Arundel assert his authority over the whole English church, if his support for the new and illegal regime were going to count for anything.[24]

As well as the personal hostility to Arundel, there was, of course, a substantial number of the clergy who thoroughly disapproved of the usurpation – as indeed they should. It was not difficult for Arundel to transmute hostility to himself into hostility to Henry and *vice versa*.

For a man of the archbishop's political skills, dealing with the opposition amongst the most prominent members of the church hierarchy was a 'no-brainer'. Arundel simply allowed them to fraternize with the secular opposition, and waited for the inevitable collusion to happen. It did.

Henry and Arundel released Richard's closest partisans, the Earls of Rutland, Huntingdon and Kent, out of prison and handed them into the custody of the Abbot of Westminster. Doubtless such clemency reflected credit on the usurper and his chief accomplice, but contemporary observers may have been puzzled by the apparent foolhardiness of allowing all the new regime's chief opponents to reside together under the same roof.

It's hard to imagine that such a well-informed politician as the Archbishop of Canterbury had no idea where the Abbot of Westminster's sympathies lay. Richard's affinity with the monks of Westminster was common knowledge.

The demoted ex-Bishop of Carlisle, Thomas Merks, was also free to go wherever he wanted, and by 6 December 1399 he was most likely in hiding in London.

Didn't it occur to the king or the archbishop or their advisors, that these hostile ex-dukes and ex-bishops – all supporters of the deposed Richard – might plot together? As one historian writes: 'On the part of Henry such heroic generosity can only be explained by excessive confidence in his strength, or by excessive weakness, but fortunately for him, his enemies lost no time in openly abusing his clemency ...'[25]

Or was that the whole point? Perhaps Henry was actually waiting for his clemency to be abused. The events that unfolded over the next couple of months all panned out so conveniently for Henry and Arundel's purposes that one can't rule out the possibility that the whole thing was orchestrated – or at least allowed to happen. Perhaps Henry and Arundel were deliberately giving their potential enemies enough rope to hang themselves. Whether it was intentional or not, that is exactly what Richard's supporters did – all most conveniently.

They conveniently plotted Henry's death around the Abbot of Westminster's dining table. The plot was then conveniently revealed to the king, before Henry could be harmed. And – even more conveniently – the rebel lords all took to their heels and were then conveniently caught and beheaded by various mobs in various cities so that Henry didn't even have to stain his hands with bloodshed.

All this and Henry had also made a convenient profit out of the lands and property confiscated from the executed rebels. The castles, manors and personal belongings of the Earls of Kent, Huntingdon and Salisbury and the rest were

Westminster Abbey as it would still have appeared in the sixteenth century, situated on Thorney Island and separated from the rest of London.

duly parcelled out amongst Henry's sons and supporters, even down to the last beds, bolsters, coverlets and curtains. 'It is gratifying evidence of the increasing humanity of the age,' writes the historian J.H. Wylie, 'that in every case sufficient provision was made for the children and widows of the ill-fated traitors.'[26] But, in fact, Henry was merely offering conscience money, because he (and, one suspects, his chief adviser) was trampling underfoot one of the conventions of English justice. 'It was of course essential that the criminal be convicted according to proper judicial process. If a misdoer, on being taken in flight, was executed summarily by his captors, none of his possessions went to the king. This virtually assured all criminals of a proper trial.'[27] Thus in 1352, one Adam Peshale was arrested by agents of the crown, but was beheaded before he could be brought before the Council. Because the accused had not been brought to trial, Edward III felt obliged to order that his lands and possessions should pass to Adam's son and heir rather than to the crown. Henry, pointedly, did not follow his grandfather's equitable example.

Of course, the most convenient thing of all about this revolt (which is often referred to as 'the Epiphany Uprising') was that, after such a dastardly attempt on Henry's life, no one could reasonably expect Richard to be allowed to go on living. Richard's death was now a foregone conclusion.

The whole thing was equally convenient for Archbishop Arundel. As far as he was concerned, he now had his most prominent opponents in the English church well and truly under his thumb. The various abbots, bishops and ex-bishops who were hostile to him, including Roger Walden the deposed Archbishop of Canterbury, had been given a thoroughly good scare. They'd tasted imprisonment and had probably been forced to contemplate the possibility of execution – the Bishop of Carlisle had been under sentence of death in the Tower for four months. The fact that they had escaped by the skin of their teeth put them

Richard II's funeral.

fairly and squarely in the debt of the archbishop. Even the obstreperous Bishop of Norwich went gratefully back to his diocese, thanks to Archbishop Arundel.

On top of that, two priests, Richard Maudelyn and William Ferriby, who had been amongst Richard's closest companions and advisers, met exemplary execution at Tyburn. Thomas Arundel showed no interest in demanding respect for their clerical status – which should have protected them – and they were drawn, hanged and beheaded. It was a clear warning to the clergy not to mess with the usurper or the newly returned Archbishop of Canterbury. In the case of Maudelyn, perhaps the fact that he closely resembled Richard in 'face, size, height and build' made it doubly important that he should be disposed of.[28]

All in all, the result of the January 1400 uprising was to reinforce the usurper's control of the reins of power and to enable Archbishop Arundel to tighten his grip upon his rebellious church. Even if Henry and Arundel hadn't organized it themselves, the outcome couldn't have been more satisfactory.

WHAT DOES CHAUCER DO AS HIS WORLD FALLS APART?

Exactly how satisfactory the collapse of the Ricardian opposition and the inevitable death of Richard would have been to Chaucer we can only guess. But, in his final months, the poet was certainly not retiring from the limelight. In the build-up to the previous *coup* against Richard, in 1386–7, Chaucer had prudently given up all his court appointments and retired to distant safety, perhaps in Kent, perhaps further away. By contrast, in 1399–1400, he moved right into the centre of the storm. The very week that the Abbot of Westminster and the others were supposed to be plotting around the Abbot's dining table, Chaucer became the Abbot's new neighbour. He moved into a tenement within the sanctuary of Westminster Abbey. In other words, he placed himself right in the conspiring heart of the Ricardian opposition to Henry.

Whether or not Chaucer was actually involved in the conspiring, the brutal dispersion of the Ricardian opposition and the brief imprisonment of his landlord – the Abbot – could not have been at all reassuring for the poet.

The direction in which the returned Archbishop of Canterbury was already moving must have been not simply disconcerting for the poet, but truly alarming.

ARUNDEL CONSOLIDATES HIS POSITION

Even after the routing of the January 1400 plotters, Archbishop Arundel was still faced with a body of opinion within the church that remained solidly pro-Richard and hostile, both to Henry and to himself. Arundel needed to whip a disunited and fractious clergy into line.

As soon as he dared leave Henry to his own devices, Arundel set about persuading those members of the clergy who resented his return or who opposed the usurpation back into the fold, and in those days without telephones, that meant making personal contact.

Arundel's first official visitation in 1400 was to Chichester and Coventry and Lichfield, where the Bishop, John Burghill, was a staunch supporter of Richard II. Burghill was also, according to the chronicler Adam of Usk, a laughing-stock around the archbishop's dining table. Adam tells a scurrilous story of how Burghill is supposed to have hidden away a hoard of gold in the wall of his chamber, only to find that two jackdaws had entered by a hole in the outer wall, stolen the gold and scattered it amongst the trees and garden, 'thereby providing a lot of people with a windfall'. Adam confides: 'This is a story which I heard told one day at the table of my aforesaid lord [Arundel] by various guests of his, great men of the realm, and it caused much amusement.'[29] Bishop Burghill had not been implicated in the Epiphany Plot and hence had not been already neutralized in the way Merks and Colchester had been. Presumably Arundel had to bring him into line by other means, and a personal visit was an effective way of applying the pressure. The proud archbishop certainly wasn't visiting Bishop Burghill to check if he were still being bothered by birds.

On his way back from Chichester, Arundel made sure he passed through the diocese of Lincoln. It was in the diocese of Lincoln that Lollardy was supposed to have its hottest spots – indeed Oxford itself fell within its bounds.[30] One assumes the archbishop made the most of the opportunity to check the situation on the ground, and perhaps to apply a little influence here and there where needed.

As his grip on the church tightened, Arundel was able to turn his attention to secular matters. He quickly became the leading member of Henry's Council, and he held the office of chancellor for longer than anyone else. Even when he was not attending Council, the archbishop's advice was in demand and, on occasion, it was Arundel's authorization that was sought, rather than the king's.[31]

There remained, nevertheless, a good deal of hostility towards the powerful archbishop amongst the knights of the shire, citizens and burgesses – that is, if their choice of Speaker was anything to go by. Despite being warned against it, the Commons chose as their Speaker Sir John Cheyne. His election was a real snub for Arundel. Cheyne was a knight of Gloucester, a soldier and a married man, who had been ordained as a deacon but renounced his calling to the church without dispensation. He had become a radical critic of the Church

Commercial, and had been arrested in 1397 on suspicion of being involved in the Duke of Gloucester's death. He was a man inimical to Archbishop Arundel, and the fact that he was elected Speaker demonstrates clearly the extent to which Arundel lacked parliamentary support.[32]

THE WAR ON HERESY

Arundel desperately needed a strategy that would silence both civil and clerical dissent and at the same time consolidate support for the new regime. He fell back on a policy that has been employed by rulers since time immemorial: he fixed on a common enemy. It was a common enemy with whom he was already very familiar and against whom he already had a ground plan laid out.

In January 1401 Archbishop Arundel formally announced to Convocation that their number one objective was to be the 'war on heresy'. And there could be no halfway house. You were either with him or against him. The fight against heresy was to dominate the following decade. It changed the nature of politics. It changed the atmosphere in which ordinary men and women lived.

What is more, heresy and treason were skilfully elided so that to question the working of holy church quickly became as unthinkable for the secular gentry as it was for the parish priest or the university student.[33] Arundel was under no illusion but that the war on heresy, and in particular the litmus test of belief in the Eucharist, was as vital for keeping secular dissidents in check as it was for repressing dissension within the religious community. It may be that this was a policy which he and the Chancellor of Florence had discussed,

Heresy pictured as a devil at a preacher's shoulder.

during Arundel's enforced stay in that city. For on the 30th August 1399, at the very time that Henry and Arundel re-entered London in triumph, Coluccio Salutati dispatched a letter to the archbishop in which he seems to extol the use of religion to consolidate the citizenry – especially (and this would have been of signal importance to Arundel) where there is a lot of discord. The letter is opaque, but Salutati reminds Arundel of what he saw during his stay in Florence during his exile: that a stricter observation of religion was creating harmony amongst the normally warring factions in the city.

> Our entire city is dressed in white and done up like the city of Nineveh; all have turned to the Lord with so much devotion that all have put on sackcloth, sing hymns, visit holy places, strive for penance with marvellous earnestness, avoid meat and fast. Nor is there anyone of noble or high position who does not visit the holy places ... And this next thing is astonishing hereabouts (for we are extremely cruel avengers of blood and injury): everyone is reconciled to his brother and neighbour and all are converting themselves from mortal enemies into very special friends.[34]

The detail about the city of Florence being 'dressed in white' may be a reference to a penitential movement known as the 'Bianchi' which was then current in many north Italian cities, and rumoured (mistakenly) to have originated in England.[35] But why should Salutati be writing about this at this precise moment, when he knew Arundel was embarked upon his dangerous bid for the throne and power of England? Perhaps the significant thing is the emphasis that Salutati puts on the cohesive effect of religious fervour on a divided society. Arundel and Henry would have found themselves trying to impose law and order on exactly such a society, and the whole passage could be read as a coded reminder to Arundel to employ the same policy: use religious zeal (in Arundel's case, the 'war on heresy') to impose his authority on the warring factions of the divided nation. This, in any event, is certainly what Arundel did.

The example of Italy was very much in Arundel's mind when he thought about the use of religion for political control. In 1404, during the turbulent parliament held at Coventry, when Arundel angrily accused the royal retainers of showing disrespect for the Sacrament, he had to remind Henry of the essential role that respect for the Sacrament played in controlling the kingdom: 'While faith in the Sacrament flourished in this land', he said, 'the throne and the army flourished, and everything prospered ... it was not possible for a kingdom to last long when it neglected the Sacrament.'

This was not empty rhetoric. It was a statement about the vital nature of the war on heresy to curb dissent within the state as well as within the church. And to reinforce his point, Arundel goes into a eulogy about what happens in Italy: 'In Italy,' he said, 'where the people seem to be so wicked, especially in Lombardy, they treat the Eucharist with great respect ... and I think that God will spare and look more favourably on them, for the faith shown, and the reverence with which they behave towards the Sacrament.'[36]

The war on heresy, which Archbishop Arundel announced in that winter of 1401, added a new dimension to a period already characterized by fear and intimidation. Gone was the experimental and questioning 'blue skies' intellectual environment of Richard II's court, to be replaced by repression and censorship. The country slid into a regime of Orwellian thought-control and McCarthyite witch-hunting. As Paul Strohm has said: 'So crucial was the Lollard heresy to the establishment of Lancastrian orthodoxy and legitimacy that, had it not existed, they would have had to devise something in its stead.'[37]

And although the archbishop only announced the drive against heresy officially in 1401, the long shadow of repression had fallen across the realm of England from the moment Arundel had stepped back onto English soil. Whatever deal he had struck with Henry before they launched their rebellion, there was no mistaking the changed relationship between court and church. Henry had made a Faustian pact in which, in return for the ex-archbishop's legitimization of his illegal regime, he would give Arundel and the church all the secular support that had been lacking in the previous regime. Arundel's opening speech to Henry's first parliament spelt it out: in future, government would not be 'by the voluntary purpose or singular opinion' of the king alone but by 'the advice, counsel and consent' of 'the honourable wise and discreet persons of his realm'. In other words, Henry and Archbishop Arundel were a double act.[38]

Since at least 1395 Arundel had been trying to persuade the secular authorities to help stamp out the spread of English translation of the Bible, and to allow for heretics to be burnt at the stake. But as long as Richard held power, no matter how much he denounced heresy in public, the crown never provided any legislation with teeth to combat it, and, as Peter McNiven says, 'Richard gave no impression from 1397 onwards that he numbered persons of suspect religious inclination among the enemies who must be eliminated.'[39]

By contrast, in that same first parliament, the usurper declared himself 'willing to punish heresy as far as lay in his power'. Henry also announced 'that he was resolved to preserve all the liberties of the church', and he sent the constable and marshal to the Convocation (the meeting of the church leaders) 'explaining that henceforth the clergy should not be subject to tax, talliage, or benevolence, except under urgent necessity ...'[40]

We do not need to see Henry as a pious layman, supporting the church he loved. He was simply paying off his debt to Archbishop Arundel for all the latter's help in stealing the throne.

The battle-lines against the heretics were already in preparation in October of 1399, while Chaucer and his fellow Londoners must have been still trying to take stock of the calamitous upheaval that had so suddenly engulfed them. Surely Chaucer himself must have felt the chill of a colder intellectual clime closing around him along with the winter.

On Thursday 15 January 1400, the intellectual skies over London darkened even further, as a long file of bishops and abbots, led by Archbishop Arundel, celebrated Henry's triumphant return from his victory against the so-called 'Epiphany' rebels. The ecclesiastics conducted the usurper to St Paul's to sing *Te Deum* in his honour. As the sounds of praise lifted to the roof, there must have been many in the congregation who joined in with growing unease. An intellectual like Chaucer, who had flourished under Richard II, must have found his heart in his boots as he listened to the archbishop order special thanks to the Virgin for her intervention in 'rescuing the most Christian king from the fangs of the wolves and jaws of wild beasts, who had prepared above our backs a gallows mixed with gall, and hated us with a wicked hate'.[41]

Thomas Arundel's war on heresy was to dominate not just the early years of Henry IV's rule, but the whole of the fifteenth century as well. The intellectual landscape of England was changed in a way that would have been unimaginable in Richard II's reign.

Nor was 'heresy' a cut-and-dried commodity. 'Heresy' was all about what those in power deemed it to be, and Arundel used it unashamedly as a political tool. He radically redefined heresy in order to isolate and identify his enemies. In doing so he cast his net over a wide range of beliefs and opinions – inevitably writers and thinkers who had functioned without inhibition in the previous decade would become entangled. In those early days no one could be quite sure who would, and who would not, be pulled in.

Arundel's definition of heresy was to concentrate on certain key issues, including especially the refusal to worship the cross or images, the denial of the need for pilgrimages and the rejection of indulgences, the preaching and reading of the Gospels in English, the refusal to pay tithes to priests who were already wealthier than the tithe-payer or who were in a state of sin, and – in pride of place – the question of the exact nature of the Eucharist.

As it began to dawn on his fellow countrymen that they would be called to account for where they stood on these issues, there must have been many who had expressed themselves freely in former times, who now began to regret that they had made their opinions quite so clear. No one more so, perhaps, than Geoffrey Chaucer.

CHAPTER 10

Chaucer in the eye of the storm

∾

The world in which Chaucer disappeared was thick with an atmosphere of intimidation and fear. At times we can see the process of intimidation operating overtly – as when Henry cries 'Havok' on the county of Chester, or when those who are reluctant to join his rebellion are despoiled of their property.[1] But once the bloody business of insurrection was over, the usurper was remarkably successful in removing all the evidence of his utilization of terror. We can usually discern only faint tracks – occasional traces of blood caught inadvertently upon the page.

HENRY INTIMIDATES THE CHRONICLERS

For instance, we know that Henry ordered a thoroughgoing censorship of the chronicles not because his orders were written down (well, you wouldn't, would you?) but because one of the chroniclers ingenuously lets slip that the king sent out letters to have the chronicles inspected. Of course the letters didn't actually say: 'And your chronicles had better not contain anything favourable to Richard or detrimental to Henry.' The monks, after all, could not only read – they could also read between the lines.[2]

Sometimes we can see the intimidation manifesting itself in absences. The fact that not one single English chronicle is critical of Henry's *coup* is in itself a pretty good indication that Henry suppressed hostile material. The single voice with which the English chronicles praise Henry and defame Richard after 1399 is given the lie by the contrary version of events recorded in the French chronicles. And though for most of the nineteenth and twentieth centuries this was put down to cross-Channel anglophobia, the accuracy and value of the continental chronicles has now been reappraised.

Sometimes the intimidation shows itself in blatant revision and we can actually see the process of hasty correction taking place – such as when the scribe who takes over the *Dieulacres Chronicle* tut-tuts at things the previous writer had said or when the *Kirkstall* scribe simply starts whistling to a different tune.

Elsewhere intimidation can be glimpsed in the erasures and alterations. In the *Historia Anglicana,* for example, disparaging references to John of Gaunt are altered after his son Henry seizes power – presumably as a result of 'the dread which the monks of St Albans had of falling under the displeasure of the new Lancastrian king'.[3]

And in the manuscript Royal 13.E.ix, the chronicler Walsingham 'went so far as to erase altogether even slightly compromising sentiments concerning Lancaster that had appeared in the earlier Harleian text. Opposite numerous passages in the Royal manuscript that offer reflection "cast upon the conduct of the Duke and his affairs", occur marginalia such as *cave quia offendiculum* and the like, and an erasure is then written over in less offensive tones.' So the Royal manuscript

A page from one of Thomas Walsingham's Chronicles.

'was barely finished when the revolution of 1399 made it necessary to remove the most dangerous quires, containing the *Scandalous Chronicle*, and to erase a whole series of small *offendicula*, sometimes a mere word, but often whole sentences.'[4] Here at last we catch a glimpse of the anxiety that must have been running rife through the scriptorium. We can see the supervisor nervously trying to guess what the usurper would find offensive.

Erasure, where writing on vellum is concerned, was a costlier and more time-consuming business than it is with today's word processor. It involved scraping with a knife and rubbing away until all the ink had been removed and a fair portion of the vellum too. Nobody was going to change an expensive thing like a chronicle unless they felt compelled to do so – that is, unless they felt threatened.

Sometimes, however, material was simply removed wholesale. For example, the records of the City of London for the period covering the usurpation have been interfered with. In the archive known as *Letter-Book H* two folios have been cut out and half another has been removed, cut vertically. What is the story that Henry, or whoever removed the pages, didn't want us to know? Perhaps London did not abandon Richard as easily as the usurper would have had us think. One thing is sure: Henry's heavy hand was everywhere.[5]

INTIMIDATION BY THE CHURCH

But his was not the only hand that weighed more than usual. On behalf of the church, Archbishop Arundel was as anxious to cow *hoi polloi* as he was to whip the hierarchy into line. And for some reason, when it came to heresy, both church and secular power lost their inhibitions about acknowledging the use of intimidation. The 1401 statute *De Haeretico Comburendo* set it all out in black and white: heretics were to be 'burnt before the people in a conspicuous place; *that such punishment may strike fear into the minds of others ...*'[6] Terror was its acknowledged objective.

All it took was an extremely public and well-publicized burning. Without even waiting for *De Haeretico Comburendo* to get onto the statute books, the authorities consigned the unfortunate William Sawtre (an unrepentant heretic) to the flames. The crowds flocked to Smithfield, saw the horror, and learned their lesson. They had heard, perhaps, that such evil executions were carried out in far-off lands – in France and Italy and Spain – but to see a man burnt alive in humble Smithfield was something new ... something shocking ... something altogether too near to home not to have had a terrible effect on a population unused to such a level of public barbarity over a question of personal belief.

After such a salutary lesson, not only did the leader of the church's critics, John Purvey, 'allow himself to be hustled into a public, English-language ceremony of abjuration', but other terrified opponents of ecclesiastical corruption scrambled to make public retractions.[7] The

Thomas Arundel finally achieves his ambition of being able to burn heretics.

burning of Sawtre (only four months after Chaucer disappears from the record) was a deliberate signal to the population that life had changed. Nobody, from then on, could underestimate the cost of stepping out of line.

The absolutism of the new regime bears the hallmark not so much of Henry as of Thomas Arundel. He was the control freak – the autocrat – the authoritarian.

Of course, it might be objected that Archibishop Arundel took no part in the burning of Sawtre. On the contrary, he pleaded for mercy – begging the secular powers to 'regard favourably the said William, unto them thus recommitted' – just as some nine years later he was to beg for mercy to be shown towards the heretic John Badby. In neither case were his pleas heeded. The monarch applied the full force of the law 'in detestation of this sort of crime, and as a clear example to Christians'.[8]

In fact, Arundel's pleas for 'mercy' were a cheerful fiction modelled on the example of the Inquisition. The continental inquisitors handed unrepentant heretics over to the secular power for burning, with a traditional plea for clemency. It meant nothing, but it looked good in the record books. The form of words used by the Inquisition was: 'We dismiss you from our ecclesiastical forum and abandon you to the secular arm. But we strongly beseech the secular court to mitigate its sentence in such a way as to avoid bloodshed or danger of death'.[9] It was a piece of institutional hypocrisy that may have stained the occasional ecclesiastical conscience but did not stain a single soft, white ecclesiastical hand.

Times had, indeed, changed. Even a plea for mercy had become devalued and meaningless in the hands of the cynical practitioners of raw power who now held sway in England.

NOBODY WANTS TO BE BURNT ALIVE

But the fact is the intimidation worked a treat. 'After this terrible example [the burning of Sawtre],' writes one chronicler, 'other accomplices of his recanted their heresies in person at St Paul's Cross.'[10] It seems probable that a special event was organized to show off the vast numbers of people anxious to recant. Recantation was the order of the day in the first years of Henry IV. Even Chaucer's own *Retractions* (as we shall argue later) should be seen in this context.

St Paul's Cross – a popular spot for recantations and retractions.

One of Chaucer's oldest friends, the 70-year-old Sir Lewis Clifford, was into the retraction business in a big way. Sir Lewis had been a chamber knight of the Black Prince, and throughout Richard's reign had been one of the king's closest associates. He had also been an outspoken critic of the church for over twenty years, but now he was persuaded by this newly installed reign of terror to renounce publicly his former opinions, to present Archbishop

Arundel with a list of erroneous Lollard conclusions and, what's more, to hand over a list of persons who still held such views.

The ignominy of Sir Lewis Clifford illustrates graphically how close to Chaucer the new regime struck. Clifford and Chaucer had known each other for over thirty years. Clifford had been the emissary between the French poet Eustache Deschamps and Chaucer. Together they had both survived the Appellants' *coup* of 1387 by keeping a low profile, when at least eight of their associates had met a bloody end. In the similar though even more dangerous circumstances of the 1400s, it appears that Clifford was terrified enough to abase himself before Archbishop Arundel.[11]

Chaucer was most probably (although not necessarily) dead in 1402 when Clifford recanted, but it is not hard to imagine what he would have thought of the public humiliation of his venerable friend – forced to bow the knee and grovel before the proud younger man in the robes of an archbishop. Would the poet who had made the court laugh with portraits of venal monks and lecherous friars, vain prioresses and all the rapacious deceits of ecclesiastical officers have felt at home in this new world of religious political correctness? Or would he have felt in more danger than at any time in his life – a life that had survived the perils of travel, war, espionage, treason, and court intrigue?

Before he died, Chaucer would have known that his fellow poet, John Montagu, the Earl of Salisbury, had been virtually torn to pieces by the mob at Cirencester in the wake of the abortive revolt of January 1400. These were not tranquil times. Even though he could have claimed to be a relative by marriage of the usurper, Chaucer would have known that he could not count on that to save him if Henry wished him out of the way.

WHAT HENRY WANTED FROM HIS POETS

That Henry harboured any animosity towards the poet, however, seems on the surface unlikely. It is true that, from Henry's accession, the payment of Chaucer's usual annuities seems to have been beset by delays and non-payment, and that Henry's dilatoriness in handing over actual cash rather than promises may have left Chaucer hard-up in his latter months.[12] But there is nothing to indicate that there was any ill feeling between the two. On the contrary, Henry had paid for a fine scarlet cloak for Chaucer only a couple of years before his exile, and on his accession he increased Chaucer's annuity – at least in theory.

Besides, Henry would have valued Chaucer's services. The usurper needed intellectuals and poets within his court to lend credibility and legitimacy to his regime. Chaucer, whose fame had already spread abroad, would have been a useful prop for a shaky regime. We know Henry tried to blackmail Christine de Pisan into coming to join his court. Her young son had been in Montagu's care, so the earl's untimely death released the boy into Henry's tender clutches, and the king lost no time in using him as a lure. But Christine was having nothing to do with the new and illegitimate regime. 'I was not in the least tempted to this, considering the way things were ...' she wrote.[13] If Henry thought he needed Christine to boost his court (who was not only French, but a *woman* to boot), how much better would it have been to have had Chaucer?

And Christine was right to be suspicious of Henry's literary interests. They were not pure. This was a regime that deliberately falsified the record to an unprecedented extent. Henry had not only put pressure on the monasteries to censor their own histories, he also falsified the official account of the deposition – the so-called *Record and Process*. 'Henry and his sons were committed from the outset to a program of *official* forgetfulness embracing their own dynastic origins, their predecessor's fate, the promises and opportunistic alliances which had gained them a throne.'[14]

If he was prepared to browbeat the monks into bringing their chronicles in line with his fictional account of recent history, is it not likely that Henry would have also applied the same pressure on other writers? Why would he have demanded alteration to the chronicles but not to other works?

Henry would not just have wanted famous poets and intellectuals hanging round his court and eating his food simply to add glamour to the place, he would have wanted them to earn their keep as the menials they were. And what an interesting job he had for them: they were to do nothing less than to explain why white was black.

Henry had committed double treason. He had broken his vows of loyalty and affronted the spirit of chivalry for which he was famous. He was desperate for written confirmation, to legitimize his fabricated version of events. In such a scenario it's reasonable to suppose that he would have expected all who wielded the pen to use it in support of his spurious claim to the throne.

No wonder the independent-minded Christine de Pisan stayed in France.

Of course we can't expect to find any written evidence to prove explicitly that Henry put pressure on the writers of the court. He wouldn't have sent them the sort of letters he did to the monasteries. He wouldn't have needed to. Court writers would all be only too well aware of how the political cookie was crumbling.

The best evidence we could hope to find would be to discover a writer or poet who completely changes his tune after the usurpation. But a sophisticated court poet would not want to expose himself to the charge of inconsistency in the way that the *Kirkstall* chronicler does, so we might expect such a writer to work back through his own *oeuvre*, trying to make it look as if he had changed his allegiance years before the usurpation. All this would be good evidence of pressure being brought to bear.

And we are lucky. This is exactly what happens in the work of John Gower.

JOHN GOWER: HENRY IV'S IDEAL POET?

It is possible to argue that Gower was not exactly a 'court poet'. He kept himself very much to himself in Southwark and does not appear to have spent much time in Westminster. However there is no doubt that he expected to be read by a courtly audience, and he was certainly alive to the political requirements of the moment.

Gower's comprehensive reshaping of his own political allegiances after the usurpation of 1399 has often escaped notice because he did such a good job of falsifying the chronology of his own work. Until fairly recently it was thought that Gower grew hostile to Richard in the early 1390s. As we have seen, however, internal evidence from the poems suggests that this is not the case, and that Gower altered both the *Confessio Amantis* and the *Vox Clamantis after* the usurpation.[15] So we have to clear out of our heads any idea that Gower became disillusioned with Richard during the latter's reign. There is not a scrap of solid evidence that he did. Indeed, the only things he wrote about Richard before 1399 – very much like those he wrote about Henry after 1399 – border on the sycophantic.

On the other hand, there is no reason to doubt that Gower's relations with Henry were anything but cordial. But an affable relation-

John Gower's tomb, Southwark.

ship with Henry is no indicator of antipathy to Richard. Nor would it have placed any restraint on Henry's will, once he came to power. If Henry needed the records expurgated and new panegyrics penned, no amount of cordiality would have prevented him from putting pressure on Gower to produce what he wanted.

Gower was probably ten years Chaucer's senior. In 1400 he would have been in his seventies and quite possibly going blind. Nevertheless, he seems to have fallen over himself to accommodate the requirements of the usurper – busily rewriting dedications to works already written, erasing references to Richard, and reworking passages to fit in with the new political story.[16]

Gower even dashed off a whole new work in Latin, the *Cronica Tripertita* – the *Tripartite Chronicle*. This offers an allegorical gallop through the events of 1387 onwards, rewriting the last thirteen years of history to conform to the new regime's politically correct version of what happened.

It deploys a couple of hundred lines on the magnates' revolt of 1387, three hundred and forty lines on Richard's revenge in 1397, and nearly five hundred lines on the ultimate triumph of King Henry – the great and good.

No one could accuse Gower of over-subtle characterization. Richard is 'wicked', 'greedy', 'poisonous', 'infatuated', 'false', 'cunning', 'two-faced', 'juvenile', 'violent', 'evil' – oh! and 'offensive to one and all'. He is served by 'fawning' counsellors, by 'a haughty, treacherous, greedy, wicked Earl, who was Chancellor by means of a thousand trickeries', and his 'hungry, pernicious dogs' are always ready to hand.

Henry, on the other hand, is 'noble', 'worthy', 'a friend to piety'. Here's a typical passage:

> Then the noble Henry, a friend to all honor, came into full bloom and was mightier than all. Just as the rose is the crown of flowers, he was the best of good men, the protector of the English ... the model of virtues, the most excellent of the excellent ...[17]

Well, you get the picture.

Maybe Gower was genuinely relieved Henry had seized power; maybe he was shaking in his calf-skin slippers when he wrote this. We have no way of telling. But don't forget his hysterical anti-Ricardianism is only discernible after the *coup* of 1399. And in one instance, as we saw earlier, he even takes the exact words that he once used to eulogize Richard and converts them wholesale to the praise of Henry.[18]

Yet who could blame him? This was the new order of the day. Neutrality was not enough. Wit and humour and insight were no longer viable commodities. Nothing – no scrap of anecdote – in Henry Bolingbroke's biography hints at a sense of humour. Henry's insecurity craved nothing less than the panegyric, the vilification of his predecessor, the justification of the unjustifiable and the unabashed rewriting of history. At least, judging from the results, it looks like that's how Gower did the maths.

HOW CHAUCER FAILED HENRY

What of Chaucer? If his friend Gower was thus occupied revising his works, in what resembles either a paroxysm of prudence, or just plain fear, Chaucer could scarcely have afforded to stand idly by – particularly not if, as we have argued, Chaucer's literary career was so closely bound up with Richard's indirect sponsorship.

Gower had undertaken a comprehensive overhaul of his *oeuvre* to bring it into line with the new political correctness. He had rededicated and altered the *Confessio Amantis*, rewritten the *Vox Clamantis*, penned a new work, the *Cronica Tripertita*, and tossed off several new adulatory poems in Latin. Wouldn't Chaucer have found himself in an agonisingly compromised situation? Almost his whole literary output was created in and for Richard's court – a court that was now anathema.

Fortunately for Chaucer, perhaps, the indirectness of Richard's sponsorship was reflected in a corresponding obliqueness in the way his poetry addressed the sovereign. Since Richard did not directly commission works, he apparently did not seek, or expect, panegyric. Nothing that remains of Chaucer's resembles the sort of direct flattery that Gower directed at his sovereigns – first Richard, and then Henry. In fact, there are only two occasions when Chaucer directly addresses Richard at all, and in neither case is there anything that would have got up Henry's nose.

None the less, with Gower's example as the benchmark, Chaucer must have known that tinkering with a poem or two would be scant protection against the evil eye. Henry was on the lookout for acclamation. Yet the only work that Chaucer directly addresses to the usurper is the envoy to a begging poem, which is lightyears away from Gower's purple eulogies and is, moreover, capable of a negative interpretation.

Perhaps this lack of enthusiasm explains why Henry was not in a rush to hand over Chaucer's annuities and why – just possibly – Henry might not have lost too much sleep over Chaucer's ultimate fate.

CHAUCER'S 'COMPLAINT TO HIS PURSE'

The Complaint of Chaucer to His Purse must have been one of the last poems Chaucer wrote. In it the poet playfully complains to his purse as if it were his lady-love. He says he's so sorry that she is now 'light' (with a not-altogether flattering pun on 'fickle') and that unless she makes a heavy face at him (a reversal of the usual plea for a lady's smile) he might as well be dead. The poem also plays on a secondary meaning of 'heavy' as 'pregnant'. This apparently humorous texture, however, is undershot by the sombre final line of each stanza:

Beth hevy ageyn, or elles moot I dye.

In the circumstances of 1400, when torture and execution were to be the fate of many, such a refrain might have carried all sorts of resonances. And if, in fact, within a few months the poet *was* dead – was he staring at the writing on the wall, even as his words flowed onto the page?

The envoy specifically addressed to Henry IV follows the third stanza:

O conqueror of Brutes Albyon,
Which that by lyne and free eleccion
Been verray kyng, this songe to youw I sende.
And ye, that mowen alle oure harmes amende,
Have mynde upon my supplicacion.
  The Complaint of Chaucer to His Purse, ll. 22–5
O conqueror of Brutus's Albion,
Who are by lineage and free election
Actual king, this song I send to you,
And you, that may amend all our harms,
Be mindful of my supplication.

It is often asserted that Chaucer is here simply reproducing Henry's own proclamation, in which he made a triple claim to the throne: by right of descent, by right of conquest and by right of election. But this is totally bogus. The 'proclamation' in which Henry supposedly made these claims simply does not exist. It was first conjured out of thin air by one of Chaucer's editors: Robert Bell, in his 1854 edition of the poet's works. In a footnote he wrote: 'In Henry IV's proclamation to the people of England he founds his title on conquest, hereditary right, and election; and from this inconsistent and absurd document Chaucer no doubt took his cue.'[19]

The non-existence of this proclamation notwithstanding, the story was then taken up by Chaucer's most influential Victorian editor, W.W. Skeat, and has been repeated by Chaucerians ever since. It is one of those self-perpetuating untruths that seem to have a life of their own.[20]

In 1953, for example, the highly respected scholar, M. Dominica Legge published an influential article in which she examined the relevance of Henry's triple claim to the throne to Chaucer's *Complaint*.[21] Unfortunately Legge took the triple claim on trust from Skeat and from an article by the eminent historian V. H. Galbraith, without examining its validity. The myth became further entrenched in Chaucer studies.[22]

In fact, neither 'election' nor 'conquest' played any part in the official version of Henry's claim. According to the *Record and Process* – which was circulated to all the chroniclers – Henry's claims to the throne were: (i) 'by right line of blood coming from the good lord King Henry III'; (ii) 'recovery' of his rightful realm with the help of kin and friends; and (iii) because the realm was about to be undone. The words, recorded in the *Rolls of Parliament* and elsewhere, are:

> In the name of the Father, Son and Holy Ghost, I Henry of Lancaster challenge this Realm of England and the Crown with all the members and the appurtenances, insofar as I am descended by right line of the blood coming from the good lord King Henry the Third, and through that right that God of his grace hath sent me, with help of my Kin and of my Friends to recover it: the which Realm was in point to be undone for default of Governance and undoing of the good laws.[23]

It would be a mistake to assume that this is exactly what Henry claimed in parliament, because the *Record and Process* was probably not drawn up until several months after the event. On the other hand, Adam of Usk records that Henry was careful to read his claim to parliament from a prepared script, so it may be that this *was* it. A committee (on which Usk himself had served) painstakingly worked out a formula for Henry's claim, and the wording of the *Record and Process* certainly sounds like a fudge: 'This vague concoction', remarks one historian, 'no doubt represents a compromise: it has all the hallmarks of a claim devised by a committee.'[24]

So officially there was no claim of 'conquest' – only that he had 'recovered' what was his due in the first place. And, in fact, Henry's first statement as king is actually to disavow any claim by right of conquest ... except in so far as concerns Richard's supporters. As soon as Archbishop Arundel had finished his sermon before parliament, Henry got to his feet 'in order to set at peace the minds of his subjects' and spoke (or read) the following in plain English:

> Sires, I thank God and you, spiritual and temporal lords and all the estates of the land; and would have you know that it is not my will that any man should think it is by way of Conquest I would disinherit any man of his heritage, franchise, or other rights that he ought to have, nor put him out of that which he has and has had by the good laws and customs of the Realm: Except those persons that have been against the good purpose and the common profit of the Realm.[25]

And there was a very good reason for making such a disclaimer. Henry himself had *originally* wanted to claim the throne by right of conquest, but this had been quashed by the committee appointed to work out a reasonable-sounding justification for the usurpation. The problem was that, if he claimed right of conquest, then under existing law and practice every single person's possessions and estates came into his gift. No matter how great or small, Henry would have had the right to take their property and redistribute it as he liked.

Such a situation would have been obviously unacceptable to the great lords and gentry acquiescing in the usurpation, and it appears to have been the Chief Justice, William Thirning, who pointed this out to Henry. We know this because the chronicler Thomas Walsingham inserts a little aside to this effect after Henry's statement in his version of the *Record and Process*:

> He [Henry] had proposed to claim the kingdom by conquest, but Lord William Thirning, justice, said that this was quite impossible, for by doing so he would arouse the anger of the entire population against him. This was because if he claimed the kingdom in this way, it would appear to the people that he had the power to disinherit anybody at will, and to change the laws, establishing new ones and revoking old ones, as a result of which no one would be secure in his possessions.[26]

As for the idea of 'election': Henry never claimed this, and nor was there any election. The official *Record and Process* makes no mention of one. Of course, it tries to convey the idea that there was general and unanimous acclaim for

Henry's occupation of the throne – but this is very different from *election* or due process of parliament. What happened was a challenge followed by acquiescence:

> Following this challenge and claim, the lords spiritual and temporal and all the estates there present were individually and jointly asked what they thought of this challenge and claim; to which the same estates, together with all the people, unanimously and without any difficulty or delay agreed that the foresaid duke should reign over them.[27]

A modern historian writes: 'There was no election, whatever some contemporaries liked to believe ... How wrong are those who emphasize election is suggested by the word 'challenge': 'I Henry of Lancaster challenge this realm of England.' Henry was offering to fight any rival claimant, not submitting his claim to the impartial examination of the assembly; of course no one answered the challenge ... Henry neither owed his position to parliament nor wished it to be thought that he did. He claimed the throne by *right*; acceptance of that claim was the most that he desired.'[28]

So Henry had been blocked from claiming the throne by right of 'conquest' by Chief Justice Thirning. He did not want to claim it by 'election', and the only claim he really made was by descent. Rather, he insisted, he was simply recovering that which was truly his in the first place, and was motivated solely by the dire necessity into which the realm had fallen.

COULD 'THE COMPLAINT OF CHAUCER TO HIS PURSE' BE SUBVERSIVE?

The more we examine Chaucer's address to Henry in the *Complaint*, the more absurd it becomes. Just try substituting another name for Henry's: 'Oh Adolf Hitler, who has conquered our country and been elected by free elections and also who is the rightful ruler by descent ...' It suddenly starts looking ridiculous.

In the context of 1400, when Henry was in urgent need of professional help to transform grubby history into panegyric, Chaucer's bald five lines tacked onto the end of a begging poem would scarcely have won the poet a warm place in the usurper's heart.

So why did Chaucer write the poem? There are lots of theories. One frequently championed is that he wrote the poem for Richard – but had not yet sent it when Richard was deposed. Being reluctant to waste good material, goes the theory, Chaucer simply tacked the envoy on and sent it to the new king.

But even so, the usurper would surely have required the master poet of the previous regime to make his peace with something grander than these five bare lines. Surely Chaucer couldn't really have thought such a cursory offering would prompt the new king to speed up his annuity payments – payments owed him by Richard?

But then perhaps it wasn't a begging poem at all. Without the envoy, it looks much more like a number of other poems written at about the same time by various poets, all of which are similarly humorous treatments of money.[29] So it might have been a generic verse on a topical theme – except of course for the envoy.

Another possibility is that it was a poem that Chaucer threw off for the encouragement of Richard's supporters. For this to have been the case, the timing of the composition is crucial. Both genre and style suggest it was written late in the century, and there is no reason to suppose any long gap between the writing of the three humorous stanzas and the *envoy*, which couldn't have been written before the usurpation.

This means our best bet is that Chaucer composed the entire poem in late 1399 or 1400. In this case, he was most probably writing it while Richard was still alive, and, what is more, Chaucer could have been writing from the comparative security of the Westminster sanctuary. The sanctuary itself was a stronghold of Ricardian opposition to the new regime, and Chaucer may have composed the *Complaint* around the time the plotters met at the Abbot's house to discuss bringing Richard back.

Viewed in this context, when Richard's return was still a very real possibility to many people, some of Chaucer's lines acquire an allusive quality that would not have been lost on friends of the deposed king:

Now voucheth sauf this day or hyt be nyght
That I of yow the blisful soun may here
Or see your colour lyke the sonne bryght
That of yelownesse hadde never pere.
Ye be my lyf, ye be myn hertes stere.
Quen of comfort and of good companye,
Beth hevy ageyn, or elles moot I dye.
     The Complaint of Chaucer to His Purse, ll. 8–14

Grant now, this day, before that it is night
That I your blissful sound may hear
Or see your colour like the sun bright
That of yellowness had never a peer.
You are my life, you are my heart's guide.
Queen of comfort and of good company,
Be heavy again, or else must I die.

One of Richard's badges was the sun in splendour, and his hair was yellow or red
– so that Richard was frequently associated with the sun. Gower makes the same
allusion in the first version of the *Vox Clamantis*,
written while Richard was still king, and Chaucer
does it himself, in the F Prologue to *The Legend of
Good Women*.[30] And of course 'hertes stere'
alludes to Richard's other badge – the white hart.

So, on the one hand, *The Complaint of Chaucer
to His Purse* is a playful poem, but on the other it
carries resonances for the troubled times in which
it was written. Chaucer equates his fortunes with
Richard and urges both to return before the night

*Richard II's badge of the sun in
splendour (detail from his tomb).*

really sets in – the metaphorical night of an
England ruled by Henry and Arundel. If you don't, says the poet, I'm a dead
man. And so he may well have been, within a few months.

If this was indeed the context of the poem, the envoy to Henry begins to look
ironic. It certainly doesn't seem like something designed to endear Chaucer to
the usurper.

WAS CHAUCER COMMENTING ON THE NEW AGE?

Of course, literary interpretations and theories like these are never going to be
proved categorically. One thing, however, which we *can* say about Chaucer's
Complaint is that it is quite unlike anything else he wrote to or about Richard. In
particular, Chaucer never wrote a begging poem to Richard, and perhaps this is
the most significant point. By directly begging Henry for remuneration – Chaucer
was severing the magic circle of the literary world of Richard II's court.

The poem implicitly acknowledges a return to a former mode of patronage –

harking back, in fact, to the old days of the minstrels, when the relationship between the courtiers and the poets was that of hired and hirer.[31]

In Henry's court, poets and artists were quite bluntly (and Henry, by all accounts, was the bluntest of men) once again to become servants. By openly soliciting Henry IV for money, Chaucer was declaring that the arrangement, in which he had flourished and written his greatest work, was dead.

The *Complaint* can thus be seen as a tiny elegy to a vanished court society and culture. In *that* way, it is a cry of despair, written from within the sanctuary of Westminster, as Chaucer stared out at a bleak, dangerous and unfamiliar world. He wonders if his purse, since it isn't going to be his 'treasurer' (that is, if it can't protect his money for the future), couldn't at least help him escape from the current circumstances?

> Now purse that ben to me my lyves lyght
> And saveour as doun in this world here,
> Out of this toune helpe me thurgh your myght
> Syn that ye wole nat ben my tresorere.
> For I am shave as nye as any frere.
>   *The Complaint of Chaucer to His Purse*, ll. 15–19.
> Now purse, that are to me light of my life
> And saviour, as far as down in this world here,
> Help me flee from this town with your might,
> Since that you cannot be my treasurer.
> For I am shaved as close as any friar.

It is worth noting that the appeal to his purse as his 'saviour', as far as this world is concerned, is an image that toys with the blasphemous to make its joke. Henry IV, however, wasn't a laughing man, and *The Complaint of Chaucer to His Purse* was not a poem that he would have particularly wanted to hear. Where was the flattery? Where was the justification of the new regime? Where was the condemnation of Richard?

GOWER AND HENRY'S TRIPLE CLAIM TO THE THRONE

One mystery remains in the poem, however, and that concerns once again Henry's claim of triple title to the throne. Even though it was not a feature of Henry's official claim, the fact is that Gower cites exactly the same triple title – conquest, election and right – in his *Cronica Tripertita*:

All the earth sang out in jubilation and praised God and the just and pious Henry, strong and bold. Why he was crowned is approved by *threefold right: he conquered the realm*, and because of this, right is clearly on his side; *he succeeded as heir to the kingdom and has not abdicated from it; in addition, he was chosen by the people and this firmly established*. In order that there might be agreement, no legal measure was omitted. Everything was in accord, and gave solemn promise of Henry's rights.[32]

Now, *that* was more like it! But why should both Chaucer and Gower contradict the official version of Henry's claim to the throne?

There are several intriguing possibilities. One is that the *official* version, enshrined in the *Record and Process*, was not entirely to Henry's satisfaction. We know that Henry would have liked to have been known as a conqueror, but was prevented by Chief Justice Thirning, and it's possible that this was an open secret throughout the land. We have a record of a petition, from the wretched inmates of Ludgate Prison, addressed to 'our very gracious, very excellent lord King Henry the gracious conqueror of England'.[33] Now, if even the *prisoners* knew to call Henry 'conqueror' when they wanted something from him – word had obviously got around.

So here's a possible scenario: it's common knowledge that Henry wants to be conqueror, legitimate king and everybody's hero all rolled into one. He also wants his ego massaging on an epic scale. Gower bites the bullet and hands in the required encomium, oblivious to the internal contradictions of the triple claim, but Chaucer can't bring himself to do it. The whole situation sickens him: Richard in the dungeon, men of letters transformed overnight into dancing bears, to the tune of an usurper's pipe ... Then he has an idea. He'll praise Henry exactly as he wants – use all the pregnant terminology without comment, in as brief a space as possible. He then attaches it to a poem about money that also carries messages to rally Richard's faithful encoded in its midst. Who knows? Perhaps Henry won't even spot the joke and will stump up what Richard owes. (Which, incidentally, Henry promised to do. He granted Chaucer forty marks a year, beginning the day he was crowned.)[34]

Another possible scenario is that Gower was first to write his panegyric and Chaucer, amused or irritated by its self-serving illogicalities, penned his *reductio ad absurdam* as a riposte.

A third possibility is it happened the other way round. Chaucer penned his tongue-in-cheek eulogy. Gower didn't spot the joke and – taking the master poet's work at face value – copied the triple claim with a straight face into his own panegyric.

Of course it may not have happened in any of these ways. We don't even know for certain if Henry saw the *Complaint* at all. We certainly don't know whether it spurred him into rewarding Chaucer or if it convinced the usurper to rid himself of a mischievous Ricardian troublemaker.

Perhaps all we can say is: if Henry was demanding the sort of panegyric that Gower felt compelled to offer up, it may well be that Chaucer fell far short of the sycophancy required by the new regime.

Chaucer, perhaps, was a deep disappointment to Henry IV. It is noticeable that, for all Henry's lavish promises, the only money Chaucer actually received from him was a gift of £10 for Michaelmas 1399 and £5 in June 1400 against his new grant – and this despite the fact that Chaucer had otherwise enjoyed an above-average success rate in obtaining money owed to him by the previous regime.[35]

But whatever Henry's opinion of Chaucer, there was one other person to whom Chaucer must have been anathema. A very powerful person. A very dangerous person: Archbishop Thomas Arundel ...

CHAPTER II

The Canterbury Tales as death-warrant

≈

For all his grip on the reins of power, Archbishop Arundel was still battling to gain control over his church at the time of Chaucer's disappearance. To do so he put heresy at the forefront of the religious agenda and established an iron rule in which anything other than his official line was not to be tolerated. It has been said that he 'attempted no less than a wholesale transformation of the religious culture of his day'.[1]

The watchwords of religious life were no longer to be enlightenment, understanding of the Gospels, or appreciation of Christian concepts, or even love of our Lord. From now on there was to be only one watchword: obedience. Obedience to the church – and that meant obedience to Archbishop Thomas Arundel. You could love Jesus all you liked, but unless you agreed to the exact formula of the Eucharist as prescribed by Thomas Arundel, you were a heretic. The archbishop was not interested in common men becoming familiar with biblical texts. What he demanded was that they accept without question the authority of the Roman Catholic church. *His* authority. 'Complete and unequivocal submission' was his goal.[2]

THE THOUGHT POLICE ARE CALLED IN

The terms of the Act *De Haeretico Comburendo*, which Arundel must have framed, give the tone of the new era. The Act not only introduced the ultimate punishment of burning alive, it also attempted to control public debate in a way that would have been unthinkable in King Richard's days.

The Act forbade anyone to

preach, hold, teach or instruct anything openly or secretly, or make or write any book contrary to the Catholic faith ... nor make conventicles nor hold ... schools, and also that none henceforth shall in any way favour such ... and that all and singular having such books or writings of such wicked doctrines or opinions shall ... deliver ... such books and writings to the diocesan of the same place within forty days from the time of the proclamation of this ordinance and statute ... [3]

But even *De Haeretico Comburendo* did not bring the sort of absolute control that Arundel sought. A few years later he was drafting an even more hardline measure. His *Constitutions* of 1409 formed 'one of the most draconian pieces of censorship in English history'.[4] The *Constitutions* sought not only to control what people taught, read, and discussed, they also sought to control what people *thought*. The study of Wyclif's works was naturally forbidden, as was the study of any book not approved by a panel of twelve theologians. Limits were set on the discussion of theological questions in schools, and a monthly inquiry was to be held into the views of every student at the university:

Every warden, head, or keeper of a college or principal of a hall or hostel ... shall inquire diligently every month at least in the college, hall or hostel over which he presides, whether any scholar or inhabitant of any such college, hall or hostel, has held, defended, or in any way proposed any conclusion, proposition, or opinion, sounding ill for the Catholic faith or good customs.[5]

The Thought Police had been called in. It was to be a different world.

It would, from now on, be illegal to preach without a licence, and preachers were to be discreet, condemning the failings of the clergy only to clergy, and limiting themselves to the offences of laymen when preaching to the laity. No dirty linen in public, please!

No one was to question or debate anything ordained by the church, and henceforth no one was to translate any text of Holy Scripture into the English language on their own authority.

And Arundel achieved all this in 1409 with a breathtaking example of Orwellian doublethink. He announced that henceforth all sermons and all teaching in schools should be confined to the topics listed in Archbishop Peckham's Syllabus of 1281. Arundel made it appear that he was taking the church and country back to a previous doctrinal purity – but it was a trick. Arundel was actually standing the truth upon its head.

Peckham's Syllabus was an instrument to *extend* knowledge amongst the laity, not to limit it. It was 'part of the great educational drive initiated by the

Fourth Lateran Council of 1215'. Peckham was setting down the *minimum* that non-clerical Christians should know. Arundel deftly turned it into the *maximum* they should know. He invoked Peckham as an instrument of ignorance instead of knowledge.[6]

Students at the University of Bologna.

Now although all this happened several years after Chaucer's disappearance, it gives a flavour of where the world was heading, when Chaucer disappeared from it in 1400. The *Constitutions* may not have been published until 1409, but the spirit that produced them had already seeped into the centres of power while Chaucer and his contemporaries were still trying to come to terms with how their world had deteriorated.

What would Arundel, at this moment, have made of Geoffrey Chaucer's work? In particular what would he have thought about the *chef d'oeuvre* on which the master poet was currently engaged – *The Canterbury Tales*?

WHAT WOULD ARUNDEL HAVE THOUGHT OF 'THE CANTERBURY TALES'?

Henry might have been disappointed with the quality and quantity of panegyric that the most famous English poet was willing to dish up for him – especially when measured up against a star performance like John Gower's – but the Archbishop must have regarded Chaucer's masterwork as anathema.

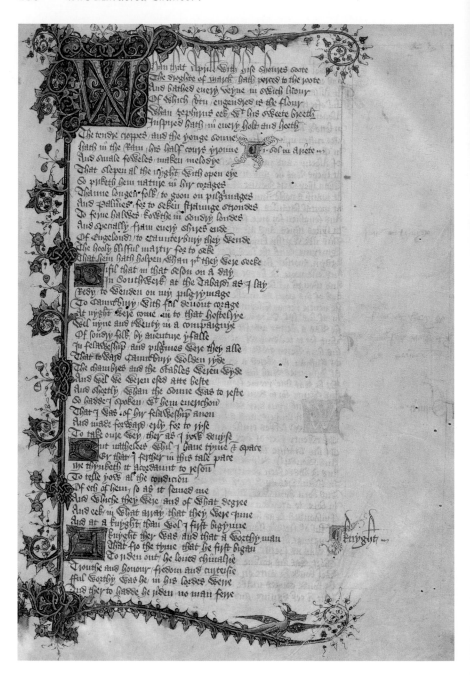

The Ellesmere MS: the beginning of 'The General Prologue'.

Chaucer had been writing his *Tales* in a entirely different age and climate – in the 1380–90s – 'in an intellectual and theological environment in whose febrile variety and shifting tensions the poem is fully engaged,' as one critic puts it.[7]

He had been actively engaged in translation and thus, whether he intended it or not, in the dissemination of knowledge and ideas to a section of society to whom these things had previously been a closed book. Criticism of the church and its servants rolled off Chaucer's pen as easily as did the fun he made of merchants, bailiffs, inn-keepers and guildsmen.

Chaucer and Arundel stood at opposite political and cultural poles. There can be no doubt that the two men knew each other – Chaucer was twice witness in legal proceedings involving the transfer of property owned by Arundel – but what they thought of each other we can only imagine.[8]

On the other hand we can make a pretty good guess as to what the Archbishop would have thought about the great work on which the poet was currently engaged, when Henry made his grab for the throne. Chaucer's easy-going, self-confident, anti-hierarchical world was essentially the antithesis of all the authoritarian Arundel stood for. As one recent critic writes: the book of *The Canterbury Tales* itself 'playing, as it so disruptively does, with the most important contemporary arguments over teaching and religious authority – was product not simply of a Ricardian world (with all that has been made to imply) but also of a world that was crucially pre-Arundelian'.[9]

Chaucer's freewheeling, socially subversive masterpiece had been overtaken by events. It suddenly belonged to another time and it was no longer welcome. It represented everything that Archbishop Arundel was trying to put the lid on.

Even the very framework of *The Canterbury Tales* would have been enough to make his crozier curl.

THE POLITICS OF PILGRIMAGE

Whan that aprill with his shoures soote
The droghte of march hath perced to the roote,
And bathed every veyne in swich licour
Of which vertu engendred is the flour;
Whan zephirus eek with his sweete breeth
Inspired hath in every holt and heeth

The tendre croppes, and the yonge sonne
Hath in the ram his halve cours yronne,
And smale foweles maken melodye,
That slepen al the nyght with open ye
(So priketh hem nature in hir corages);
Thanne longen folk to goon on pilgrimages.

> *The Canterbury Tales, The General Prologue*, ll. 1–12

When that April with his showers sweet
Has pierced the drought of March unto the root
And bathed every vein in that liquor
Out of whose strength engendered is the flower;
When Zephirus too, with his sweet breath,
Has breathed to life, in every copse and heath,
The tender shoots, and when the young sun
Has in the Ram his half-course run, [Ram=Aries: 12 March–11 April]
And small fowls make their melody
That sleep all through the night with open eye,
For nature pricks them so in their courages; [hearts]
Then longen folk to go on pilgrimages.

Reading those famous opening lines today, six hundred years later, it all seems so innocent and filled with light. How could Archbishop Arundel find anything objectionable in that?

It's an April day, the sun is up, the birds have been hard at it all night long, the sap is rising, it's Spring and – as we all know – in Spring a young man's fancy turns to thoughts of ... well ... of going on pilgrimage. Wait a minute! Stop right there!

This is exactly the sort of disrespectful attitude that the Archbishop was trying to stamp out. It was the sort of attitude for which he was prepared to burn men alive – and did.

Chaucer cheerfully equates the urge to go on pilgrimage with the natural urges of sex and love, and although it may seem like a fairly innocuous literary joke to us, it would have been politically charged to readers in the 1390s. By 1400 the same

How about my place?

joke would have become downright dangerous. Now, a man could be burnt at the stake for saying such things. William Sawtre *was*.

Pilgrimage was a sensitive subject. Arundel made it one of the key factors in his definition of heresy. The church advised that your chances for salvation were strongly enhanced if at least once in your lifetime you went on a pilgrimage. It was supposed to be a penance, but by Chaucer's day a trip to Walsingham or to Canterbury was not too much of a hardship, and indeed could even be seen as an enjoyable adventure. It was certainly the one excuse the lower members of society had for leaving the narrow confines of their own villages. In an age which placed restraints on travel, the pilgrimage was the one officially condoned outing that all could and should undertake. It may even have been one mechanism by which the peasants of 1381 organized their revolt.[10]

The Church Commercial, of course, had a vested interest in promoting pilgrimage. It made a lot of money out of it. A great centre like Canterbury could expect to make at least £1,000 a year out of visitors.[11] Activity increased in Chaucer's day – perhaps because those who had survived the Black Death felt impelled to make the journey:

> The hooly blisful martir for to seke
> That hem hath holpen whan that they were seeke.
> *The General Prologue*, ll. 17–18
> The holy blissful martyr for to seek,
> Who helped them out when they were sick.

The church's profits came not only from the offerings given by grateful pilgrims at the shrines they visited, but also from fines imposed for commuting vows to go on pilgrimage. For example, William le Scrope was absolved from his vow to go on pilgrimage to Rome on condition that he converted both the expenses of his journey and the offerings which he would have made at St Peter's to repairing a church door.[12] Indeed, the inducements offered to pilgrims seem to modern eyes unashamedly commercial. Here, for example, are a few of the Bargains of the Month on offer at the monastery of Shene:

> *Item*: In the Feast of St John the Baptist whosoever will come to the said monastery and devoutly say a Pater-noster shall have ninety days of pardon ...
> *Item*: Whosoever will come to the said monastery in the Feast of St Paul the Apostle, say one Pater-noster and one Ave Maria, shall have one hundred days

of pardon ... *Item*: In the Feast of Mary Magdalene whosoever cometh to the said monastery shall have one hundred days of pardon granted by Bishop Stafford, Archbishop of Canterbury ... *Item*: In the feast of St Thomas the Apostle and in the Feast of St Michael the Archangel they shall have three years and forty days of pardon.[13]

It is perhaps little wonder that the reformers objected to the emphasis the church laid on the commerce of pilgrimage. 'Confessors', wrote one of Wyclif's followers, '... attach more importance to foolish vows of pilgrimages and offerings and the breaking of such vows, than a vow made to God, in our Christendom, to keep God's commandments and forsake the fiend and his works, for they give light penances for the breaking of God's laws, but the breaking of these foolish vows and the absolving of them is reserved to high worldly clerics.'[14]

The reformers encouraged would-be pilgrims instead to stay at home and give the money they would have spent on the journey and offerings to the poor. No self-respecting churchman of rank was going to tolerate that sort of thing, however, and the bishops were soon threatening offenders with eternal damnation. As one reformer complained:

They tell the people that they will be damned if they put the costs of their pilgrimage to a better use, and yet that is lawful by God's law and man's law and reason ... and more help to poor men and far better than making offerings to such false sticks and to rich, worldly clerics, who are not in need ...[15]

The church took pilgrimage extremely seriously indeed. The careless way in which Chaucer cheerfully equates pilgrimage with lovemaking in the very opening lines of his masterwork was deeply subversive of Arundel's world-view – not to mention his financial base. In fact *The Canterbury Tales* – as a whole – is shot through with an anti-clericalism that would have had Archbishop Arundel reaching for his summons book.

ANTI-CLERICALISM IN 'THE CANTERBURY TALES'

Most modern scholarship tells us that Chaucer's anti-clericalism was conventional and based in a mainstream of anti-ecclesiastical satire that stretched back centuries. There is a critical consensus that Chaucer was in no way attacking orthodox religious beliefs and that his own religious views were unexceptional. 'Far from drawing new inspiration from real life,' we are told, 'Chaucer seems to have been most stimulated by the possibility of exploiting a rich literary tradition.'[16] However, in the white heat of the usurpation, when the new rulers desperately needed to control the boiling cauldron of resentment they had stirred up, it's arguable that Archbishop Arundel would not have taken such a calmly erudite view.

Whether or not similar satire had been aimed at the church fifty or a hundred years before, in the context of 1399–1400, it was dangerous and seditious – especially if you saw the world through Archbishop Arundel's eyes.

And the closer we look at Chaucer's men of the cloth – the Pardoner, the Friar, the Summoner, the Monk, the Oxford Clerk, and the Poor Country Parson – the worse it gets.

THE PARDONER

There are no two ways about it, Chaucer's Pardoner is a rogue and a scoundrel. In his wallet he's got an old pillow-case that he says is the veil of the Virgin Mary. He also claims to have a bit of the sail from the boat that St Peter was fishing in when Jesus called him to higher things. And then there's a glass jar full of pigs' bones – and goodness only knows what he claims those are.

It's all a sham, and yet with these phoncy relics he can earn more money in a day than a poor country parson would see in two months.

In church the Pardoner tells stories and reads lessons and sings and preaches so well that the money just pours in. On top of all this, the Pardoner has a suspiciously close relationship with that other *The Pardoner.* church officer, the Summoner.

The abuses that pardoners practised in Chaucer's day were notorious. We imagine pardoners today (if we imagine them at all) as church officers who went around selling pardons – or *indulgences* to use the correct term, forgiving sins and preaching in village churches to raise cash from credulous villagers. In fact all three of these activities were prohibited and not what a *questor* – the official name for a pardoner – was supposed to do.

Of course, prohibited or not, it's precisely what they did do. From shire's end to shire's end, they sold pardons, preached and forgave sins. Everyone knew they did, but *they weren't supposed to.* That was the point.

In theory, pardoners were supposed to be merely messengers who bore the paperwork of indulgences granted by the pope or by a bishop to the repentant sinners who had proved they deserved them. The problems came in the practice, no matter how the church tried to prevent it .

And the problem was exacerbated by the fact that their services were useful to those who ought to be controlling them. Pardoners were great fundraisers. They were always better at tapping into the purses of parishioners than a local man. So when there was a hospital to be built or a bridge to be repaired, there was always the temptation for religious houses and institutions to call in their services and then to split the profits. The very presence of pardoners in the system was a corrupting influence.

Pope Innocent III was the first to try to control their activities. In 1215, at that famous Fourth Lateran Council, he made it canon law that all *questors* should carry letters of licence from the pope or a bishop. They were not permitted to preach but only to read out their letters. What's more (and here was the really bad news if you were a *questor*) they had to amend their lives and cease living in taverns!

A further papal edict tried to stop pardoners intimidating village priests. From 1267 on they were no longer allowed to demand shelter from the local clergy and they were forbidden to order the local priest to summon the people to hear them.

In 1311–12 further legislation was passed to curb their activities: from then on bishops would have the power to examine every pardoner's credentials before they granted them the freedom of their diocese and the bishops were allowed to punish any pardoner who stepped out of line.[17]

So if the church establishment was so aware of the abuses practised by pardoners, and so keen to curb their worst excesses, why would Archbishop Arundel have objected to what Chaucer had to say?

Partly it's a question of *when* Chaucer said it. The 1380s and 1390s were a sensitive time to criticize the church – especially if you were calling into question the whole business of indulgences and holy relics. Which brings us to the key question: was Chaucer criticizing specific abuses of which the church itself was painfully aware, or was he criticizing the whole rotten system?

IS CHAUCER CRITICIZING ONLY PHONY PARDONERS?

Critics have spent a lot of time proving that Chaucer's portrait of a fraudulent pardoner was meant to be a satire only on fraudulent pardoners and not a satire on *all* pardoners. This rather misses the point. It assumes there were such things as saintly pardoners who stood apart from fraudulent ones. In practice, the only thing that distinguished the fraudulent from the 'saintly' pardoner was possession of a licence.

The Bishop of Durham circulated a letter to his diocese in 1340 – it rails against certain fraudulent *questors* who are going boldly around *on their own authority* to 'distribute indulgences to the people, dispense with the execution of vows, absolve the perjured, homicides, usurers, and other sinners who confess to them; and, for *a little money* paid, grant remission for ill-atoned crimes, and are given to a multitude of other abuses'.[18] Of course those words 'for a little money' may indicate that the good bishop was mainly concerned that these fraudulent pardoners were undercutting the price of a *bona fide* indulgence. Certainly his main complaint was that these fellows were operating without the proper letters and licence provided (for a fee) by himself. In other words he – quite rightly – wanted his cut.

But all the fraudulent pardoners had to do was obtain a licence from the bishop and hey presto! they ceased to be fraudulent. There is the case of one pardoner by the name of Alexander de Derby: he was 'apprehended by the Chapter of Beverley Minster and confessed that he had collected in the Chapter's name without any authorization. Yet two months after the suspension of sentence, he was duly licensed and collecting for Beverley Minster ... The only real distinction between a true and a false pardoner is the possession of a licence.'[19]

Church institutions, like monasteries, hospitals and so on, desperately needed the funds that pardoners raised, but they could not officially condone the means by which they raised them. So (with a few honourable exceptions) the ecclesiastics turned a blind eye to the abuses that the pardoners practised. Pardoners had become a necessary evil to the functioning of the church.

And that was the nub of the argument that the church's critics pursued: the very existence of pardoners was indicative of the corruption within the church itself. Everything that Chaucer's pardoner does is theoretically illegal. His confession – which is what *The Pardoner's Prologue* is – begins:

'Lordynges,' quod he, 'in chirches whan I preche,
I peyne me to han an hauteyn speche ...'
   The Pardoner's Prologue, ll. 229–30
'Lordings,' quoth he, 'in churches when I preach,
I try to be impressive in my speech ...'

For pardoners or quaestors, preaching in the church had been forbidden since 1215. Pardoners were only permitted to read out their letters. Yet this Pardoner is proud to be able to say that he knows everything by rote (l. 332).

Then he shows them his warrants:

'That no man be so boolde, ne preest ne clerk,
Me to destourbe of Cristes hooly werk.'
   The Pardoner's Prologue, ll. 339–40
'So no man is so bold – neither priest nor clerk,
To stop me carrying out Christ's holy work.'

It's precisely this sort of intimidation that was outlawed by the 1267 legislation. And so the catalogue of abuses goes on.

THE PARDONER'S FAKE RELICS

The Pardoner's main stock-in-trade, however, is holy relics. They're all as fake as a salesman's smile, but he can make them work wonders.

He knows exactly what his audience's main preoccupations are and he hits them straight away with his brand-leader: a shoulder bone from a sheep that belonged (oddly enough, considering the rampant anti-semitism of the times) to a 'Holy Jew'. Now, if this shoulder bone is dipped in a well, the water from that well will cure any cow or calf or sheep or ox of anything from worms to pustules to mange. And what's more, if the good man who owns the beasts drinks the water himself before cock-crow, every week, his animals will multiply!

Nor is that all, ladies and gentlemen! He has a mitten here – just slip your hand into it, and next time you sow wheat or oats they'll multiply too! – providing of course you offer pence or – even better – some silver groats worth four pennies each!

Can it be that Chaucer is attacking only those charlatans who travelled the countryside duping the people with fakes and frauds? Yet here we come to a mystery. False relics don't figure in the official records. Pardoners were legally permitted to carry relics, and while clearly most of them must have been fakes hardly anyone mentions it: 'Although one may find the standard abuses of pardoners repeated over and over again, the abuse of false relics does not appear amongst them. There is no mention of it in any of the manuals which treat of the pardoner, and it is noticed in only a few church councils.'[20]

A reliquary diptych containing bones.

One reason for this may have been that it was an abuse the church had firmly under control. In 1287 the Synod of Exeter, for example, had ruled that anyone encouraging people to venerate false relics should be treated as a heretic, and nobody wanted that – even in the days before heretics could be burnt.

But another and perhaps more compelling reason for the church's silence on the subject of false relics was that it was a can of worms that it did not wish to open. For a start: how did you prove whether a relic was real or false?

According to an inventory of the period, Canterbury Cathedral itself could boast amongst its relics: 'Aaron's rod ... Some of the stone upon which the Lord stood when He ascended into heaven. Some of the Lord's table upon which He made the Supper. Some of the prison whence the Angel of the Lord snatched the blessed Apostle Peter. Some wool which Mary the Virgin had woven. Some of the oak upon which Abraham [sic] climbed to see the Lord. And some of the clay out of which God fashioned Adam.'[21]

With authenticated wonders like these locked in one of his cupboards at Canterbury, small wonder if Archbishop Arundel preferred to avoid the question of false relics. If people were to start being sceptical of the Pardoner's pillow-case, they might well start asking questions about the Archbishop's lump of clay. If Chaucer invited people to laugh at his Pardoner's jar of pigs' bones – heavens above! – people might start making fun of the Virgin Mary's knitting!

Arundel was interested in obedience. If the church said something was a holy relic, you'd better believe it. The spirit of cynicism was definitely not something the custodian of Aaron's rod wished to encourage.

In an age when huge numbers of churches and abbeys had become famous for their relics, it is not surprising that the only people impertinent enough to bring up the subject of phoney relics were those who disapproved of the whole business – and that included venerating sacred images. The orthodox had no hesitation in branding such critics as Lollards.

'It was a characteristic of that sect of Lollards', writes the chronicler Henry Knighton in the 1380s, 'that they hated and inveighed against images, and preached that they were idols, and spurned them as a deceit, so that when one of them referred to St Mary of Lincoln, or St Mary of Walsingham, he would call them ... "The witch of Lincoln, and the witch of Walsingham" ... '[22]

As far as Wyclif had been concerned, there *was* no distinction to be made between true and false relics; they were all false and to be done away with along with what he called the cult of saints: 'With the fall of the cult of saints, the evils of relic worship and of shrines emblazoned with jewels and gold will also pass. Such "wealth foolishly lavished on shrines might be distributed to the poor to the honour of the saints".'[23]

To Arundel, any attack on pardoners would have smacked of Lollardy. After all, hadn't the Dreadful Doctor's followers preached this very attitude? 'When a pardoner comes along with stolen bulls and false relics, granting more years of pardon than come before doomsday in exchange for worldly wealth donated to rich places that don't need it, he's given help and welcomed by curates in return for a share of what he makes ... '[24]

And if, in these passages, Chaucer was only criticizing those pardoners without licences and those who dealt in false pardons, where in his oeuvre does he indicate the benefits to be gained from licensed pardoners and real relics? The answer, as both the poet and Archbishop would have been aware, was: nowhere.

THE PARDONER'S PARDONS

It was theoretically prohibited for the Pardoner to sell pardons. He could certainly not forgive sins. Penance involves three acts: contrition, confession and satisfaction. A 'pardon' or 'indulgence' is merely a way of reducing or removing the temporal punishment or '*poena*' which is left after the sacrament of confession and absolution has removed the moral guilt or '*culpa*'.[25]

So to attack the corrupt practice of selling pardons was not theoretically a departure from the orthodox position. Indeed, even in the next century, the orthodox Dr Thomas Gascoigne could write: 'Modern sinners say: I do not care what and how many sins I commit for I can easily get a plenary indulgence granted me by the pope, whose writing I grant I have bought for fourpence or sixpence or for a game of tennis.'[26]

But at the end of the fourteenth century these were sensitive issues. A critical atmosphere surrounded the very theology and practice of indulgences in which Chaucer's Pardoner had set up his corrupt *modus vivendi*. This theology and practice actually made his fraud possible. Without them he simply could not exist.

And the words with which the Pardoner concludes his *Tale* would have done nothing to soothe Archbishop Arundel's digestion:

> 'And Jhesu Crist, that is oure soules leche
> So graunte yow his pardoun to receyve,
> For that is best; I wol yow nat deceyve'
>   *The Pardoner's Tale*, ll. 916–18
> 'And Jesus Christ, that is our soul's physician,
> Grant that you his pardon shall receive,
> For that is best, I will you not deceive.'

Who, it might be asked, could possibly argue with the statement that Christ's pardon is the best? Well, Archbishop Arundel could! Though not, of course, in so many words ... He'd have to agree with the proposition in principle, but that wouldn't mean that the subtext had escaped him. If *Christ's* pardon is the best, any other form of pardon is necessarily inferior. In other words, the pardons offered by the church are a poor substitute for Christ's forgiveness.

This was not at all the sort of proposition that Thomas Arundel was interested in circulating amongst the common people. It was more like the sort of idea those dreadful followers of Wyclif were always pushing: 'There comes no pardon but from God for good living and for ending in charity, and this cannot be bought and sold in the way that prelates buy and sell them these days.'[27]

Wycliffites would have held this emphasis dear – that Christ's pardon is best, and yet, horrifyingly for them, the Pardoner – a conman from start to finish – has used it as part of his sales pitch. Could it be that the outrage provoked by the Pardoner grows in proportion to its scope for offending the religious outlooks *of whatever camp*, whether of the conservative orthodox or the radicals alike?

Or is Chaucer employing here the device in which he allows the arch-deceiver to tell the truth? After all, that is what the Pardoner is doing throughout his *Prologue*: liar that he is, he is telling the truth about his deception.

Not only is the Pardoner's professional corruption exposed through this invocation of Christ's pardon, but the standard, orthodox theology of indulgence is left looking very sickly.

It was definitely not the sort of proposition that Archbishop Arundel would have wanted to see in a popular work of literature.

THE PARDONER'S OFFER TO THE PILGRIMS

The archbishop would have been even less amused if he turned over the leaf to the end of *The Pardoner's Tale*, where the Pardoner turns his skills upon the pilgrims themselves and offers to absolve them from their sins.

'You don't even have to stop and kneel,' he tells them 'I can absolve you as we ride along – in fact I can give you new, fresh pardons at the end of every mile! You are so lucky to have me riding with you because should one of you fall off his horse and break his neck, I can give him the greater and the lesser absolution as his soul leaves his body!'[28]

Illegal as it was for the Pardoner to sell his pardons, it was totally out of order for him to claim to be able to forgive sins, but this final offer to supply the last sacrament would have struck Chaucer's contemporaries as an unbelievable obscenity. It was the ultimate in cold-hearted mercenary deception. The Pardoner is knowingly offering to deprive his victims of their last chance to reach heaven. He is little better than a devil incarnate condemning their souls to hell.

The Pardoner's sprightly indifference to what happened to the souls of those he fleeced is also spelt out in his confessional *Prologue*:

> 'I rekke nevere, when that they been beryed,
> Though that hir soules good a-blakeberyed!'
>   *The Pardoner's Prologue*, ll. 405–6
> 'I don't care in the least, when they are buried,
> Even if their souls go a-blackberrying!'

This again was a common complaint raised by critics of the church, namely that mercenaries like the Pardoner couldn't care less about what happened to the souls they trafficked in: 'If men's souls go to hell by breaking of God's commandments no matter, as long as the pennies come fast to fill their hands and coffers,' observes one Wycliffite author. And another: 'If they have money and gold to their liking, by extortion and robbery, they don't care how foul devils devour Christian souls.'[29]

And if Archbishop Arundel's smile had frozen on his thin lips by now, the Host's reply to the Pardoner would have wiped it off his face altogether.

'Thou woldest make me kisse thyn olde breech,
And swere it were a relyk of a seint,
Though it were with thy fundament depeint!
... I wolde I hadde thy coillons in myn hond
In stide of relikes or of seintuarie.
Lat kutte hem of, I wol thee helpe hem carie;
They shul be shryned in an hogges toord!'
  The Pardoner's Tale, ll. 948–55
'You want to make me kiss your old breeches
And swear they're a relic of some saint,
Though they've been painted with your fundament!
... I wish I had your testicles in my hand
Instead of relics or reliquary.
Let 'em be cut off, I'll help you carry them;
They shall be enshrined in a hog's turd!'

This is exactly the sort of disrespect for the church's officers that Arundel was attempting to stamp out. What's more, it's couched in the sort of language that demonstrates the contempt in which so many common men held the church in those days. Archbishop Arundel certainly would not have wanted such stuff repeated at dinner tables throughout the land – let alone enshrined in the masterwork of the country's foremost poet.

THE PARDONER AND ARCHBISHOP ARUNDEL

There is one further aspect of the portrait of the Pardoner that might have got up Arundel's nose.

Chaucer's Pardoner is not – as far as we know – a fraudulent pardoner in terms of his licence. We are given no reason to doubt that his letters of authority have not been duly approved by the diocesan bishop. And since the pilgrims are riding to Canterbury, this would mean (in 1396–7 and after 1399) the approval of Archbishop Thomas Arundel himself.

Of course, it's all a fiction, and these are fictional characters riding on a fictional pilgrimage, but Canterbury is real and, as far as the archbishop was concerned it may all been a bit too close for comfort.

Any disrespect shown towards an appointed officer of the church would have been intolerable to Thomas Arundel under any circumstances. The accident of fiction which makes Arundel himself the licensing bishop of this reviled charlatan would almost certainly have been something the archbishop would have wished to suppress by every means that lay in his power.

THE PARDONER AND THE SUMMONER

But lest we had any doubt about what Chaucer is criticizing – the individual conman or the whole corrupt institution – the *General Prologue* spells it out for us in the relationship between the Pardoner and the Summoner.

The Summoner was another official of the church. His job was to deliver citations to people who were due to appear in the ecclesiastical courts. If the recipients were members of the laity, this usually meant that they were being summoned for failing to pay their tithes or death duties, or that they stood accused of some sexual offence, or were involved in some marital dispute or else accused of perjury.[30] While the tribunals were in session, a summoner would act as usher or beadle.

In other words, the Summoner is a law enforcement officer, acting on behalf of the church. He represents the Church Police.

So perhaps it is significant that Chaucer depicts the Pardoner and the Summoner as the best of friends. In fact they are such *very* good friends, that many readers suspect a sexual liaison between them:

> With hym ther rood a gentil pardoner
> Of rouncivale, his freend and his compeer,
> That streight was comen fro the court of rome.
> Ful loude he soong com hider, love, to me!
> This somonour bar to hym a stif burdoun;
> Was nevere trompe of half so greet a soun.
> *The General Prologue*, ll. 669–74
> With him [the Summoner] there rode a pardoner
> From Rouncivale, his friend and his compeer,
> Who'd come straight from the Court of Rome.
> Full loud he sang: 'Come Hither Love to Me!'

This Summoner bore to him a stiff bass;
Was never a trumpet of half so great a sound.

The symbolism of the relationship could hardly be clearer. Here is the corrupt Pardoner, openly flouting all the laws that were supposed to govern his trade, riding side-by-side with the law enforcement officer who should be arresting him. In fact, not only should the Summoner have arrested the Pardoner, he ought to have thrown him into the archbishop's prison as well. And yet here they are – singing in close harmony! 'Before our eyes, Crime and Justice, the Pardoner and the Summoner, amble together in vinous jocularity down the road to Canterbury.'[31]

If the point is lost on some recent scholars, it would very likely not have been lost on Chaucer's contemporaries. This unholy alliance between the Pardoner and the Summoner opens up the vista of a corrupt chain of collusions – a canker riddling the orthodox church – which could be traced right up to Rome itself.

As one seminal study puts it: 'Chaucer's satire is not directed against false pardoners or against pardoners of any particular establishment, but against the state of institutional decay which made the existence of the pardoner possible.'[32]

It is not a stance that would have made the poet at all popular with Archbishop Arundel. In fact, it is exactly the sort of criticism that the archbishop was determined to crush … and crush with all the means and power at his considerable command.

THE SUMMONER

Of all the people that the Pardoner could have taken up with, it is another crooked church official that Chaucer has him select as his 'compeer'. There is surprisingly little satirical material about summoners until Langland's *Piers Plowman* – perhaps because the office wasn't introduced into England until the thirteenth century. However, summoners represent for Langland and Chaucer, as for Wyclif and his followers, yet another example of the thoroughgoing corruption of the minor officers of the church.

Summoners threaten to send people to the ecclesiastical courts on false pretences in order to extort their money. They are thoroughly familiar

Summoner delivering a summons.

with the sexual misdemeanours of the lower classes, and they exploit that familiarity to summon lechers to the archdeacon's court where they can be relieved of their money. Summoners by reputation were also eminently bribable, whether with cash or sexual favours.[33]

Chaucer goes into greater detail than Langland in the actual day-to-day mechanics of how the corruption of the Summoner is manifested. This particular Summoner has got all the young people – or perhaps the young women – under his thumb. They come to him for advice and he can make them do what he likes. If a fellow has a mistress, the Summoner will turn a blind eye to it for a good twelve months in return for nothing more than a quart of wine – and then excuse him to the full.

Now these are all abuses that Archbishop Arundel probably disapproved of himself. Indeed he might well have tried to put a stop to them wherever he could. In a way there was probably little difference between the Archbishop and the critics of the church about whether or not such abuses should be curbed. The difference would come, however, in the question of how one aired the problem. Archbishop Arundel might want to stamp out the corruption of summoners, but he also wanted to stamp out the public chatter about such corruption.

As we'll see later, even where Arundel would not have disputed the truth of Chaucer's satire, he would have objected to the fact that Chaucer had written it down – and particularly the way in which he'd written it down.

There is, however, one passage in the portrait of the Summoner to which Archbishop Arundel might have taken particular exception. That is Chaucer's little aside about the nature of excommunication.

> And if he foond owher a good felawe,
> He wolde techen him to have noon awe
> In swich caas of the ercedekenes curs,
> But if a mannes soule were in his purs;
> For in his purs he sholde ypunysshed be.
> 'Purs is the ercedekenes helle,' seyde he.
> But wel I woot he lyed right in dede;
> Of cursyng oghte ech gilty man him drede,
> For curs wol slee right as assoillyng savith,
> And also war hym of a *Significavit.*
>   *The General Prologue,* ll. 654–71

And if he found a good companion anywhere
He'd teach him not to be in awe
Of the Archdeacon's power of excommunication,
Unless the man's soul was in his purse,
For in his purse he would be punished.
'Purse is the Archdeacon's hell,' said he.
But well I know he lied – indeed he did –
For every guilty man should dread excommunication,
For it can slay the soul just as sure as absolution saves it,
And also let him beware of a *Significavit*.

This is one of those rare moments in *The General Prologue* when Chaucer lowers the mask of the invisible narrator and seems to speak to us directly. The intimate quality of the interjection gives the lines an intensity and urgency: Take no notice of what the Summoner says! He's lying! Excommunication is terrible and we should all beware of it.

Unfortunately, Chaucer undercuts the sincerity of this appeal to his audience with the last line: 'And also he should beware of a *Significavit*.'

Significavit is the first word of the writ by which the *civil* officers (as opposed to ecclesiastical officers like the Summoner) could arrest someone who'd been excommunicated in order to throw him into prison. The trouble with excommunication, on its own, was that it had become increasingly ineffective in an age that was troubled by disillusion with the established church. The Wycliffites did not want to belong to the church – they regarded it as the source of all evil.[34] Excommunication from a church you didn't want to belong to in the first place was about as much use as punishing an exhibitionist by taking away his clothes.

The church had for many years relied on the civil authorities to provide the extra pressure of imprisonment to persuade miscreants to come to heel. Until 1382, this co-operation between lay and ecclesiastical powers was governed by a piece of legislation called *De excommunicato capiendo*. Once a wrongdoer was excommunicated, a bishop could obtain a writ from the local sheriff to hold the offender in prison until he absolved himself in the eyes of the church. There was a holding-off period of forty days, in which the offender could appeal before he was thrown into prison.

The revolt of 1381 concentrated everyone's minds wonderfully, and the church's powers to deal more effectively with heretics were considerably enhanced. After 1382, anyone excommunicated by an ecclesiastical court could be *immediately* arrested – by application of the writ *Significavit*– and thrown into prison until he made his peace with the church. Making your peace with the church, of course, usually involved either an act of contrition and recantation – or else a payment.

The humour of these four lines from *The General Prologue* lies in the fact that Chaucer adopts a tone of great sincerity and great piety. He tries to convince his readers of the terrible nature of excommunication – how it will slay the soul as sure as absolution will save it. He then cheekily reminds them that if fear of punishment in the next world doesn't persuade them to cough up the required fine, they should still watch out for the very real punishment that could attend them in this world.

Chaucer was hitting a very contemporary button. The idea that fear of imprisonment by the secular power could be more effective than threats of excommunication might have been something Arundel secretly agreed with, but the disrespectful tone in which Chaucer expresses it, and the fact that he does so at all, would certainly not have gone down at all well with the archbishop.

He would have said it smacked of Lollardy.

THE FRIAR

Friars had not been around as long as monks. While the monks, secluded in their cloisters, could trace their origins back to the third century of Christianity or even earlier, the mendicants (friars), tramping around the countryside, could

only trace their existence back to 1154 – when the Carmelite order was founded in Palestine. The Franciscans were founded by St Francis in 1209 and the Dominicans by St Dominic in 1214–15. This made friars very much the *parvenus* of the religious world – as their critics never failed to point out.[35] What is more they owed their creation not to Christ but to papal favour.

The word 'mendicant' comes from the Latin *mendicus*, meaning 'beggar'. In actual fact friars were supposed to live by the work of their hands and only to seek alms as a last resort. Originally

The Friar.

they were forbidden the ownership of property, even in common: no lands, no possessions, no fixed sources of income. The Franciscans in particular were wedded to the ideal of 'absolute poverty'.[36]

Though this sort of programme might not appeal to modern tastes, in the thirteenth century the concept was a stunning success from the start, and within a generation of the deaths of St Francis and St Dominic there were tens of thousands of friars all over Europe. For example, it has been calculated that there were about 25,000 Franciscans alone in various parts of the world before the Black Death.[37]

They tended to be highly educated and they worked in the poorest localities and amongst the most destitute and desperate of the poor – to begin with at least. The movement of mendicant friars represented a return to the simplicity of life and poverty of Christ and his Apostles.

That, at least, was the theory.

In practice, by the time Chaucer came to write *The Canterbury Tales*, the begging orders represented, in the eyes of a large portion of the population, the nadir of religious hypocrisy. The ultimate practitioners of apostolic poverty and abstinence had become great landlords living off the fat of the land, and great womanizers, dressed in the finest clothes. Of course, even though they lived in luxurious houses, furnished with the best, they themselves didn't own a thing. The pope did their owning for them. The friars only had the 'use' of everything – not the ownership. And by this pleasant fiction they could still pretend to themselves and to others that they were living out the letter of St Francis' vision.

It is little wonder that making fun of the friars had become a stock-in-trade of writers of all persuasions by the early fourteenth century. You didn't necessarily have to be a church reformer to find plenty of laughs at the expense of the 'poor' friars.

So it's no surprise that the main attributes of Chaucer's Friar Huberd are mostly well-worn jokes that everyone would have heard a hundred times before. He is a lecher, a snob, a flirt, a liar, a flatterer and a grifter. He will impose himself on a parish curate, claiming to have more powers of confession than the priest, and he knows the taverns in every town.

These self-same accusations had been flying around the heads of friars for many a year. But just because something has been said before doesn't mean that it isn't true. The satirists may have been making the same old jokes about the same old failings of the friars for over a century, but if the friars didn't change their behaviour, why should the criticisms change?

MAKING FUN OF FRIARS IN THE 1390S

What is even more important, though, is the way the same criticisms can take on different resonances, depending on when and how they are made and who exactly is making them.

In Chaucer's day, the world had polarized. Wyclif had stirred up the hornets' nest of dissent. He had at first maintained a friendly relationship with the friars but, around 1379, that collapsed and the former friends became the bitterest of enemies.[38] The Dominicans (who had provided the theological muscle for the Inquisition on the Continent) led the assault on Wyclif's Eucharist ideas. At the same time, friars and monks – 'private religions' as the Doctor called them – became a prime target of the Wycliffites.

The Peasants' Revolt of 1381 galvanized the authorities – secular and religious alike – into action against the troublemakers. And, unlike modern historians, the conservatives of Chaucer's day made no distinction between political trouble-makers and religious troublemakers. To the worldly bishops and powerful lords of the 1380s they were all tarred with the same brush. Thus by the 1390s to criticize friars and monks – even in a general sort of way – was no longer a safe subject of ribaldry. It was to risk being identified with the radicals.

This is why there is no need to ask the question: 'Was Chaucer a Lollard?' That assumes a secret sect to which it was possible to subscribe. The opposition to church corruption was a varied and heterogeneous amalgam of laymen and clerics, nobles and churls, by no means all of whom would have agreed with everything that Wyclif proposed.

The prelates, who wished to squash the widespread criticism of ecclesiastical abuse, wanted to create a situation of 'You're either with us or against us'. It was *they* who wished to simplify the opposition into one identifiable 'sect'.

The only question that need concern us is: would Archbishop Arundel have called Chaucer a 'Lollard'? Or to put it another way: would he have *wanted* to call Chaucer a Lollard?

As far as Arundel was concerned, the very fact that Chaucer satirizes the mendicant orders would have been enough to place him in the opposing camp. The friars had become the archbishop's allies against Wycliffism and rebellion. Chaucer's own opinion of Wyclif's ideas would have been irrelevant. In the 1380s and 1390s even the traditional jibes against the friars carried new connotations.

There are three details of the portrait of Friar Huberd in *The General Prologue* that would have had Arundel reaching for his 'WARNING – LOLLARDY!' stamp – if such things had existed then.

First there is the question of Friar Huberd's luxurious dress – his 'semi-cope' of 'double worsted'; that is, 'his short cloak cut from a very expensive cloth':

> ... he was nat lyk a cloysterer
> With a thredbare cope, as is a povre scoler,
> But he was lyk a maister or a pope.
> Of double worstede was his semycope,
> That rounded as a belle out of the presse.
>   *The General Prologue*, ll. 259–63
> ... he was not like a cloisterer
> With a threadbare cope, as is a poor scholar,
> But he was like a master or a pope.
> Of double worsted was his semi-cope
> As round as a bell out of the casting mould.

Boccaccio had criticized virtually the same thing forty years before.[39] So there is nothing original about Chaucer's remarks. But to make the observations in 1351 (when Boccaccio was writing) was one thing. For Chaucer to do it when he did was very different. In the late 1380s, it was the kind of opinion to be found only in radical tracts like *Jack Upland* (a poem attributed to Chaucer in later centuries).[40] When John Ashwardby, the vicar of the University Church of St Mary, Oxford, was attacked for urging ordinary folk not to give alms to friars who wore expensive cloaks, his views were branded as those 'of the lollard sect'.[41]

Another detail about Friar Huberd you'd only find in Wycliffite writing at this period concerns the small knives and pins that the Friar has stuffed into his tippet (or hood):

> His typet was ay farsed ful of knyves
> And pynnes, for to yeven faire wyves.
>   *The General Prologue*, ll. 233–4
> His hood was always stuffed full of knives
> And pins, that he could give to pretty wives.

One Wycliffite tract tells us that the friars have become:

pedlars bearing knives, pins, and girdles and spices and silk and precious fleeces and furs for women, and they take small high-bred dogs, to win their love and to get many great gifts in exchange for little or nothing; they wickedly covet their neighbours' goods.[42]

A third aspect of Friar Huberd which was closely associated with Wycliffite polemic is the way he is so pleasant when he says his '*in principio*':

> For thogh a wydwe hadde noght a sho,
> So plesaunt was his *in principio*,
> Yet wolde he have a ferthyng, er he wente.
>   *The General Prologue*, ll. 253–5
> For though a widow had not a shoe
> So pleasant was his *in principio*
> Yet would he get a farthing, before he went.

'*In principio*' refers to the opening words of the Gospel according to St John, which was a favourite text for friars upon entering somebody's home – presumably because it continues: 'But how many ever received him, he gave to them power to be made the sons of God.'[43] To the friars' critics the words usually prefaced an attempt to defraud the unsuspecting of cash – at least that's what the Wycliffites said. *Jack Upland* tells us that friars 'win more with *In principio* than Christ and his apostles and all the saints of heaven'.[44]

In Principio: from the Gospel according to St John.

Chaucer also adds one unique detail: he mentions Huberd's harping and singing:

> And in his harpyng, whan that he hadde songe,
> His eyen twynkled in his heed aryght
> As do the sterres in the frosty night.
>   *The General Prologue*, ll. 266–8
> And in his harping, when that he had sung,
> His eyes would twinkle in his head aright
> As do the stars in the frosty night.

This is not a traditional feature of satires against the friars. One Wycliffite tract from around the 1380s mentions harping as one of the many wiles of friars to seduce women:

> On holidays they devote themselves to magic tricks or witchcraft or vain songs and singing and harping, playing guitars and dancing and other vain trifles to get the stinking love of damsels and steer them to worldly vanity and sins ...[45]

But otherwise musical accompaniment is not recorded as a widely recognized failing of the mendicant orders. About the only other writer who mentions it is Boccaccio, who has his lovesick friar Rinaldo composing 'canzonets and sonnets and *ballades*' and singing 'various songs'.[46]

Whatever the inference, it looks as if it might have been a sensitive enough issue for the owner of the Ellesmere MS to have the illustration of the friar's harp removed sometime at the beginning of the fifteenth century. [47]

To have painted a satiric portrait of a friar in the political atmosphere of the 1390s was to pin your colours to the radical opposition to the church. It was perhaps something that Chaucer was regretting by the year of his death.

Friar Huberd, however, was by no means Chaucer's only satire on the mendicant orders in *The Canterbury Tales*. And when he returned to the task of ridiculing the friars in general, he took the gloves off and focused his criticism – quite literally – below the belt.

THE DEVIL'S ARSE

The Friar hates the Summoner – no doubt about it. Chaucer peels away Huberd's affable exterior like a chemical stripper rolls back old paint. 'A summoner', says the Friar:

> '... is a rennere up and doun
> With mandementz for fornicacioun,
> And is ybet at every townes ende.'
> *The Friar's Prologue*, ll. 1283–5
> ' A summoner is a runner up and down
> With written orders for fornication,
> And is beaten at the end of every town.'

'With mandementz for fornicacioun' could mean: 'with summonses to appear in court on charges of fornication' but could equally be read: 'with written permissions for fornication'. It's such a low blow that even the Host calls the Friar to order:

'A, sire, ye sholde be hende
And curteys, as a man of youre estaat.'
    The Friar's Prologue, ll. 1286–7
'Ah, sir, you should be noble
And courteous, considering your importance in society.'

Chaucer gives no special reason for the animosity between the Friar and the Summoner, but none was needed. It was an all-too-familiar criticism that the orthodox clergy and their agents, when they were not in active collusion, were habitually at each other's throats. It was yet another sign of Antichrist's presence within the established church: 'The members of Antichrist tread upon each other,' observed Wyclif.[48]

To rub it in, Friar Huberd tells a tale about a summoner who, falling in with the devil, proves himself to be the worse of the two. In telling such a story, as it happens, Huberd not only exposes the vices of summoners, he also exposes himself. Against the Host's explicit directions, the Friar tells a 'churl's' tale, fixing himself in a *milieu* of minor extortions, briberies and illicit sexual relationships – matters with which he seems only too familiar.

When the Summoner seizes his chance to revenge himself on the Friar, Chaucer uses the opportunity of speaking through the voice of a 'churl' (i.e. non-noble) to open the floodgates of anti-mendicant invective:

'This Frere bosteth that he knoweth helle,
And God it woot, that it is litel wonder;
Freres and feendes been but lyte asonder.'
    The Summoner's Prologue, ll. 1672–4
'This Friar boasteth that he knoweth hell,
And God knows! That is little wonder!
For there's little difference between friars and fiends.'

Next the Summoner tells an anecdote about a friar being shown around hell by an angel. The friar remarks to the angel that he doesn't see any friars in hell, and asks if that is because they all go to heaven? 'No,' says the angel, 'there are millions of friars in hell!' and he takes him down to Satan, who has a tail as wide as a ship's sail. 'Hold up your tail, Satan!' commands the angel. 'Show forth your arse and let the friar see where the nest of friars is in this place!' Twenty thousand friars swarm out. Like bees from a hive, they buzz around hell and then swarm back as Satan claps his tail shut again.[49]

There was a story then current about a Cistercian monk who went up to heaven and found his brothers dwelling under the cloak of the Virgin Mary, and it's possible that Chaucer has wickedly inverted this to produce his outrageous calumny against the whole order of friars.[50] Chaucer may blame the 'churl's mouth' for the outrage, but that's unlikely to have satisfied Archbishop Arundel.

This is one of the very few passages in *The Canterbury Tales* that has no known source (other than this last anecdote mentioned) so we must assume Chaucer made it up. If so, it provides an unusual insight into his thoughts at the time.

Under the Virgin Mary's cloak.

Whoever he might have blamed for the story, it is a fair bet that Archbishop Arundel would have marked Chaucer down for giving it so public an airing and for making it so rude. But then, as one recent commentator puts it: 'Chaucer at his most vulgar is often Chaucer at his most provocative and in many ways his most serious.'[51]

A FART FOR RELIGION

And as the archbishop turned the page or listened to his acolyte reading *The Summoner's Tale*, his indigestion would have hardly improved.

As with *The Summoner's Prologue*, there are no sources or even close analogues for *The Summoner's Tale*. It is one of those rare moments when Chaucer apparently writes from his own invention, and it must, therefore, carry some weight as an indicator of the poet's mindset.

The Summoner's Tale is not really a tale. It is more like a piece of journalistic reporting: 'The Full Inside Story! How A Friar Works on the Infirm, the Aged and the Poor! Be Warned! This Can Happen To You!'

The story stars a certain friar by the name of Friar John, and it begins with a description of his working methods. Friar John, like Friar Huberd, travels around the churches in a certain area, preaching and extracting whatever money he can out of the congregation. Then he's off on his rounds:

> With scrippe and tipped staf, ytukked hye,
> In every hous he gan to poure and prye,
> And beggeth mele and chese, or elles corn.
> *The Summoner's Tale*, ll. 1737–9
> With satchel and metal-tipped staff, and coat tucked in his belt,
> In every house he began to peer and pry,
> And begged for meal and cheese, or else some corn.

Friars customarily travelled in pairs and Friar John has with him a sidekick who carries 'a pair of ivory tables' – that is, a folding set of writing tablets, coated on one side with wax. On these he inscribes the names of the Friar's benefactors so that the holy men can forever remember them in their prayers. Once they get round the corner, however, Friar John's assistant is busy rubbing out the names.[52] It's so near the bone, Friar Huberd can't hold back his fury:

> 'Nay, ther thou lixt, thou Somonour!' quod the Frere.
> *The Summoner's Tale*, l. 1761
> 'Nay! There you're lying, you Summoner!' cried the Friar.

Whether Friar Huberd is incensed because of the truth of the accusation or because of its injustice, we don't know, but we can guess.

Chaucer's Summoner, however, has only just started his assault. He proceeds to spill the beans about the rest of Friar John's scams. In great detail he describes the Friar's visit to one particular house, where he finds the good man, Thomas, sick in bed. The whole passage is a lexicon of the stratagems that friars used to con money out of innocent people.[53]

For example, Friar John claims at one point that the prayers of friars are more acceptable to God than the prayers of ordinary people, because friars 'are wedded to poverty and abstinence' (ll. 1906–14). The sick Thomas responds by pointing out that for all the money he's spent on friars he doesn't seem to have felt any benefit. Whereupon Friar John triumphantly wades in with the argument that the whole problem is that Thomas has been spending on *too many* friars – he should concentrate it all on one friar – i.e. Friar John – for a farthing divided into twelve is nothing. Everything is stronger when it is whole (ll. 1966–71).

Eventually Thomas gets so fed up with this sales pitch, that he decides to teach the friar a lesson. He says he'll give Friar John a contribution to his house but on condition that it is shared out equally with his brother friars. Friar John swears by his faith that he will share it out, and then Thomas tells him to feel down the back of his bed beneath his buttock. As Friar John does so, Thomas farts into his hand. Friar John leaps up, beside himself with rage, and is chased out of the house.

Ivory tables such as the Friar's would be used to write down names of donors.

Friar John then complains to the local lord. The lord, however, is tickled by the philosophical problem that Thomas has presented to the friar. By what means can the sound or smell of a fart be equally divided (ll. 2220–37)?

The lord's squire offers a solution. He suggests that they should get a cartwheel with hollow spokes, and that all twelve friars in the house should kneel down and firmly apply their noses to the outlets of the spokes, and then Thomas can sit on the middle of the wheel and fart. But Friar John himself shall kneel beneath the middle of the wheel and receive the 'first fruit' of the fart, because 'he is a man of great honour' (ll. 2276–7).

The lord, the lady and everyone there – apart from Friar John – agree that the young squire has spoken like a true Euclid or Ptolemy. As for Thomas the churl, they all say he was no fool nor possessed of a devil, but has spoken with intelligence and subtlety (ll. 2286–92).

Now, modern scholars have pointed out that this passage is a parody of the descent of the Holy Spirit as a great wind to the twelve Apostles on the day of Pentecost. Here is a slightly modernized version of the Wycliffite translation of *Acts* 2:

When the days of Pentecost were filled, all the disciples were together in one place. And suddenly there was made a sound from heaven, as of a great wind coming, and it filled all the house where they were sitting ... And all were filled with the Holy Ghost, and they began to speak in diverse languages ...[54]

By the 1390s, the Pentecost story had become caught up in the increasingly bitter debate over biblical translation. For the Wycliffites, the Pentecost wind rendered many languages comprehensible to all – God desires to communicate with everybody and therefore *Acts* 2 provides biblical authority for the translation of the Bible into English. For the orthodox church, on the other hand, the Pentecost story demonstrated just the opposite: God's desire is to communicate only through a select band of interpreters. Hence it was a cue for suppressing the translation of the Bible into English. The church establishment used the Pentecost story 'to reinforce the authority of the church'.[55]

So, by writing *The Summoner's Tale* in the heightened religio-political climate of the 1390s, Chaucer was not sitting on the fence. However he might claim that it was the churlish Summoner speaking, there would be no getting around the disrespect for orthodox teaching and the utter contempt for the mendicant orders which the tale flaunts.

What is worse, Chaucer was writing in English.

For Archbishop Arundel this would have been Chaucer's besetting sin. Not only did Chaucer hold the views he did, not only did he demonstrate disrespect for the officers of the Holy Church, not only did he pour mockery and scorn upon sacraments and icons that underpinned the authority of the church – he also wrote it all in a language that anyone could understand.

From the moment Arundel first sniffed *The Summoner's Tale*, Chaucer's card would have been well and truly marked. Perhaps when he wrote it, if he gave the Archbishop a thought at all, Chaucer must have felt himself beyond Arundel's reach – protected as he was in the late 1390s by an ever more powerful court, and finally by the exiling of the Archbishop himself.

But by 1400, the ball game had completely changed. Chaucer might have thought he was playing cricket, but suddenly he was involved in a war game – a war game in which the other side was making up the rules as it went along and using live ammunition.

THE MONK

The Monk, says Chaucer the Narrator, was a handsome man. In fact, it's almost impossible not to like him. He's such a cheery character and fond of all the things everybody likes: fine food, luxury clothing, and first-class travel – which, in those days, meant horses. Nowadays it's easy to appreciate the Monk's casual disregard for the old monastic values of abstinence, withdrawal from the world and hard work.

The Monk is not the sort of man to be confined to the cloister – he is an 'outrider', one of the brothers whose duties take him outside the monastery to deal with the extensive business matters of a rich monastic order.[56] For him the key question is not 'How shall God be served?' but 'How shall the world be served?' (*Gen. Prol.*, l. 187).

Chaucer is focusing on one of the key issues of the day: the involvement of the clergy in the affairs of the state and of the world. It was an issue which influenced the character of the nation's government and which often dominated the everyday life of ordinary people.

A Victorian interpretation of the Monk and the Friar.

The rise in the numbers and influence of the Church Commercial, the so-called 'worldly bishops' and other prelates, provoked outrage and criticism from many quarters. Of course, in one way it was not surprising that kings and lords wanted to use clerics in positions of counsel and power, since the clerics were the most educated group in society. But the critics of the Church Commercial pointed the finger at the conflict of interests implicit in serving two masters: the church and the state.[57]

The so-called 'Lollard manifesto', posted on the doors of St Paul's and of Westminster in 1395, took special aim at the 'Caesarian clergy' – the Wycliffian name for the Church Commercial. The sixth of the 'conclusions' stated: 'A king and a bishop all in one person ... make every realm out of good rule ... temporality and spirituality are two parts of Holy Church and therefore he that has taken himself to one should not meddle with the other "because no man can serve two masters"...' The manifesto therefore petitioned that all curates – both high and low – should be relieved of their temporal offices and occupy themselves solely with their spiritual affairs.[58]

No wonder that, on reading this Lollard manifesto, the Chancellor, Thomas Arundel (who at that time also happened to be Archbishop of York) rushed off to Ireland to try to spur Richard II into action against the church's critics.[59] Any assault on worldly prelates was an assault on Thomas Arundel.

Criticism like this found its intellectual roots, of course, in the writings of John Wyclif.[60] But it was not restricted to the followers of the Evil Doctor. Even the friars sometimes joined in the fray. So too did Chaucer's one-time patron,

John of Gaunt, and also his friend John Gower.[61]

In fact, Thomas Arundel must have found it extremely irksome that so few writers and intellectuals came to his aid. There *was*, of course, that elderly Benedictine monk, Uthred of Boldon (d. 1397), who actually defended men of the church participating in secular government. But that didn't exactly constitute popular support.[62]

For the most part, Arundel had to put up with smart-alecs, like Geoffrey Chaucer, having fun at his expense. 'Well,' he must have thought, 'let him enjoy himself while he can.'

THE MONK'S FINE HORSES

The keeping of fine horses adorned with costly harness and silver ornaments by supposedly abstemious men of religion had been criticized at least since the twelfth century when St Bernard of Clairvaux contrasted the pomp of riding bishops with the plight of poor men walking .[63]

But by the time Chaucer came to create *The Canterbury Tales*, the 'proud horse' theme had become so familiar in the mouths of the Wycliffite critics of the church that it had begun to be regarded as a hallmark of Lollard polemic – at least in the eyes of the orthodox. One radical writer complains that: 'Bishops and friars accuse poor men [a coded way of referring to Wyclif's followers] of saying that men of the church should not ride on such strong horses, nor use so many jewels, nor precious clothes, or delicate food ...'[64]

And little wonder, for the theme was ever upon the tongues of the Oxford radicals. Nicholas Hereford, for one, attacked the lifestyles of clerics like Chaucer's Monk. These men, railed Hereford, 'want to be called "Lord" and to ride about on fine horses'. Robert Lychlade thundered from the pulpit in 1395: 'I would lie if I said that I had never seen one abbot lead sixty horses and more in his entourage.' That same year Lychlade was expelled from Oxford for his opinions.[65]

This contemporary contrast between the humble *pedestrian* cleric and the proud *equestrian* one finds its echo in *The General Prologue* where the Monk tears around the countryside on his fine horses with his jingling harness and hounds, while Chaucer's Parson plods around his wide parish *on foot*. It suddenly looks as if this little detail is not a mere fleck of local colour.

To criticize the clergy for their fine horses and luxurious trappings had once been an orthodox commonplace, but in the hothouse of the 1390s, when the

Caesarian Clergy had taken over the seats of power, it meant criticizing the Chancellor and the Archbishop of York or (by 1396) the Archbishop of Canterbury ... for they were one and the same man. Archbishop Arundel, who rode into exile with an entourage of twenty horses, would not have taken kindly to the juxtaposition of the hunting Monk and the foot-slogging Parson. Beneath the fun and banter of Chaucer's pilgrims, the great prelate would have smelt the burning fuse of dissidence. [66]

THE CLERK OF OXFORD

Amongst this gallery of venal, sybaritic and corrupt churchmen, there are, however, two clerics of whom Chaucer clearly approves. These are the Clerk of Oxford and the Poor Parson. And what controversial choices they would have been in Chaucer's day.

The word *clerk* was applied to anyone who could read and write, so it could be applied to both students and ecclesiastics. In this case, the Clerk of Oxford is a university student. Education at Oxford or Cambridge was intended as a preparation for holy orders, but in fact many graduates did not become priests.

The attitude of many medieval conservatives towards students seems to have been rather similar to that of the British tabloid press today: they were all spongers, living the life of Riley at other people's expense. The medieval satires pictured them 'tavern-haunting, drinking and gambling, whoring, playgoing' and 'aimlessly wandering around!'[67]

Chaucer's Clerk of Oxford is a remarkable exception. He's as poor as a church-mouse, thin as his horse, and dressed in a threadbare coat. He hasn't got himself a church position, and he's not interested in a lucrative job working for the crown. He just wants to concentrate on his studies: Aristotle and logic. If he gets any money he spends it all on books and studying, though he takes time

The Clerk of Oxenford.

to pray for anyone who supports him. He doesn't parade his learning in front of less well-read mortals, but speaks only when it's necessary and no more than he needs to.

There's nothing in such a description to have set Archbishop Arundel's teeth

Oxford, hotbed of religious radicalism.

on edge – except … *Where* was this paragon of scholastic virtue studying?

Oxford was the nest of Satan, as far as Arundel was concerned. It was the hotbed of religious radicalism – 'the source and centre of intellectual religious dissent'.[68]

It had spawned the dreadful Dr Wyclif and a hydra-headed school of disciples – men like Philip Repingdon, Nicholas Hereford, John Aston and a host of others. These were men of the church who were prepared not only to countenance destruction of the church's wealth but to talk also about such terrible things openly, in public *and* in the English language!

Archbishop Arundel's predecessor, the aristocratic William Courtenay, had experienced no end of trouble with those Oxford scholars. He called the place 'the nurse of heresies'. Way back in 1377, as Bishop of London, Courtenay had had to go through that humiliating business in convocation, when he tried to discipline the ringleader of the Oxford dissidents, John Wyclif, only to have that wretched John of Gaunt threatening to drag him out of St Paul's by his hair. As soon as Courtenay came to power as Archbishop of Canterbury, he set about eradicating Wyclif and his whole bandwagon. Courtenay laid the blame for the Peasants' Revolt squarely on the Wycliffites at Oxford, and from then on he was locked in a power struggle with the university. He eventually managed to get some sort of control over it, and finally made an official visitation (in other words, an *inspection*) in 1389.[69]

In that most troublesome year of 1395, however, the university made a bid to regain its academic freedom, and obtained a papal bull giving it exemption from ecclesiastical jurisdiction. The next year, Arundel became Archbishop of Canterbury, and took up the quarrel with Oxford once more. With typical hubris, he overruled the papal bull, and rejected out of hand the 'absurd privilege of exemption'. He summoned the Chancellor of Oxford to appear before him, but – as he was announcing his decision – the Chancellor walked out on him.

This was a mistake. Archbishop Thomas Arundel was not the sort of man you walked out on – ever.[70]

From then on the quarrel was personal. Charges of Lollardy were levelled at the university once again, and within a month Arundel had Oxford on its knees. It was forced to apologize in writing to the incensed prelate, and a royal order soon followed preventing the university from having recourse to the papal bull. Shortly after the king ruled that the archbishops of Canterbury had the right to inspect Oxford whenever they felt like it – for ever.

Chaucer was writing the *The General Prologue* throughout these upheavals. The fact that he places his idealized Clerk as a student of Oxford – rather than the safer and more orthodox Cambridge – was not an accident of detail his readers could have ignored.[71]

For Archbishops Courtenay and Arundel alike, Oxford was a dissident university, the spawner of Lollardy. The Clerk of Oxenford, as an idealized figure, would have been a red rag to a bull.

THE POOR PARSON

But if Arundel found the portrait of the Clerk of Oxenford hard to swallow, the portrait of the Poor Parson would have stuck firmly in his gullet. The Poor Parson is a living rebuke to everything that a worldly bishop like Thomas Arundel represented. He is the very antithesis of Arundel's character, values and way of life.

The Poor Parson.

The Parson may be poor but he is rich in holy thought and works. He's a learned man – a clerk – and he truly teaches Christ's Gospel. He's benign and diligent and patient in adversity. He is loath to excommunicate folk because they can't pay their tithes (the tenth of their income due to the church) and he would rather give them from his own income and property. He can survive on very little. Even though his parish is a big one he walks everywhere on foot and visits the great and the humble. He teaches by setting an example and he doesn't run off to London where he could make more money singing masses for the dead in a chantry in St Paul's or getting himself hired by a guild. He is a shepherd and not a mercenary. He isn't scornful of sinners, but kind – trying to draw people to heaven by fairness – though he'd tell someone off if he thought they warranted it – be they high or low. He doesn't look for any pomp or reverence, and his conscience is clear.

> A bettre preest I trowe that nowher noon ys.
> *The General Prologue*, ll. 524
> A better priest I swear there nowhere is.

Every single item in that checklist was an affront to Archbishop Arundel's being.

Modern readers often seem disappointed with the portrait. As one of our most perceptive and influential scholars writes: 'The Parson's portrait, in comparison with those of the Monk and Friar, is like a drink of cold water after being excited and fuddled by wine; satiric ambiguities and ironic tones vanish in favour of a simple purity.'[72]

Chaucer's contemporaries would probably not have agreed. For them the Parson's portrait would have seemed like a dangerously heady cocktail of controversial ideas and contemporary issues. It was, perhaps, the most subversive portrait in the whole gallery. Thomas Arundel would certainly have considered it inflammatory and odious.

'Had Wyclif set out to versify his own ideals,' writes one of the major historians of Wycliffism, 'he could not have wished to alter any of this, [Chaucer's description of the Poor Parson].' What is more, considering that he was writing within a few years of Wyclif's death, when the controversy over his ideas was still raging, Chaucer's omissions from the Parson's portrait are as significant as his inclusions: 'There is no mention of the Parson's administration of the mass, no allusion to his role as confessor.'[73] Today's reader might pass over such omissions, but to Chaucer's immediate audience, alive to the public uproar of the times, the riots and power struggles in which church and university and a newly literate population were then engaging over these very matters, their absence would have been provocative.

Belief in the nature of the Eucharist and the manner of celebrating Mass had been made a touchstone of heresy for the orthodox inquisitors. Similarly, the act of confession and the role of the clergy as intermediaries between man and God was a cornerstone of an orthodoxy still buffeted by the continuing though weakening assault of Wycliffite brickbats. By passing over such key issues in silence, Chaucer was sailing extremely close to the wind of heresy. As James Joyce said: 'Absence is the greatest form of presence'.

Indeed, whenever the Parson appears, we hear the then current language used by and about the Wycliffites. 'Chaucer, with his acute ear for linguistic idiosyncracies ... has deliberately chosen to surround his parson with a suggestion of Wycliffism, a suggestion that no contemporary reader or listener could have missed ... To an educated Londoner in the 1390s, for whom Chaucer was writing, such language, such satire and the unabashed admiration for such ideals must have recalled Wyclif and his followers.'[74]

Certainly the other pilgrims on the road to Canterbury have no difficulty in pinning down the Parson as a Wycliffite. When the Host calls the priest to tell a tale, the Host swears by 'Goddes bones' and 'Goddes dignitee'. The Parson answers:

'Benedicite!
What eyleth the man, so synfully to swere?'
  The Epilogue of The Man of Law's Tale, ll. 1170–1
'Benedicite!
What ails the man so sinfully to swear?'

The Host is onto him in a flash!

'I smelle a Lollere in the wynd,' quod he.
'Now! goode men,' quod oure Hoste, 'Herkenneth me ...
This Lollere heer wil prechen us somwhat.'
  The Epilogue of The Man of Law's Tale, ll. 1172–4
'I smell a Lollard in the wind,' quoth he.
'Now! good men,' quoth our Host, 'Harken to me ...
This Lollard here will preach to us somewhat.'

At this point, that well-known defender of orthodox religion, the Shipman (who steals wine from his clients and has no qualms about throwing his passengers overboard) jumps in with the *Sun* reader's estimate of this newfangled doctrine – regurgitating the words he would have heard from pulpit after pulpit, as orthodox priests denounced the radical reformers.

'Nay, by my fader soule, that schal he nat!'
Seyde the Shipman, 'Heere schal he nat preche;
He schal no gospel glosen here ne teche.
We leven alle in the grete God,' quod he;
'He wolde sowen som difficulte,
Or springen cokkel in our clene corn.'
   The Epilogue of The Man of Law's Tale, ll. 1178–83
'Nay, by my father's soul, that shall he not!'
Said the Shipman, 'Here shall he not preach;
He shan't explain the gospel nor teach.
We all believe in the great God,' quoth he;
'He would sow some difficulty,
Or sprinkle cockle (a weed) in our clean corn.'

THE ORIGIN OF THE WORD 'LOLLARD'

In that last line the Shipman touches on the derivation of the word 'Lollard', from the Latin *lolium* meaning 'cockle, tares or darnel' – weeds that spring up in fields of wheat.[75]

In 1377 Pope Gregory sent a bull to the Chancellor of Oxford University berating him for allowing Wyclif the oxygen of publicity. In the communication he introduces the idea of the Wycliffites sowing *cockle* amongst the clean corn of the orthodox wheat – an image which in turn is taken from the New Testament. It is worth noting that the pope himself (or at least his scribe) spells *lolium* throughout as *lollium* (with a double *l*):

> We are obliged to wonder and lament that you ... have through some idleness and sloth permitted cockle [lollium] to spring up among the clean grain on the campus of your said illustrious school, and, what is worse, even to mature; nor, as we have heard recently, do you show any concern about the eradication of this cockle [hujus lollii] ... And what distresses us more bitterly is the fact that the growth of this cockle [lollii] is learned of in Rome before a means of extirpation has been applied in England where it was born.[76]

The chronicler Henry Knighton also spells *lollium* with a double *l*, perhaps deliberately to accentuate the wordplay. It must have been a commonplace amongst the orthodox preachers of the day.[77]

Presumably one reason for the popularity of this pun amongst the conservative sections of the clergy was that it covertly encouraged the idea of burning such heretics, for the parable as told by St Matthew concludes: 'I will tell the reapers: "Gather the darnel first, and tie it in bundles for burning".'[78]

Had Henry Knighton read *The General Prologue* (which is just possible), he might even have felt he could identify the Poor Parson. The Parson's habit of trudging around the countryside on foot would have reminded the chronicler of one of Wyclif's followers, whom in the mid 1380s Knighton described thus:

> The renowned Master John Aston, disregarding bodily ease, rejected the use of a horse, and went about on foot, walking with a staff, tirelessly visiting churches all over the kingdom with his phial of poison, lest harnessing a horse, or taking time to feed it, should delay his journey or distract his mind from the work he had undertaken. Thus rather, like a dog springing up from rest, ready to bark at the slightest sound, he sped on his way, a busy and contentious bee always ready for argument.[79]

The Poor Parson's foot-slogging habits put him at the opposite pole from the finely horsed Monk, but he should also be seen in apposition to the Friar. The Parson is in many ways more of a mendicant than that mendicant himself. He certainly lives out St Francis's Rule more closely than the Friar – whose sybaritic lifestyle dishonours that ideal. The portrait of the Friar rings with the language of commerce: 'good pitaunce', 'silver', 'profit', 'al with riche', and 'purchas', while the Poor Parson's is rooted in the ideal of apostolic poverty: 'povre Persoun', 'riche ... of hooly thoght and werk', 'povre parisshens', 'in litle thyng have suffisauce'.

St Francis insisted that his community follow and imitate the life of Christ and his apostles, and that is precisely what the Parson does. How different from the Friar and the Monk and the Prioress, but how different, too, from a Caesarian cleric like Arundel!

The Parson's qualities are further enhanced by association with his brother – a man of the soil, the Ploughman. The very occupation of ploughman had acquired at this time a whole counterpoint of social and spiritual significance – mainly through the prestige of Piers Plowman, the hero of William Langland's eponymous poem.

ARCHBISHOP ARUNDEL AND THE POOR PARSON

As Archbishop Arundel listened to or read Chaucer's description of his ideal priest, he would have found himself staring at an image that was the exact opposite of himself.

The Parson gladly embraced poverty, while Arundel's whole life had been one of luxury and wealth. Indeed, he had used the church and therefore the tithes of poor parishioners to achieve that luxury and wealth. The Poor Parson 'waited after no pomp and reverence', whereas those two elements were inextricable from Arundel's lifestyle. The Poor Parson scorns the commercial mechanics of the church, in which generous remuneration rewards those who desert their parishes and dedicate themselves to singing for the souls of the dead in well-endowed chantries in St Paul's, or who attach themselves to tradesmen's guilds in London. Such scorn for the basic financial traffic of the church would have touched Arundel where it hurt him most.

Tithe barns needed to be big.

So too would the Parson's lamentably cavalier attitude to the payment of tithes. Archbishop Arundel would have been scandalized by his reluctance to excommunicate his parishioners for failure to pay their tithes. For goodness sake! Such behaviour was a direct threat to the whole financial structure of the church. Tithes were what its wealth was based on. It was only the church's critics who attacked them. The Wycliffites said that tithes need not be given to clerics who were in a state of sin. John Ball said that tithes need not be paid by someone whose income was less than the priest to whom the money was supposedly due.

Yet here was the Poor Parson not only avoiding excommunicating the church's debtors but even preferring to give away his own worldly goods to the needy!

> Ful looth were hym to cursen for his tithes,
> But rather wolde he yeven, out of doute,
> Unto his povre parisshens aboute ...
> *The General Prologue*, ll. 486–8

Full loath were him to curse to get his tithes
But rather would he give, without a doubt,
Unto his poor parishioners about ...

Heavens above! If everyone started doing that, the church would be reduced
to apostolic poverty in no time!

Arundel would also have been alive to the Parson's readiness to quote from
the Gospels:

He was also a lerned man, a clerk,
That Cristes gospel trewely wolde preche ...
This noble ensample to his sheep he yaf,
That first he wroghte, and afterward he taughte.
Out of the gospel he tho wordes caughte ...
But Cristes loore and his apostles twelve
He taughte, but first he folwed it hymselve.
    The General Prologue, ll. 480–1, 496–8, 527–8
He was also a learned man, a clerk,
That Christ's Gospel truly would preach ...
The noble example to his sheep he gave,
That first he acted, and afterwards he taught.
Out of the Gospel he those words had caught ...
But Christ's law and his apostles twelve
He taught, but first he followed it himself.

Within a few years, Arundel was to make mere knowledge of the Bible an
indicator of heresy.[80] Even in the 1390s access to biblical material was being hotly
contested. The Prologue to the Wycliffite translation of the Bible, possibly written
at the same time that Chaucer was painting his portrait of a perfect parson, tells
us that knowledge of Holy Writ is a dangerous business if you don't happen to
be a learned cleric:

Though covetous clerics are mad by reason of simony, heresy, and many other
sins, and despise and stop Holy Writ as much as they can, yet the unlearned people
cry after Holy Writ, to know it and keep it, with great cost and peril of their life.[81]

What is more, the Parson's emphasis on the Gospels (Matthew, Mark, Luke
and John) rather than the Bible as a whole, and his insistence on the supremacy

of 'Christ's law' rather than the church's, would have rung another warning bell in Archbishop Arundel's mind – for hadn't Wyclif himself held that 'the core of the Divine message was to be found within the four Evangelists', and didn't his followers stress the duty of preaching the Gospels as opposed to the whole length of the Bible? Wasn't that why Wyclif was sometimes known as *Doctor Evangelicus*?[82]

The Parson's emphasis (in the *The General Prologue*) on man's relationship to God and to the Gospels would have seemed to short-circuit the role of the clergy, who over the centuries had devised an elaborate system of offices, sacraments and services to translate God's Scripture into messages which only *they* could pass on to the laity.

Chaucer may have felt pretty safe in the 1390s in making his Parson such an exemplary and subversive figure, but the events of 1399 were to turn it into a high-risk undertaking. Once Arundel returned to power, he was not likely to tolerate the criticisms of Caesarian clergy like himself, implied in the portrait of the Poor Parson.

ARUNDEL AND CHAUCER

In short, Archbishop Arundel would have found plenty in *The Canterbury Tales* to object to. And it's not surprising. Chaucer 'was part of the same fourteenth-century literary scene that included the authors of the religious texts Arundel sought to suppress'.[83] *The Canterbury Tales* were 'crucially pre-Arundelian' because they plunged into the treacherous waters of contemporary religious controversy, and they made waves that rocked the boat of the established church in the plain sight of all. And that, to Thomas Arundel, would have been the final straw. Chaucer was making the church a laughing-stock – was making *him*, Archbishop Arundel, a laughing-stock – and doing so in the language of the common people.

Once Thomas Arundel had his grip on the reins of power, he set about prohibiting biblical translation and unauthorized quotation, he forbade public criticism of the clergy and set limits on the discussion of theological ideas. All of these prohibitions Chaucer had transgressed as a matter of course throughout *The Canterbury Tales*. But by 1400, England had undergone a sea change. As the *Cambridge History of Medieval Literature* observes: 'Lines that read wittily in the 1370s might seem problematical in the 1380s and perilous ten years later.'[84]

We have no evidence that Arundel chose to suppress Chaucer's work, but it would be most surprising if he hadn't wanted to.

He suppressed vast quantities of other material – why shouldn't he have tried to suppress *The Canterbury Tales*? Nor would it be surprising if he didn't totally succeed. There must have been many enthusiasts and admirers of Chaucer's work – ready to risk concealing whatever they could. There must have been noble families like the DeVeres, who probably owned one of the earliest and best manuscripts of the *Tales*, who would have been able to maintain copies of valued manuscripts without investigation.

Perhaps if Arundel had succeeded in confining *The Canterbury Tales* to the houses of the nobility, he would have considered that sufficient. At least he would have removed them from the reach of the general public. He would then have been able to get on with his business of tightening control on the minds and reading habits of learned clerks without the threat of an opposition rallying around a counter-culture such as Chaucer provided.

And if Arundel *did* wish to suppress *The Canterbury Tales*, the one thing he could have done was strike at its core – because that was near to hand in London. He could have confiscated Chaucer's manuscripts of his work-in-progress as easily as he called in other works to assess for heresy, or as easily as Henry called in the chronicles. The disappearance of Chaucer himself from the scene – whether from natural causes or foul play – would have made the disposal of the manuscripts a foregone conclusion.

As we shall see in the next chapter, the available evidence of the manuscripts that remain makes such a scenario at least possible – if not probable.

CHAPTER 12

What happened to Chaucer's work?

~

Henry's 'program of official forgetfulness' looks, in practice, more like a programme of wholesale obliteration.[1] When something has been obliterated, of course, it is always hard – often impossible – to assess what has been lost. When it's gone, it's gone. But there is no reason why we should be generous to Henry. He disrupted the peaceful succession of the crown with an illegal and dishonourable grab for power. He falsified the record, rewrote history and tried to erase much of the past. Why should we give him the benefit of the doubt?

THE DESTRUCTION OF RICHARD'S COURT
AND THE MISSING ROYAL LIBRARY

The few clues that have survived the violence of the usurpation suggest a deliberate vandalism designed to destroy the cultural achievements of Richard's court. Whether this destruction was achieved through direct orders from the usurper, or whether it was undertaken by individuals who were fearful of any association with the previous regime, the result was the same.

'Conscious efforts were made to eradicate the king's [Richard's] memorial presence from English culture after 1399.'[2] We find portrait after portrait of Richard defaced or removed. In the famous picture of Chaucer reading *Troilus and Criseyde* to the court, Richard's face has been obliterated. Richard has also been effaced from a portrait in the book of geomancy which

Richard II's face has been effaced.

he commissioned and owned. And when the portrait of Richard that hangs in Westminster Abbey was taken down for repairs in 1866, it was discovered that the portrait 'had been wantonly mutilated by hacking as if with an adze or hatchet'.[3]

At Warwick Castle, Henry IV destroyed the white hart emblems which the king's half-brother, Thomas Holland, Duke of Surrey, had set upon the gates. Of course this may simply have been normal practice, since it is exactly what Roger Walden did to Arundel's banners and emblems when he moved into Lambeth Palace, and, indeed, exactly what Arundel did to Roger Walden's when he returned.

Perhaps more interesting for our investigation is the possibility that Richard's library might have been deliberately destroyed. The fact that there are few survivals from his library is not unusual – no royal libraries from before the time of Edward IV have survived intact or in any quantity but the disappearance from the record of books which we know were in his possession only a few years before the usurpation might suggest a wilful destruction of the collection. In 1395, the French chronicler Jean Froissart describes how, while he was staying at Richard's palace in Eltham, he presented a book of his love poems to the king:

> I presented it to him in his chamber, for I had it with me, and laid it on his bed. He opened it and looked into it with much pleasure. He ought to have been pleased, for it was handsomely written and illuminated, and bound in crimson velvet, with ten silver-gilt studs, and roses of the same in the middle, with two large clasps of silver-gilt, richly worked with roses in the centre.[4]

It is not necessarily surprising that the book no longer exists – anything could have happened to it in the last 600 years – but what seems strange is that there is no further record of such a valuable item. It just disappears. If it had been stolen and then given to someone else, we would expect it to turn up in a will or in library records, but it doesn't. If it was in Richard's possession in 1395, one might expect it to have been still in his possession four years later, but there is no mention of it. The possibility remains that it was destroyed deliberately along with the rest of Richard's library.

Another book which we know must have been in Richard's possession is a panegyric composed by John of Gaunt's confessor, Richard Maidstone. It commemorated the great pageant that celebrated the restoration of good relations between the king and the Commons of London after their quarrel in 1392.[5] We would surely have expected the records of such an important occasion to have been carefully preserved in the royal library, and the fact that it too disappeared at this time must be at least suspicious.

Of course, it's hard to draw definite conclusions from the fact that things aren't there. That's precisely why usurpers destroy the evidence of former regimes in the first place. But the testimony of Richard's missing royal library is reinforced by the fact that other literature, composed within Richard's court, also seems to have disappeared shortly after the court's destruction.

One of Richard's best-loved chamber knights, Sir John Montagu, Earl of Salisbury, composed balades, songs, rondeaux and lays. Christine de Pisan, who knew him so well that she entrusted the care of her son to him, called Montagu: a 'humble, sweet and courteous' man, 'a gracious knight, lover of writing, and himself a graceful writer'.[6] The Lancastrians, however, seem to have found him particularly obnoxious, and the chronicler Walsingham writes him off as 'the friend of Lollards, the derider of images, the scoffer at sacraments' who got his just deserts at the hands of the mob and died 'miserably, refusing the sacraments'.[7] Perhaps it is little wonder that none of his verse survives.

Christine de Pisan writing in her study.

Similarly Sir John Clanvowe, another favourite chamber knight of Richard's, a friend of Chaucer's and a poet of some note, is represented by only one poem, *The Boke of Cupide,* and yet we can be pretty sure he wrote more. Even with *The Boke of Cupide,* no manuscript survives from Richard's reign, and the poem is preserved in just five mid- to late-fifteenth century manuscripts, all associated with Chaucer.[8] The lack of manuscripts of Clanvowe's work, or of Montagu's poetry or – come to that – of the *Gawain* poet's in isolation would mean nothing, but when taken together a pattern emerges that is suggestive of a policy of deliberate destruction. Given the context of the usurpation and the determination of the usurper to obliterate the glories of the former regime, such a policy would not be surprising.

It has been suggested that one of the main factors in the destruction of these poets' works was the fact that they were so closely associated with Richard's court, and that this might also apply to Chaucer: 'The haphazard preservation of his lyrics and even the important dream-vision poems suggest that courtly connections may have worked against their survival when the court in question, Richard II's, suffered such a catastrophic reversal of fortunes.'[9]

We have already seen that Archbishop Arundel would have been extremely hostile to the collection of tales on which Chaucer was then currently engaged. He would have had no interest whatsoever in the protection of Chaucer's text. It now appears that Henry too, although perhaps not antipathetic to Chaucer himself, had no desire to preserve the culture of the previous regime. Indeed, he went out of his way to destroy all trace of it. The destruction of the most renowned cultural icon from Richard's court would have fitted in with his overall strategy. Both king and archbishop would have had their reasons for obliterating Chaucer's output.

Perhaps they tried to do just that.

WERE CHAUCER'S MANUSCRIPTS DESTROYED?

It is a curious fact that none of Chaucer's poetry survives in a manuscript written by his own hand during his lifetime. One might have thought that when such a renowned author died, someone would have made great efforts to preserve his collected manuscripts.

What is even more curious, however, is that until recently it has been generally accepted that no manuscript of his poetry copied by *anybody* during his lifetime has survived. If this is so then it is a remarkable situation. We have manuscripts of Langland, Gower, Lydgate, Hoccleve, Boccaccio, Petrarch, Deschamps, Machaut – all either in the author's own hand or dating from his lifetime. But there are none of Chaucer's.

Some manuscripts of Chaucer's prose works – the *Treatise on the Astrolabe* and his translation of *Boece* – were 'almost certainly' copied before 1400, judging from the style of their handwriting and decoration.[10] And it has even been suggested that a comparatively recently discovered manuscript, *The Equatorie of the Planetis,* is actually in Chaucer's own hand, but the jury is still out on the matter, and the editor of *The Riverside Chaucer,* for one, decided against it.[11] In any case the survival of two or even three prose treaties contemporaneous with a great poet seems surprisingly little – especially in comparison with the survival rate of manuscripts attributed to his contemporaries.

Gower and Langland both left behind manuscripts of their poems created during their lifetimes. There are two copies of Gower's *Confessio Amantis* from the late fourteenth century and two dated 1400. Of Gower's Latin works, three manuscripts are dated *c.* 1400 and two 1408 (the year of Gower's death). It is

Chaucer from the Ellesmere MS.

also likely that two manuscripts of *Piers Plowman* are pre-1400 and therefore date before the likely year of their author's death.[12]

So we have contemporaneous manuscripts of Langland's poems and a number of Gower's, at least one of which, it has been argued, bears corrections in his own hand. It is clear that copies of Chaucer's poetry were circulating during his lifetime, but none have survived.[13] Why on earth not?

Recently, however, some scholars have proposed a pre-1400 date for the earliest manuscript of *The Canterbury Tales*, known as the Hengwrt. Kathleen Scott has closely examined the border of the Hengwrt MS and concluded that the decoration should be dated *c.* 1395–1400. She adds: 'the implication is of course that Hengwrt was made before the death of Chaucer'. Whilst the illumination of the second earliest manuscript of *The Canterbury Tales* she brings forward to 1400–05 with the implication that work must have begun on the manuscript before then.[14]

Opening of 'The General Prologue' from the Hengwrt MS.

Following on from Kathleen Scott's work, Estelle Stubbs, the editor of *The Hengwrt Chaucer Digital Facsimile* (on CD-ROM), speculates that Chaucer himself may even have had a hand in supervising the early production stages of the Hengwrt. She also points out that the hands of the two scribes who copied out the Hengwrt resemble those of the clerks in the Privy Seal Office at Westminster and that Chaucer would have had access to the Office.[15]

But even if both the Hengwrt and the Ellesmere manuscripts were, indeed, begun (neither was completed) while Chaucer was alive, this is still a remarkably low survival rate of texts from an author's lifetime.

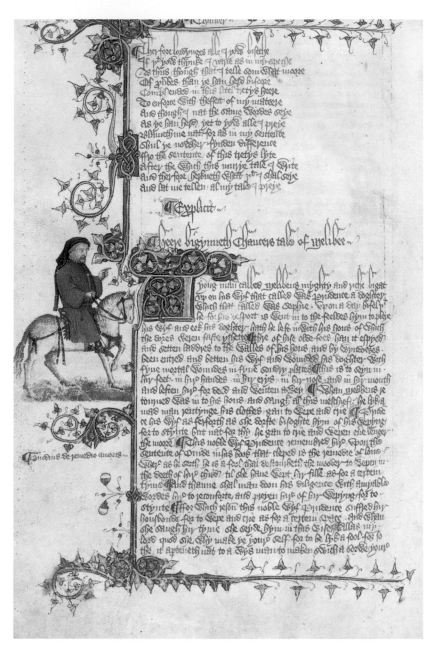

The Ellesmere MS.

Why should this be?

Two solutions are usually offered. The first is that Chaucer was diffident about publishing his material and that once it had been written down and read out he cared little about it. The second is that before 1400 the English language lacked prestige and that it was Henry IV and his son Henry V who encouraged English as a deliberate royal policy to engage the support of parliament and the English citizenry for a questionable usurpation of the throne.[16]

Neither of these propositions seems very satisfactory. We have already seen (see p.35 above) that Richard II cultivated the vernacular as a prestigious language in line with royal policy throughout the courts of Europe. A counter-movement, however, sprang up in ecclesiastical circles as English began to be associated with the spread of criticism of the church. The return to power of Archbishop Arundel in 1399 and the usurper's reliance on that powerful and autocratic prelate ensured the supremacy of the anti-vernacular forces, but only for as long as Arundel lived.

What is more, as we shall argue later, the revival of Chaucer's reputation seems to have owed nothing to Henry IV but everything to his son, the Prince of Wales, and his attempts to seize power from his father and Arundel (see pages 259 ff. below).

So what about the other proposition, that Chaucer was diffident about publishing his work?

THE MYSTERY OF CHAUCER'S OWN COPY OF 'THE CANTERBURY TALES'

Scholars seem to agree that when the first manuscripts of *The Canterbury Tales* were copied there was no definitive authorial text available to copy from. Charles Owen writes: 'What the manuscripts tell us is not of one copy text, preserved in a single volume, available to scribes and editors in the years immediately following Chaucer's death. Rather it is of a collection of fragments, tales and groups of tales, reflecting the different stages of a developing plan for the whole work.'[17]

Ralph Hanna points out that this means that none of the surviving manuscripts can offer us a definitive order for the tales: 'none of the tale orders we have received necessarily reflects Chaucer's plan (if indeed he had arrived at one); rather, they are evidence of the difficulties manuscript supervisors had trying to make a text left manifestly incomplete at its author's death look like a continuous whole (see Owen 1982).'[18]

Charles Owen suggests that the *Tales* were circulated exclusively in booklet format and that, since these booklets were relatively insubstantial, they failed to survive the wear and tear of readers down the centuries. This would certainly help to explain the lack of contemporary manuscripts of the complete *Canterbury Tales*, even if it leaves *Troilus* and the other major poems unaccounted for.

Owen's final conclusion, however, is more debatable. He suggests that Chaucer *himself* did not compile and keep his own authorial collection of *The Canterbury Tales* – otherwise it would have been used by the early compilers.[19]

But it is one thing to establish that an authorial copy-text was not available to the compilers of the earliest surviving manuscripts, and quite another to assume that there therefore *was* no authorial copy of the text at all. If an authorial text did indeed exist, or had existed, but was unavailable to a scribe such as the Hengwrt scribe, so shortly after (or even so shortly *before*) Chaucer's death, one may rightly ask the question: what happened to it?

It is difficult to imagine that Chaucer himself would not have kept at least one up-to-date collection of his own tales – even if just for his own satisfaction. What author doesn't? Besides, he was one of the few poets to record his concern for the preservation of his work:

Adam scriveyn, if ever it thee bifalle
Boece or Troylus for to wryten newe,
Under thy long lokkes thou most have the scalle,
But after my makyng thow wryte more trewe;
So ofte adaye I mot thy werk renewe,
It to correcte and eke to rubbe and scrape,
And al is thorugh thy negligence and rape.
  Chaucers wordes unto Adam, his owne scriveyn
Adam, scribe, if ever it befalls you
Boethius or Troilus for to write out anew,
Under your long locks, may you have the scabs,
If you don't copy out my writing more true;
So often every day I must your work renew,
To correct and also to rub and scrape
And all is through your negligence and haste.

Chaucer was, by his own account, a careful, exacting author. Could he really have been the sort of artist who would have been content to cast his masterwork to the wind in the form of insubstantial booklets and nothing else?

> Go, litel bok, go, litel myn tragedye,
> Ther God thi makere yet, er that he dye,
> So sende myght to make in som comedye!
> But litel book, no makyng thow n'envie,
> But subgit be to alle poesye;
> And kis the steppes where as thow seest pace
> Virgile, Ovide, Omer, Lucan, and Stace.
>
> And for there is so gret diversite
> In Englissh and in writyng of oure tonge,
> So prey I God that non myswrite the,
> Ne the mysmetre for defaute of tonge;
> And red wherso thow be, or elles songe,
> That thow be understonde, God I biseche!
>   *Troilus and Criseyde*, ll. 1786–98
> Go little book, go, my little tragedy,
> May God yet send your author before he dies
> The power to create some comedy!
> But little book, don't go vying with other poems
> But be humble before all Poetry:
> And kiss the steps where you see pace
> Virgil, Ovid, Homer, Lucan and Statius.
>
> And because there is so great a diversity
> In English and in the writing of our tongue,
> So I prey to God that none miswrite thee,
> Nor ruin your metre through faulty language;
> And wherever you are read, or else are sung,
> I beseech God that you may be understood.

It is hard to credit the author of these lines (for all their conventional content and debt to Boccaccio) with having a cavalier attitude to his text. Besides, can we really believe that a writer who had embarked on a work with such a complex framework as *The Canterbury Tales* would not have preserved the elements together for final assembly at some happy future date? Even if he didn't give a hoot about his life's masterwork, he'd surely need to keep the growing pile of tales and links beside him for reference. Otherwise how on earth would he have remembered who'd said what to whom or where they were in the journey or even how many tales they'd each told?

The question is even more puzzling in view of the fact that, by Chaucer's day, the preservation of an authorial collection had become *de rigueur* for any

self-respecting writer.[20] Since at least the mid-fourteenth century authors had begun to assert themselves as identifiable and individual voices – they had thrown off the cloak of anonymity, and were actively embracing the fame of authorship. Alongside this new assertiveness there naturally developed a need to compile and preserve an authorial collection which would act as the foundation stone of that fame.

The Man of Law.

The trend had perhaps started in Italy and was taken up by the French writers. Chaucer himself follows suit on several occasions in his own work – identifying himself, listing his works and sometimes commenting ironically on his fame and obsession.

Chaucer even has one of his pilgrims, the Man of Law, refer to his creator's fame and obsession:

'... But nathelees, certeyn,
I kan right now no thrifty tale seyn
That Chaucer, thogh he kan but lewedly
On metres and on rymyng craftily,
Hath seyd hem in swich Englissh as he kan
Of old tyme, as knoweth many a man;
And if he have noght seyd hem, leve brother,
In o book, he hath seyd hem in another.'
  Introduction to The Man of Law's Tale, ll. 45–52
'... But nevertheless, for certain,
I cannot tell a suitable tale right now
That Chaucer, though he knows but little
About metre and clever rhyming,

Has not told them in such English as he knows
Long ago, as many a man knows;
And if he has not said them, dear brother,
In one book he has said them in another.'

Chaucer clearly identifies himself with the new tradition of assertive authorship. Why would he have stopped short of making his own authorial compilation?

All the writers with whom Chaucer most identified took great care to preserve their output: Dante, Boccaccio, Petrarch, Guillaume de Machaut, Froissart, Eustache Deschamps all deliberately preserved their work and compiled authorial collections which they guarded jealously. In a manuscript dating from around 1350, Machaut sought to commemorate his own poetic achievement by compiling a book complete with a list of contents headed: 'Behold the order that G. de Machaut wants there to be in his book.'[21] Gower did the same, and his constant revisions and production of new manuscripts are so voluminous that it has been suggested that he must have had a whole scriptorium working under his direction. And, of course, he is represented on his tomb with his head resting on his three books – his claim to immortality in this world.

It seems inconceivable that Chaucer would not have taken meticulous care of his own work. Not only was it the literary fashion, it was also common sense. No author spends long hours reading and translating material which he then tosses away. If that is true today – how much more so in the days before mechanical reproduction. How could he not

John Gower. His head rests on his three books: one in Latin, one in French and one in English.

have made an authorial compilation? He was, by his own confession, first and foremost a translator and 'a compilator' (as he calls himself in his introduction to *A Treatise on the Astrolabe*).[22] What would be the point of compiling and translating the books of foreign authors, if he did not both publish and preserve them? Chaucer *must* have had an authorial collection.

Some scholars have speculated that perhaps Chaucer wrote his rough drafts on wax tablets, such as were used in schools, and then had his scribe write out fair copies.[23] It has even been suggested that this is the process that is being described in *Chaucers wordes unto Adam, his owne scriveyn*. But it has to be said that there is nothing in that short verse to suggest that Chaucer is referring to anything other than the normal production of copies for private circulation. Moreover it is hard to imagine any writer using such a limiting medium as wax tablets, capable of carrying no more than twenty or thirty lines at a time, for such ambitious and often lengthy works as *Troilus and Criseyde*, the *Melibee* or *The Knight's Tale*. Besides even if that had been the process, it still meant he had an authorial copy – albeit not in his own hand – so what happened to it?

Of course, as far as *The Canterbury Tales* was concerned even Chaucer's authorial collection would not have contained the complete poem, because when Chaucer died it was still a work-in-progress. Some scholars have suggested that Chaucer had decided to finish it off, however, because he gives such an air of finality to *The Parson's Prologue* and *Tale*.[24] But even if he had chosen this tale as his ending, it doesn't mean he wasn't intending to write others. There is no reason to suppose that he was writing in strict chronological order.

If he had decided to use *The Parson's Tale* as his finale, he'd naturally give it an air of finality, but we shouldn't let that deceive us into thinking he had done with the whole enterprise.

Of course, it's also possible that *The Parson's Tale* was indeed, by chance, the last thing that Chaucer wrote, even though he was intending to go back and insert more stories and treatises into the framework. Perhaps something interrupted him.

DOES THE HENGWRT MARK CHAUCER'S DEATH?

In fact, we have good evidence that this is exactly what happened. In both the Hengwrt and the Ellesmere MSS, there is a clear break in the copying of the texts. The scribe begins to transcribe *The Cook's Tale* but only gets to line 58 before he stops abruptly. However, in both cases he leaves space in the manuscript in the expectation that he will be receiving further copy.

Now it could have been that the scribe simply assumed that there was more copy to come when there wasn't. Maybe Chaucer had got bored with *The Cook's Tale* and decided to abandon it. But there is no evidence that Chaucer was bored with the tale. And the *Tale* itself promises to be anything but boring – most readers finish the 58 existing lines with more than a passing interest in what Perkyn Revelour is going to get up to with his friend's promiscuous wife who keeps a shop for appearances' sake, but really makes her living out of sex.[25]

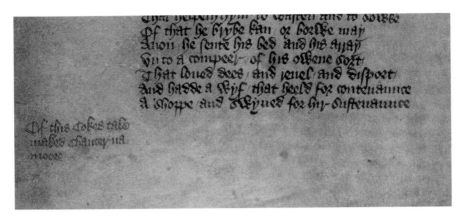

The moment Chaucer died? The unfinished 'Cook's Tale'.

Besides, a scenario in which the scribe did not know that Chaucer had already abandoned the *Tale* would imply a lack of communication between the scribe and Chaucer. Whereas the latest research suggests the opposite: that there was good communication, if not with Chaucer himself then with whoever was supplying the texts to be copied.[26] That supervising presence would have known if *The Cook's Tale* was a false start.

There again, if Chaucer himself *was* involved in supplying the material but had not yet finished composing *The Cook's Tale*, why would he have gone to the expense of having it copied? What author in his right mind would start having a fair copy made of something he hasn't yet finished? Beginnings have a nasty habit of needing revision in the light of endings.

And then, suppose Chaucer had abandoned *The Cook's Tale* – why on earth would he have wanted to have the little bit he'd written copied? Who wants an aborted project like that hanging around on public display as a permanent reminder of one's failed inspiration? It simply wouldn't make sense.

If Chaucer was indeed involved in some way with the production of the Hengwrt up to the end of *The Cook's Tale*, and if he supplied the scribe with the opening section, then it seems reasonable to assume that he must have completed *The Cook's Tale*.

So what happened to it?

Could it be that the abrupt ending marks the moment at which Chaucer disappeared from the scene? This is certainly what the editor of *The Hengwrt Chaucer Digital Facsimile* imagines to have happened. She further conjectures that Chaucer's death may also have 'caused the break in continuity in the copying and illumination of the Ellesmere'.[27]

So what if whatever caused Chaucer to disappear also caused his authorial collection to disappear at the same time – taking with it the remainder of the as yet uncopied *Cook's Tale*? Wouldn't that explain why the copyist of the Hengwrt and Ellesmere started the *Tale*, left room for its completion, but never completed it?

We are thus presented with a third possibility to explain the shortage of contemporaneous Chaucer manuscripts – and given the political circumstances at the time Chaucer died it seems a pretty obvious one. As we have seen, Henry IV and Archbishop Arundel were both busy suppressing and controlling the written word, each for his own particular ends, so why would they have stopped short of suppressing the words of the most famous poet of the previous regime? When the usurper and his henchman were determined to obliterate the material legacy of Richard's court, why would they have refrained from suppressing the work of the poet who – more than anyone else – epitomised the spirit of that court? Moreover, why should Archbishop Arundel have turned a blind eye to a writer who had held the church hierarchy up to such withering ridicule as had Chaucer?

Could it be that the core of Chaucer's manuscripts was deliberately destroyed?

Against this hypothesis is the fact that in the margin of the Hengwrt MS one of the scribes wrote: 'Of this Cokes tale maked Chaucer namoore.' It seems a pretty definite and well-informed statement. On the other hand, judging from the differences in the inks used for the comment and the main text, the comment appears to have been inserted at a later date – probably many years later – during the final stages of the manuscript's compilation.[28] It may therefore be less literally accurate than it sounds – a shorthand version of what happened. In any case, the truth by then may well have been politically sensitive and not something any scribe would wish to put down in writing during dangerous times: 'Of this Cokes tale maked Chaucer an end but sothe is he disappeared and his manuscript too ...'

One thing seems clear from all the latest research on the Hengwrt and the Ellesmere: the abrupt end to *The Cook's Tale* marks a major disruption in the production of both manuscripts. In the Ellesmere, for example, the decoration suddenly undergoes a radical change. One particular artist is replaced by another, and another painter – who may have been the master limner (or illuminator) all but ceases to work on the project.[29] In the Hengwrt the copying ceases to have the guiding hand of the supervisor (who may or may not have been Chaucer) and the ordering of the tales becomes somewhat confused.

All of this suggests that whatever happened to Chaucer was sudden and unlooked for.

THE DESTRUCTION OF CHAUCER'S OEUVRE?

If Chaucer's own compilation of his works had simply disappeared sometime in the last six hundred years, there would be little to say on the subject. But the fact is that the earliest manuscripts of *The Canterbury Tales* appear to have been assembled in their initial stages from the best texts and under authoritative supervision, but later in their production to have been cobbled together piecemeal from something less than an authorial compilation. This suggests that Chaucer's own manuscripts were missing at the time of his death or shortly after. If this is so, something drastic must have happened to such valuable and precious things. They must have been lost or destroyed – either by accident or on purpose.

Given Chaucer's fame and social standing at the time of his death, it is hardly conceivable that his authorial collection could have evaporated into thin air overnight. When a famous man of letters dies today, there are always ardent readers, agents, executors or relatives anxious to preserve his literary estate. How much more important would it have been then, in the fourteenth century, when the very books themselves were such prized objects. An author's manuscript wasn't valuable just as an object of interest – it was an asset to be passed on, to be inscribed in wills, a thing to be given to kings and emperors. No one in the fourteenth century would have casually thrown away a pile of manuscripts because the author had passed on.

A scenario in which Chaucer's works came under threat might also explain the apparent haste with which the later sections of the Hengwrt MS appear to have been transcribed: 'There are obvious signs of haste in the writing ... in the course of some pieces ... after careful opening stretches, which suggest that, while eager to maintain a high standard where it would be most noticeable ... he [the scribe] was not at indefinite leisure to do the copying deliberately.'[30]

Perhaps the pressure came from trying to create (possibly in secret) as complete a record of the master's work as possible, before the agents of destruction could obliterate the entire canon?

WHO MIGHT HAVE DESTROYED CHAUCER'S MSS?

If Chaucer's authorial collection was, indeed, destroyed around the time of his death, we do not have to look far for the perpetrators. As we have seen, both Archbishop Arundel and the usurper Henry IV would have had their reasons for wanting it out of the way. The fact that so few manuscripts of the poetry that Chaucer could have held in his own hands exist today may be an indication, not that Chaucer's work was uncirculated during his lifetime, but that the censors and political agents succeeded in eradicating a good portion of it.

If this surmise is correct, one might further speculate that admirers of his poetry would have done what they could to preserve whatever was left. The compilers of the Hengwrt were clearly doing their best to produce a definitive text – until their supervisor ceased to be involved. Then it looks as if suddenly work was carried out against the clock, and from scraps and booklets as they came to hand.

Might it be too fanciful to imagine that John Lydgate could have slipped a reference to the destruction of Chaucer's authorial manuscript into his *Troy Book*, when he talks there of Chaucer's 'boke *that is left be-hynde*'? Could he be implying that, although Chaucer's own pages were destroyed, yet the work survived, in a copy like the Hengwrt? Of course it's most likely that Lydgate was reaching for a rhyme, or that he simply meant: 'Chaucer may be dead but he is survived by his poetry.' None the less it is a curious

John Lydgate as a Canterbury pilgrim.

line – with the tantalizing possibility that it could – just – be an allusion to the disappearance of Chaucer's works at the same time as the poet himself vanished.[31]

And perhaps it is no coincidence that the work (in English, French and Latin) of John Gower survived in manuscripts 'often significantly grander ... larger in format, on finer vellum, with more elaborate layout and decoration, often carried out according to a systematic model'[32] whilst Chaucer's masterpieces went underground – preserved only in booklets or in unfinished, unbound manuscripts such as the Hengwrt – hidden away in a drawer and left untended long enough for the vellum to have been gnawed on by rats.[33] But then Gower was prepared to eulogize the new regime, to eradicate the past from his work and to toe the line of the new political correctness ...

If the usurping regime decided to eradicate Chaucer's works, is it possible that they also took it upon themselves to eradicate the man?

They would have been careful to leave no evidence, and we should not expect any. There is no evidence that Richard II came to a sticky end, but we're pretty sure he did; all we can do is surmise from the circumstantial details that surround the king's disappearance. In Chaucer's case we can say almost the same thing. There is no evidence of foul play, but there are many circumstantial details that build up a picture of a man in the wrong place at the wrong time (see Chapter 15).

Did 'they' take his manuscripts and destroy them? The history of the Hengwrt MS suggests a hurried attempt to complete the manuscript and then a long period of neglect – until safer times, perhaps, when Chaucer's name was once more revived.

And the Ellesmere? We have proof that tampering fingers were laid upon this most elegantly finished of Chaucerian manuscripts.

CHAPTER 13

How the Ellesmere MS was censored

~

We may not be able to prove beyond a shadow of doubt that Chaucer's own copy of *The Canterbury Tales* was deliberately destroyed, but we can say categorically that one of the earliest and most famous manuscripts of it was censored – probably soon after 1407.

Recent microscopic analysis shows that significant changes were made to the Ellesmere manuscript – possibly around the time that Archbishop Arundel was stamping on all criticism of the church and outlawing the English language as a medium for theological debate. We do not know why the owners (or someone else) went to the expense (and possible risk) of having it altered. But is it possible that, along with its author, the Ellesmere manuscript in its original form was once thought to be dangerous material?

The Ellesmere MS is celebrated for its illuminations – particularly for the miniature portraits of the Canterbury pilgrims affixed to the beginnings of their tales. In 2001, the Huntington Library, where the Ellesemere

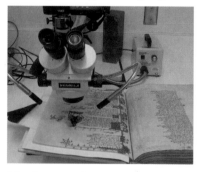

*The Ellesmere under the microscope.
It is open at The Monk's Tale.*

manuscript is housed today, very kindly allowed us to make a microscopic examination of these famous images. Two of the miniatures have been tampered with. And most probably a third has, as well.

Two of the altered images are of religious figures – the worldly Monk and the harp-playing Friar – and it's easy to see why such anti-clerical caricatures might have been considered problematical, during those perilous years of Archibishop Arundel's ascendancy and his clampdown on anti-clerical material.

But the third portrait, that of the Knight, must have been changed for some other reason, and this gives us a possible dating for the alterations.

THE KNIGHT

Although there are often small discrepancies of detail between the pilgrims' painted portraits in the Ellesmere manuscript and how Chaucer describes them in his text, none of the illustrations diverges as radically from what Chaucer wrote as do those of the Monk and – especially – the Knight.

There is something fundamentally wrong with the painted miniature of the Knight in the Ellesmere MS. Not only does the illustration look like no other depiction of a knight from that period, but it is also totally contrary to the character of the Knight as Chaucer took pains to present it in the *General Prologue*.

All that Chaucer tells us about the Knight's clothing in the *Prologue* is that he is wearing a fustian jupon which has been marked or stained in some way by his coat of mail. The 'fustian jupon' was a tight-fitting, padded garment of thick material, worn as much for defence as anything else. It was not showy. It was just standard issue. Most of Chaucer's scholarly interpreters have pointed to the Knight's 'besmotered' jupon as evidence both of his humility and of his religious devotion – *The Ellesmere Knight.* he comes home from his travels and why! he's off on a pilgrimage without even a thought to his clothes!

But in Chaucer's time a fustian jupon could send other messages as well. Typically it identified its wearer as a non-noble professional man-at-arms.[1] For Chaucer's contemporaries, the fustian jupon symbolized the decline of chivalry, the disappearance of the colourful pageantry of the chivalric nobility and their replacement by the mercenary captains who had every good reason to rejoice in the battlefield anonymity the common jupon provided.[2]

Chaucer thus describes his Knight in the *Prologue* as a down-to-earth, unchivalric soldier wearing his ordinary working clothes.

The Ellesmere illumination, however, shows us almost the exact opposite: a man dressed in the height of fashion. He wears a piece of material that stretches from his hat to his shoulder – a high-fashion accessory known in the fifteenth century as a *liripipe*, an item as functional as a modern-day necktie.

The same is true of the wide, baggy sleeves that the Ellesmere Knight is sporting. Long, wide sleeves were the height of fashionable folly, according to contemporary moralists. They are totally inappropriate for the sober Knight of Chaucer's verse. It's his son, the

Fustian jackets were illustrated by either vertical or horizontal lines.

Squire, who is the fancy dresser – and indeed it is the Squire whom Chaucer describes as wearing long, wide sleeves. So why did the Ellesmere artist give them to the Knight as well?

The answer is that he didn't – or at least not when he first painted the image. Even with the naked eye it is possible to see that the shoulder and torso of the Knight have been altered – either by the original artist or by somebody else. Under the microscope, what was done becomes absolutely clear.

If we look closely at the right-hand side of the Knight's neck, we can see that the double line of the collar has been thickened to a single broad black line at the point where it crosses the red *liripipe*. At the same time the line jumps slightly to the right. Moreover, a partly erased line is faintly visible where we would expect

the shoulder to be. (Follow the vertical double line of the neck down across the *liripipe* to see it.) Falling away from this descending line on each side are curved lines which represent the natural form of the shoulder. It is quite clear that the thick black line has been drawn over the original shoulder and carried on to become the long wide sleeves which dominate the picture. The thick line and the wide sleeves are both clearly an addition made to the original picture at some later date.

Microscope detail showing the over-painting of the Knight's shoulder.

The discoloration of the sleeve at this point also indicates that originally there was a shorter sleeve. The smudging to the right of the thickened line suggests that the alteration was made inexpertly, or perhaps in a hurry.

Again, on the right hand side of the torso, in the area of this light discoloration, it is possible to see yet another vertical line, to the left of the thick added line, which looks as if it might once have marked the original waist-line, which is exactly what we might expect of a 'fustian jupon' (a thick padded jacket) such as Chaucer describes in the text. Indeed, the usual way of depicting such a garment was to draw vertical lines down the torso – which is exactly what we find on the Ellesmere Knight. The sleeves ought to be tight to the arm – wide baggy sleeves made out of the same material would simply not make sense.[3]

Then there is the *liripipe* itself, which forms the intersection of the double line of the neck and the thickened, over-drawn line. It is a little curious, to say the least. A *liripipe* was a fashion feature which fell away from the hat to the back and was often draped forward across

The whole of the Knight's sleeve has been added on. The original sleeve is probably indicated by the lighter area under the over-painted sleeve.

the shoulder. In the case of the Ellesmere Knight the reverse appears to be the case. The *liripipe* appears to *start* at the shoulder, and to be drawn up, and straight across the front of the hat. It is an impossible feature – one that looks suspiciously as if it has been introduced simply to obliterate the hat.

With the over-painted alterations – the long, wide sleeves and the *liripipe* (as well as other 'fashionable' features, such as the long pointed shoes and the gold tassels, unmentioned by Chaucer) – stripped away, the Ellesmere miniature begins to look more like the Knight of *The General Prologue*.

It also looks more like another famous painting of a fourteenth-century knight – the portrait of Sir John Hawkwood, by Paolo Ucello, that hangs in the Duomo in Florence.

Sir John Hawkwood was one of the most famous mercenary captains of his day. He had fought in France for Edward III and, following the conclusion of peace in

Sir John Hawkwood by Paolo Ucello.

1361, had set up his own business hiring out a freelance army to the various warring despots of northern Italy. He was, unusually for his calling, a man of probity – someone you could trust – and a brilliant commander. By the time of his death in 1394 he had been general of the troops for the Republic of Florence for fourteen years. In gratitude the Republic commissioned a grand, marble monument to his memory from the artists Agnolo Gaddi and Juliano Arrighi. When, however, Richard II requested, on behalf of Hawkwood's widow, that the body be returned to England for burial in 1395, the Republic sensibly decided it would be a waste of good florins to go to all the expense of a marble tomb, and so compromised by placing a painted version of the Gaddi–Arrighi design for the tomb-that-would-have-been on the wall in the Duomo.

By 1435, however, Gaddi's painting was deteriorating, and the Commune of Florence ordered Paolo Ucello to do another portrait, reproducing the Gaddi design. Moreover, the Commune apparently wanted the new portrait to look like the older one, for Ucello's first attempt was found unsatisfactory, and he was sent back to the cathedral to re-do it.[4]

Sir John Hawkwood, from the Croniche del Sercambi.

We can further deduce that Ucello was reproducing the same picture as Gaddi had painted because there is another, similar portrait of Hawkwood – dating from the 1390s – which appears in miniature in a manuscript of a work called the *Croniche del Sercambi*, currently housed in the State Archives at Lucca. Sir John Hawkwood is presented in the manuscript miniature in the same posture and with his horse in the same pose as in Ucello's portrait.

Either the Sercambi portrait was based on the original Gaddi design or both were based on a now lost template. Since the Ellesmere portrait could not have been based on the Ucello painting, because that was not executed until 1435, it is clear that the Ellesmere image of the Knight must have been based either on the template or else on a sketch or memory of the Gaddi memorial. The Gaddi, the Sercambi and the Ellesmere images are all part of an interconnected series.

The fact that the correspondence between the image in the Ellesmere manuscript and the Ucello image hanging today in the Duomo has gone unnoticed for six hundred years is a tribute to the success of the alterations to the manuscript.

*When one of the images is flipped
the similarity becomes more obvious.*

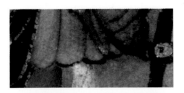

But as soon as we flip one of the images, the similarity becomes more obvious. Strip away the long wide sleeves, the *liripipe*, the pointed shoes and the medals, and there can be little doubt that the Ellesmere miniaturist and Ucello were drawing with the same model in view.

There are too many similarities for it to be coincidence: the posture of the horses, the posture of the riders (with the rod of office removed in the Ellesmere case) and the 'three scallops' theme worked into both picture and miniature. One of the inexplicable elements of the Ellesmere illumination is that the Knight appears to be wearing a strange skirt – it is quite unlike any garment worn at this period. If, however, we compare the 'skirt' with Sir John Hawkwood's saddle in the Duomo portrait, we can see that the 'three scallops' design Ucello worked into the saddle has been transformed into the odd garment of the Ellesmere Knight. Now, a visual transposition of this sort is exactly what we might expect from someone reproducing an image from memory, or from a hasty sketch, in which a 'minor' detail has been misinterpreted. But it might also be something else.

The 'three scallops' wouldn't necessarily have been a 'minor' detail. The Hawkwood family emblem was three scallops of the shellfish variety. Ucello's scalloped saddle is probably a visual pun on Hawkwood's emblem. So the 'skirt' of the Ellesmere Knight may originally have been intended as a reference to Sir John Hawkwood, the most famous of English mercenary captains.

Microscopic analysis also provides further corroboration of a connection between the Ellesmere portrait and the Duomo wall-hanging of Sir John Hawkwood. The Duomo portrait has red harness and bridle for Sir John's horse,

The microscope reveals that the harness was originally red – as in the Duomo portrait.

whereas the Ellesmere miniature shows them black. But *underneath* this black pigment, using the microscope, red pigment can clearly be seen in the Ellesmere manuscript on all sections of the horse's harness.

Assuming Ucello to have copied this feature of the harness colour from the original Gaddi memorial, the alteration adds credibility to the idea that the Knight's portrait in the Ellesmere was changed to diguise its resemblance to Sir John Hawkwood.

But why would anyone have wanted to alter this image?

WHY WAS THE KNIGHT'S IMAGE ALTERED?

The reason may have been a family matter. It is believed that the Ellesmere manuscript once belonged to the DeVere family – the Earls of Oxford. Now the DeVeres lived at Castle Hedingham in Essex, and by a strange coincidence this meant that their nearest neighbours were none other than the Hawkwoods, who lived in Sible Hedingham – just a mile down the road.

The two families were not merely next-door neighbours – they were intimately connected. Sir John's elder brother (also confusingly called John) was the steward of the DeVere household and also acted as executor for Thomas DeVere in 1371.

The connection between the two families even extended beyond the grave. The same year that Richard requested the return of Hawkwood's body, he also brought home the remains of his former favourite, Robert DeVere, who had died in 1389 after escaping the fury of the rebellious magnates in 1387. The bodies of Hawkwood and Robert DeVere were buried within five miles of each other and in the same year. Shortly before he died Hawkwood gave orders to sell the Leadenhall in London, which he owned, and use the proceeds to set up a chantry of two priests to sing for his soul 'in the Priory of Hedingham Castle'.[5]

It is not certain whether Hawkwood's widow, Donina (daughter of the Milanese tyrant Bernabò Visconti), came to England for the funeral, but their son did return and was duly naturalized and knighted by Henry IV in 1407.[6]

If the DeVeres, in Castle Hedingham, possessed the Ellesmere MS at this time, it might simply have been socially embarrassing to be in possession of a caricature of the Grand Old Man now his son-and-heir was their new next-door neighbour; especially when the fictional son of the fictional Knight is also illustrated and ridiculed (though affectionately) in the figure of the Squire. Perhaps it would have been even more embarrassing if everyone knew that the Grand Old Man in question was familiar to the author of *The Canterbury Tales*, since Chaucer had met Sir John Hawkwood – indeed was specifically charged by the King to meet with him – on his 1378 journey to the court of Bernabò Visconti.

It may, on the other hand, have been more serious than that. It may have been *politically* embarrassing to have had an image of the father of the newly knighted master of Sible Hedingham on the pages of a book that was so closely associated with the old regime – especially if you were a family like the DeVeres already trying to live down uncomfortably close ties with the deposed king. Or, there again, perhaps it was simply thought to be unwise to have a likeness of the next-door neighbour's dad in a book of questionable theological outlook.

Whatever the reasons for the changes to the Ellesmere illumination of the Knight, the fact that they were made suggests a sensitivity about the nature of *The Canterbury Tales* – datable to some time around the year 1407. In the case of the Knight it is likely that the sensitivity was about identification with an individual, and was a matter of perhaps only local concern. But there are two other portraits which have also been tampered with. The use of the identical black pigment on the harness suggests that these alterations were done at the same time, and they provide evidence that the book of *The Canterbury Tales* was perceived as something that could have drawn down the wrath of the all-powerful Archbishop Arundel.

THE MONK

The Ellesmere illustration of the Monk is palpably unlike the description in the text. The *Prologue* describes an extrovert, good-living prelate, with a bald head and a twinkle in his eye. He is dressed in the very best that money can buy and he is wearing a gold brooch under his chin.

The Ellesmere portrait, by contrast, shows a figure shrouded from head to toe in black. He looks more like a hermit than a worldly priest. He is wearing a hat and seems to have a veil covering his face – even though, as far as we know, no monk ever took the veil. The Ellesmere portraits – the one of words and the other of paint – are so different that one critic has been forced to conclude that 'we must reject the

The Ellesmere Monk is completely contrary to the character described in the text.

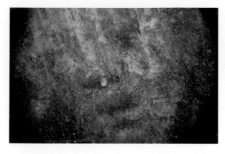

The microscope reveals a character totally consistent with Chaucer's description: a bon viveur with red nose, red cheeks and red lips.

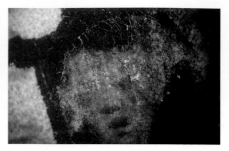

Back-lighting shows what might have been the Monk's bald head.

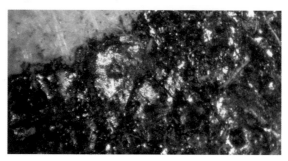

Under the microscope, the Monk's gold jewellery, described in the text, shines out as new.

commonplace assumption that the purpose of the miniatures was to illustrate *The General Prologue*'s text with "fidelity" ...'[7]

Microscopic analysis of the illustration, however reveals a totally different picture – one that is in complete accord with the description in *The General Prologue*.

Beneath the microscope, it is immediately apparent that the whole portrait has been subjected to heavy over-painting with a thick, black pigment. This pigment has been washed over the face of the Monk, giving the appearance of a veil. But under that 'veil' of pigment are all the characteristics we would expect to see of this *bon viveur* – this 'manly man', as Chaucer deems. His eyes are bright and shining, he has a red nose and red cheeks, and possibly a grin all over his face.

The application of a back-light to the manuscript reveals further that, under the black pigment of the hat, there is the outline of a round head – presumably the bald head of Chaucer's text.

Lower down, under the Monk's chin, where Chaucer's text describes a 'full curious pin', the microscope reveals gold leaf shining out, bright as new, from under the black over-painting.

Someone, without a shadow of doubt, has covered up the Monk's forbidden jewellery, as well as the all-too-apparent signs of good living revealed in his physiognomy.

It's exactly the kind of image it would have been dangerous to own in the years when Archbishop Arundel was on the warpath against any criticism of the church – particularly around 1407, when he was not only Archbishop of Canterbury but also Chancellor of the realm.

THE FRIAR

The other figure that seemed to have been altered is the Friar. In his case it appears that he was originally carrying a harp, as befits his description in Chaucer's text.

> Wel koude he synge and pleyen on a rote;
> Of yeddygnes he baar outrely the pris ...
> And in his harpyng, whan that he hadde songe,
> His eyen twynkled in his heed aryght
> As doon the strerres in the frosty nyght.
> *The General Prologue*, ll. 266–8
> Well could he sing and play upon the strings;
> His ballads always carried off the prize ...
> And in his harping, when that he had sung,
> His eyes would twinkle in his head aright,
> As do the stars upon a frosty night.

The illustration of the Friar shows him carrying a staff which is nowhere mentioned in the text, but which 'fills a place where a musical instrument could have been represented'.[8] The Friar's cope also forms an odd configuration which fits the outline of a 'harp', which in those days could be 'any of several ancient stringed instruments' of which the most likely for the Friar would probably be the *psaltery* – a sort of medieval version of the zither, which could come in many shapes and forms.[9] It may well be that the harp was painted out and the irrelevant staff inserted.

Again microscopic inspection strengthens the impression that the Friar is hugging such a 'harp'. There is also a whitish-

The kind of 'harp' the Friar would be holding.

grey line forming a right angle visible in the centre
– suggesting that originally his arm was crooked
to hold the instrument and that both the arm as
we now see it and the oddly angled hand holding
the pike have been added.

It may also be that the Friar was originally
dressed in white (as a Carmelite, or possibly grey
as a Franciscan) and has been again over-painted
with the ubiquitous black pigment that has been
used on the Monk.

*The strange rectangles of the Friar's cope
may have been a psaltery.*

Of course, it goes without saying that a friar
was supposed to be preaching the Word of God to the people – not plucking a
harp or strumming a zither to accompany popular ballads. One critic postulates
that Chaucer was describing a particular friar who was musically accomplished.[10] If so, that would be one explanation for the removal of the offending
instrument from the illumination.

But there is a much more obvious reason. The elements that have been removed
from the Friar, as in the case of the Monk, are those that betray the worldliness
and veniality of these ecclesiasts.

The criticism implicit in each image has thus been censored.

WHEN WAS THE ELLESMERE CENSORED?

Sensitivity to the ridicule of religious figures could be expected at almost any time
from 1400 onwards. Arundel's attempts to clamp down on any criticism of the
church would have made any manuscript-owner a trifle nervous of possessing
such explicit material. It was bad enough having criticism within a text – but in
an age when only a small portion of people could actually read, that was a con-
trollable problem. To have visual depictions of such criticisms, however, sitting
on the page large as life for all to see would have been tempting fate.

The alterations could have been made at any time in the first half of the fifteenth
century, though an earlier rather than a later date seems most likely. The alterations to the Knight's portrait suggest sometime around 1407, the same year that
Archbishop Arundel took over complete control of both church and state,
although they could equally have been done at the time of Arundel's *Constitutions*
in 1409, in which it was prescribed that:

Preachers were to be discreet, condemning the failings of the clergy only to clergy, and limiting themselves to the offences of laymen when preaching to laity ... No book or tract composed by John Wyclif or anyone else in his time or since then ... shall henceforth be read in schools, halls, hostels or other places whatsoever ... No one henceforth shall translate any text of Holy Scripture into the English language on his own authority ... No one ... of whatever grade estate or condition ... shall assert or propose any conclusions or propositions sounding contrary to the Catholic faith or good rules ... [11]

When such draconian measures were first announced, there must have been many a book-owner who wondered whether the volumes on their shelves would fall foul of the authorities. No one holding a copy of *The Canterbury Tales* could be blamed if they erred on the side of caution.

The one thing these alterations illustrate is that there was a nervousness about owning this particular manuscript of *The Canterbury Tales*. Did this nervousness apply to *The Canterbury Tales* in general? Did it apply to all of Chaucer's works?

At first sight, the reverse would seem to be the case: Chaucer's writing was positively championed by the Lancastrian regime. The fifteenth century was the time when his reputation grew and when his manuscripts started to proliferate. If Archbishop Arundel or the usurper Henry IV were in any way implicated in the liquidation of the poet, we might expect to find Chaucer's reputation and works neglected throughout the Lancastrian rule. And yet we find the opposite.

The answer to this conundrum presents us with a vivid glimpse of medieval princely politics.

CHAPTER 14

Chaucer as a political icon

~

If Henry IV and Archbishop Arundel did, indeed, attempt to suppress Chaucer's work, and in particular *The Canterbury Tales*, why were the Lancastrian poets so vocal in their celebration of Chaucer? Time and again, both Thomas Hoccleve and John Lydgate acknowledge him as their teacher, inspiration and never-to-be-surpassed master.

Lydgate, a monk of Bury St Edmunds, is forever telling his unfortunate readers how much better what they are now reading would have been had it been written by Chaucer rather than his humble self:

Chaucer – a portrait made specifically to record his likeness.

> Whan we wolde his stile countrefet,
> We may al day oure colour grynde and bete,
> Tempre our azour and vermyloun:
> But al I holde but presumpsioun ...
>   John Lydgate, *Troy Book*, II, ll. 4715–18
> When we would his style counterfeit
> We may all day our colours grind and beat,
> Adjust our azure and vermilion,
> But I say it's all but a presumption ...

Chaucer's superiority is a recurrent theme with Lydgate throughout his *Troy Book*:

Was neuer noon to this day alyue
To reckne alle bothe yonge & olde
That worthi was his ynkhorn for to holde ...
John Lydgate, *Troy Book*, V, ll. 3528–30
There's been no one living to this day
Counting all both young and old
That worthy was his inkhorn for to hold ...

The other major Lancastrian poet, Thomas Hoccleve, was similarly fulsome in his praise of Chaucer:

O maister deere and fadir reuerent
My maister Chaucer flour of eloquence ,
Mirour of fructuous entendement
O vniversal fadir in science ...
Thomas Hoccleve, *The Regement of Princes*, ll. 1961–4
Oh master dear and father reverent
My master Chaucer, flower of eloquence
Mirror of fruitful learning
O universal father in knowledge ...

If Archbishop Arundel and Henry IV intended to suppress Chaucer's name and works, surely they wouldn't have allowed *this* sort of thing to go on? So how is it that Chaucer's reputation seems to have been so high with the Lancastrian poets?

An examination of the chronology suggests that Chaucer's promotion in the early fifteenth century has, in fact, nothing to do with Henry IV, but everything to do with his son, the Prince of Wales, and – what's more – with the prince's struggle to wrest power from his father.

What is remarkable is the lack of references to Chaucer that are connected with Henry IV. There are only two citations of the poet before 1410.[1] One is in a charming poem called 'The Flower of Courtesy', which has been attributed to Lydgate and dated at 1400, but neither the date nor the attribution are at all reliable. It may well have been composed a good deal later.[2]

If we put this poem to one side, the only recorded literary allusion to Chaucer before 1410 is one made by an old friend of the poet's, Henry Scogan, and the context in which Scogan makes his allusion gives us a good clue as to what was going on.

HENRY SCOGAN'S 'MORAL BALADE'

Henry Scogan was a man of some property, he had seen military service and was, like Chaucer, an esquire of Richard II. He became tutor to Henry IV's sons, and Chaucer addressed one of his poems to him.[3]

Scogan's eulogy to Chaucer came in 1407, when Scogan was probably approaching seventy.

It's uncertain whether he was giving a sort of after-dinner speech, in the form of a recitation, or whether he'd written the poem for the occasion, but perhaps by reason of illness was unable to read it himself. A note in one of the manuscripts by John Shirley (*d.* 1456) reads: 'Here foloweth next a Moral Balade, to my lord the prince, to my lord of Clarence, to my lord of Bedford, and to my lord of Gloucestre, by Henry Scogan; at a souper of feorthe merchande in the Vyntre in London, at the hous of Lowys Johan.'[4] The poem itself begins:

My noble sones, and eek my lordes dere,
I, your fader called, unworthily,
Sende un-to you this litel tretys here
Writen with myn owne hand full rudely.
   Henry Scogan, *A Moral Balade*, ll. 1–4
My noble sons, and my dear lords too,
I, who am unworthily called your father/tutor,
Send you this little treatise here
Written, very simply, in my own hand.

It sounds as if he were sending the poem as a letter. It is also possible, of course, that the usurper's sons were not present at the dinner and Henry Scogan was simply reading out a poem that he'd sent them.

However it was delivered, and whoever was listening, the important point is that it was dedicated to the Prince of Wales and his brothers.

At this time, Prince Henry had already locked horns with his father. It was a conflict that darkened Henry IV's later years. The king was already wracked with guilt over the usurpation and tormented with debilitating fits, which he possibly attributed to his own evil deeds. The father-son antagonism sprang, in part, from the prince's affection for, and loyalty to, Richard II.

After his father had been exiled in 1398, as we have seen, the 11-year-old Henry was taken under Richard's wing, and accompanied him to Ireland. The prince seems to have developed a genuine and lasting affection for Richard which he apparently did not feel for his father. Henry Bolingbroke had been off 'crusading' for much of the boy's childhood, and the prince had lived with his mother in Peterborough – seldom seeing his father. Even when Bolingbroke returned to England, the prince saw relatively little of him, and in fact spent more time with his grandfather, John of Gaunt.[5]

It is thus scarcely surprising if the boy should have developed an ardent affection for a substitute father-figure who, by all

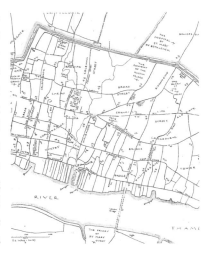

Sketch map of London at the time of the Peasants' Revolt (1381) showing Vintry, where Henry Scogan recited Chaucer's poem 'Gentillese'.

reports, treated him with more warmth and respect than did his own father.

When Henry invaded England, the prince was summoned to Chester to confront both his father and the captured King Richard. One chronicler records how the 12-year-old knight respectfully welcomed his father but then attended on Richard, whom 'he loved entirely'.[6] Even when ordered by the usurper to abandon Richard, the prince refused to obey until Richard himself reminded him of his duty to his father.

The young prince's affection for Richard may well have been the basis – or even the cause – of the growing estrangement between the Prince of Wales and Henry IV. His high regard for Richard certainly endured into his adulthood, and one of his first acts, as Henry V, was to bring back Richard's body from its obscure grave in Hertfordshire to rest at last in the tomb Richard had prepared for himself and Queen Anne in Westminster Abbey.[7]

We can well imagine that Henry IV would have found his son's allegiance to the man he had murdered hard to stomach. But though the origins may have been purely personal, the conflict inevitably took on its own political dimension.

By 1407, Prince Henry had become the nominal head of a gathering opposition, which consisted for the most part of a younger generation of baronial interests. Henry IV was growing more and more incapacitated by fits – possibly the result of a cerebral embolism – or it may have been syphilis.[8] As the usurper relinquished his grip on government, Archbishop Arundel had begun to take more of the reins of power into his own hands. At the beginning of 1407 he accepted the office of chancellor, and between 1407 and 1409 frequently acted as the ailing king's deputy. To the baronial opposition, who had thought that the archbishop was their chief spokesman against the royal prerogative, this looked like a betrayal.[9]

Henry V – the man who revived Chaucer?

The 19-year-old Prince Henry was already convinced that he was soon to become king, and rumours of a change of monarch were rife. Just the year before, Henry Beaufort, Bishop of Winchester and one of the prince's closest advisers, had told the French court in confidence that the king would soon either die or pass on the government of the realm. Meanwhile the prince had to put up with his father's seemingly endless relapses and recoveries.

It is against this background that Henry Scogan, the prince's old tutor, stood up in the house of Lewis John the Welshman and recited (or had recited on his behalf) a poem addressed to the Prince of Wales that must have made his listeners' ears stand on end!

Scogan casually recalls what his master Chaucer said: when a man dies he can't bequeath his virtues to his heir along with his house:

> My mayster Chaucer, god his soule have!
> That in his langage was so curious,
> He sayde, the fader which is deed and grave,
> Biquath nothing his vertue with his hous
> Unto his sone ...[10]
>
>   Henry Scogan, *A Moral Balade*, ll. 65–9

> My master Chaucer, God save his soul!
> Who was so sophisticated in his language,
> He said: the father who is dead and buried,
> Bequeaths nothing of his virtue with his house
> Unto his son ...

In 1407, the tense situation between the usurper and his son would have charged any talk of inheritance with topical electricity – and yet here is Scogan, claiming to be talking directly to the young Prince Henry.

Of course, Scogan phrases it very politically, saying the father cannot bequeath his virtue to his son, along with his house. But for the prince – anxious as he was to escape the shadow of obloquy under which his usurping father now dragged out his days – the sub-text would have been obvious: if a father couldn't pass on his virtues to his son, neither could he pass on his sins.

The prince, from very early on, had been concerned to distance himself from his father's shameful usurpation. The chronicler Walsingham tells the story that, when news of Henry Bolingbroke's arrival back in England reached the king in Ireland, Richard told the young prince, who was with him, that his father was putting his inheritance in jeopardy. The prince reportedly replied that he was 'totally innocent of any complicity with his father'.[11] Even if this were a later invention by Walsingham, it's a good summary of the way the future Henry V regarded his father's moral status *vis à vis* the usurpation.

Scogan's 'Moral Balade' presents the Prince of Wales with a blueprint for the unimpeachability of his claim to the throne. No matter what his father was guilty of, young Henry could not be tainted with his father's crimes.

Scogan then quotes in its entirety Chaucer's poem *Gentilesse* – and once again the context of 1407 gives the poem a whole layer of new meaning. In fact, in the context of 1407 it begins to look downright subversive.

If Archbishop Arundel had been present, he would have been outraged. Then at the height of his autocratic powers, he was already drafting his infamous *Constitutions*, by which he intended to shackle the intellectual activity of the nation. His view was simple: ecclesiastical authority was there for one purpose – to be obeyed without question, and with deference. According to Arundel, the mitre and crozier conferred by the church bestowed upon the occupant of episcopal office the right to wield power – in the same way that the crown and the sceptre bestowed upon the king the right to rule. But Chaucer's poem offered a very different reading:

> For unto vertu longeth dignitee
> And noght the revers, saufly dar I deme,
> Al were he mytre, croune, or diademe.
>   *Gentilesse*, ll. 5–7
> For high honour belongs to virtue
> And not the reverse, I can safely say,
> Though he wears mitre, crown or diadem.

Don't forget that 'gentilesse' in this context means 'nobility'. That constant refrain, 'Al wear he mitre, crown or diadem', would have been quite shocking to the merchant-guests listening that night in the Vintry in London Town. To question the authority of the bishops might have been acceptable in the 1390s, but it was a different matter in 1407. To argue that no one could claim rightfully to hold office unless they could prove themselves worthy of it – be they bishop, king or emperor – was the sort of argument that John Wyclif and his followers had been trying to push thirty years previously! Hadn't that all been put beyond the pale of discussion? Hadn't *De Haeretico Comburendo* silenced all that sort of dangerous chatter?

Evidently not. Not, at least, at a dinner in the City in the home of the Welshman Lewis John.

In fact, even the location Scogan chose for this first public celebration of his old friend, Geoffrey Chaucer, may have had some resonance. Lewis John was an associate of Chaucer's son, Thomas.[12] Indeed, there is every reason to think that Thomas Chaucer would have been at the event – he was, after all, Prince Henry's second cousin once removed and a friend of Lewis John. But to be in the house of a Welshman would not have been a neutral piece of happenstance. It might – just possibly – have carried overtones of defiance.

The Welsh were in their seventh year of open rebellion against the English crown – which meant rebellion against Henry IV's rule, his usurpation, and also against King Henry himself. Welshmen hadn't been exactly *personae gratae* since the revolt began, and the king had found a number of ways to make it plain to Lewis John and his countrymen that London was not their kind of town.

Could it be that the home of Lewis John was an apt venue for those who opposed the king in 1407?[13]

Lewis John himself was a respectable enough man who mixed with equally respectable people. Thomas Chaucer, for example, was not only Henry IV's butler in that year, but also Speaker of the House of Commons.[14] John seems to have been an ambitious sort, busily tying his star to young Prince Henry's. It's possible that the two had met during the prince's lengthy campaigns in Wales. As a Welshman, John would have needed all the help he could get. One of Henry IV's first acts after taking power in 1400 was to deny all Welshmen the right to own real estate in London. Since John was a vintner (as were Geoffrey Chaucer's father, and – nominally – his son Thomas, too), being unable to own warehouses would have seriously crimped his business.

But not being able to own property would have had another consequence which Lewis John might have considered more serious: without property ownership, a man couldn't rise far in London politics. Judging from the track of his subsequent career, this must have rankled.

What else we know about Lewis John is that his manoeuvring seems to have worked. Almost immediately upon the succession of Henry V, good things began to rain down upon him from heaven. Within a month of Henry IV's death, Lewis John was appointed Keeper of the (new) King's Exchange in the City of London and the town of Calais, and Keeper of the King's Mint in the Tower of London and also Calais.[15] Thomas Chaucer stood surety for him at the time.

A year later, in April 1413, Lewis John was elected to parliament.[16] In November 1414 he successfully petitioned parliament to be exempted from the ban on Welshmen owning real property in London. At the same time, he, Thomas Chaucer and another vintner, John Snypston, entered a formal complaint to parliament to recover over £800 owed them for wine supplied to the court of Henry IV.[17]

And on 26 May 1414 Lewis John was granted a three-year exclusive right to issue letters of exchange for anyone going abroad. This cost him 200 marks a year, payable to the Exchequer, but no doubt it was worth it.[18]

So, judging from how quickly, after Henry Prince of Wales ascended the throne, the star of Lewis John also rose in the heavens, we can say that the gathering at John's in the Vintry must have been politically charged and with high hopes for the young prince's future.

This little 'souper' in 1407, then – the first properly attested literary recollection of Chaucer since his death – had all the earmarks of a 'power dinner'. Certainly every guest we know about, or can guess at, had larger agendas, none of them favourable to either the authority of the ailing king or of the ambitious archbishop-cum-chancellor. And right in the middle of that wheeling-and-dealing, almost like a centrepiece, is a poem by Chaucer.

Scogan was no Romantic – rolling out verses because 'feelings' got the better of him. He was an old courtier cagey enough to have survived the Appellants, the Merciless Parliament, the bloody days of Richard's deposition and murder, and the dangerous ins and outs of serving an increasingly paranoid king obsessed with suspicions of traitors all about him.

So if Scogan settled on a poem of Chaucer's as the pigeon to carry a message to the prince, he didn't do it casually. It would be perverse of us, then, not to ask why he did it.

Could it be that by reviving the reputation of Chaucer Scogan was also reviving the spirit of King Richard's court? After all, it was to Richard rather than to his father that Prince Henry looked for legitimacy. He had grown up in Richard's court – been happy there by all accounts – and Geoffrey Chaucer, as we have seen, was an unavoidable part of it, central to a *familia Regis* which connected the arts and freedom of thought with what it meant to be a king.

Perhaps Chaucer's *Gentilesse* – with its emphasis on moral worth rather than privileged birth – represented a rallying cry for those around the Prince of Wales: and for the prince himself, an image of the new Camelot that he would establish.

Could it also be relevant that in this same year, 1407, Thomas Chaucer, as Speaker of the Commons, openly challenged Archbishop Arundel's authority in parliament by seeking to make the office of chancellor subject to review?

In the paranoid climate of those days, with power slipping between their fingers, what would Henry IV and Thomas Arundel have thought about Lewis John's little *soirée*? Did their spies report back to them? Did Henry Scogan go peacefully in his bed, when he died a few weeks later?

Might there as well have been another, darker purpose in linking the dead poet with the theme 'The son cannot bear guilt for crimes committed by the father'? Was Scogan hinting at something *else* concerning Geoffrey Chaucer and Henry IV and his henchmen – some other guilt which, in any case, young Henry would not have to bear?

Of course, we cannot say for sure what the answer is to any of these questions. One thing we can say, however, is that commemoration of Chaucer in the first decade and a half of the fifteenth century appears mainly in poems addressed to the Prince of Wales, and, with the exception of Henry Scogan's recitation, not until 1410 – the year Prince Henry took over control of the government from his father.

By the time parliament met at Westminster on 27 January 1410, the prince's party had turfed Archbishop Arundel out of the chancellorship and the disgruntled king had gone to stay with him in Lambeth. For almost the next two years, from January 1410 to November 1411, a council made up of the Prince of Wales and his friends administered the country in the king's name.[19]

Many of these friends were Beauforts, led by Henry Beaufort, Bishop of Winchester. The Beaufort clan were the children of John of Gaunt and Katherine Swynford, which made them Henry IV's bastard siblings and maternal cousins of Thomas Chaucer. So the Chaucer family star was firmly fixed to the prince's party – by blood, as well, perhaps, as by temperament.

THOMAS HOCCLEVE AND 'THE RULE OF PRINCES'

The ascendancy of the prince's party in 1410 seems to mark the shift of the wind for Chaucer's posthumous reputation. About this time, his memory begins to be revived in other poems directly addressed to the Prince of Wales. The major celebrant was Thomas Hoccleve, a civil servant working in the Office of the Privy Seal. He was quick to offer himself as 'a sort of proto-laureate'. In true laureate style he dedicated a 'how-to-rule' book to young Henry called *The Regement* ['Rule'] *of Princes.* The initial cause of Hoccleve's sudden devotion was probably venal. As one scholar puts it: 'Hoccleve – perhaps in the spirit of political opportunism, despairing of ever having his annuity paid by the *ancien regime* – casts his lot in with Prince Henry.'[20]

The poem is 'unabashedly partisan on [Prince Henry's] behalf' and 'wholly consistent with the prince's own programme of self-representation as a peerless exemplar of orthodoxy'.[21]

Hoccleve peppers his poem with flattering references to Chaucer. In fact Chaucer figures in the poem no less than five times. By contrast, the *Regement* is very lukewarm about Henry IV. It refers to him only

Thomas Hoccleve presents his book to Henry V.

as 'the king which that is now'. Henry IV has been 'gracious ynow' to Hoccleve, the poet dutifully says, but has failed to make sure that the annuity granted to him has been paid!

> 'My lige lorde, the kynge wich that is now,
> I fynde to me gracious ynow;
> God yelde him! he hath for my long seruise
> Guer-douned me in couenable wyse.
>
> In thé schequér, he of his special grace,
> Hath to me grauntid an annuitee
> Of xxti mark, while I haue lyues space.
> Mighte I ay paid ben of that duetee,
> It schulde stonde wel ynow with me;

But paiement is hard to gete adayes;
And that me put in many foule affrayes.'
  The Regement of Princes, ll. 816–26
My liege lord, the king which that is now,
I find to me gracious enough;
God save him! he hath for my long service
Rewarded me in the proper way.

In the Exchequer, he of his special grace
Hath to me granted an annuity
Of 20 marks, while I have life's space.
Had I been paid any of that duty
It would be well enough for me,
But payment is hard to get nowadays,
And that has put me in many foul affrays.

In fact, the *Regement* goes beyond being lukewarm about Henry IV. It contains
passages that can be read now – and presumably could have been read then – as
veiled criticisms of the king.

By 1410 Henry IV had surrounded himself with a narrow circle of advisers –
the narrowness of Henry IV's court compared to the Prince of Wales's was one
of the standard contrasts drawn in the chronicles.[22] His propaganda machine
had rewritten history to his own glorification and he had surrounded himself with
flattering poets. How then to read these lines from *The Regement of Princes*?

The moste lak that han the lordes grete,
Is of hem that hir soothes shuld hem telle;
Al in the glose folk labour and swete;
Thei stryuen who best rynge shal the belle
Of false plesance, in that hir hertes swelle;
And swich deceyt, lordes blyndly receyue.

The worldly riche men, han no knowleche
What that their bene of his condicioun;
Thei ben so blent with fauelles gar speche,
Wich reportith to hem, that hir renoun
Is euerywhere halwid in the toun,

That in hem-self they demen gret vertu,
Where as ther is but smal or naght a gru,
  The Regement of Princes, ll. 1926–39
The greatest lack that great lords have
Is of those who'll tell them the truth;
Everyone labours and sweats at deception;
They strive to see who best can ring the bell
Of false pleasantness, to puff up their lords' hearts;
And such deceit, lords blindly accept.

The worldly rich men has no knowledge
Of how his situation really is;
They are so blinded with flattery's ensnaring speech,
Which reports to them that their renown
Is everywhere hallowed in the town,
That they believe themselves full of great strength,
Whereas there is but little or not a grain.

A few lines further on, the poem commemorates Chaucer's memory in a way that is clearly associated with the prince's struggle against his father and Thomas Arundel. Writing soon after Arundel's *Constitutions* came into effect, Hoccleve complains that he is very nervous about attempting to compose anything in English 'With hert as tremblyng as the leef of aspe' ('With heart as trembling as an aspen leaf'). What follows is a lament for Chaucer, framed as a lament for the English language. In 1410 the political overtones must have been dynamite:

But weylaway! so is myn herte wo,
That the honour of englyssh tonge is deed,
Of which I wont was han conseil and reed.
O, maister deere, and fadir reuerent!
Mi maister Chaucer, flour of eloquence ...
  The Regement of Princes, ll. 1958–60
But wellaway! My heart's so full of woe,
That the honour of the English tongue is dead,
From whom I used to get counsel and advice.
Oh, master dear, and father reverent!
My master Chaucer, flower of eloquence ...

With the *Constitutions* only recently introduced to outlaw the use of English in religious debate, it is not hard to imagine what resonance was carried by 'the honour of englyssh tonge is deed'! Of course, the poet deflects criticism by representing the loss of the English tongue as being Chaucer's tongue, but few could have read or heard these lines in 1410–12 without understanding the wider implication of the lament.

JOHN LYDGATE AND CHAUCER

Around the same time, the other major English poet of the day, John Lydgate, also starts to lament Chaucer's death in public:

> ... thof my hert pleyne
> Vpon his dethe, and for sorowe blede
> For want of hym, nowe in my grete nede
>> *The Life of Our Lady*, ll. 1644–6
> ... thereof my heart laments
> Upon his death, and for sorrow bleeds
> For want of him, now in my great need.

No one is quite certain when Lydgate was writing this poem.[23] Scholars are divided about whether it was 1409–11, 1421–2 or even as late as 1434. The earlier date is certainly possible, since we know the young prince took an interest in Lydgate from at least 1406–8, and perhaps knew him as a fellow student at Oxford from 1398.[24] If the date is 1409–11, then, the 'nede' that Lydgate has for Chaucer goes beyond mere pious platitudes. The poem is part of the fight-back against Archbishop Arundel's assault on the English tongue.

Prince Henry clearly saw the English language as an important part of his political agenda. In 1412, just before ascending the throne, he commissioned from Lydgate a book on the theme of ancient Troy – a trophy poem to put English on equal footing with the dominant cultural languages, Latin and French:

> By-cause he wolde that to high and lowe
> The noble story openly wer knowe
> In oure tonge, about in every age,
> And y-writen as wel in oure langage

As in latyn and frensche it is.
  Troy Book, Prologue, ll. 111–15
Because he wished that to high and low
The noble story might be openly known
In our tongue, everywhere in every age,
And written as well in our language
As it is in Latin and French.

Like Hoccleve's, Lydgate's poem is thoroughly partisan towards the prince and even allows itself to indulge in a swipe at the prince's father:

O myghti God, that with thin inward loke
Sest every thing thorugh thin eternal mught,
Why wiltow nat of equite and right
Punish and chastise so horrible a thing,
And specially the mordre of a kyng?
  Troy Book, V, ll. 1046–50
Oh mighty God, that with your inward look
Sees every thing through your eternal might,
Why do you not, in equality and right,
Punish and chastise so horrible a thing,
And especially the murder of a king?

The poem took eight years to complete and this passage comes towards the end, so presumably Lydgate didn't write it until Henry IV was safely buried. In fact, we know exactly when Lydgate began writing his *Troy Book* because in his Prologue (ll. 125–46) he includes accurate astrological co-ordinates, that tell us he began on 31 October 1412 – a Monday – at four o'clock in the afternoon. Henry IV died barely five months later.

Dead usurpers never take offence.

HOCCLEVE'S PORTRAIT OF CHAUCER

What seems clear is that Chaucer was being used as an icon by the Prince of Wales to rally the opposition to his father and to Arundel. Indeed Chaucer does become an icon – quite literally – because Hoccleve integrates into *The Regement of Princes* an actual image of the poet. We know exactly where the picture goes because Hoccleve tells us in the text: 'I have here his likeness made.' And where it comes is after an astonishing passage in which Hoccleve warns the prince that, if he wants to win the hearts of his people, he himself needs to 'bowe' to God; moreover, any king so reckless as to offend God on purpose will be disobeyed:

> … To god your herte bowe,
> If ye desire men hir hertes bende
> To you. What kyng nat dredeth god offende,
> Ne naght rekketh do hym desobeissaunce,
> He shal be disobeied eeke perchaunce.
> *The Regement of Princes*, ll. 4973–7
> … Bow your head to God
> If you desire men to bend their hearts
> To you. Whatever king does not dread to offend God,
> Nor cares not about disobeying Him,
> He shall be disobeyed also, perchance.

Was there *anyone* drawing breath and able to read in 1411 who might have missed this shot at Henry IV? In a couple of lines, Hoccleve has summarized the whole usurpation: in reckless disobedience to the Divine Plan, Henry dethroned the anointed King Richard – and murdered him! – thereby offending God and bringing rebellion down on his head from every quarter of the realm (and also, by extension, on his own body, as the curse of his withering illness was commonly understood, even by Henry IV himself).[25]

The whiff of 'ungodliness' had long hung around Henry's court and Arundel had more than once taken it upon himself to reprimand Henry for the behaviour of some of his followers. Perhaps more importantly, 1410 was the year in which the Prince of Wales began to move away from his heterodox supporters and to make his bid for the orthodox territory until then dominated by the formidable Arundel.

Hoccleve's lines were designed to distance the prince from his father and, at the same time, to spell out his new agenda – claiming legitimacy from Richard and espousing ecclesiastical orthodoxy.

And in the very next stanza, Hoccleve introduces Chaucer as the founder ('firste fyndere') 'of our faire langage'. Remember this is the very year the *Constitutions* swept the land! Not only that, but Hoccleve also claims that everything he has just written – presumably about usurpation being a curse on king and country – Chaucer has said already, better and often ('Hath seyde in caas semblable, & othir moo/ So hyly wel').

It is exactly here that we find the portrait of Chaucer in the manuscripts.

Why does Hoccleve do it? Well, he tells us: It's 'to put othir men in remembraunce' – those, that is, who have forgotten Chaucer's achievement ('thei that haue of him lest thought & mynde') – so that they 'By this peynture may ageyn him finde.' In other words, they – we, all of us – will get Chaucer back. Not literally of course, but he *is* talking about a kind of miracle here – a political one. What the prince needs, what the realm needs, what everyone needs is the return of Chaucer's wisdom and advice. That, of course, is what *The Regement of Princes* was – a book of advice for princes.

Chaucer: the portrait commissioned by Hoccleve so that no one would forget what the great poet looked like.

The Regement of Princes was copied *a lot* from the outset. Over 45 fifteenth-century manuscripts still exist today with it whole or in fragments.[26] Three of them have portraits, the same portrait, in the same place. They seem to have been owned by influential men who were supporters of the prince – scholars believe, in fact, that they were deliberately distributed by the prince. It's a fair guess, however, that he didn't send one to his father, or to the archbishop. There was altogether too much in *The Regement* about that subversive Chaucer being 'slaughtered' and 'quenched'.

What is clear is that Hoccleve's poem is part of the prince's bid for power. And Chaucer was central to its message, central enough to warrant an expensive picture within the text. His memory was being turned into the regimental colours for those opposed to the current regime.

DOES THE HENGWRT MS CHART THE RETURN
OF CHAUCER'S STAR?

There is one other item of material evidence to help us piece together the revival of Chaucer's reputation around 1410. It may also provide us with a tantalizing clue as to what had been happening to his manuscripts prior to that time. It is a piece of evidence that links Hoccleve's *The Regement of Princes* to the Hengwrt MS of *The Canterbury Tales*, which we were considering earlier. And since it involves the activities of a group of rats, perhaps we had better first describe what happened to the manuscript during its early life – at least as far as scholars have been able to deduce from detailed examination of it.

The Hengwrt MS was compiled over several years. At least two scribes had a hand in it, under a supervisor's watchful eye. We do not know who the supervisor was, but it has been suggested that he might even have been Chaucer himself. Several inks are used, indicating what appears to be several passages of time between copying, and the whole manuscript is 'a series of parts'. Two of the tales appear to have been copied for a different collection but then pressed into service to complete the Hengwrt.[27]

One of the tales, *The Cook's Tale*, breaks off abruptly, and thereafter the regime of production seems to have changed and the supervisor drops from view. There are signs of haste in the later stages of copying, and signs that the final scribe tried to give the manuscript the appearance of a complete work.[28]

Even more intriguing, there seems also to be evidence that the manuscript was left lying around as loose leaves for some time before it was bound.[29] Now, in itself, this was not necessarily unusual – manuscripts could be completed but not bound for many reasons. However the Hengwrt was left lying around loose for long enough for rats to have got in and gnawed at some of the leaves before it was finally bound. This doesn't indicate simply a gap in the production line – it seems to suggest a degree of neglect.

Besides the rats' teeth-marks, there was another contribution to the Hengwrt MS before it was first bound, and this brings us back to Thomas Hoccleve. *The Monk's Tale* had been copied without the stanza about Adam. While it was still in loose leaves, someone has added the missing stanza in the margin. The handwriting is tiny, and appears to be the work of the same scribe responsible for the presentation copy of Hoccleve's *The Regement of Princes* made in 1412–13.[30]

Now, if the Adam stanza were copied into the Hengwrt around the same time, it means that the Hengwrt MS remained neglected in loose leaves throughout the ascendency of Henry IV and Archbishop Arundel, and was only rescued from the cellar (or wherever it was) after Prince Henry made his bid for power.

Was it neglected simply because Chaucer was no longer fashionable – or because Chaucer was no longer approved of? Could it be that the manuscript had been hidden away during those first dark and dangerous years of the fifteenth century? Could it be that, in the history of the making of the Hengwrt MS we have a sketch map of the rise and fall and rise again of Chaucer's early reputation?

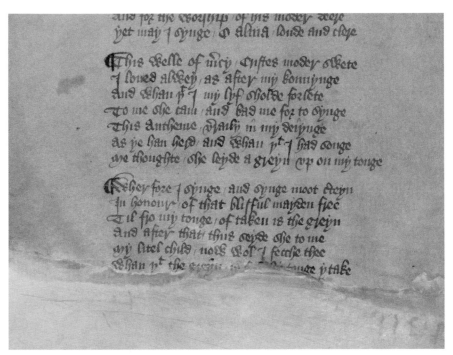

The section of the Hengwrt MS gnawed by rats, indicating a lapse of many years between writing and binding.

CHAPTER 15

Chaucer's final days

≈

Out of this toune helpe me thurgh your myght ...
The Complaint of Chaucer to His Purse, l. 17

In spite of his *Complaint*, Chaucer didn't in fact manage to get out of London – at least not as far as we know. But then we know very little of his final days upon this earth. That is part of the problem.

It is not just that there is no official record of Chaucer's death; there is, indeed, no *contemporary* record of it either. He simply disappears. One might have expected some documentation concerning such a famous man. But there is nothing. The last mention of the great poet and intellectual is that he received £5 owing on his annuity from the hand of Henry Somer, a clerk of the Exchequer on 5 June 1400. After that: silence.

WHY DIDN'T CHAUCER LEAVE A WILL?

Perhaps the oddest thing is that Chaucer does not appear to have made a will. His friends and contemporaries did. John Gower left one. So did Sir Lewis Clifford. Even Piers the Plowman made a will![1] Surely a meticulous civil servant, like Chaucer, would not have died intestate if he could possibly have helped it.

In 1378, before he embarked on his journey to Italy, he appointed attorneys to look after his affairs (John Gower was one), so we know that he took these matters seriously. If by the end of the century he found himself lying on his deathbed, it seems improbable that he would not have put his affairs into order.

Of course, documents can get lost with the passage of time, and so nothing conclusive can be adduced simply from the lack of a will; yet it is curious that despite extensive searches in the public records nothing relating to the winding-up of Chaucer's estate has been found.[2]

'The absence of a will for Chaucer strikes me as a bit puzzling,' writes Nigel Saul, Richard II's biographer:

> Wills become fairly common by the end of the fourteenth century. Indeed, it was generally the practice for every man of property to make one with the onset of old age. An appropriate moment in Chaucer's life would have been his entry into that property in the precincts of Westminster Abbey in 1399.
>
> A great many wills have been lost, of course. But the incidence of survival is highest among those who were resident in London and the south-east. From London there is the great series of wills in the rolls of the Court of Husting ... which begins long before Chaucer's death and continues long after.[3] At Lambeth Palace there are the wills irregularly enrolled in the archbishops' registers, and above all there is the long series of Prerogative Court of Canterbury Wills in the registers at the Public Record Office.[4] It is a reasonable surmise that Chaucer's will, if he had made one, would have been enrolled in one of these registers. After all, he resided for long periods in London and, at least for a while, in Kent at or near Greenwich.[5] But evidently no will was enrolled.
>
> The objection could be raised that Chaucer probably did not actually own property; he leased it. The distinction is a fair one, but it does not have any bearing on the making of a will. A will – strictly speaking, a testament – was concerned with the disposition of the testator's moveable assets, not with real estate. The latter was generally taken care of separately, in a codicil or by an enfeoffment to use.
>
> Late medieval wills are principally concerned with disposing of the testator's moveable wealth to the maximum benefit of his soul. The objects disposed of include plate, bed hangings, tableware, clothing, livestock, sometimes books – any items of value. Commonly, gifts are made to the church: it is usual to find small sums left to the four orders of friars and to parish churches and hospitals in the testator's neighbourhood.
>
> These are the sort of bequests that Chaucer might be expected to have made. Yet we have no evidence of them.[6]

Four of the knights accused by the chronicler Walsingham of being Lollards not only failed to leave wills, but also failed to be recorded in the Canterbury

Register, which another historian regards as 'a little mysterious'. He suggests, however, that a violent, unexpected end, such as Montagu met with at the hands of the Cirencester mob in 1400, could explain such a lack.[7] Might the same be true of Chaucer? After all these were people he knew – perhaps even close friends. Not necessarily that Chaucer was lynched by a violent mob, of course, but that he met some sudden or unforeseen end?

We know that Chaucer had things to leave. He tells us himself that he had a substantial library, for example. In the *Prologue* to *The Legend of Good Women* the God of Love admonishes Chaucer for being unable to write anything complimentary about women, despite his having such an extensive library – sixty books, no less!

> Was there no good matere in thy mynde,
> Ne in alle thy bokes ne coudest thow nat fynde
> Som story of wemen that were goode and trewe?
> Yes, God wot, sixty bokes olde and newe
> Hast thow thyself, alle ful of stories grete ...
> *The Legend of Good Women*, ll. 270–4
> Was there not good material in your mind,
> Nor in all your books could you not find
> Some story of women that were good and true?
> Yes, God knows! Sixty books both old and new
> You own yourself, all full of long stories ...

Sixty books was almost a king's library. Henry V possessed a library of 110 volumes at his death – and he was an educated king who valued books.[8] Of course, it's not necessary to take the remark in the *Legend* as the literal truth, but there is, on the other hand, no reason to think it impossible. One would expect a serious 'makir' like Chaucer to own books. And even twenty books in the hands of a commoner would still have brought his heirs a pretty penny.

Chaucer clearly had things to leave. We would expect him to have made a will. It was what others of his class and background were doing at the time, and it seems uncharacteristic of Chaucer to neglect his affairs to such an extent. The lack of a will therefore suggests three possibilities. Either the will has been accidentally destroyed or lost sometime after Chaucer's death; or Chaucer didn't make a will because his death was so sudden; or that he made one, met a sudden end, and his will was deliberately destroyed, along with all his other papers.

THE 53-YEAR LEASE

Chaucer certainly didn't seem to have been expecting to die in December 1399, for he took out a 53-year lease on a house at that time. Now, of course, he wasn't expecting to live for another 53 years either, but it is not the act of a man at death's door.

Derek Pearsall (in *The Life of Geoffrey Chaucer*) refers to the 'inexplicable circumstances in which Chaucer took a fifty-three-year lease' on a house and goes on to suggest that perhaps Chaucer was subconsciously trying to fend off the approach of death both by expanding the scope of *The Canterbury Tales* and by taking out the long lease.[9] And that is quite possible. On the other hand, the length of the lease might simply be the act of a man who doesn't think he's anywhere near dying – and if, as has been suggested, Chaucer did indeed make a trip to Calais in early 1400 he is unlikely to have been in poor health.[10]

The impression persists that Chaucer may have met a sudden, unexpected death, and it is reinforced by the testimony of his fellow poets writing after the Prince of Wales takes power in 1410. If we return to the memorials of Chaucer penned by Lydgate and Hoccleve, we find they not only align Chaucer politically with the Prince of Wales against Henry IV, they also convey a remarkably consistent impression of his death and its suddeness.

CHAUCER'S SUDDEN DEATH

For a start, why do the fifteenth-century poets go on about the *tragedy* of Chaucer's death? It's one thing to sing his praises and to acknowledge his superiority and his importance in turning the English language into a recognized vehicle for poetry, but why go on about the *tragedy* of his being dead – ten, twenty years after he died? It seems as if Lydgate and Hoccleve cannot mention Chaucer without regretting his death – as if there were something about it which they cannot actually address.

The consistent theme of their eulogies is that the death that took Chaucer away was unanticipated and sudden. Thus Hoccleve:

> That combre-world, that the, my maistir, slow,
> Wold I slayn were! Deth was to hastyf
> To renne on thee, and reue the thi lyf.
> *The Regement of Princes*, ll. 2091–3

That Vexer of the World, who killed you, my master,
I wish he were slain [himself]! Death was too hasty
To run at you and rob you of your life.

Of course, untimeliness is one of the 'great themes' in eulogies. There is a special kind of mourning to be done for those whose lives are cut short of full achievement. In English, Milton did it best in 'Lycidas'. Untimeliness is as common as grass in eulogies.

But eulogy allows other approaches as well. Some eulogies, while acknowledging the sadness of a passing, emphasize the peace that comes from a life fulfilled – death's *timeliness*, precisely. Think of Tennyson's 'Crossing the Bar'. So poets have a choice; and when, like Hoccleve and Lydgate, they keep hitting on the same note, in high-strung language and for a long time, there *may* be something to it.

In this case, what jumps off the page is Hoccleve's image of death as a street mugger 'running at' Chaucer one-on-one to rob him of his life in an isolated, senseless criminal act. Street crime and the fear of sudden, unexpected attack amidst familiar surroundings were as commonplace for Londoners of the fourteenth century as today. Perhaps more so. Chaucer himself had had first-hand experience: he'd been mugged while making his rounds as Richard II's Clerk of the King's Works.[11]

Death as a street mugger

But for Hoccleve to use such a violent image here – in a eulogy – suggests that both poet and readers understand that Chaucer did not meet his fate as an ailing old man on his deathbed. Could it even be that for a small but informed audience, the allusion is to an actual, little-publicized meeting with death on the road, that took Chaucer by surprise?

In any case, Hoccleve's eulogy is clearly not of the 'well-earned rest in the bosom of God' genre. Whatever happened to Chaucer overtook him too soon and suddenly. Nor could the verbs be chosen to more violent effect:

What eiled deth? Allas! Why wolde he sle the?

O deth! thou didest naght harme singuleer,
In slaghtere of him; but al this land it smertith;

But nathelees, yit hast thou no power
His name sle; his hy vertu astertith
Unslayn fro the, which ay us lyfly hertyth,
With bookes of his ornat endyting,
That is to al this land enlumynyng.
   The Regement of Princes, ll. 1967–74
What ailed Death? Alas! Why would he slay thee?

O death! You didn't do an individual harm
In slaughtering him, but all this land suffers by it.
But nonetheless, you still have no power
To slay his name. His great force springs up afresh
Unslain by you, which ever gives us new heart,
With books of his highly embellished writing
Which has been illuminating to all this land.

Chaucer the 'gentle master' is not allowed to go quietly – Hoccleve has him 'slaughtered', the word applied most often to animals killed for a purpose. Chaucer didn't just die; death was brought upon him by another agent. The impression is reinforced later when Hoccleve says 'his lyfe be queynt' – his life was *quenched* – snuffed out.

Moreover Chaucer's 'slaghtere' has national impact: 'but al this land it smertith'. It is a tragedy of the highest scale which, in a sort of backhanded way, Hoccleve puts into perspective in the following stanza:

Hast thou nat eeke my maister Gower slayn,
Whos vertu I am insufficient
For to descreyue? I wote wel in certain,
For to sleen al this world thou haast yment;
   The Regement of Princes, ll. 1975–81
Have you [Death] not also slain my master Gower,
Whose virtue I am insufficient
To describe? I know well and certainly
That you have meant to slay all the world;

Gower died quietly of old age in his lodgings at the Priory of St Mary Overie in Southwark. His loss to poetry earns him a mention – it's sad, but not a tragedy. Everybody dies, Hoccleve continues, even Christ! But that's just the

point, isn't it? Hoccleve isn't saying Chaucer should
have lived for ever. Only that he shouldn't have died
when he did.

A few lines further on the description gets even
more interesting. Hoccleve intriguingly turns death
into a female figure who has deliberately taken
Chaucer away because 'she' knew he could not be
replaced:

Death and the Lady.

> She myghte han taried hir vengeance awhile,
> Til that sum man had egal to thè be.
> Nay, lat be that! sche knew wel that this yle
> May neuer man forth brynge lyk to the,
> And hir office needes do mot she;
> God bad hir so, I truste as for the beste;
> O maister, maister, god thi soule rest!
> *The Regement of Princes*, ll. 2094–107
> She [Death] might have stayed her vengeance awhile,
> Until some man had been equal to thee [i.e. Chaucer].
> Nay, let that be! She knew well that this isle
> Will never bring forth a man like thee,
> And her office she needs must do.
> God bid her so, I trust as for the best;
> Oh master, master, God give thy soul some rest!

Of course these lines are capable of a perfectly neutral interpretation. They
could simply be a generalized lament against death: 'Why couldn't Death have
waited until we had another poet equal to Chaucer ... But no, Death had to do
her office.'

But what are we to make of the following?

> Nay, let that be! She knew well that this isle
> Will never bring forth a man like thee ...

Hoccleve seems to be saying that death *deliberately* took Chaucer away because
'she' *knew* that England would never produce another like him – as if, in other
words, death had a choice. This is an odd thing to imply. Death is usually portrayed

as even-handed – without respect for rich or poor, for virtuous or evil, or for young or old (and Hoccleve does indeed cover those possibilities in the previous stanza). Why then give death such an exceptionally specific motivation, unless it's to flag some hidden meaning? Why should death *care* about whether Chaucer could or could not be replaced? The motive makes more sense in the world of human politics for which *The Regement* was written than in the mythic world of life and death. For what if Arundel were death?

In other words, Arundel wanted to silence the critics of the church; he knew that there was no one who could match Chaucer; and that is why Chaucer had to die. There was no one else capable of mobilizing such open mockery, of carrying out such a serious onslaught against the corrupt practices of the established church. Remove Chaucer, and Arundel would rid himself of the most articulate, informed and effective opposition that the Church Commercial faced.

And the clever thing was that, from the established church's point of view, the deed was being done in the name of God – as part of the drive to stamp out heresy. 'God bad hir so' – it could almost be a coded reminder that the impetus for Chaucer's death came from the ecclesiastics![12]

Death must carry out her office because God (or the church) ordered 'her' to. And who are we to question the actions of the church? The smoke was still rising over John Badby's ashes when Hoccleve was writing. Archbishop Arundel had made it clear that we must accept without question what the church ordains ('I trust as for the best'). But oh! master, master ...

And her office she needs must do.
God bid her so, I trust as for the best;
Oh master, master, god thy soul give rest!

The stumbling lines, the sense of loss and the anger against 'death', all combine to suggest that something is not quite right with the way Chaucer died ... that there is some underlying injustice that cannot be articulated.

Lydgate too emphasizes the *tragedy* and the suddenness of Chaucer's demise in his *Troy Book*: But he adds another – slightly sinister – ingredient: 'envy', which in those days meant 'ill-will' or 'hatred':

Gret cause haue I & mater to compleyne
On Antropos & vpon hir envie,
That brak the threde & made for to dye

Noble Galfride, poete of Breteyne,
Amonge oure englisch that made first to reyne
The gold dewe-dropis of rethorik so fyne,
Oure rude langage only tenlwmyne.
To God I pray, that he his soule haue,
After whose help of nede I moste crave,
And seke his boke that is left be-hynde
   Troy Book, II, ll. 4694–700
Great cause have I and reason to complain
Against Anthropos and her envy
That broke the thread and caused to die
Noble Geoffrey, poet of Britain,
Who first made reign in English
The gold dew-drops of rhetoric so fine,
Only to illuminate our language.
To God I pray, that he keeps his soul,
After whose help of necessity I must crave,
And seek his book that is left behind.

As an isolated passage this could, of course, be passed off as totally conventional, but when it is read in the context of so many other laments on the same lines, there is reason to treat the conventional phrases with respect.

In Lydgate's later works, written after 1420, the emphasis moves away from the complaint over Chaucer's death to the celebration of his greatness. This seems to support the idea that the earlier bitterness over Chaucer's untimely death was more than a conventional posture and that it did indeed contain a sub-text of topical allusion which faded as the years passed.

When Lydgate finished the *Troy Book* in 1420, Henry IV had been dead for seven years and Thomas Arundel for six. Recruiting Chaucer's memory to muster opposition to the king and archbishop had value in 1409–12, but such tactics undoubtedly lost their attraction for the prince once he put on the crown. Keeping alive old murders, whether Richard's or Chaucer's, would have been detrimental to Henry's own goals of self-legitimation, national unity and success in his war with France.

Seventy-nine years later, the printer William Caxton had a memorial fixed to a pillar above Chaucer's grave. On it was inscribed a poem by the Italian poet Stephen Surigo (Stefano de Surigone) which read: 'Pierian Muses ... lament the cruel fate of the bard Geoffrey Chaucer. Let it be a crime to refrain from weeping.'[13]

This could be yet one more conventional platitude. After all, death is inevitable, and the usual medieval reflection was: 'This will happen to us all – Death is the great leveller.' Alternatively we might see it as a surviving memory, a hint at some untold story that Chaucer somehow suffered an untimely death – one that simply shouldn't have happened when it did.

LACK OF A MONUMENT

William Caxton was the first person to mention Chaucer's tomb, and when he did so it was to say that he did not regard it as a satisfactory memorial for the 'worshipful fader and first foundeur & enbelissher of ornate eloquence in our englissh.' He therefore commissioned Surigo, an Italian scholar from the University of Milan then teaching Latin Eloquence at Oxford, to write some suitable verses, to be inscribed on 'a tablet of verses' and attached to one of the columns in Westminster Abbey.[14]

There is no very good record of what marked Chaucer's grave before this. Caxton refers to it as a 'sepulture' (which could just mean 'grave') 'standing before the Chapel of Saint Benedict'. The antiquary John Stowe, writing some-time before 1598, says Chaucer was buried in the cloister (as was, Stowe also notes, Chaucer's old friend Henry Scogan), but gives no description.[15] The only other detail we have from anywhere near the period is from Surigo, who calls it 'a tiny grave'.

But we *do* have an interesting account from a gentleman of the early eighteenth century named John Dart. Mr Dart was a bit of a history buff, with a particular focus on Westminster Abbey. Dart reports that Chaucer was buried under the floor in the south transept, beneath a single slab so simple that, when it was removed in 1700 to make room for the elaborate tomb of John Dryden, it was subsequently 'sawn to mend the pavement'.[16] Unfortunately, Dart makes no mention of which pavement received the mending – or of anything that might have been found a few feet further down.

So, all we can infer is that Chaucer's burial was a comparatively humble one. John Gower, in contrast, had been buried at St Mary Overie, Southwark, in an elaborate tomb – complete with his effigy resting its head on his three books – which still stands to this day in what is now Southwark Cathedral.

Of course, we should bear in mind that Caxton was Chaucer's publisher, and the table of verses may have been simply part of a publicity campaign, but if we take Caxton's indignation over Chaucer's memorial at face value, then we may draw one of two conclusions. One is that the funerary arrangements were following Chaucer's own expressed desires – in which case he seems to have leant towards the funeral simplicity demanded by many so-called Lollards in their wills. The second possible inference is that he was buried without ceremony so as not to draw attention to his death – an official brushing under the carpet perhaps?

Such a burial might be extraordinary for a figure as famous as Chaucer, but it would not be extraordinary for someone whom the usurping regime disapproved of – or even feared. Henry IV seems to have so feared the symbolic resonance of Richard's burial site that he hid the body away on his own private estate at Kings Langley, a safe twenty miles out of London. Almost a hundred and fifty years later, the same treatment was meted out to Galileo Galilei, when Pope Urban's intervention prevented Galileo's patron, the Grand Duke of Tuscany, from erecting a monument in the Church of Santa Croce in Florence, with the result that the remains of the great man 'were quietly hidden away in the basement of the church bell tower for almost a century'.[17]

Those who wield power – and especially those who wield it with questionable legitimacy – are seldom keen to allow splendid memorials to those they perceive as their critics.

DID CHAUCER SEEK SANCTUARY IN HIS FINAL MONTHS?

According to *Chaucer Life-Records*, being buried in Westminster Abbey at this period did not denote appreciation of Chaucer as a poet; the world-renowned 'Poet's Corner' is a much later invention. Nor was there anything particularly remarkable about Chaucer being buried in the abbey, since Richard II had been turning it into a burial place for courtiers and royal officials. But the fact that Chaucer was buried in Westminster did demonstrate that his allegiance was to the old regime. Westminster was Richard II's special church.[18]

In fact, Chaucer's association with Westminster began the previous year when he took out the famous 53-year lease. The house in question was in the garden of the Lady Chapel of Westminster Abbey. What is more, it was situated within the sanctuary of Westminster. So the intriguing question is raised: did Chaucer move into the sanctuary of Westminster because it was a nice house, or because it offered sanctuary? His lease is dated 24 December 1399 – less than two months after Henry had seized the throne. It was a time when the poet found himself in a highly dangerous and exposed situation. Is it possible that he was trying to avoid political fallout from the new regime?

There is no need to think that the tenement Chaucer rented was not an extremely pleasant place. It is true that there were more expensive properties, but at least this particular house was not situated in the quarters where most of the sanctuary-seekers were gathered.[19]

And with good reason. 'Sanctuarymen', or 'grithmen', were not always the cream of society. 'Thither fled the traitor and the murderer, the thief and the debtor, and there they dwelt secure from the king's justice or their victim's vengeance.'[20]

The bounds of the sanctuary at Westminster.

Certainly Londoners didn't think much of the 'sanctuarymen'. In 1402 they petitioned the Commons to remove the franchise of the other great sanctuary in London, St Martin's-in-the-Fields, where, they claimed:

> ... murderers, traitors and disturbers of the king's peace are received ... By day they hide, and by night they break out to do their murders, treasons, robberies and felonies not only within the Franchise of the City but also outside it.[21]

Many years later, in the time of Henry VII, a Venetian visitor to England 'found it hard to believe that so many villains were permitted to conduct organized criminal activities under the shelter of the church ...'[22]

During Chaucer's lifetime there was a constant tussle between church and state over the question of sanctuary. The validity of the concept was regularly challenged. In 1378, for example, Sir Alan Buxhill, Keeper of the Tower, broke into the abbey with forty soldiers to recapture two escaped 'debtors', Robert Haulay and John Shakyl – a clear violation of the sanctuary of Westminster. Buxhill and his men chased Haulay all over the abbey until they eventually killed him – along with the sacristan who was trying to defend him. Three months later, John Wyclif was rolled out at the Gloucester Parliament to make the theological argument against the applicability of sanctuary in cases of debt.[23]

In the Haulay-Shakyl case the argument was clear-cut with the bishops condemning the breach of sanctuary and the crown defending its invasion – although wheeling in a churchman to argue their case. But a few years later a curious inversion was to occur.

Westminster Abbey always remained jealous of its privilege of sanctuary, which arose from the fact that the land around the abbey was an independent liberty. Royal writ did not extend there, and royal officers had no authority.[24]

And yet, as Richard's reign progressed, it came about that the main defender of sanctuary was the king, while the chief opponent of it was a churchman – no less a figure than the Archbishop of York – later Archbishop of Canterbury – Thomas Arundel.

In 1388, while Arundel was still Chancellor of the Realm, a Suffolk parson, William de Chesterton, 'went into sanctuary at Westminster for his personal safety'. He had made the mistake of writing a letter to the pope in which he badmouthed the chancellor. Arundel read the offending letter out in parliament and there was an explosion of indignation, for the parson had also foolishly touched on some matters that could be regarded as treasonable. Arundel and parliament demanded the clerk be delivered up from sanctuary. Richard, however, opposed this, saying: 'It is not for us to drag anybody out of a holy place or punish him in it; and his punishment must accordingly be left to the discretion of the person who has the keeping of that place.'[25]

That same year, Sir Robert Tresilian, the Chief Justice of the King's Bench, fled from the wrath of the Lords Appellant. Discovered hiding in disguise in the house of a tenant of the sacristan of Westminster, Tresilian was dragged out by force and then executed forthwith. Richard II pleaded for the Chief Justice's life, arguing that his pursuers were guilty of breach of sanctuary, but William Wykeham, Bishop of Winchester and Thomas Arundel, newly created Archbishop of York, poured scorn on the idea, saying if this were allowed, all sorts of criminals would be able to scheme against the royal majesty. Wykeham and Arundel were, apparently, content to forgo this particular privilege of the church when it suited them.[26]

Sanctuary was thus not a foolproof guarantee of safety, especially when Thomas

The execution of Robert Tresilian.

Arundel was around, but it was at least some sort of bolt-hole.

What is more, most sanctuaries in the country could offer only a temporary refuge – forty days was the maximum stay. The sanctuary at Westminster, however, was one of the 'chartered' sanctuaries and could therefore offer more or less permanent refuge. The inmates were 'only subject to slight regulation, and although their members sometimes helped with daily chores it seems that little attempt was made to control or reform them. Since the sanctuarymen were not convicts, they could lawfully carry on trades while "inside"; some simply used the church as a safe base for continuing criminal activities. It is little wonder that the system was a subject of constant complaint.'[27]

The tenement which Chaucer rented, however, was not situated amongst the riff-raff of the sanctuarymen. Their places of abode were in a gated enclosure – huddled up against the wall that bordered the aptly named 'Thieving Lane'. Entry to the enclosure was by two main gates: Broad Gate to the north, and one by the Abbot's gaol at Tothill Street.

Chaucer's house was on the other side of the abbey, amongst the salubrious establishments of the well-to-do. But none the less it was within the sanctuary of Westminster, and as such gave the tenant certain 'privileges and immunities' for which he in turn had to give certain undertakings. Chaucer was bound by the terms of his lease, for example, 'not to receive without permission persons seeking protection because of the privileges and immunities of the abbey'.[28]

The fact that Chaucer took up residence in this location does not necessarily mean that he needed to – all sorts of people seemed to have lived there – but there is no getting away from the fact that, had he wanted to, he could have claimed whatever protection sanctuary might afford.

WESTMINSTER ABBEY AND THE KING

One thing is undeniable, however: by moving into the precincts of Westminster Abbey, Chaucer was unequivocally nailing his colours to the mast of Richard II's sinking ship. In fact, he was doing more than that, as it turned out. At the very moment that Chaucer moved into his tenement, Westminster Abbey was fast becoming the focus for Ricardian opposition to the new illegimate regime. 'The sympathies of the Abbot, William Colchester, were strongly on the side of Richard II, and he allowed his abbey, at the very centre of the administration of the kingdom, to become the headquarters of rebellion.'[29]

On Wednesday 17 December 1399 the Earls of Huntingdon, Kent, Rutland,

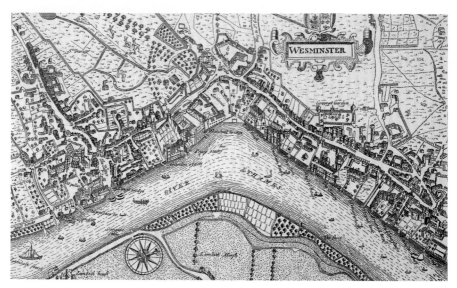

John Norden's bird's-eye view of London, 1593. You can see how even in the sixteenth century Westminster was separated from the City of London by fields.

and Salisbury met in the Abbey House at Westminster. There they were joined by the deposed Archbishop of Canterbury (Roger Walden), the ex-Bishop of Carlisle, and William Colchester, the Abbot of Westminster. J.H. Wylie, Henry IV's biographer, adds that there was also 'Richard Maudeleyn, a priest ... who had been one of King Richard's most intimate personal companions. This man bore a remarkable likeness to the late king both in face and figure ... Two others were present at the Abbot's house: the one a French physician, "John Paule" ["Master Pol"], whom Richard had left at Wallingford as one of the specially trusted guardians of his queen – the other, Sir Thomas Blount, "a sage baron" of Oxfordshire.'[30]

Even if Chaucer were not seeking asylum within the abbey confines when he took out his lease at the back-end of the year 1399, he was placing himself in the centre of rebellion. Is it conceivable that Chaucer could have been unaware of what he was doing? Chaucer was a man who had acted as diplomat and spy for two monarchs. He was a man with his finger on the pulse of every stratum of society (look at *The General Prologue*). He was a squire of the chamber – a man who knew enough about what was going on in 1386 to take a low profile when the magnates rebelled against Richard.

Chaucer would have known that Westminster Abbey was Richard's special church – the one where he had planned to be buried alongside his beloved Queen Anne. Chaucer may possibly have also known that as much as it was loved by Richard, it was disliked by Henry.[31]

Chaucer would also have known that there was no love lost between the Abbot of Westminster, William Colchester, and Archbishop Arundel. They had clashed on more than one occasion.[32]

Surely, then, Chaucer would have been aware that by throwing in his lot with the Abbey of Westminster, he would have been aligning himself with Richard's camp – at least in the eyes of the new king and archbishop.

Would Chaucer have done this if he were trying to curry favour with the new regime? Or did he consider it to be a risk worth taking? For we should not forget that at this moment, when Chaucer makes his move, Richard is still alive. The hopes of those loyal to him must have also been still alive. The possibility of reinstating Richard and destroying the usurper would not have seemed so far-fetched at that moment as it does to us today. Richard's supporters were not to know, as they gathered in the Abbot of Westminster's house, that it was to be the failure of their *coup* that would trigger Richard's death.

In such troubled times, Westminster and its sanctuary may or may not have offered a fragile but welcome security to the literary spokesman of Richard's court, but the move there would certainly have made clear where Chaucer's allegiance lay.

OTHER TENANTS OF CHAUCER'S HOUSE

It is generally claimed, however, that the tenement which Chaucer occupied so briefly could have had little to do with seeking sanctuary, since it appears to have been subsequently leased by loyal servants of the usurper. John Gardner records that Chaucer's successors in the house in the abbey grounds included Paul de la Mounte who, he tells us, was Henry IV's chief clerk and physician.[33] And the usual clincher is that the longest-holding tenant was Chaucer's son, Thomas, whom Henry appointed (among other titles) Chief Butler to the king in 1402. In that office Thomas served Henry IV for most of his reign, and was reappointed by his son Henry V upon the usurper's death in 1413. As the *Chaucer Life-Records* say, 'The general nature of the tenement can be judged by the type of people who occupied it. Those near to Chaucer in date resembled him socially, in that they had some official connection with the court.'[34]

If the tenement was occupied by favoured members of Henry's household, the argument goes, then clearly it was not being used *as* sanctuary. It may have been merely a nice house in a convenient location.

But the list of tenants is not as straightforward as that. John Gardner, for example, appears to have misread the entry in the *Chaucer Life-Records*: Paul de la Mounte was Richard II's chief clerk and physician, not Henry's.[35] Perhaps more significantly, he was also the 'Master Pol' listed as present among the 'Epiphany plotters' who met in the Abbott's house on that week before Christmas 1399, to plan the usurper's assassination. The good physician probably had every reason to keep out of the Henry's way in the winter of 1400–01.

Moreover, the next tenant after 'Master Pol' also had close ties to Richard. He was one William Horscroft, the chief skinner, who had supplied Richard with 'enormous quantities of furs, cloaks and hoods' and who was rich enough to stand surety for many 'prominent and wealthy people' during Richard's reign.[36] It seems that Chaucer's two successors to the tenement were both men aligned with the previous regime and men, therefore, who needed to tread carefully in the new and perilous times.

But what of the tenant who held the lease for the longest period – Chaucer's own son, Thomas? Surely Thomas Chaucer was a trusted retainer of Henry IV's – he would have had no need to seek sanctuary at Westminster. Well, probably not from the king … no …

Thomas Chaucer was a man of affairs at court and in the city, who must have inherited some of his father's diplomatic skills. There is no question that they served him well in the early days of the usurpation. Three days after his coronation, Henry appointed Thomas Chaucer Constable of Wallingford Castle for life. On 5 November 1402, Thomas was appointed Chief Butler to the King, a significant position which he held intermittently until his death in 1434, having been several times renewed and reappointed by Henry IV, and then later by Henry V.[37]

Among other duties, the Chief Butler was empowered to supply wine for the king's table, and perhaps more importantly, to appoint deputies with exclusive rights to buy wine for the king in specific ports – an authority Thomas exercised to put his friends (like Lewis John and John Snypston) in the way of good profits.

As Chief Butler, Thomas also became *ex officio* Coroner of the City of London, though the position, as with most *ex officios*, seems to have been primarily honorific. No one believes that he spent time reviewing the cases of everyone in London who passed away, any more than that he spent his days waiting at Henry's elbow with a pitcher of wine.

But these were dangerous times, and no matter how skilful a politician Thomas Chaucer may have been, he was having to swim in extremely murky waters. And whatever *bonhomie* may have existed between Henry IV and his Chief Butler, it was not shared by the king's right-hand man, Archbishop Arundel.

In 1407, Thomas Chaucer – then Speaker of the House of Commons – clashed in parliament with Archbishop Arundel, newly reappointed as Chancellor of the Realm. The issue Thomas raised was specifically to demand accountability to parliament of the King's Council, over which Arundel, as Chancellor, had just gained control. Not surprisingly, given his rather negative views on power-sharing, Arundel cut Thomas Chaucer off in mid-speech. It was a vehement enough reaction to have been noted for the record. And perhaps not surprisingly, too, Thomas Chaucer ceased to be Speaker in 1408.

Two years later he must have made himself even more unpopular with the archbishop. In January of 1410 Thomas Chaucer, once again elected Speaker, had a new job: this time to lead the Commons as they presented a bill to dis-endow the church (and the Caesarian clergy) – a bill so notorious that in some circles it acquired a nickname: the 'Lollard Disendowment Bill'.

It would be difficult to imagine a more comprehensive way to antagonize the church establishment and Archbishop Arundel in particular. The bill envisioned doing everything that was most abhorrent to him. It proposed taking away from the church all of its property and possessions and redistributing them amongst the court and laity. The Commons reckoned that with the proceeds of the dis-endowment, and the temporalities 'occupied' and 'arrogantly wasted' by the bishops, abbots and priors, the king could acquire 'fifteen new Earls, 1,500 knights, 6,200 esquires and a hundred new alms houses. In addition, he could draw from the same sources an additional annual income of £20,000, plus £2,000 for each Earl and for every knight £200 ... '[38]

There is no record of Archbishop Arundel's precise reaction to this breathtak-ingly radical proposition – not that it's difficult to guess. Henry IV, however, banned all discussion outright. If the Commons had hoped that the economic benefits of disendowment would appeal to the cupidity of the king and his empty purse, their hopes were quickly dashed. They were four Henrys too soon. The usurper, evincing all signs of being scandalized, decided to adopt the orthodox stance. Some members of the king's affinity got even hotter. Henry's esquire, John Norbury, urged the archbishop to 'take up the Cross against the enemies of the Cross' and wage holy war against them. The Commons were forced to grovel in apology, and Thomas as Speaker was forced humbly to request the return of the Disendowment Bill.

But parliament – and Thomas Chaucer – got off lucky. And to make sure that everybody knew just *how* lucky, Henry and his archbishop did a little promotional advertising. It had all the earmarks of a typical Arundel campaign. As Peter McNiven, in his book *Heresy and Politics in the Reign of Henry IV*, argues forcibly, the burning of one John Badby, in March 1410, was nothing less than a direct warning to the Commons.[39]

What happened to Badby was probably what Arundel would like to have done to the ringleaders of the Commons – amongst whom Thomas Chaucer, as Speaker, must have been one of the most vulnerable. Thomas would no doubt be mindful of the fate of the last Speaker of the Commons in Richard's reign – Sir John Bussy, who had read out the accusations of treason that led to Archbishop Arundel's exile under Richard. Bussy was executed without trial by the all-conquering Henry on the 29 July 1399.[40] Nobody ever accused Thomas Arundel of having a short memory.

Is there any wonder that by September of 1411 we find that Thomas Chaucer has availed himself of the lease on his father's old tenement 'within the sanctuary' of Westminster?[41] Whether Thomas intended to use it or not, he must have thought it not imprudent to keep a bolt-hole within the sanctuary of Westminster, at such an inauspicious time.

He had evidently offended the king, as well as the archbishop, because two months after he took up the lease on the tenement, just before the November parliament, Henry warned '[Thomas] Chaucer in particular that he would tolerate no sort of innovation in this parliament'.[42]

This was certainly a dangerous time for Thomas, for this was the parliament in which the party of the Prince of Wales lost its grip on power – perhaps as a result of the rash proposal that the king should abdicate in favour of his eldest son. Henry IV reasserted control and reinstalled Archbishop Arundel as Chancellor. Thomas Chaucer would need all the sanctuary he could get.

The parliament finished with the Commons obviously fearful of recriminations and petitioning the usurper that he would declare himself satisfied with the loyalty of those who had attended both this parliament and its predecessor.

In the long run, however, Thomas seems to have done himself no harm with the king, for he was retained as Chief Butler until Henry IV died in 1413. None the less, however we look at them, the events of 1410 and 1411 were dangerous and difficult to negotiate. The fact that Thomas took up his father's old lease within the sanctuary of Westminster at this time suggests that the availability of sanctuary may have been a consideration.

To return to 1400. We cannot say categorically that Geoffrey Chaucer took out the lease on the tenement in the sanctuary of Westminster Abbey in order to make use of the protection that it offered, but we *can* say that the potential was there, should he have needed it. The sanctuary was certainly used for political asylum. In 1413 an extraordinary character by the name of John Wyghtlok, a former groom of Richard II's, installed himself in a safe-house in the sanctuary, and used it as a base to disseminate broadsides proclaiming that King Richard was still alive and well in Scotland.[43]

We can also say that there is some evidence that others who leased the same tenement may have had reason to be interested in its location within the sanctuary. And we can *certainly* say that by moving into Westminster, Geoffrey Chaucer was identifying with the Ricardian party rather than with the new regime of the usurper.

And so we are left with one last question to address about the poet's final days, and that is: Did Geoffrey Chaucer really die in 1400?

CHAPTER 16

Did Chaucer really die in 1400?

≈

There is a single-page manuscript in the collection of the British Library. One side of it has a rather attractive, full-length portrait of Geoffrey Chaucer standing on what looks like a prodigious golf divot, staring thoughtfully down at a conical pen case (known as a 'penner') in his right hand, and holding a rosary in his left. The manuscript bears the rather unprepossessing title of BL MS Additional 5141, but the image it carries is instantly recognizable because for years it graced the cover of the Penguin edition of Nevill Coghill's much-reprinted modernization of *The Canterbury Tales*.

Apart from its general familiarity as 'what Chaucer looked like' for generations of paperback readers, though, very little is known about BL MS Add. 5141. It arrived at the Library (then the British Museum) in 1786 as half of a two-part gift of manuscripts from one George Steevens.[1] The other manuscript was a *Canterbury Tales* (now BL MS Add. 5140) which, records show, Steevens purchased for nine guineas at auction. He didn't buy the portrait at the same auction, however. No mention of the portrait is made in the sale catalogue, and the fact that the Museum bound it separately instead of with the *Canterbury Tales* copy Steevens donated suggests that, at the time, someone (presumably Steevens) knew more than we do now about the fate of the larger manuscript from which the portrait was cut. We'd like to know a lot more about that of course – even though we probably won't, ever – because there is a lot more to BL MS Add. 5141 than the Penguin front cover reveals.

The portrait of Chaucer from BL MS Add. 5141.

CHAUCER'S MOST INACCURATE BIOGRAPHY?

To begin with, in the top corners of the page there are items the Penguin graphics designer saw fit to excise for the book cover, to make room for the title and Chaucer's name. To the left of the portrait in the manuscript is a shield bearing the arms of the Chaucer family, a chequerboard of irregularly sized diagonals of red and white. To the right, there is an English daisy, a marguerite, with four leaves, one opened bloom and two buds; and over the daisy, the Arabic numbers '1402'.

More intriguing, on the back of the page is a brief *vita* of the poet, written in a late sixteenth-century hand, as follows:

Hactenus Chauceri vita

He lyved some parte of Richarde the second his tyme, in the lowe cuntryes of Holland and Zellande by reason of some disgrace that happenyd unto hym, as a man suspected to be spotted with the rebellion of Jack Straw and Watte Tyler. From thence he travailed into Fraunce where he proffited so much in the Frenche tongue and grewe into such singularitye of knowledge in their Phrase of Speatch, and Methode of writinge, as they had hym in wonderfull admiration for his wisdome, and to this daie havinge his works in thayre owne Language they do mutch esteame them. He returned out of Fraunce in the Latter ende of Ric. The 2. His reigne accompanied such a wonderful fame of his well doinges as the unseparable companyon of his vertues. The rest of his Lief (which was not longe) he spent at his Mannor at Ewhellme in Oxford shyr and his castel of Dunnyngton in berkshyer the which were both his and other landes to the valewe of L 1000 by the yere the which out of the discent of his Lyne came all to the Duke of Suffolke, and by his attendor to the Kinge. He had a house in Woodstock where he dyd Lye mutch when the courte was there, it is at this daie still cauled Chaucers house beinge a house of great receipt and next adioyninge to the courte and havinge a pryvye waie thorowe the parck to the courte the which argued his great estimacon with the kinge, (or rather with the Quene as some thought). There is yet in Dunyngton Parck an Oke still cauled Chaucers Oke where many tymes he toke delight to visite his boke and exercyse his memory. After he had lyved to very olde age he died at London and is buryed in Westmynster /A[nno domini] /1402 / A[nno] regni Regis henrici 4ti/Quarto/. Whose Lief was so good, and vertues so rare, as God defende that ever tyme should decaye his prayse, or weare out the worthy memorye of so excellent a

man as his worckes yet extant and in Printe do sufficientilie prove him. A sub-
tile and wittye Logycyan, An eloquent and Swete Rethorycyan, A delightful
and pleasant Poete, A grave and modest Philosopher, A moste religious and
holye devyne, So that (Leonem ut in proverbis est [homines] ex lipsis aestiment
Ungrisus). His worckes unprinted and not to be founde

Chronicon conquestus Anglici   De Leonie et eius dignitate

Inobitum Blanchiae Ducissae   Dantem Italum transtutlit

De Vulcani veru   Jack Upland inveighing against Freeres

Alia plura fecit in quisq[ue]   ocia, Missantium iam magnam
　　　/Monacho[num]

... Ititudinem, horas non intellectas, Reiliqias, perepgrinationes, ac ceromonia

... probavit   Praedicat Algerum merito Florentia Dantem
　　　　　　　Italia and ... meros tota Petrarche tuos
　　　　　　　Anglia Chaucerum vera ... a Partam
　　　　　　　... Veneres debet patria ... suas

Anyone familiar with the story of Chaucer's life, as pieced together by modern
scholars, will know that this poor Renaissance biographer got nearly every detail
wrong. No recent scholar has ever placed Chaucer in the Low Countries as a
political exile, on the run from Richard II's soldiers; neither does any modern
biographer have him seeking asylum in France. None of the estates awarded him
in BL Add. 5141 belonged to him, according to presently accepted accounts – but
rather to his son, Thomas Chaucer. Nor does any present-day scholar of Geoffrey
Chaucer believe he wrote the 'lost' works attributed to him by the manuscript,
except perhaps the *Inobitum Blanchiae Ducissae* (if that is in fact *The Book of
the Duchess*) and *De Leonie et eius dignitate* (the long-lost *Book of the Lion*?).
About his death in London and his burial in Westminster, some refreshing verity
creeps in – *but in the year 1402?* In all respects, the document seems wildly idiosyncratic. One wonders where the writer of BL Add. 5141 got such stuff.

WHERE DID THE ANONYMOUS BIOGRAPHER GET HIS INFORMATION?

Actually, we do know a bit about the sources of the BL Add. 5141 *vita* – enough
to hazard a few guesses, anyway, at some of its tantalizing secrets. It seems our
Renaissance biographer was a careful scholar, despite how nearly everything he

wrote completely contradicts what everyone believes today. Apparently he looked into all of the published sources available *c.* 1598 to compile the single-page *vita*. These sources were: John Leland (1506–52), Henry VIII's library-keeper and tireless researcher into the nation's antiquities, John Bale (1495–1563), one-time vicar of Swaffham, Norfolk and author of a history of English writers, Thomas Speght (*fl.*1598), schoolmaster and an early editor of Chaucer's works, and possibly William Thynne (*d.* 1546), clerk of the kitchen to Henry VIII and the first editor of Chaucer's works.

From each (except Thynne) he quoted directly, or paraphrased unmistakably, so we know he used them; and in these writers we find the same confusion of Geoffrey Chaucer with his son Thomas as owner of the estates mentioned, and so forth. So he (or she) had done the homework.

Of course, such thoroughness, to consult so many sources to create so brief a document, is unusual. It suggests someone with access to a fine collection of books, who took his Chaucer very seriously. This amateur biographer of the Renaissance clearly wanted to get the facts correct about Chaucer's life. Despite all of what seem like howlers to us, we can accord him (or her) a measure of respect for a task carried out in earnest.

And the same can be said about the BL Add. 5141 biographer's sources: Leland, Bale, Speght and even Thynne all wanted to report accurately about the life and death of Chaucer.

But knowing that the author of the BL Add. 5141 *vita* relied on the printed accounts of Leland, Bale and Speght (and maybe Thynne) answers

Title page to Thynne's 1542 edition of Chaucer's works. This copy records that this book exchanged hands in the Talbot Inn on 12 November 1610.

questions only temporarily and partially. For we might ask as well after the sources used by these earliest of biographers, themselves. If, as seems likely, Bale borrowed here and there from Leland, and Speght here and there from both, what sources did Leland find, to get his information in the first place? Or, when Bale disagrees with Leland, what was his authority? Moreover, what can we say about the material in BL Add. 5141 which appears uniquely, and in no other earlier written source known to us today?

And then finally, in an inquiry into a possible murder, do any of these questions matter?

DID CHAUCER DIE IN 1402?

Let's take the date 1402 first. The anonymous Renaissance biographer states that Chaucer 'died at London & is buried in Westminster/ An[no domini] 1402 / A[nno] regni Regis henrici 4ti/Quarto' (emphasized by the '1402' on the portrait side, where it must be intended to indicate the final year of Chaucer's life). In so doing, he opposes directly the authority of Speght's edition of 1598, which we know he used, and the inscription of Chaucer's official tomb in Westminster Abbey (which he must have gazed upon): Both have Chaucer dying on 25 October 1400.

So probably the Renaissance biographer was following his other source, John Bale, who also holds with the 1402 date of death.

But why choose Bale over the tomb inscription (and Speght, who takes his death date from the tomb) – unless there had been some reason, some rumour of inaccuracy, now silenced but known to the biographer of BL Add. 5141, about the date on the tomb? And perhaps during the sixteenth century there was something floating around London. Chaucer's tomb, after all, is more a monument to his memory than a sepulchre: Chaucer's bones rested in the floor of the south transept, with little or no inscription to mark the spot.[2] What we know today as 'Chaucer's tomb' was placed there in 1556, reputedly by one Nicholas Brigham, a Tudor afficionado.

We can't even be certain it ever held a body.[3]

Now, that's rather an odd thing to do: to decide to put up a tomb for Geoffrey Chaucer – out of the blue – a century and a half after he died. If it was a whim – it was a pretty expensive one. Why did he do it?

In 1556 Nicholas Brigham was personal treasurer to Mary Tudor – 'Bloody Mary', Henry VIII's eldest, and Catholic, daughter who became queen in 1553. As a trusted member of the Queen's Privy Chamber, Brigham was a power player behind the scenes of Mary's disastrous reign. He died, of obscure causes, in 1558, the year Queen Mary died.[4] As a reason for his commissioning the tomb, John Dart, the eighteenth-century antiquary and historian of Westminster Abbey, offered that Brigham was 'a Lover of the Muses'.[5]

That seems reasonable, except that in Renaissance London 'a Lover of the Muses' described every Tom, Dick and Clarence hanging around the court. Nobody else seemed to have thought of setting up a monument for Chaucer. So, why did Nicholas Brigham?

But let's first consider where Brigham discovered the 25 October death date.

It's a mystery. He didn't get it from the slab in the floor, because if it had been written there, other witnesses wouldn't have had the trouble they did deciding on when Chaucer died. He also didn't get it from Bale, who actually has three death dates: 'about 1450' and '1402' in his published works, and '4 June 1400' twice in his private diaries, which Brigham would hardly have seen – even though they were friends. In any case, why not go all the way with Bale, and use June and not October?[6]

Nor could Brigham have got his date from Leland. Leland, in fact, is uncharacteristically cautious about describing Chaucer's death, and gives no date at all for it. Leland says carefully: 'At this time Chaucer grew hoary, and felt himself afflicted by old age; wearied by that, while attending to his affairs in London, he died and was buried on the south side of the church of St Peter, Westminster.'[7] Since Leland offers death dates for other, less famous writers whose lives he wrote, his silence (and Bale's confusion) about Chaucer's circumstances seems odd.

After all, shouldn't the facts about the death of the most famous poet in England be easier to obtain than about men of lesser reputation?

Actually, John Bale and the BL Add. 5141 biographer must have thought 'getting the facts' should have been easier, too. Something like frustration comes through in the number of sources the little *vita* required. In Bale's case, the number of times he changed his mind may tell a similar story. Bale published a catalogue of British writers in 1548 in which he says Chaucer died 'about the year of man's redemption, 1450, under Henry the Sixth'. In 1557 he published a much-revised and expanded version which was again reprinted, with changes, in 1559.[8]

Somewhere in the revising process, Bale changed his mind – twice. In his diaries, he considered the 4 June 1400 date; and in the final editions of the catalogue, Bale says that Chaucer 'lived until the year of the lord 1402, as is revealed in the letter of Cupid (*charta Cupidinis*)'.[9]

Now, if the 'charta Cupidinis' Bale had in mind was the 'Letter of Cupid', a poem most Chaucer scholars attribute today to Thomas Hoccleve, its final stanza goes like this:

Written in th'ayr, the lusty month of May.
In our paleys (wher many a millioun
Of loveres trewe han habitacioun)
The yere of grace joyful and jocounde
A thousand and four hundred and secounde.
    Thomas Hoccleve, *The Letter of Cupid*, ll. 472–6

Written in the air, the lusty month of May [*either* in great haste *or* whilst flying!]
In our palace (where many a million
Of lovers true have their habitation)
The year of grace, joyful and pleasing
One thousand, four hundred and two.[10]

The most likely place for Bale to have turned up a copy of the 'Letter of Cupid' would have been in either the 1532 or the 1542 versions of Chaucer's works compiled by William Thynne. Apparently to Thynne – in those innocent years before there was a tomb inscription to look at – the notion that Chaucer was still writing in 1402 wasn't a problem.

And in fact, it doesn't get to be a problem until the great Victorian editor of Chaucer, Walter W. Skeat, excommunicated the 'Letter of Cupid' from the Chaucer canon, reasoning (like the good Victorian parson that he was) that a poet whose tombstone said he died in 1400 couldn't have been still writing in 1402. Certainly, now, that's logical.

To Bale, however (who after all lived a lot closer to Chaucer's time than Skeat did) the stanza seems to have sent exactly the opposite message. It convinced him – logically enough – that in order to write it, Chaucer must have been still alive in 1402. And what about the 4 June 1400 date in Bale's private diaries? Well, scholarly opinion holds that the diaries were working notes for the revised editions – so that, for whatever reason, Bale's final assessment of Chaucer's death date was what he published in 1557/1559 – that is, 1402.[11]

From this record offered us by the decisions of Thynne, Leland and Bale, then, two conclusions seem likely. First: the early editors and biographers of Chaucer – that is, pre-Brigham's tomb – had no hard proof of when Chaucer died. For some, like Thynne, who compiled the poems but offered no 'Life' of the poet, this wasn't a complication – although who knows? If Thynne had had a documented date of death or a date on the slab, would he have tried his hand at biography? Did the lack of certifiable birth/death dates make him nervous?

Not knowing precisely when Chaucer died certainly seems to have made Leland nervous. At any rate, as we have seen, he waffled inconclusively about it. His 'while attending to his affairs in London, he died' gets to the end of the story, but in a rather unsatisfying way.

So anyone wanting to know when – exactly – Chaucer died must have relied on traditional, hearsay accounts – and anything they could get their hands on that looked like real evidence, even scraps of poems. Hence John Bale, who seems to have been keen to get hold of solid facts, seized upon the date in the 'Letter of Cupid'.

The second conclusion is that at least two 'lines' of such hearsay accounts (with variations) must have existed, to be pondered over until eventually one was chosen. One 'line' asserted 1400, but in different months – June? October? – and the other claimed 1402, with no specific month of death. This would have been the 'line' Bale accepted, although clearly from the number of stabs he took at it, he must have felt beset by ambiguity until the end. Nor was he alone.

Perhaps the most striking example of this ambiguity, next to Bale, is John Pits, an antiquary-historian who published his *History of the English* (*Historicarum de rebus Anglicis*) in 1619. In his biographical sketch of Chaucer, Pits says the poet 'went to sleep in God, and at Westminster was buried with honor, the twenty-fifth day of October in the year 1400'. But in the *Index Universalis cum Anno Domini Adiecto*, an index of authors and their death dates Pits added as a reference guide at the end of his book, some 350 pages removed from the 'Life' of Chaucer, he gives 1402 as the year of death.

Was that his final answer? Or was Pits simply trying to hedge his bets?

Then there is the odd behaviour of John Foxe, whose *Acts and Monuments of Martyrs* was *the* book to read for gory details about how centuries of Protestants lived and died under the heel of sanguinary Catholics. Foxe published his *magnum opus* in 1563 – and he lived in London, so he had plenty of time and opportunity to look at Brigham's tomb. In fact, in his account of Chaucer, Foxe quotes from the inscription, and – as part of the quotation of the words on the tomb – gives the 25 October 1400 date for Chaucer's demise.

But Foxe also points out that the tomb was the project of 'one Mr Brickham' in 1556, and curiously he opens his account of the death of Chaucer (and Gower) like this: 'Albeit concerning the full certainty of the time and death of these two, we cannot finde ...'[12]

John Foxe.

So if there weren't any 'facts' given out, of the official sort, about when Chaucer was laid in his obscure spot in the floor of the Abbey – at least not any that satisfied the earliest of Chaucer's biographers – why are modern Chaucer scholars solidly agreed about 25 October 1400? Well, because they look it up in the *Chaucer Life-Records*.

But that account, in the *Chaucer Life-Records*, is a reconstruction from scant evidence. It reads: 'Under the date of 5 June 1400 the exchequer clerks entered a payment of £5 to Geoffrey Chaucer by the hands of Henry Somer. This is the latest known reference to Chaucer as living. It represents the payment of an instalment of the arrears on his annuities, £10 of which had been paid through Somer on 21 February 1400 ... The traditional date of Chaucer's death is 25 October 1400. The lack of any evidence of the Michaelmas or later payments on his annuities supports this date.' What exactly is meant by the 'tradition' which has given us 25 October 1400? 'The date 25 October 1400 as that of Chaucer's death', the editors write, 'rests upon the now illegible inscription based upon the tomb, which according to John Stow, was erected by Nicholas Brigham in Westminster Abbey in 1556.'[13]

So there it is: a 'now illegible inscription' on a tomb not actually Chaucer's, reportedly put up more than 150 years after the fact by an obscure Tudor gentleman whose own role is known only from a third-party account. There's not much hard evidence here to nail down Chaucer's last day.

But what of the unstated premise of the *Life-Records*, that if Chaucer's annuity went untouched at Michaelmas, then at Michaelmas he was dead? How could a man eat, with no money to pay for sustenance? The logic seems impeccable. Chaucer must have been dead before Michaelmas, and so needed no further funds. Into this scenario, a death date of 25 October 1400 fits very well.

But let's suppose Chaucer were no longer paying his own way. What if someone else were 'responsible' for his care and feeding during his last months – or years?

Here's a hypothesis. Beginning some time after June 1400, Chaucer was under arrest, in some secret place – perhaps house arrest in the abbey itself?

Or perhaps he was in Saltwood Castle, the forbidding stronghold of the Archbishops of Canterbury, that had a prison regularly used by Courtenay and Arundel as a handy hideout for interrogating dissidents. The Wycliffites John Purvey and Nicholas Hereford were tortured there.[14] It was there, too, that Arundel interrogated the suspected Lollard William Thorpe, who left the written account of his interrogation, mentioned earlier. Thorpe reports that at Saltwood he was threatened with burning and drowning, among other methods employed to make him talk. Thorpe clearly took the threats seriously. Not many who went in walked out of Saltwood. Thorpe may have been a notable exception. We do not know how he died. John Foxe, however, opined in 1563 that Thorpe never saw the light of day again – he was 'secretly made away with', is how Foxe put it.[15]

If Chaucer was in Saltwood, did he leave on his own two legs?

Of course he needn't have been in either of these places. Chaucer could have died in any number of nasty prisons, sometime between when we last hear of him in June 1400 and 1402. But wherever he was, if he was a prisoner he could have been living at someone else's expense, and would be in no position to pop along to collect his annuity.

Archbishop Arundel's prison was at his home at Saltwood Castle.

Another hypothesis is that Chaucer was murdered outright in 1400 – perhaps one of the archbishop's agents 'ran at him and robbed him of his life' (as Hoccleve had it) one dark night as he was walking home down Thieving Lane? – but the body (and so the act itself) was concealed until 1402, when burial could be effected on the quiet under the floor of Westminster. And it must have been done on the quiet, since we have no report of Chaucer's funeral, which is another odd thing, given Chaucer's importance.

Chaucer, in other words, might have suffered a fate strikingly similar to that of Richard II: kept out of sight and then starved to death in Pontefract Castle (a murder that leaves no marks), his body months later, after being exhibited around the country, to be interred without ceremony in an out-of-the-way Dominican friary at Kings Langley.

So the king and the archbishop had experience of making people disappear and disposing of them quietly.

It always helps to know what you're doing ...

WHY BURY CHAUCER IN WESTMINSTER ABBEY?

Of course, there remains the question: if Chaucer was murdered, why go to the trouble of burying him in Westminster Abbey – even obscurely? Why not just pitch his body down a hole somewhere in the dead of night, and cover it up?

It may be that the fate of Richard II provides an answer. Undoubtedly there were those among Henry's intimates who would have loved to fit the dead Richard with the equivalent of a pair of concrete shoes, dump him in the Thames and be done with it, but that was impossible. Too many people were watching. Langley Abbey may have been out of the way, but it was still *somewhere*. No one could accuse Henry of being a monster who wreaked his anger on the dead body of the king.

There would have been too many people watching and wondering about Chaucer, too. If he had died in custody, there would have to be a body – and a burial. And in 1402 – after 5 November 1402, to be exact – there was a pressing reason for having Chaucer's body in its final resting place. For on that date his son, Thomas Chaucer, became Henry's Chief Butler, and so also *ex officio* Coroner of the City of London. The post was an important sinecure, of course, but it put Thomas Chaucer in at least nominal charge of investigating the deaths of London citizens. Nobody wanted him investigating his own father's death – perhaps least of all Thomas himself.[16]

But if there were going to be a problem, why appoint Thomas Chief Butler at all? Surely there were lots of other wine merchants around who could serve up a decent vintage on demand, if that was all there were to it.

Henry must have had his reasons. Perhaps one of them was that Thomas was family: he was the son of Henry's father's second wife's sister. That is: Thomas Chaucer's mother, Philippa, was sister to Katherine Swynford, mistress and then wife to John of Gaunt. That made Thomas kin to all sorts of influential people, including the king, young Prince Henry, and the notorious Beauforts.

Another possible reason for bringing Thomas into the court circle was his considerable influence among the Commons. Thomas's budding political career, which led him to become Speaker by 1407, could scarcely have been overlooked by a careful politician like Arundel, who might have found it prudent to bring this man on board, and gain his influence over the very burghers whose support the regime so badly needed?

Except for the lingering problem of his awkward father …

So if our speculations are right – if there was something suspicious about Chaucer's death – it would have been important to get the body buried before 5 November 1402. Perhaps, in fact, a fortnight or thereabouts earlier – say, on October 25? In time for everything to be finished and done with before Thomas's appointment?

Perhaps, indeed, we may surmise that is why the date 25 October came to be passed down through the years until, in 1556, Nicholas Brigham *almost* got the whole thing right.

DID CHAUCER HIDE OUT IN HOLLAND?

Setting aside these conjectures for the moment, let us consider the most absurd claim of the Renaissance biographer of BL Add. 5141. Namely that Chaucer was a political exile in the Low Countries.

> He lyved some parte of Richarde the seconde his tyme, in the lowe cuntryes of Holland and Zellande by reason of some disgrace that happenyd unto him, as a man suspected to be spotted with the rebellion of Jack Straw and Watte Tyler ...

It seems quite likely that our anonymous biographer got most of this from Thomas Speght, who claims in his 1598 edition of Chaucer's *Workes* that the poet, 'favouring some rash attempt of the common people', was forced to flee into 'Holland, Zeland and France, where he wrote most of his bookes'.[17]

Without hesitation, we ought to label this spurious. Nothing exists, as far as we know, to corroborate the claim that Chaucer had to flee the country to avoid persecution for supporting the Peasants' Revolt of 1381 (and in fact we have documentary evidence showing that, rather than being out of favour with Richard II, after the revolt, Chaucer's star as a civil servant was never brighter.)

Nevertheless, Speght and the biographer of BL Add. 5141 both seem confident of these facts, and about their consequences. Where did their information come from? Did Speght find it first, and did the BL Add. 5141 biographer draw only on Speght – or, since they were writing at the same time, did they have access to the same information and so corroborate each other?

We know the anonymous biographer didn't always follow Speght unless he felt Speght had it right – the 1402 death date being one case in point, Speght's claim that Chaucer 'wrote most of his bookes' overseas (which goes unmentioned in BL Add. 5141) being another. Conceivably if the anonymous biographer were just following Speght, he would have done so all the way. So it seems we have two considered opinions when both Speght and the biographer locate Chaucer in the Low Countries and France, for what sounds like political reasons. And they seem confident about it – none of the bet-hedging Leland offers sometimes.

Why would they both be so sure?

One reason may be that the two of them aren't entirely wrong. Chaucer didn't go to Holland and Zeeland and France to hide from Richard's wrath in 1381 – but he might have gone there in 1388, to hide from somebody else's – just as Robert DeVere, Richard's great friend, did. After his defeat by the rebellious magnates' forces at Radcot Bridge in 1387, DeVere escaped to London, and from there to the Netherlands and Paris, eventually to settle in Louvain.[18]

1388, of course, was the year of the Merciless Parliament, and an excellent moment to be away from London if you were a friend of Richard II's. Very prudently, scholars and biographers have long agreed, Chaucer spent the time in rustication somewhere – probably in Kent.

There are many reasons why Chaucer might have removed to Kent. It was familiar territory. He had held various appointments there, had been elected to parliament from Kent, he was on the peace commission from Kent, and apparently owned some property there. In 1388 Chaucer was named in four separate actions in the Court of Common Pleas, one of which cites Chaucer as being resident in Kent.[19]

Case proved you might think – but it isn't as clear-cut as that. The Court action is the only firm evidence for Chaucer's whereabouts in 1388, and it's not a record of Chaucer being in court. It is, in fact, a record of Chaucer *never showing up*.

In one of the cases, Chaucer was a 'mainpernour' – which meant that, should the defendant fail to appear in court, Chaucer along with others was liable to arrest instead, 'body for body' ('*corpus pro corpore*'). But the case didn't get that far, and Chaucer's presence wasn't required.

Mainpernors were often drawn by attorneys from standing lists of persons who had given blanket permissions to be named in such cases, perhaps for a fee. Since most cases, like this one naming Chaucer, would be settled ahead of time, the assumption was that those standing surety would seldom, if ever, have to report. Some mainpernors may not even have known their names were on the record for a particular case, if the case never got called.

The other cases are more interesting, since in each writs of *capias* were issued for Chaucer. *Capias* came in three sizes – *capias, capias sicut prius*, and *capias sicut pluries*.[20] Basically these were summonses of increasing urgency: if all three were issued for you, it meant that you had missed two court dates. Your next failure to appear would bring an arrest warrant. Chaucer received a *capias sicut pluries* in one case in 1388, as well as a *sicut prius* in another, which apparently settled before it went further.

No one likes to be sued for debt, especially if the means are lacking immediately to pay it off, so it's possible that Chaucer stayed away from the law courts because he was afraid of meeting his creditors face to face. But whatever his reason, one thing is clear: what the court records actually show is *not* proof that Chaucer was in Kent because he was in court, but rather that Chaucer could have been *anywhere* (including Kent, of course) precisely because he was *not* in court.

CHAUCER NEEDS SOME MONEY IN A HURRY

Other court records of the time may suggest an ominous context for Chaucer's departure from London in 1388. On 1 May 1388 court records show that Chaucer transferred his annuity in full to John Scalby, apparently in exchange for a lump-sum payment in cash.

Such transfers were a common 'means of getting ready money', and it has been proposed that perhaps Chaucer used the cash to pay off the debts for which he was being sued – and so that's why the cases didn't proceed. Unfortunately the remaining records don't say why the suits were dropped.[21]

But trading in your annuity for a lump sum would make sense for other reasons too – especially if you weren't expecting to be around for a while to claim it yourself, quarterly, at the Exchequer Office.

Chaucer's annuity transfer to Scalby was carried out on 1 May 1388, but consider what was occupying the courts elsewhere in London, other than the Common Pleas. On 5 May 1388 Sir Simon Burley, Richard II's former tutor, close counsellor and Chaucer's friend and a co-member of the Kent peace commission, was condemned to death for treason. The former Mayor of London Sir Nicholas Brembre (who worked alongside Chaucer at the custom house) was executed in February. Another of Chaucer's friends, a fellow poet and member of Richard's court circle, Thomas Usk, was likewise arrested, tried and beheaded in 1388. And Robert Tresilian, Chief Justice of the King's Bench (and yet another member of the fateful Kent peace commission with Chaucer and Burley), was dragged out of sanctuary so he could be tried and executed.

All these deaths were the sensations of the day: the queen begging for Burley's life on bended knee, Brembre the former mayor dying above a vast throng of his constituents, the sanctuary rights of Westminster Abbey violated to bring Tresilian to his execution ...

Perhaps in that bloody year of the Appellants' power, it seemed to Chaucer that Kent, where his residence was public knowledge, even to the Court of Common Pleas, wasn't rustication enough. DeVere, after all, had run to France and the Low Countries, and DeVere was still alive ...

So while it seems likely that Speght and the biographer of BL Add. 5141 were wrong about Chaucer running away from Richard because of his support for the rebels in 1381, they may have been more accurate than they are given credit for when it comes to Chaucer's whereabouts between 1 May 1388 and 1389.

Certainly the orthodox wisdom among Chaucer scholars has nothing concrete to offer about what he was up to in Kent, or why – if he was there, just a short journey away from London – he didn't present himself before the bench when summons after summons arrived in the post. This, for example, is what the 'Chaucer's Life' section in *The Riverside Chaucer* edition has to say about Chaucer's 'withdrawal into Kent':

> Chaucer was not entirely free from official duties: he was still a member of the Kent peace commission. But between 1386 and 1389 he had leisure in which he could work on the General Prologue of *The Canterbury Tales* and a number of the tales themselves.[22]

Maybe, indeed, he *was* 'at leisure' in Kent, obliviously cranking out *The Canterbury Tales* while his old friends were being slaughtered one by one a few miles away, not even *imagining* that a midnight knock on the door might come for him as well.

But it's equally possible that Kent didn't seem far enough away, after all.

CHAUCER'S DUTCH CONNECTIONS

What we would really like, of course, is some hard evidence that Chaucer was in Holland or France or both. (A passport with entry stamps would be nice.) But possibly there are one or two clues still left lying about unnoticed. The case in the Court of Common Pleas, in which Chaucer was listed as a 'mainpernour', might offer one. The person for whom he stood surety was one Matilda Nemeg or Nemghen, a servant girl whose surname indicates her place of origin as Nijmegen, in the Netherlands.

Why would Chaucer (or his attorney) submit his name to stand for a Dutch servant girl? It seems odd that a gentleman of his stature would do that. If she ran off, Chaucer would have to pay the consequences, *corpus pro corpore*. But perhaps he knew her family? And if so, did he owe them a favour – like harbourage, for instance?

Nijmegen is in Gelderland, up in the far north-eastern part of Holland. Undoubtedly if he could have got there, it would have been a pretty fair place to lie low, simply because it's so remote. If, on the other hand, Chaucer had wanted to stay a little closer to civilized life while enjoying some local protection, he might have gone a bit farther south, almost down to the French border, to Hainault.

Chaucer's in-laws were from the Low Countries. His wife Philippa was some-times called Philippa Pan in the records, but this stood for her father's name, Sir Paon de Roet, a knight of Hainault who came over with the retinue of Philippa, Edward III's queen. 'When Chaucer married Philippa Roet in 1366,' we read, 'he became part of the Hainault Connection and fell into the permanent protection network of what really was – only because of the long and close family ties stem-ming from a specific geographical area – a kind of Hainault mafia.'[23]

Hainault would certainly have been a good hide-out for someone on the run: many miles from danger, surrounded by a protective 'family'. Did Chaucer pay a visit to Philippa's people in 1388? Did he meet Matilda Nemeg, or some of her relatives there? Did Philippa go along – and not come back? It is one of the minor mysteries of Chaucer's private life that his wife of twenty-one years disappears from the historical record at about this time. At least, we know of no documented evidence to place her after 5 July 1387. The usual assumption is that she died. But where? If she died in England, where is she buried? And if she died in Hainault – perhaps nobody has been looking in the right places?

Could this be where Chaucer hid out in 1388?

CHAUCER'S DUTCH TALES

And then there are *The Canterbury Tales* themselves – specifically, the tales of the Miller, the Reeve and the Merchant. Recent scholarship has been tracing lines of connection between these tales and Middle-Dutch narratives and farces. It now seems that three of Chaucer's greatest triumphs have Dutch sources.[24]

Now certainly there were plenty of 'Flemings' in the boroughs of London, and Chaucer surely knew a number through his wife's family; he presumably also met quite a few in the course of his official duties in the custom house, where the ability to speak Low Country languages must have been an asset – the wool trade being dominated on the Continent by Flemish merchants. So he had plenty of opportunity to hear Dutch stories in London.

On the other hand, at least one of his sources is a farce, and a farce requires actors and performances. Were there Dutch theatricals in London? Or is it more likely that Chaucer saw the farce 'live', while on an enforced sabbatical in the Low Countries?

We cannot yet answer these questions, but there are more to come.

If the author of BL Add. 5141 and Speght might have been right about Chaucer's flight to the Low Countries and France, but wrong about the year and about who the executioners were, we are still left to ask: why is the anonymous author so certain of 1402 as the date of Chaucer's death?

WHY WAS THE ANONYMOUS BIOGRAPHER
SO SURE ABOUT 1402?

When BL Add. 5141 came to the British Museum in 1786 it was a single page, just as it is now. It seems to have been cut from something else, and it appears to be a copy – maybe early sixteenth-century, maybe earlier – of another picture.[25] But obviously its origins are older than the little *vita* on its back.

There is some evidence that the BL Add. 5141 portrait served as the model for the frontispiece of Thomas Speght's 1598 edition of Chaucer – despite the fact that the engraver, John Speed, claims he copied it from the portrait Thomas Hoccleve had painted onto a page of his *Regement of Princes*. It seems likely that BL Add. 5141 belonged at one time to Robert Cotton, the great seventeenth-century antiquary whose manuscripts became the core of the British Museum collection. Since Cotton, Speed and Speght were all friends and fellow members of the Society of Antiquaries, which Cotton formed, it would have been natural for Speed to borrow the portrait from Cotton to do the work for their mutual friend Speght.

Sometime in the early eighteenth century what sounds like BL Add. 5141 was found pasted into another of Cotton's manuscripts.[26] The man who found it (another engraver by the name of George Vertue) dated it at 'about 1400'.[27] That would make it, or its original, and the manuscript from which it was cut, contemporaneous with Chaucer himself. *What happened to that manuscript?* It seems to have disappeared, in the same way that most of the other fourteenth-century manuscripts of Chaucer's writings have disappeared.

Do we have BL Add. 5141 (later copy or not) today because someone liked the picture – and thought it harmless? Or was the one who sliced it loose an admirer of Chaucer's, who under duress threw the book away but secreted the portrait for safe-keeping?

Probably we'll never know.

But let's suppose *you* cut BL Add. 5141 out – perhaps at some risk – and took it home, to lock the door and admire. Wouldn't you, when you showed it to a handful of your most discreet friends, tell a tale about it, an *histoire* of where it came from, and what the flowers meant, and the coat of arms ... and the date? And also, of course, how you knew?

And when that single page of vellum was passed down to your children, and your children's children – wouldn't the *histoire* go with it?

And wouldn't that *histoire* have spread a bit, once the archbishop was safely dead himself, and Henry V was king – enough so that the 'true' date of Chaucer's death (and perhaps a few juicy bits about him) would have stayed around, despite Nicholas Brigham and his artificial tomb, long enough into the following century so that people who really wanted to know the facts, who *really* asked after them – people like John Bale and the anonymous Renaissance biographer of BL Add. 5141 – might have found them?

It's a possibility. There is one more odd thing about whoever wrote the *vita* on the back of BL Add. 5141: since he relied on Speght's 1598 *Workes* for some of his information – like the flight into Holland and France – the anonymous biographer is probably one of the few who ever had Speght's book and the model for its frontispiece in his hands at the same time. He had to have had Speght's book open as he wrote, because some of his phrasing is nearly word for word the same as Speght's. He must have looked back and forth from one to the other as he copied, compared them ...

So what are we to make of the fact that Speght, plain as day, in black and white, says right there that Chaucer died 25 October 1400, straight off the tomb; and yet our man – this unknown biographer – just like that! – writes down 1402?

What made him do it? What did he know, this anonymous Renaissance author of BL Add. 5141, to put his trust in the '1402' at the top of the little portrait, instead of the tomb of Brigham and the published opinion of the learned Mr Speght?[28]

Perhaps the answer lies with Mr Brigham and why he would have wanted to build a monument to Geoffrey Chaucer in Westminster Abbey in 1556 in the first place.

WHY DID BRIGHAM BUILD THE TOMB IN 1556?

To be truthful, nobody has ever answered this question. Nobody, in fact, seems to have ever asked it.

Brigham was by no means the first admirer to pay his tribute to the great poet in the sixteenth century. One of Chaucer's greatest fans seems to have been Henry VIII. Celebrating the greatness of English letters was a central part of Henry VIII's nationalist mythologizing, just as it had been of Henry V's. And Chaucer was crucial to this as England's first poet laureate and 'the father of the English language'. Indeed, to this end Henry sent out Master William Thynne (who seems to have been otherwise an overseer of kitchens), to go round through the libraries of the monasteries Henry was closing and bring together all the poems of Chaucer he could find. The result was Thynne's collected *Works of Geffray Chaucer*, which he dedicated to the king in 1532. Always a fool for more of a good thing, Henry in 1533 created the office of 'King's Antiquary' and installed in it John Leland, heretofore the royal chaplain. Leland's assignment was to rummage around in the dissolved monastic libraries again for more Chaucer, if he could find any, but mostly in order to produce a kind of critical survey and history of English literature, to establish once and for all the international worthiness of English writers and their work. Leland spent six years at it, and before dying insane in 1552 produced three books filled, he noted rather breathlessly, with 'a whole world of things very memorable'.[29]

Chaucer's tomb.

In 1531, Henry VIII announced himself the 'protector and supreme head of the church and clergy of England', as well as head of state. That year and the next he invoked the law of *praemunire*: from then on, anyone in holy orders who objected to Henry VIII being head of the church could be tried as a traitor. Religious dissent – once again – became political dissent, and punishable as treason.

Undoubtedly, Archbishop Arundel would have admired the efficiency.

Under *this* Henry, however, it would not do to have Chaucer turn out a papist. But a populist? Yes! because English was the language of the common people (Good King Harry! Bully beef and mustard!) then, now and forever. And a Wycliffite? Yes! because Wyclif's project was to translate the Bible into English, and redistribute church wealth, and put heat on the friars and see in the Eucharist only symbolic blood and flesh … every one of which was policy under Henry VIII.

So a reputation attached to Chaucer as a religious radical and a proto-Protestant, with radical works being attributed to him that have since been excluded from the canon.[30]

But when did Brigham install the tomb? He obviously did it with full authority of the reigning monarch and yet he did it right in the middle of the five-year rule of Bloody Mary, who was – dare we say – hellbent on re-establishing Roman Catholicism throughout the realm. In her battle for the hearts and minds of Englishmen, the queen presided over the burning of nearly three hundred of her countrymen for heresy – men and women who had dutifully become Protestants to avoid being burnt by her father, Henry VIII. And Roman Catholic Brigham, as Queen Mary's treasurer and a member of her Privy Council, must have lent his vote to this.

We can see the problem. Resuscitating Chaucer as the voice of English letters was a pet project of Henry VIII's, and it involved establishing him clearly as a Protestant poet. And though Nicholas Brigham may have been a 'Lover of the Muses' – it *definitely* couldn't have been a *Protestant* Muse that Bloody Mary's treasurer wanted to hear singing 'with a vois memorial in the shade'.[31]

What then was the logical thing for a fanatical Catholic 'Lover of the Muses' to do about this terrible confiscation of England's genius by the adulterous Henry VIII and his devil-serving Protestants? The answer, obviously, was to take him back. And one way to do that, it may have occurred to Brigham, was to get everybody's focus away from that miserable, Lollard-looking grave-slab in the floor of the South Cross and provide Chaucer with a proper monument – a good, big, honorific sort of monument, the kind Catholics have always liked to fill up churches with.

In fact, the tomb Brigham selected for Chaucer was an anachronism when he installed it. It is an altar-tomb, of a kind popular in friars' churches in the late fifteenth century. It is almost identical to the tomb of the Duchess of Northumberland, in Chelsea Old Church. Both have been described as 'Marian works', leading one early archaeological survey to conclude that Chaucer's tomb 'was certainly connected with the restoration of the old regime'.[32] Under the canopy to the right of the altar-like raised stone, there is a space provided for a priest to say masses for the dead inhabitant. 'Choosing such a tomb for Chaucer', Derek Pearsall has observed, 'was obviously a way of associating him with a specifically late-medieval Catholic practice.'[33]

1556 was a very good year for resuscitating Chaucer's Catholic reputation, especially at Westminster Abbey. The year earlier Queen Mary ratcheted up her campaign to eradicate Protestantism by several quick notches. On 4 February 1555 Arundel's statute *De Haeretico Comburendo* was revived, and the first Protestant was burnt at the stake. On 26 September 1556, Mary abolished the chapter of Westminster Abbey and re-established the monastery to house twenty-eight monks; on 10 November the endowments were put into the hands of the monastery, under a new Roman Catholic abbot, one John Feckenham. Brigham's new tomb for Chaucer, modelled on those of a pre-Protestant age, must have fitted right in with the times.[34]

And as for the date: well, if there *were* still rumours floating around London in 1556 that Chaucer had perished in prison in 1402 – or even that he'd been cut down in the street by 'muggers' on a mission – one way to put them to rest, perhaps, would have been to inscribe 'October 25 1400' in large letters on the new tomb. Exactly how that might have settled anything isn't clear, after all these years; but it may help explain why nobody before John Bale specifies when Chaucer died.

WHY DID NOBODY KNOW WHEN CHAUCER DIED?

Thynne says nothing. Neither does Leland – even though he notes when other English writers died. And Thynne and Leland were the closest in time to the actual event, closer than Bale or Brigham by half a generation.

History may have the answer to this, as well. Both Thynne and Leland were producing their command-performance books for the king between 1531 and 1539, precisely while Henry VIII was busiest beating his particular brand of Reformation into the popular consciousness. They were especially bloody years, too, and dangerous, with Anne Boleyn, Cromwell, Sir Thomas Moore, all once mightily exalted, now tried for treason and killed. It would have been pretty hard for a Thynne or a Leland to know which way to step, even on a matter as simple as the date and manner of Chaucer's death. *If*, of course, there *were* a 'matter' of Chaucer's death. (Maybe trying to figure it all out helped tip poor Leland into insanity).

But John Bale is different. He was a Protestant – a Carmelite friar who 'reformed' in 1533, and later became Anglican Bishop of Ossory in Ireland, where he devoted himself to rescuing Catholics from the Roman Powers of Darkness. He earned the nickname 'bilious Bale', and a mob of his diocesan faithful once attacked his house and killed five servants, just to show their appreciation for all he was doing for them.

It is this Bale who finally settles on 1402 as the year Chaucer died, and who also seems to be the primary source for the 'Life' on the back of BL Add. 5141. So perhaps it all comes together: the silence of Thynne and Leland, the conflicting certitude of 1400 on (Catholic) Brigham's monument versus (Protestant) Bale's and the anonymous Renaissance biographer's persistent 1402.

Could there have been some other lingering bit of rumour, combined with a partisan loyalty which made the biographer choose Bale's date over the 1400 of the learned Speght and the inscription on the tomb?

If either Bale or the author of the BL Add. 5141 *vita* believed Chaucer had been taken out by papists they would have screamed it from the house-tops, but if it was a cover-up they were dealing with – it is one that has successfully convinced everybody for 600 years.

On the other hand, every cover-up, even the best, leaves a telltale bit or two exposed, some ragged end to pull the giant ball of string apart.

Is 1402 just such an end?

Could the date of Bale and BL Add. 5141 be the true year Geoffrey Chaucer passed from this earth?

CHAPTER 17

Did Chaucer repent?

~

'Chaucer before his death often cried out, "Woe is me! For I shall not now be able to revoke or destroy those things that I have wickedly written concerning the wicked and filthy love of men for women and which will now be passed down for ever from man to man, whether I wish it or not." And so complaining he died.'

This is how Thomas Gascoigne, Chancellor of Oxford University, pictured Chaucer's last moments in a book that he wrote some thirty to fifty years after Chaucer's death.[1] The statement is sometimes taken as supporting evidence for reading Chaucer's *Retractions* at the end of *The Canterbury Tales* as a true death-bed repentance. On the other hand, it is equally likely that Gascoigne simply took his cue from the *Retractions* itself. We have no way of knowing, although Gascoigne's choice of vocabulary (he was writing in Latin) might suggest the latter.

The whole question of Chaucer's state of mind at the end of his life is necessarily speculation. We can't be sure what he was writing in those final months, and we do not know whether or not what he did write was a reflection of his own situation.

We can, however, place Chaucer's last moments into a political and historical context, and to a certain extent, that context may suggest which works he was then currently engaged on, and we can at least hazard a guess as to why he might have written them at that time – if indeed he did.

What the context suggests – albeit uncertainly – is that Chaucer's last works were: *The Parson's Tale*, Chaucer's *Retractions* and *An ABC*.

RETRACTION AS AN ART-FORM

The two aristocratic, worldly bishops who ruled the English church from 1381 to 1414 were not interested in the dissemination of religious knowledge amongst the lay population. Unlike some of their less worldly predecessors, Archbishops

Courtenay and Arundel did everything they could to restrict learning to its traditional practitioners: the clerics and the nobility. In Archbishop Arundel's case, the restrictions he placed on reading, preaching, discussing and even *thinking* helped to cast a shadow over the literature (secular as well as religious) of a whole century.[2]

Yet there was one literary genre which flourished under both Courtenay and Arundel: the recantation, or confession.

Retraction as an art-form probably doesn't exert much appeal for a modern audience, but towards the end of the fourteenth century and in the dangerous days at the opening of the fifteenth century, it became extremely popular.

Archbishop Courtenay was the most enthusiastic patron of the genre, and he went to great lengths to encourage some of the ablest minds of his day to experiment with it. In 1382, he persuaded Nicholas Hereford, Philip Repingdon, John Aston, and Laurence Bedeman – amongst the brightest of the Oxford intellectuals – to come up with their own particular retractions. The theme was, of course, always the same: that is, they retracted all the views which they held in common with the damnable John Wyclif – in particular, any views they might share with him on the nature of the Eucharist.

The main inducement that Courtenay offered was that he would not excommunicate them if they complied.

But it was not always easy. John Aston, in particular, had a way of turning a recantation into a restatement of what he believed in. Archbishop Courtenay had to order him time and again him to rework and revise his attempts.

What is more, the recantations were no good unless they were public. For example, it was one thing to get Philip Repingdon to deny everything that he had previously believed to a closed meeting of prelates at the House of the Blackfriars in London, but what Courtenay really wanted was for the rest of the University of Oxford to hear him denying it. So the archbishop convened the next Convocation at Oxford and then ordered Repingdon (and Aston) to appear before it and undergo the humiliation of making their retractions before their fellow scholars. The Convocation had to wait several days for the reprobate couple to find the courage to appear, but finally Courtenay was rewarded for his tenacity by the sight of the proud rebels making their confessions in public in Oxford.[3]

Similarly, when the heretic William Swinderby was arrested in Lincoln, Courtenay was concerned that his excellent recantation should not be enjoyed by only a few like-minded churchmen, and the repentant priest was ordered to read out his confession in eight churches throughout the diocese. Courtenay wanted as many people as possible to benefit.[4]

One of the easiest retractions Archbishop Courtenay obtained was one from an Irish knight by the name of Sir Cornelius Cloyne. Cloyne had been a great supporter of Wyclif's ideas – particularly Wyclif's extraordinary assertion that after the wine and bread were consecrated during the Mass they did not cease being wine and bread. It was the 1 June 1382, two days after Courtenay had organized a barefoot procession through the streets of London to hear the condemnation of Wyclif's heresies read out aloud. Sir Cornelius Cloyne got up after the sermon and told the astonishing story of how – only the day before – he had been at Mass and when the priest held up the bread and the wine, as usual, he'd suddenly seen – there in the priest's hands – flesh and blood!

As the Leicester chronicler Henry Knighton describes it: 'on the breaking of the bread the knight looked again, and saw with his own eyes, in the hands of the celebrant friar, true flesh, raw and bleeding, divided into three parts. Greatly wondering, and astonished, he called his squire, that he too might see it, but he saw nothing but what he was accustomed to see. The knight, however, looking at the third part saw it white as it had been before, but then ...' (and this is the incredible part) 'saw in the middle of that piece the name of Jesus written in letters of flesh, raw and bloody, which was wonderful to behold.'[5]

Of course, the fact that Sir Cornelius Cloyne was heavily in debt and had had to obtain protection from his debtors only three weeks before, had nothing to do with Archbishop Courtenay. Nor did the fact that Cloyne afterwards obtained a pension from the court of 40 marks a year have any bearing on his sharpened powers of perception.[6]

In 1388 Courtenay visited the pleasant town of Leicester, where an anchoress by the name of Matilda had made her home in a cell in the churchyard of St Peter's. She was brought before the archbishop charged with Lollardy. Her subsequent recantation, however, pleased Courtenay so much that he waived any penance and even offered forty days indulgence for anyone who might contribute to her support.[7]

Sometimes, however, it was harder work to persuade people to try their hand at recantation. Take Nicholas Hereford for example. He'd been one of the main authors of the Wycliffite Bible, so one might have thought he would have a professional interest in perfecting a literary genre. His original recantation in 1382, however, had been far from satisfactory, in Archbishop Courtenay's eyes, and he'd been ordered to reappear alongside Repingdon and Aston, but by then Hereford had left the country to appeal to the pope. A spell in the pope's prison of St Angelo must have convinced him of the futility of trying to appeal to God's Vicar on Earth, but by a stroke of good luck he'd managed to escape jail during an anti-papal riot in the city. Back in England he'd been re-arrested in 1386 but had escaped prison yet again. In 1388 Hereford was finally captured and thrown into Archbishop Courtenay's prison of Saltwood, in Kent, alongside the other most important Wycliffite of his time – John Purvey. There he was 'grievously tormented' with the result that, in 1390, Hereford finally submitted and agreed to have a go at a real, full-blooded, public recantation at St Paul's Cross.[8]

The main thing, as far as Courtenay was concerned, was that it had to be public. Back in Leicester in 1388, he'd made William Smith (the one who'd once used an image of St Catherine as firewood) and Roger Dexter and his wife Alice, parade around the town in their underwear, genuflecting and kissing images of the cross. It wasn't the punishment Courtenay was interested in, it was the publicity. In fact, because of the cold weather, he allowed them to put their clothes back on once they got into the church – so long as they kept their feet bare and their heads uncovered.[9]

The chronicler Henry Knighton acknowledged the importance of Courtenay's role in achieving these confessions, which, he noted, had come about 'more from fear of the archbishop than for the love of God'.

Nor was Courtenay interested in whether the confession was genuine. All he wanted to achieve was a public forum for a good recantation. Knighton – who still remained in Leicester after Archbishop Courtenay had packed up his bags and gone home – noted that the recanters weren't really convinced: 'their hearts persisting nevertheless in their old delusions, which flourished greatly in secret when they dared to entertain them'.[10]

Sincerity was never a major consideration in the exercise of recantation. In 1402, for example, a priest by the name of Richard Wyche was invited by the Bishop of Durham, Walter Skirlaw, to have a shot at abjuration. When Richard refused, according to his own account, the bishop sent a knight to persuade him to take the oath whilst maintaining in his mind whatever reservation he had about the details. Wyche must have felt he was being asked to compromise his artistic integrity, for he refused.[11]

Durham Castle.

The art of recantation got a great boost when Thomas Arundel took over as Archbishop of Canterbury. He was able to introduce a major new inducement to potential recanters, retracters and abjurers: the offer of not being burnt at the stake.

This was a turning-point in the popularity of the genre.

Within a few months of Chaucer's disappearance from the record, the unfortunate William Sawtre was burnt alive for refusing to come up with a satisfactory retraction and for persisting in claiming that the bread and wine remained in the host after consecration alongside the body and blood of Christ.

The burning of Sawtre finally persuaded John Purvey to have a stab at retraction. Doubtless that was the intention behind the burning – it had been hurried up to take place a mere three days before Purvey was due to stand trial. The *De Haeretico Comburendo* Act hadn't even hit the statute books. But Purvey, as Wyclif's heir, was the most prestigious heretic the church could lay its hands on. His retraction was worth far more in terms of publicity value than his martyrdom. Yet he had remained obdurate in prison for several years, even undergoing torture. The execution of Sawtre finally convinced him to submit and he allowed himself to be put on display at St Paul's Cross, where he made a full and humiliating public recantation in English – affirming with his heart and with his mouth before his master, Archbishop Arundel of Canterbury. And, he said, he signed the testimonial with his own hand, freely and willingly.[12]

After the 'terrible example' of Sawtre's burning, says one of the chronicles, others of his accomplices came to St Paul's Cross and publicly retracted their heresies.[13] It wasn't just John Purvey who decided to turn to recantation. It seems probable that Archbishop Arundel staged some sort of high-profile, public mass recantation in an elaborate ceremony at St Paul's Cross.[14]

And these were by no means the only instances. The large number of trials shows 'how frequently Lollards abjured their heresy; for one suspect persistent and unlucky enough to deserve burning, there are fifty or more who renounced their opinions and practices'.[15]

Around the time of Chaucer's disappearance, recantation or retraction was possibly the most popular form of public statement in the land. Even one of Chaucer's closest friends was induced to have a go at it. The 72-year-old Sir Lewis Clifford was forced to make a spontaneous and grovelling submission to Archbishop Arundel in 1402. He retracted his twenty-year association with Lollardy and pleaded that it had been all a mistake – made through ignorance and the simplicity of his heart.

As a further earnest of his good faith he was also persuaded to append a list of heretical beliefs which he claimed were common amongst Lollards, and was even encouraged to turn informer by handing over a list of persons who still claimed such views.[16]

It had come to this: the sophisticated, intellectual courtier, the high-flying chamber knight and counsellor of Richard II, royally connected through marriage, and the friend of poets, must turn informer and apostate. The man by whom the French poet Eustache Deschamps had sent his famous honorific poem to Chaucer, the father-in-law of Sir Philip de la Vache to whom Chaucer addressed his poem *Truth*, the man who was possibly the godfather (or even the father) of the 'little Lewis' to whom Chaucer dedicated his *Treatise on the Astrolabe*, was humbled in his old age before the proud archbishop. Such a turn-about could only have been the result either of miracle or the fear of death.

CHAUCER'S 'RETRACTIONS'

If Arundel squeezed a recantation out of one of Chaucer's closest friends, why should it surprise us if he also squeezed one out of Chaucer himself? At the end of *The Parson's Tale* Chaucer attaches his own personal confession or recantation. He calls it his 'retracciouns' (retractions). Rather than a straightforward confession of religious belief, however, Chaucer's *Retractions* form a literary recantation, and can be seen as following a tradition of medieval Latin, French and German writing in which an author, embarking on a religious topic, regrets the follies of his youth and his writings of worldly vanity. As such the *Retractions* can be read as entirely conventional.[17]

As always with Chaucer, however, the contemporary context is crucial. If Chaucer had written this in the 1350s, then it would indeed have been seen as entirely conventional. But he didn't write it in the 1350s; he wrote it (most probably) in 1400. At such a critical moment, the *Retractions* must be seen in the context of who else was recanting and retracting at the same time. There may have been literary precedents, but in the 1400s the people who were busiest recanting and retracting were those who stood accused of heresy.

Burning at the stake for heresy had been practised on the Continent but was an innovation in England in 1401.

After 1401, especially, the fear of death by fire became a terrifying reality that urged unprecedented numbers to the public ordeal of recantation. If, indeed, Chaucer had lived on until 1402 he would have witnessed the first bloody fruit of *De Haeretico Comburendo* and the (very) public immolation of William Sawtre. He might also have witnessed or heard of his friend Sir Lewis Clifford's humiliating recantation. The pressure to recant would have been overwhelming.

Of course, we don't actually know when the *Retractions* was written – we can only guess, but even if it were earlier – sometime in the late 1390s – the same argument would apply. Chaucer's literary recantation was composed at a time when public disavowal was one of the most important issues of the day. The daily pressures of enforced religious orthodoxy and the regular inquisition of ordinary people's faith and beliefs cannot be separated from Chaucer's urge to confession at the end of *The Canterbury Tales*.

THE ENIGMA OF 'THE RETRACTIONS'

Chaucer's *Retractions* have always posed certain problems – one of which is that in them he disavows almost his entire canon. Why should he have wanted to revoke *The Book of the Duchess*, *The House of Fame*, and *The Parliament of Fowls* or even, come to that, *Troilus and Criseyde*? Indeed, many critics have found it so hard to believe that Chaucer would want to retract these works that they have been driven to wonder whether he really wrote the *Retractions* or whether it wasn't the interpolation of some officious monk, either interfering after Chaucer's death or else trying to put things in order as Chaucer lay on his death bed. At least one critic has even been moved to see the whole thing as ironic.[18]

General critical opinion today is that the *Retractions* are by Chaucer. We find them in practically all manuscripts that contain *The Parson's Tale* in its entirety, and the fact that the piece begins: 'Now I pray to them all that hear or read this little treatise' seems to indicate that it is intended to follow the treatise on the three stages of confession: penitence, confession and satisfaction, that the Parson has just delivered. The *Retractions* further echoes *The Parson's Tale* when Chaucer pleads to be granted 'grace of verray penitence, confessioun, and satisfaccioun'. The poet seems to be acting out the three stages of penitence as prescribed in the preceding treatise.

That opening line, however, begs another question. Why does Chaucer frame his address in the third person plural? Elsewhere, in this sort of invocation,

Chaucer invariably addresses his audience directly, as he does before embarking on *The Miller's Tale*:

> And therfore, whoso list it nat yheere,
> Turne over the leef and chese another tale ...
> Blameth nat me if that ye chese amys.
>   *The Miller's Prologue*, ll. 3176–7, 3181
> And therefore, whoever doesn't want to hear it,
> Turn over the leaf and choose another tale ...
> Don't blame me if you should choose amiss.

Chaucer usually writes as if he intends to recite his verse himself. He addresses his audience directly, just as if he himself were reading the material out aloud in public.[19] The start of the *Retractions*, however, sounds like someone who is talking at a distance – someone who is no longer able to address his audience directly. His 'litel tretys', or somebody else reading from it, is going to have to do his talking for him:

> Now I pray to all of them that listen to this little treatise, or else read it, that if there is any thing in it that pleases them, they should thank our Lord Jesus Christ for it, from whom all wit and goodness proceeds. And if there be anything that displeases them, I pray them also that they attribute it to my lack of learning and not to my will ...[20]

Why this exceptional change of location for the narrator? Why the third person rather than a direct address? Is it because he is lying on his deathbed, unable to get to the court, where he would find his audience? Or is it because the court he knew is no longer there? Or could it be that he is holed up in his tenement within the sanctuary of Westminster, and doesn't dare stir outside? Perhaps he's just given up public reading because of old age or ill health. Or perhaps he's lying in the prison of the Archbishop of Canterbury.

Of course, we don't know, and it may be none of these reasons, but it is significant that Chaucer does not seem to anticipate declaiming the 'treatise' himself in front of an audience. It is true that he relapses back into the second person a few lines later – 'Wherefore I biseke yow mekely, for the mercy of God, that ye pray for me that Crist have mercy on me and foryeve me my giltes ...'[21] – but this seems to be no more than a conventional invocation.

What, then, about the works that Chaucer chooses to reject?

He 'revokes' almost his entire canon: *Troilus and Criseyde*, *The House of Fame*, *The Legend of Good Women*, *The Book of the Duchess*, *The Parliament of Fowls*, and *The Canterbury Tales* – at least 'thilke that sownen into synne' ('those that tend toward or are conducive of sin'). There really isn't much left, especially when he throws in for good measure 'my translaciouns and enditynges of worldly vanities' ('my translations and writings of worldly vanities'). What's left? *Anelida and Arcite* and *A Treatise on the Astrolabe* both count as translations. *The Romaunt of the Rose* is not only a translation but also a work about worldly vanities. That leaves only the short poems, and Chaucer dismisses most of those as 'many a song and many a leccherous lay'. The only work that he is prepared to claim by name is his translation of Boethius' *Consolation of Philosophy*. Otherwise he mumbles about 'othere bookes of legendes of seintes, and omelies, and moralitee, and devocioun' but it's as if he can't really be bothered to mention them – whatever they are.

What exactly does Chaucer mean by *The Canterbury Tales* that 'sownen into synne'? Presumably the only ones that don't are *The Tale of Melibee*, *The Monk's Tale*, and *The Parson's Tale*. Can those really be the only works that Chaucer does not want to disavow?

In any case, why name in detail the works he's ashamed of but only one of the works he's glad to have written? Could it be that what he is really doing is establishing the canon of his works – but doing so under the pretence of humility and confession?

Then again, what on earth is so sinful about *The House of Fame* or *The Book of the Duchess*? Of course, there had always been some conservative churchmen prepared to regard as sinful any work of literature that was not specifically on a religious topic. Any secular work could be deemed to be about worldly vanities – especially if they included pagans. Boccaccio berates those opponents of works of fiction: 'These enemies of poetry', as he calls them, 'utter the taunt that poets are liars ... my opponents curse the poet and clamour for the extinction of poetry as replete with pranks and adulteries of pagan gods.'[22]

Presumably such enemies of poetry would have found Chaucer's rejection of works like *The House of Fame* or *The Book of the Duchess* perfectly compatible with his total conversion to a wholly orthodox religious perspective. As one twentieth-century Catholic critic sees it, Chaucer here displays 'a delicate conscience that has reawakened after a long sleep'.[23]

'I REVOKE IN MY RETRACCIOUNS'

It may be, however, that Chaucer's *Retractions* were not quite as drastic as they seem. He certainly asks for forgiveness for his 'guilts' in making translations and in writings about worldly vanity, but he tempers this with the reminder that the Bible says: 'Al that is writen is writen for oure doctrine',[24] which could be taken to mean that even translations and secular writings can teach us something.

But in any case, that damning phrase: 'the which I revoke in my retracciouns' is by no means as cut-and-dried as it would appear to modern readers.

The word 'revoke' had more meanings in Chaucer's day than it does now. It certainly had the modern sense of 'retract' or 'disown' which it took from the Old French *revoquer*. But it also had another meaning, from the Latin *revocare*: 'to recall to mind' or 'to rescue' or 'to bring back, revive'.[25] In fact, the only other time Chaucer uses the word, he uses it in this latter sense. In *Troilus and Criseyde*, Criseyde revives Troilus from a fainting fit:

> She ofte hym kiste; and shortly for to seyne,
> Hym to *revoken* she did al hire peyne;
> And at the laste, he gan his breth to drawe,
> And of his swough sone after that adawe.
>   *Troilus and Criseyde*, III, ll. 1117–20
> She kissed him oft, and shortly for to say,
> She did all she could to *revive* him;
> And at the last, he began to draw his breath,
> And out of his swoon soon after that awoke.

So the only other occasion that Chaucer uses the verb *revoken*, he means to say: 'revive', 'recall' rather than 'withdraw'.

The word 'retraccioun' is also an interesting choice here. It had, as far as we know, never been used before in vernacular English in this way. In fact, the *Middle English Dictionary* gives no other instance of it at all. In Old French *retraire* had come to mean 'to withdraw', 'to disavow'. But *retraire* may not have been the source word Chaucer had in mind.

St Augustine had used the Latin form – *Retractationes* – as the title of one of his books. *Retractatio, -onis* had a range of meanings: 'a revision, correction ... reconsideration, remembrance'.[26] The word was also used in this sense by Bede and by Geraldus Cambrensis, both imitating Augustine; an English version was used by John Capgrave in 1451. It is clear that people in England were well aware of this Latin meaning in Chaucer's day.[27]

What *retractatio* did *not* mean, interestingly enough, is what we mean by 'retraction' today: a 'denial', a 'rescinding', a 'taking back', a 'revocation'. It is *just* possible that this meaning was already in use orally in the fourteenth century, but the *OED* does not record a written use of *retract* to mean 'revoke', 'withdraw' or 'rescind' until the mid-sixteenth century.

Augustine's *Retractationes* was well known when Chaucer wrote and Chaucer seems to be following in a tradition of imitating Augustine's work. He contracts the word to 'retracciouns', but the fact that he uses it in the plural undoubtedly alludes to St Augustine's title.

St Augustine.

St Augustine's *Retractationes* is not a 'retraction' (in our modern sense) or 'denial' of his earlier works; it was actually a review of his literary output, in which he offered corrections and comments, as Augustine explains in his Prologue.[28]

It follows, then, that when Chaucer wrote 'the whiche I revoke in my retracciouns', it is just about possible that he meant: 'which I withdraw in my retractions', but it is much more likely that he meant: 'which I recall to mind in my *Review of Work*'.[29]

Archbishop Arundel wasn't much of a scholar, but he would probably have understood the reference to St Augustine, and would probably have been aware that after Augustine has explained his *Retractationes* as a catalogue of works with critical commentary, he says 'Therefore, what remains for me to do, is to judge myself under my single Master, whose Judgment I desire to escape, for all my offences.'[30]

If God was Augustine's judge, Archbishop Arundel was Chaucer's. It was a comparison that Arundel would not have resented in the least.

VAGUE, VAGUE ...

There is one other conundrum in Chaucer's *Retractions*. If one of his purposes was to establish the canon of his work, why is he so vague about *some* of his work – in fact, even inaccurate at one point?

Take his claim to have composed a regrettable 'book of the XXV Ladies'.

Presumably this refers to *The Legend of Good Women* – even though, as far as we know, only nine legends exist (or ten, if you count as a separate legend the brief story of Medea, clumped in with that of Hypsipyle). Now, some scholars have argued that this inaccuracy is a scribal error, a slip of the pen – perhaps, it has been suggested, a mix-up of XXV with XIX – although just how that makes anything clearer is puzzling, since it still leaves the count ten short.[31]

Of course, it may be that more legends existed once. In fact, it seems most likely that there were indeed originally XXV since that is the number that Edward, second Duke of York, remembered, in his prison cell in 1405.[32] If some were lost it shouldn't come as a surprise, given how many things of Chaucer's, including his own copies of all of his writings, were going missing at the turn of the century.

WHAT WAS 'THE BOOK OF THE LEOUN'?

'The book of the Leoun' is another example of something getting lost. Everything else Chaucer mentions by title in the *Retractions* has been identified, and copies have eventually turned up. But not 'the book of the Leoun'. Chaucer, however, seems to have thought it was important enough to list by name – unlike the many 'songs and many a leccherous lay' which he tosses willy-nilly into the *Retractions*.

So what was 'the book of the Leoun'? Can its disappearance shed any light on whether (and by whom) Chaucer may have been murdered?

One thing we can say for certain is that 'the book of the Leoun' has been missing for a long time. None of the early biographers or editors claim to have seen it, or have published a scrap of it. And they would have if they could – people were printing everything they could conceivably attribute to Chaucer's hand, even things we now think of as absurdly unlike Chaucer's work.

Undoubtedly people were looking for it. The title was there – bold as life – in the *Retractions*. How frustrating then (as it has been ever since) to have to keep listing 'the book of the Leoun' among 'His worckes unprinted and not to be founde'.[33] Why, then, couldn't they find it, even with the advantage of starting over five hundred years ago?

The simple answer is, because it was gone. There can be a host of reasons for that, of course. The medieval written record is everywhere fragmentary. Things getting lost isn't necessarily sinister.

Medieval scholars, however, have a rule-of-thumb about estimating what has been lost: if there were multiple copies of any given work, the chances are good that one at least will have survived. The more copies of something we have today, the greater number, it can be guessed, existed once. Perhaps when Chaucer died there weren't many copies of 'the book of the Leoun' around.

Again, there are many benign reasons why that might have been. One possibility is that 'the book of the Leoun' simply wasn't very good, and nobody much wanted copies. 'The book of the Leoun' could have been Chaucer's great mistake, and he was stubborn about admitting it – *ergo*, he listed it in his *Retractions*. Or maybe just the opposite: by calling attention to his 'Lion book', Chaucer was thinking especially like St Augustine, in the *Retractationes*, and flagging a correction.

Still another possibility is that the 'Leoun book' was composed with a limited audience in mind, a *coterie* poem, in other words. But then even a *coterie* poem – if it were by Chaucer – stood a good chance of being copied and thus surviving. *The Book of the Duchess* was probably written, initially at least, for an audience of one: John of Gaunt. Nevertheless, four copies of *The Book of the Duchess* survive. Not an overwhelming number, but it makes the absence of any copies of 'the book of the Leoun' all the harder to understand. There are, however, two other possibilities to consider.

WHAT COULD 'THE BOOK OF THE LEOUN' HAVE BEEN ABOUT?

One scenario is that 'the book of the Leoun' was a very late work – perhaps only just finished. Maybe he hadn't circulated it to anyone yet, and the single copy, his working copy, was destroyed along with his other sole authorial copies.

Another scenario, however, is that 'the book of the Leoun' was singled out because of its inflammatory content. If 'the book of the Leoun' was a political allegory about the events of 1397 or 1399 which made Richard look good, and Henry IV and Archbishop Arundel look less than saintly, that would certainly have guaranteed its almost instant disappearance under the new regime.

The standard line offered by Chaucer scholars about

Guillaume De Machaut.

'the book of the Leoun' is that it had French sources: 'It could have been a redaction of Machaut's *Dit dou Lyon* or of Deschamps' *Dit du Lyon*, perhaps freely adapted as a compliment to Prince Lionel on the occasion of his marriage,' we are told.[34] That would have been the prince's second marriage to the daughter of Bernabò Visconti, despot of Milan, in 1368 – and certainly the 'lion=Lionel' identity has its attractions.

It also, however, has its problems. If Chaucer wrote 'the book of the Leoun' in 1368, it would make it his earliest recorded poem, and it seems likely that, in that many years, copies would have been made in sufficient numbers for one, at least, to have survived. Moreover, if 'the book of the Leoun' was written for

Eustache Deschamps.

Lionel in 1368, Chaucer couldn't have been influenced by Deschamps' 'Dit du Lyon' (or *La Fiction du Lion*, the title Old French scholars prefer today) because Deschamps didn't begin writing it until 1382.[35] So if 'lion=Lionel' in 1368 it would have to have been based on Machaut's *Dit* which is usually dated about 1342.[36]

The confusion about Deschamps' poem is worth pointing out, because it reminds us of how misinformation sometimes gets passed on and established in the official canon of scholarly explanations. And it gets more interesting still if we look more closely at the poems Machaut and Deschamps actually wrote. Here's a summary of Machaut's *Dit dou Lyon*:

> Awakened one morning by the chirping of birds, the Narrator takes a walk. He crosses to an island where he is assaulted by a Lion. The Lion turns out to be friendly, however, and leads the Narrator through a wasteland (where they must endure the snarling of wild beasts) to a *locus amoenus* ['a place of love']. There they are received by a beautiful Lady and her retainers. The Lady and one of her knights explain the secrets of the island. The Narrator intercedes on the Lion's behalf: the poor animal adores the Lady but is rendered despondent by the envious wild beasts who torment him. The Narrator then returns to his own side of the river.[37]

To turn that plot into a poem celebrating the marriage of Prince Lionel to a daughter of the Visconti, Chaucer would have had his work cut out for him. Machaut's Lady is much-older than the Lion – she has raised him from a cub – and so has trouble taking the Lion's passion seriously.[38] The love the Lion eventually wins from the Lady in the *Dit dou Lyon*, then, is nothing much like what most husbands want from their wives on their wedding-day – even if the marriage is (as Lionel's clearly was) a political and economic alliance.

So if Chaucer used Machaut's *Dit dou Lyon* as a source or a model for 'the book of the Leoun', he probably wasn't attracted to it by the occasion of Lionel's marriage in 1368.

The plot of Deschamps' *La Fiction du Lion* is even less likely to inspire a marriage poem:

> *La Fiction du Lion* is a didactic, nostalgic hymn to the lost Golden Age of Charles V, who died in 1380, using a 'Roman de Renart' frame. Charles is Noble the Lion. A Golden Age of grace, harmony, and frugality gives way to one of violence and tyranny. Lady Nature, in a lengthy speech, bewails the decadence which has prevailed since the death of Noble the Lion, during the new regime of Charles VI: Charles the Wise gives birth to Charles the Mad.[39]

That's definitely not a marriage poem. So if Chaucer did borrow ideas from either or both of these two poems, what kind of a poem was he writing?

The answer is: political allegory.

That's what both *La Fiction du Lion* and *Dit dou Lyon* are – neither celebratory nor amorous. And if Chaucer was drawing on Deschamps' poem, the political events he had in mind to allegorize took place well after 1382.

Considered as political allegory based on an amalgam of Machaut's and Deschamps' poems, Chaucer's 'book of the Leoun', might have looked like this: the Lion guards an island kingdom; he is noble, but is constantly tormented by a noxious crowd of lesser wild beasts: dragons, buffalo, camels, tigers, panthers, elephants, bears, leopards, dogs of several kinds, beavers, snakes, scorpions and some unnamable whatsit with two horns ('une autre beste a deus cornes',

l. 390). They threaten the Lion, malign and slander him, attack him with their claws, hooves, etc. Amidst all of this the Lion, who could destroy them all with a single paw, remains stoic. The snarling mob acts this way because (according to Machaut) they are envious of the Lion's superior character and social position. Essentially, what they want is his crown.

'Animals as political allegory' seems to have become a fashion in the late fourteenth and early fifteenth century.

There it is: all you have to do if you're Chaucer is mix-and-match from Machaut and Deschamps – plug in Richard II as the Lion, England as the island, and the rebellious magnates, Gloucester, Arundel and Warwick and co., as the envious wild beasts. The poem could have celebrated Richard's final triumph over his enemies in 1397 with the deaths of Richard, Earl of Arundel and Gloucester, and the exiling of Archbishop Thomas Arundel and Warwick.

Such a political allegory would certainly have fitted well into Richard's own vision of what had taken place. In 1398 he described to the emperor Manuel Palaeologus the way in which, since his minority, he had been surrounded by envious magnates and nobles who had made attempts upon his throne and even directed their malevolence against his person:

> Wherefore when we could no longer endure their rebellion and wantonness, we collected the might of our prowess, and stretched forth our arm against these our enemies; and at length, by the aid of God's grace, we have by our own valour trodden on the necks of the proud and haughty, and with a strong hand have ground them down, not to the bark only, but even to the root; and have restored to our subjects peace, which they had troubled, and which by God's blessing shall endure for ever.[40]

A 'book of the Leoun' would adapt very easily to that sort of scenario.

Or could Chaucer have only just finished writing 'the book of the Leoun' when he disappeared? In that case, his subject might have been the ten years 1389–99 as the lost Golden Age following Richard's outmanoeuvring of the Appellants, and the usurpation as the time of violence and tyranny that comes after – and name your envious beasts.

Of course, Chaucer's skill in keeping his head below the parapet had kept him alive in parlous times when others were losing theirs. So one might ask why should this consummate politician suddenly, in the *most* parlous times of all, write a political allegory that could get him into trouble? Maybe he just had to stand up and be counted? Maybe he knew the game was up and – sink or swim – he had to write something to rally the troops?

In this regard it is interesting to remember that, whether Chaucer wrote his 'book of the Lion' in 1397 or 1399, John Gower at just that time saw fit to write something very similar in conception – although of course since Gower was writing as an apologist for the new regime, the rebellious nobles who surround Richard are not ravening wild beasts but noble creatures of heraldry: the Swan

(Thomas of Woodstock, Duke of Gloucester), the Bear (the Earl of Warwick), and the Horse (Richard, Earl of Arundel, brother to Archbishop Thomas).[41] All of these animals are derived from the badges each man wore – just as King Richard's would have been, if he were the Lion of 'the book of the Leoun'. Horses and bears and swans are some of the beasts which attack the Lion in the *Dit dou Lyon*. Gower and Chaucer, we know, often exchanged poems. Could some of the inspiration for Gower's *Tripartite Chronicle* have been the long-lost 'book of the Leoun'?

This sort of bestiary-cum-political allegory seems, in any event, to have caught on about this time. In the radical populist work known as *Mum and the Sothsegger* (*c.* 1403) we find: Warwick the Bear, Gloucester the Swan, Robert Arundel the Horse and Richard II as the Hart (taken from the badge the king designed for himself).[42] The same sort of political zoo opens its gates again in another anonymous political poem, 'On King Richard's Ministers' (1401). It is not impossible that others were written which have not survived. Whether these were inspired by Chaucer's lost poem or whether they were all part of the same literary fashion for political irony, it is easy to imagine how unpopular Chaucer's offering would have been with the new regime. There is therefore the possibility that 'the book of the Leoun' was what got Chaucer killed.

... AND VAGUER STILL ...

Of course, all this is supposition heaped on supposition, but what do we make of Chaucer's vagueness further on in his *Retractions:* 'and many another book, if they were in my remembrance ...' This parallels the ritual of confession, but at the same time it sounds like someone talking at a distance from his authorial collection. If he had his books beside him, why didn't he just flick through them and include more titles to make sure the canon of his works was complete?

Chaucer's choice of words here recalls the distant-sounding phrasing of the opening lines, where he addresses his readers or listeners in the third person, as if he doesn't expect to confront his audience in the flesh. So here, he seems to have lost access to his own works. Could it be that he has genuinely lost them? Or could they have been taken from him? Or is he simply stuck someplace where he cannot get to them? Could he be in prison? Or could his authorial collection have already been destroyed?

Whatever the truth of the matter, we shall probably never know the answers to these questions. But one thing we can say: Chaucer's authorial voice in *Retractions* has a ring of finality – the sound of someone who doesn't seem to expect to meet his audience any more, who does not have access to his own works and who, perhaps, doesn't expect to write any more. Whether Chaucer was ill or in prison we can only guess.

At the same time, it is not necessary to see the *Retractions* as Chaucer's total rejection of his own work. It is simply a review of his output – a recalling to mind of what he had achieved, set in a conventional religious confessional framework of submission before Christ. Following in the steps of Augustine, for all its omissions, it represents Chaucer's most complete record of his own works.

If Archbishop Arundel had been looking for a retraction of all the anti-ecclesiastical content in *The Canterbury Tales*, or a full abjuration of Chaucer's religious beliefs, of the sort that he was demanding from so many other people, the *Retractions* would not have satisfied him.

But perhaps Chaucer tried to make his peace with the triumphant Caesarian clergyman in other ways.

CHAPTER 18

Chaucer and Archbishop Arundel
(*An ABC* and *The Parson's Tale*)

∾

Of all Chaucer's works, perhaps the two least likely to be placed in a political context are *An ABC* and *The Parson's Tale*. The former is generally written off as an early work, and the latter universally regarded as a great bore and quite often even omitted from editions of *The Canterbury Tales* altogether – as if it didn't really have a serious place in Chaucer's masterwork.[1]

Yet when viewed in the stormy context of Henry of Lancaster's usurpation and Archbishop Arundel's determination to beat his fellow countrymen into intellectual, religious and political submission, it is possible that both works shed new light on those last dark months of Chaucer's existence.

Archbishop Thomas Arundel.

They could be crucial works, if we are to understand what confronted Chaucer in his final days and what his ultimate fate may have been.

'AN ABC'

Chaucer's short poem known as *An ABC* is in fact an English version of a French poem by Guillaume Deguilleville, which was contained in a very much longer poem (said to be the original for Bunyan's *Pilgrim's Progress*) called *The Pilgrimage of the Life of Man* (*La Pèlerinage de la vie humaine*). Deguilleville completed his poem in 1335, so the original clearly could not have reflected the events of 1400. But, as always with Chaucer, the political and social context is all – or quite a bit of it, anyway – and even a translation of Deguilleville could be made relevant to the times.

In any case, Chaucer's poem seems less like a translation to modern eyes than a very free adaptation. He uses the same alphabetical format as Deguilleville and commences most stanzas with the same word as in the French. But Chaucer makes additions and changes that may be significant.[2]

An ABC, it used to be generally agreed, was one of Chaucer's very first poems, but there are some good reasons to suppose that isn't so. In the first place, the major support cited for this early dating is that Chaucer's editor, Thomas Speght, claimed that *An ABC* was 'made, as some say, at the request of Blanche Duchess of Lancaster, as praier for her privat use'.[3] Speght was writing two hundred years after Chaucer's death, and even though he may possibly have had access to a now lost manuscript, his testimony is hardly proof. Duchess Blanche was John of Gaunt's first wife. She died – we know exactly – on 12 September 1368. Probably Chaucer composed *The Book of the Duchess* to console John of Gaunt. Now, *The Book of the Duchess* is usually said to be Chaucer's earliest known poem. But obviously if *An ABC* were written for Blanche's 'privat use', she would have to have been alive to use it. And that would make *An ABC* Chaucer's earliest poem.

Those Chaucer scholars who have bothered themselves about *An ABC* (of which there are not many) have mostly been content to get pretty much everything they have to say about the poem from the explanatory notes in standard editions. And once enshrined there, Speght's speculation that Chaucer wrote the poem for the devotions of Duchess Blanche has served quite handily to slam the door on any further poking about in a slightly embarrassing neighbourhood.

Virgin and child.

Because the fact is that Chaucer's *ABC* is 'liked' (rather as the gentleman in *Death of a Salesman*) 'but not *well* liked'. It gives every indication of being precisely what it appears – an expression of its author's devotion to the Virgin Mary, offered without a hint of self-consciousness or irony. For most of Chaucer's later readers, that has proved an unacceptable thing to think about Chaucer.

Reformation Englishmen turned him into a proto-Protestant. John Foxe, for example, while 'canonizing' Chaucer in his *Book of Martyrs*, didn't even acknowledge *An ABC* as his: such unabashed image-worship would hardly do. In the twentieth century, proudly secular and 'objective', *An ABC* was still unpopular, because religious emotion had itself become slightly embarrassing.[4] Nobody – New Critics, Freudians, Marxists, feminists, *nobody* – wanted to get tarred with that.[5]

All of this lugubrious history tells us why Speght's linking of *An ABC* with the Duchess Blanche has been gospel for so long. There are scarcely any more effective ways of dismissing a poem than to call it 'an early work'. 'Ah, the rashness of youth. Chaucer knew better later, of course.'

In fact, the closer we look at *An ABC* the less it looks like a poem for Blanche. In the first place, the poem *sounds* like a man addressing a woman. It's hard to imagine the Duchess Blanche saying to the Virgin Mary: 'Ladi, tak hede!' or using the courtly address: 'thou mighti debonayre' or 'Help, lady bright'.[6] It is true that there is always a certain licence allowed in prayer-poems to adopt a persona, but why should he give the Lady Blanche a male persona for her private use?

Then there is the verse form. In *An ABC* Chaucer uses a stanza which otherwise is found only in his late work. It's been called the '*Monk's Tale* stanza', from its most famous example, and Chaucer also employs it in three minor poems: 'The Former Age', 'The Complaint of Venus', and the 'Lenvoy de Chaucer a Bukton'.[7] All of these are unequivocably datable to the last years of Chaucer's life, with the possible exception of *The Monk's Tale* itself, which some critics suggest he might have begun somewhat earlier. But that raises the question of why Chaucer composed *An ABC* in '*Monk's Tale* stanza' in 1367–8 and nothing else in it again until *The Canterbury Tales* and the three minor poems – surely he didn't forget how to write it for thirty years?

And finally there is the sophistication of *An ABC*, which points toward later composition. As a few more scholars have begun to pay attention to it, *An ABC* begins to look more manifestly a richer poem. Of course there's no reason to suppose Chaucer incapable of sophistication in 1367. He would have been in his middle twenties then – no 'juvenile' even by modern standards, and being around the court he would in any case have seen a lot. But the recent drift of scholarship about *An ABC* makes it out to be a poem of Chaucer's maturity.[8]

So it is possible – if not likely – that the poem was written late; and if it was, might it have any relevance to the situation in which Chaucer found himself in 1399–1400?

The demise of Richard II and the annihilation of his court had taken the rug from under Chaucer's feet. His current work-in-progress was shot through with often vituperative anti-ecclesiastical invective and satire, and yet now dissent against the church was being equated with dissent against the usurping king. It had become dangerous.

So could it be that Chaucer wrote *An ABC* as an attempt to give himself a theological make-over? Could *An ABC* be seen as an act of reparation on the part of someone with a theologically flawed past? Not that he wasn't being sincere, but just that he was trying to square his own beliefs with those currently being imposed from above?

Pilgrim assaulted by vices, from Deguilleville's 'The Pilgrimage of the Life of Man'.

Deguilleville pictured a penitent abased before the Virgin Mary. Mary is the exalted summit of mercy and perfection, while the penitent is an abject suppliant. God's justice is harsh *because* it is just ('So hidous is his rightful rekeninge', l.132) and there is no mercy without the intercession of the Virgin: 'God ne graunteth no pitee/ Withoute thee' (l.136–7). The orthodoxy is unquestionable and Chaucer follows Deguilleville to the letter in all this. Clearly, both poets could hope to make their peace with the heavenly hierarchy.

But might Chaucer *also* have been hoping to square himself with the more immediate hierarchy here on earth, as represented by that guardian and definer of orthodoxy: Archbishop Arundel?

This is, perhaps, where Chaucer's additions to Deguilleville's text are important. One thing that Deguilleville does not mention – but Chaucer does – is that, in addition to the penitent's assorted sins and shortcomings, a singular black mark against him is the fact that he was *in error*. 'Error' in Chaucer's time was the standard word used to categorize belief that was out of step with orthodox Catholic teaching. In other words, 'error' was the common term for 'heresy'.[9]

Now, to be sure, Heresy appears also in the *Pèlerinage de la vie humaine*, but in a very different way from what we find in *An ABC*. Deguilleville personifies Heresy as an old woman carrying a faggot of wood (with which to light the fire that will eventually consume her) and running backwards and squinting because she is purblind. Her father is Satan, who appears as a hunter laying traps to catch the unwary. But Deguilleville's Pilgrim evades the snares and nets (any wonder Bunyan loved the *Pèlerinage*?) – diving into the stormy sea to escape, and that's that. It's all over in one episode. Heresy is one thing of which Deguilleville's Pilgrim is not guilty.[10]

In contrast, Chaucer's Penitent (or is it the poet himself?) returns to the subject of his heresy – his 'error' – three times in the course of *An ABC*. The effect, in Chaucer's poem, is to make 'error' more of an issue.

Glorious virgine, of alle floures flour,
To thee I flee, confounded in errour.
   An ABC, ll. 5–6
Glorious virgin, of all flowers flower,
To thee I flee, confounded in heresy.

And he's come to the right person because, since at least the thirteenth century, the Virgin Mary had been celebrated as the antidote for heresy.[11] Sixty lines further on, Chaucer spells out this aspect of Mary's efficaciousness:

I wot it wel, thou wolt ben oure socour,
Thou art so ful of bowntee, in certeyn,
For whan a soule falleth in errour
Thi pitee goth and haleth hym ayein
   An ABC, ll. 65–8
I know it well, thou wilt be our succour,
Thou art so full of bounty, for certain,
That when a soul falls into heresy
Thy pity pulls him out again.[12]

Towards the end of the poem, Chaucer outlines the role that Mary will play in absolving his suit:

Virgine, that art so noble of apparaile,
And ledest us into the hye tour
Of Paradys, thou me wisse and counsaile
How I may have thi grace and thi socour,
All have I ben in filthe and in errour.
   An ABC, ll. 153–7
Virgin, who are so noble of character,
And who leads us into the High Tower
Of Paradise, teach me and counsel me
How I may get your grace and help,
Though I have been in filth and in heresy.

Also in contrast to Deguilleville, Chaucer has his penitent speak as if he were presenting a case at law. The imagery of *An ABC* is legalistic. It is hard to imagine that, to any reader in the 1400s, lines 153–60 would have failed to summon up some reminder of the ecclesiastical courts that were then working overtime up and down the land, probing into heresy on behalf of Archbishop Arundel. Nor would the implicit comparison have been favourable:

Presenting a case at law.

> Ladi, unto that court thou me ajourne
> That cleped is thi bench, O freshe flour,
> Ther as that merci evere shal sojourne.
>   *An ABC*, ll. 158–60
> Lady, summon me to that court
> That is called your magistrate's bench, O fresh flower,
> There where mercy always stays.

There are moments when the poem actually becomes quite funny. For example, Chaucer can't resist taking a little swipe at the cost of legal fees. The Virgin is our only advocate, he says, and – minor miracle! – she works cheap. All she wants is an Ave-Maria or two!

> We han ...
> Ne advocat noon that wole and dar so preye
> For us, and that for litel hire as yee
> That helpen us for an Ave-Marie or tweye.
>   *An ABC*, ll. 100–04
> We have ...
> No other advocate willing and with courage enough
> To plead on our behalf, and that for as little hire as you
> Who help us for an Ave-Maria or two!

Of course, to place *An ABC* in the context of Arundel's pursuit of heresy in 1400 is a matter of speculation. If Speght were somehow to be proved right and the poem dates from before Duchess Blanche's death in 1368, then the legal imagery that runs like a *leitmotif* through the poem is nothing more than a literary conceit.

However, official concern about 'error' did not begin to play any real part in national affairs until ten years after Blanche's death. And it was not until 1382 that the ecclesiastical courts and, indeed, the secular courts, began to see the first legal proceedings against heretics in any number. The linkage between legal proceedings and heresy, which is crucial to *An ABC*, therefore also suggests a later date of composition.

So to sum up: some critics have asserted that in *An ABC* the historical Chaucer is ventriloquizing through the faceless penitent. If this is indeed the case, then we witness in the poem Chaucer's confession of a lapse into theological *error*, and this at the feet of heresy's traditional remedy, the Virgin Mary. The poem's language is noticeably legalistic, which makes best sense if *An ABC* were composed after 1382. Its penitential resonances only deepen if, in the dark days of heresy-hunting at the start of the fifteenth century, Geoffrey Chaucer were writing it in fear for his life – in the next world and also, very immediately, in this.

Read as an attempt to win favourable judgement on two levels, *An ABC* exhibits characteristic Chaucerian complexity. It makes good sense to see it as a product of a faithful man's last days and, on another level, as a desperate attempt to square himself with the newly triumphant church whose flagrant excesses he had criticized with such gusto, and sometimes even contempt, in freer times while Richard II was king.

'THE PARSON'S TALE'

In American football parlance, there's a thing called a 'Hail Mary play': with the game on the line and no other chance of winning, you send everybody eligible downfield and heave the ball as hard and as far as possible in their general direction – and pray. Sometimes somebody catches it. More often they don't. That may have been Chaucer's situation in 1400. If we're right about what he was up to in *An ABC* – a wing and a prayer – it can help us understand what may have been his plan for *The Parson's Tale* and the *Retractions*, too. The other pilgrims immediately identify the Parson as a Lollard. 'I smelle a Lollere in the wynd,' cries the Host, Harry Bailly, the moment the Parson opens his mouth. And, it's true; as we have already seen the Parson's vocabulary and attitudes echo with 'Wycliffite' resonances. Even his response to the Host's demand for a story – 'Telle us a fable anon, for cokkes bones!' – displays a scorn for fiction that his contemporaries would have regarded as Wycliffite:

Thou getest fable noon ytold for me,
For Paul, that writeth unto Thymothee,
Repreveth hem that weyven soothfastnesse
And tellen fables and swich wrecchednesse.
　　The Parson's Prologue, ll. 31–34
You'll get no fable told on my behalf,
For St Paul wrote to Timothy
Reproving those who turn aside from truth
And tell fables and such wretchedness.

Nor will our Parson tell a romance in alliterative verse – and God knows! – we'll get nothing from him in rhyme, either: rhyme is 'but little better!' (*The Parson's Prologue*, ll. 43–4).

Poetry and fiction had been long regarded with suspicion by some ultra-conservative Christians in a tradition that, as the Parson himself points out, stretched back to St Paul's advice to Timothy: 'Have nothing to do with those godless myths, fit only for old women.'[13] But in Chaucer's time such objections had become the preserve of the religious reformers rather than the conservatives. A typical Wycliffite sermon complains: 'Some preach fables and some vain stories; some abridge holy writ and some make up lies; and so God's law is all put aback.'[14]

The Poor Parson.

There are other things about the Parson, however, that seem to run contrary to this 'loller' identification. For a start, if he's a Wycliffite, what's he doing on a pilgrimage? Scorn for pilgrimages was one of the most common characteristics distinguishing the Lollards. No card-carrying Wycliffite would even consider going on one.

But the oddest thing of all is that when the Parson – this manifest 'Lollard' – comes to tell his *Tale*, it turns out to be a thoroughly orthodox treatise on confession – a sacrament which Wyclif and his followers rejected out of hand.

In other words, Chaucer's Parson *looks* like a duck, *walks* like a duck, *quacks* like a duck – but sets up his stall with the wolves.

What *is* going on?

WHY IS CHAUCER'S PARSON ON A PILGRIMAGE?

Let us take the question of why he is on the pilgrimage first. This is, perhaps, not such a serious contradiction.

The pilgrimage of *The Canterbury Tales* is, after all, a literary device. They are not there to perform some modern idea of a realistic social event. There is plenty of realism in Chaucer's depiction, of course, but it would be a mistake to look for a dramatic structure or development in the actual pilgrimage. At the functional level it is a convenience designed to provide book-ends for the tales.

Of course, it *is* fascinating how the pilgrims interact with each other and how they reveal themselves within their own tales to a greater or lesser extent. But in our enthusiasm for the modernity of Chaucer's ability to record patterns of speech and the interplay of dialogue, we shouldn't lose sight of the fact that a medieval book was not like a modern book. A medieval 'book' was usually a collection of works. In a way, it was nearer akin to a Victorian album than to any book on the shelves of a modern bookstore. Before the age of printing most 'books' tended to be the bringing-together of pieces that the compiler thought were worth preserving.

The Canterbury Tales is no different. It just happens to be one of the most complex and ingenious collections. In such a context, the pilgrimage to Canterbury is a convention, and to say that the Poor Parson should not be on it if he subscribes to Wycliffite ideals is not really the point. One might as well say that it would be most unlikely for the Monk to join in such a pilgrimage, or for the Friar or the Prioress.

For that matter, why is the Poor Parson riding a horse, when one of his most striking characteristics is that he goes everywhere on foot?

For the sake of fitting every representative of society in between the 'book-ends', we have to suspend our disbelief about the composition of this particular pilgrimage. The Parson shouldn't be on it, but if he weren't we wouldn't have a representative of his social type.

But though we should beware of reading too much into the Parson's presence on the trip to Canterbury, the fact that the 'tale' he tells turns out to be a perfectly orthodox treatise on confession is surprising, and much more interesting…

THE POLITICS OF CONFESSION

The Parson's Tale is not really a 'tale'. He warns the other pilgrims in his Prologue that they won't get a work of fiction out of him, and he offers them instead a 'meditacioun'. In Chaucer's day a 'meditacioun' was a learned treatise – either for private study or for reading aloud. The Parson acknowledges this when he refers to his 'meditacioun' as a written text: 'as I bigan in the firste chapitre' (X, l. 957).

Chaucer doesn't even *pretend* that this is something someone would actually tell on the road to Canterbury.

The subject of this particular meditation is the theory and practice of penitential confession. In 1400 this would have been highly significant.

Now 'confession' may strike the vast majority of modern readers as a pretty unfortunate choice for what is the longest of *The Canterbury Tales*. Couldn't Chaucer have found some more exciting topic to end his poem with? Even Gower – not noted for excitement – makes his last and longest tale in the *Confessio Amantis* about incest. Why confession?

The answer is that in the fourteenth century it was one of the most pressing issues of the day – a highly charged and highly politicized activity.

The Fourth Lateran Council of 1215 had insisted on the importance of the Sacrament of Penance and that every man and woman – 'everybody of either sex' ('*omnis utriusque sexus*') is how it begins – must go to confession at least once a year, preferably some time around Easter. Ever since then, the authority to administer confession had become a powerful and attractive tool for the priesthood. Apart from preaching, it was the most effective channel for the clergy to communicate with and advise their parishioners. But it also became so much more than that.

Confession.

The knowledge of people's transgressions

obtained during confession, and the guidance and advice that might be offered, conferred on the priesthood extraordinary power. Confession turned into a means of monitoring the population: the priest could find out – was *supposed* to find out – what was going on in people's lives and minds, and then tell them what to do next. Whatever the high-minded intentions of the Council of 1215, it is hardly surprising that the administration of confession eventually became a source of rivalry between the local village priests, like the Poor Parson, and the mendicant friars.

The three orders of clergy – monks, friars and parish clergy – had long had a history of rivalry, especially where money was involved. Most of the parish clergy were short of it; the monks had plenty of it; the friars took as much of it as they could. Cloistered in their monasteries, the monks were not considered a threat by the parish clergy, but the nomadic friars, whose sustenance came from begging as they walked around the country, were in direct competition for the often scarce resources of the parson's parishioners. There was an explosive and often bitter rivalry between them.

The parish priest's heart must have sunk whenever he heard that a friar had turned up in the parish. He would have to give over his church to him and stand by to watch as the visitor charmed and cajoled his congregation – for these friars were often highly educated men of the world. Like Friar Huberd of *The General Prologue*, many of them became skilled in making their visitations agreeable events in the lives of the simple people of the parish. Something to look forward to … someone who would bring a breath of the exotic world beyond the parish boundary into humdrum lives.

The village priest would also know that the friar would be making a pitch for the rich pickings (or even not-so-rich pickings) to be had out of his parishioners.

For one thing, many a villager preferred to confess sexual infidelities with their neighbours to someone who came from outside the area and whom they might never see again, rather than confess to the resident priest. The priest would be there next Christmas … and next summer … and – what is worse – knew their wives and husbands and children …

Then, for another thing, the friars offered many inducements. They often claimed they had more power than the parish clergy when it came to confession – that is, they could forgive graver sins or give more days of absolution. And what would *really* irritate the local priest was that frequently the friars would go out of their way not to be censorious when hearing the confessions of sinners.

They would be full of understanding and magnanimity, and then, when the nasty business of confession was over, would give surprisingly light punishments – especially in households where they anticipated a generous offering (a fat chicken, say, or a ham or a string of sausages) from the repentant sinner. Chaucer's Friar is one of these:

> Ful swetely herde he confessioun,
> And plesaunt was his absolucioun:
> He was an esy man to yeve penaunce,
> Ther as he wiste to have a good pitaunce.
>   *The General Prologue*, ll. 221–5
> Full sweetly he heard confession,
> And pleasant was his absolution:
> He was an easy man to give penance,
> Wherever he knew he'd get a good offering.

It's pretty clear on whose side Chaucer comes down in this contest. All his criticism is aimed at the friars and the worldly ecclesiastics. Just look at the tales he gives to the Friar and to the Parson, respectively. To the Parson he gives a prestigious and intellectually weighty tale. To the Friar he gives a scurrilous story that places the Friar (for all his skills in social climbing and his impressive appearance) firmly amongst the company in the tavern and the market square.

And since the sacrament of confession was such a bone of contention between the friars and the parish clergy, the fact that Chaucer has his Poor Parson deliver a learned treatise on it means that he is in a very obvious way continuing his criticism of the mendicant orders. In *The General Prologue* Chaucer parades before the public gaze the sleaze and connivance of the Friar's confessional practices. In *The Parson's Tale* he shows that an ordinary parson is perfectly capable of understanding the theory and practice of the confession.

ARUNDEL'S REACTION TO 'THE PARSON'S TALE'?

There are possibly things in *The Parson's Tale* that would have had Archbishop Arundel looking down his imperious nose. For a start, he probably would not have liked the attack on the mendicant orders implicit in the Parson's approach. And he might have started tapping his foot in exasperation when he came to the statement (X, l. 964) that if a priest kills a man or a woman inside the church, the church must be closed until it has been purged, and the priest should never be allowed to sing Mass again for the rest of his life.[15] Arundel did not consider the misdeeds of priests proper material for general reading.

Nor would Arundel have particularly enjoyed the portion of *The Parson's Tale* that deals with simony in the church – 'spiritual merchandise', as the Parson calls it, one of the bestselling wares of the Church Commercial.[16] But on the other hand, Chaucer was careful: the criticisms remain vague and general.

The main thing, though, that Arundel would have disapproved of was that all these things – plus the theory and practice of confession – were being explained in plain English. To blacken matters further, the Parson even quotes from the Bible in English!

English was the Great Satan to Thomas Arundel; and, as we have already seen, driving it out of his church was his Mother of All Battles. English became another of his touchstones of heresy. 'Simply to be a reader of English or to own a religious text written in English became in certain circumstances and among certain sorts of people potentially incriminating. Literacy pointed an accusing finger towards heresy.'[17]

The whole enterprise, then, of *The Parson's Tale*, and parts of it in particular, would likely have stuck in Arundel's throat – but he wouldn't have choked on it – not, that is, in the way he would have done over the portrait of the Parson in *The General Prologue*.

Indeed, what is so very curious about *The Parson's Tale* is the fact that it is fundamentally a thoroughly orthodox piece of work – not only orthodox, but often deeply conservative, as well.

THE ORTHODOX NATURE OF 'THE PARSON'S TALE'

It's very odd that Chaucer decided to put this treatise on confession into the mouth of the Parson, a man who is so readily identified as a Lollard by his fellow travellers. For Wyclif and his followers, the whole business of confession and absolution was fraudulent. It was an imposition upon the common people. Consider the ninth item from the so-called Twelve Conclusions of the Lollards, which were found nailed to the doors of Westminster Hall during the winter session of Parliament 1395, and also to the doors of St Paul's:[18]

> ... the articles of confession that is said to be necessary to salvation of man, with a feigned power of absolution enhances the priests' pride, and gives them

opportunity of private calling ... time of confession is the best time for wooing and for private continuance of deadly sin ... They say that they have the keys of heaven and hell, they may curse and bless, bind and unbind at their own will, in so much that for a bushel of wheat or 12d. a year they will sell the bliss of heaven ... sealed with the common seal.[19]

When John Purvey, arguably the most influential Wycliffite after Wyclif himself, finally submitted to Archbishop Arundel, after being tortured in the archbishop's prison in Saltwood Castle, he specifically had to abjure his objections to confession:

The second heresy that I held, wrote about and taught was this. That which I confess with my own mouth, be it in private penitence or even out loud, destroys the freedom of the gospels, and was newly introduced by the pope and the clergy to entangle the consciences of men in sin, and also to drag their souls to hell. Against which heresy I believe and acknowledge this to be the universal truth. This is that which I confess with my own mouth does not destroy but promotes the privilege of the gospels, and it was not introduced to the entanglement but rather to the liberation of human conscience from sin.[20]

The Parson's Tale, however, not only promotes the necessity of confession, but it also emphasizes the importance of the role of the priest in the process. The Parson makes it quite clear that confession has to be made before a priest to be valid. He specifically cites the priest as the mediator between God and man – something which contradicts the fundamental beliefs of the religious radicals.

What is more, *The Parson's Tale* even goes into some detail about the seating plan best suited to priest and penitent during the act of confession! The Parson tells us that the Penitent:

... should humble his outward body before the priest, who sits in God's place. For which reason, since Christ is sovereign, and the priest is the mean and mediator between Christ and the sinner, and the sinner is the last by way of reason, then should not the sinner sit as high as his confessor, but kneel before him or at his feet, unless some illness prevents it.[21]

Of course, in the days before the invention of the confession box afforded protection, penitents could all too often find themselves being groped by their confessors, so perhaps seating arrangements were important. But in this passage it is the hierarchical arrangement that is being emphasized, and it is this stress on hierarchy and on the role of the priest as mediator that is so un-Wycliffian and so foreign to everything we learn of the Poor Parson in *The General Prologue*.[22]

In fact, the whole attitude of *The Parson's Tale* towards the office of priesthood is distinctly non-Wycliffite. 'Priests are angels', says the *Tale*, 'by the dignity of their calling.'[23] The Wycliffite view was that the office conferred nothing on the holder of the office – only grace could do that.

Or consider *The Parson's Tale*'s reflections on celibacy in the priesthood. The *Tale* is treating of the 'cursed sin' of adultery – especially when one or both of the sinners are in holy orders:

> And ever the higher that he is in orders, the greater is the sin. The things that greatly aggravate their sin are the breaking of their vow of chastity, when they received their order. And furthermore, the truth is that holy orders are the chief of all the treasury of God and his special sign and mark of chastity to show that they are enjoined to chastity, which is the most precious life that there is.[24]

The Wycliffites, by contrast, regarded the vows of celibacy taken by the clergy as a source of inevitable evil. The third of the Lollards' *Twelve Conclusions* of 1395 reads: 'The third conclusion, sorrowful to hear, is that the law of continence annexed to the priesthood, which was first ordained in prejudice of women, induces sodomy in all Holy Church ... '[25]

The Parson's Tale is also perfectly orthodox on the question of absolution. It introduces, *for the only time in Chaucer's work*, a clear (though rather clumsy) affirmation of the sacrament of the Eucharist:

> Men may also reduce venal sins by receiving worthily the precious body of Jesus Christ [i.e. participating in the Eucharist] by also receiving holy water, by deeds of alms, by general confession of *Confiteor* during Mass, and at Compline, and by the blessing of bishops and of priests and other good works.
>
> The Parson's Tale, X, ll. 384–5

These attitudes and this treatise are certainly not what one would expect from a follower of Wyclif, and it is difficult to reconcile them with the character of the Parson in *The General Prologue*.

What was Chaucer playing at?

WHAT IS CHAUCER UP TO IN 'THE PARSON'S TALE'?

Why should Chaucer create a character like the Parson – so clearly a Lollard to the other pilgrims – and yet who, when he comes to tell a 'tale', delivers a perfectly orthodox treatise on a subject which was anathema to the Wycliffites?

It is tempting to see *The Parson's Tale* as Chaucer's personal testament. Reaching the end of his life, he records for posterity his final thoughts on life, death, the Universe and Everything. The *Tale* has a feeling of finality that encourages this impression. And this is indeed how many interpreters have seen it: 'Only in *The Parson's Tale* can he [Chaucer] be said to speak unequivocally from and of the truth of faith ... It is a ground-plan of salvation ... an expression of deep and orthodox piety ... The *Retraction* grows inevitably out of *The Parson's Tale*, and confirms the passing of artistic into historical consciousness. It is Chaucer's own act of satisfaction.'26

But if indeed it is Chaucer speaking from the pious heart through his Poor Parson here, then not only has he undergone a radical change of opinion on many ecclesiastical matters, but he has also experienced a drastic personality change as well.

It is hard to accept that the author of *The Canterbury Tales* genuinely believed some of the things that *The Parson's Tale* puts such great store by. For example, would Chaucer really have felt it was crucial to confession to get the seating arrangements right? Or would Chaucer really believe, as the Parson seems to believe, that sex for pleasure *even within marriage* is a deadly sin? This is what *The Parson's Tale* says:

> The third kind of adultery is sometimes between man and wife, and that is when they have no other interest in their assembling but only their fleshly delight, as says St Jerome, and they reckon of nothing but that they are assembled, because they are married and all is good enough as it seems to them.
> *The Parson's Tale*, X, l. 904

> If they [a man and wife] assemble only for amorous love and for none of the aforesaid causes, but only for to accomplish that burning delight, without reckoning how often. Truly it is a deadly sin ...
> *The Parson's Tale*, X, l. 942

The Parson even includes wet dreams and nocturnal emissions as grievous sins![27]

This is an ultra-conservative, orthodox voice that is very hard to reconcile with the opinions and attitudes that Chaucer expresses elsewhere throughout his work. Can it really be Chaucer's final reflection on the human condition?

The pointing finger of censure.

WHEN WAS 'THE PARSON'S TALE' WRITTEN?

All this is assuming, of course, that *The Parson's Tale* was one of the last things that Chaucer wrote. Many scholars in the past have dated it early, but more recent analysis of specific phrases and verses not found in the sources have led some to the conclusion that it was written after the other tales. It has recently been argued that Chaucer attempted to order the *Tales* 'after *The Parson's Tale* and the *Retraction* were written ... The composition of these two pieces implies a decision on the author's part about his poem that would naturally spark an assembling of what was then complete.'[28] Another scholar has urged that the Parson's 'meditacioun' should be removed from *The Canterbury Tales* altogether, but the general consensus is that Chaucer intended it to be, as it is in the Ellesmere manuscript, at the end of the *Tales* and followed by the *Retractions*.[29]

Perhaps the strongest argument for *The Parson's Tale* being one of Chaucer's last works is that there are signs that it was abandoned while still a work-in-progress. It's full of little errors, the kind a writer gets rid of in the process of revision – if, that is, he has the time and/or the inclination. An obvious example is the way a rubric at line 315 announces the beginning of the '*The Second Part of Penitence*', and another rubric its conclusion at line 385. There follows an unnumbered section of roughly six hundred lines on the Seven Deadly Sins, and then, at line 956, a rubric introducing '*The Second Part of Penitence*' again. Clearly Chaucer had not read through the material or had time to correct it.

At another point the writer (Chaucer? the Parson?) promises 'three good reasons' why a man and his wife are permitted to make love – but then generously provides *four*. And there are many other errors and inconsistencies.[30] As one modern editor muses: 'Often only comparison with the suggested sources will clarify Chaucer's meaning, and ... compositional flaws may be due to hasty work or a faulty source text or Chaucer's extracting material from a much longer work of complex structure.'[31]

Of course, Chaucer left a number of unfinished works – poetical and otherwise: *The House of Fame, The Legend of Good Women, The Cook's Tale*, for instance. It is often asserted that Chaucer was not over-concerned with bringing his works to a satisfactory conclusion, or else that he had no qualms about abandoning a piece when he became bored with it or found it too difficult to end. But such an idea of Chaucer doesn't really seem to be in character with the meticulous civil servant who took such pains to put his affairs in order whenever he left for foreign shores – nor with the demanding poet who scolds his scribe for sloppy copying.

What is more, some scholarly opinion now suggests that many of the works supposedly abandoned by Chaucer were actually completed but subsequently lost their endings. There is evidence, for example, that the missing ending of *The Legend of Good Women* went AWOL sometime after 1405. It has also been conjectured that the last section of *The House of Fame* was lost in an act of censorship.[32] While the most recent thinking on *The Cook's Tale* is that its abrupt breaking off is because Chaucer was working on it when he died.[33]

This is also the simplest and cleanest hypothesis for the unfinished and unrevised state of *The Parson's Tale*.

Perhaps, in *The Parson's Tale*, Chaucer was doing what so many people were doing in 1400, when they found themselves confronted by the implacable forces of religious conformity, backed by torture and imprisonment and finally the threat of being burnt alive. Like so many who discovered themselves caught in Archbishop Arundel's fine-meshed dragnet of suspicion, Chaucer may have been trying, as best he knew how, to reconcile his own beliefs with the newly-entrenched orthodox position. That is what so many other people were doing – men like the theologian Henry Crump, John Purvey and William Sawtre.[34]

In fact Chaucer has the Parson himself articulate such a claim for reconciling orthodox and heterodox. When the Host demands the Parson tell them some fable or other, the Parson replies:

> Why sholde I sowen draf out of my fest
> When I may sowen whete if that me lest?
> *The Parson's Prologue*, ll. 35–6

Why should I sow chaff out of my fist
When I may sow wheat if I want to?

The Parson is thus taking the usual jibe thrown at the Wycliffites – that they were spreading tares or weeds amongst the clean corn – and turning it on its head. In his image, *he* is the one sowing the clean wheat and eschewing the 'chaff'. It's a way of saying: look our positions are not so different after all. We are both in our way after the same thing.

Of course, those who attempted such reconciliation may or may not have known that 'reconciliation' wasn't what Archbishop Arundel was really interested in. The Archbishop had no curiosity about how differing views could be accommodated into the official programme of the Church. He had no inclination whatsoever to discover compromise. His intention lay in the opposite direction entirely.

Archbishop Thomas Arundel wanted confrontation, and he wanted – above all – to make distinctions. He wished to identify those whose views challenged the established church – that is to say: that challenged *him*. He wanted to isolate those views and he wanted to crush them.

For a while, in the 1400s, many who stood under suspicion were still laying out the stalls of their consciences for inspection, in the mistaken belief that the authorities were interested in peaceful compromise. They suffered under the illusion that if they could prove to Archbishop Arundel that their views were compatible with orthodox teaching, he would leave them in peace to carry on voicing their protests against church corruption.

It is hard to believe that Chaucer could have been that optimistic. As a tried and tested diplomat and spy, he must surely have known only too well the political reality which faced him at the end of his life.

He could not alter the past. He had written that which by 1400 he must have been regretting he had written. But there could be no putting the genie back into the bottle – no closing of Pandora's box.

Perhaps the best he could hope for was to throw himself on the mercy of the court – as he does in *An ABC*. But as another shot, he could try to show that even a man with the obvious Wycliffite sympathies of his Poor Parson could still be deeply orthodox and supportive of the church's *status quo*. 'Men are like books,' Chaucer might have told himself, 'you have to read them deeper than the cover.'

CHAUCER'S 'PC RATING' FOR THE YEAR 1400

If, in 1400, Chaucer had taken stock of where he stood in regard to Arundel's increasingly idiosyncratic definition of 'heresy', his assessment of his own chances might have looked something like this:

1. He had made fun of pilgrimages. That was a definite black mark against him in Arundel's book.

2. He had mercilessly ridiculed the idea of relics and images. That was not good news in the present climate.

3. He had attacked the mendicant orders in scurrilous and outrageous terms – consigning them to the Devil's arse. Arundel would have scored another very black mark against his name for that.

4. He had criticized the worldly clergy – in ways which directly impinged on Caesarian bishops like Courtenay and most certainly Arundel himself. That was definitely going to count against him.

5. And he had done all this clearly and plainly in the English language. That was probably his worst sin of all in Archbishop Arundel's eyes. It was certainly the hardest one to square with the new religious autocracy.

But – 'Apart from *that*, Mrs Lincoln, how did you like the play?'

On the positive side, at least Chaucer had never questioned the necessity of the priesthood. Nor – and this was his biggest asset – had he ever written against the sacrament of the Eucharist. And since denial of the Eucharist was Arundel's chief litmus test of heresy, Chaucer may have thought he stood a fighting chance.

And this is perhaps what we see in *The Parson's Tale*: Chaucer going for the fighting chance.

He takes the Poor Parson, whose life is a standing reproach to the worldly clerics, like Arundel, and puts into his mouth a treatise of unquestionable orthodoxy. Of course, it is *unfortunate* that it is in English, but perhaps that is where Chaucer had to draw the line. He could not admit to the supposed 'subversiveness' of speaking plainly in his own language. Perhaps he didn't even realize the lengths to which Arundel was prepared to go to stifle religious discussion in the vernacular.

But perhaps he was about to find out.

It may be that *The Parson's Tale* is sending a message on two levels.

On the human level it may simply be an apology for youthful indiscretions. But there's another level on which to read *The Parson's Tale*, visible in silhouette, as it were, backlit by Sawtre's flames. It's a reading that Thomas Arundel may have found less palatable for is runs like this: in spite of appearances, there is in fact no contradiction between what the Parson seems and what he says.

If it is true that every literary fiction is autobiographical in its way, then the Chaucer who wrote *An ABC* in prayer to the Virgin for help in dire need is equally his Parson and the Wife of Bath, and the Monk who loves fine horses and a well-sauced swan. He is even the Pardoner, the fiction master. They all issued forth from Chaucer – *are* Chaucer; in different times and different places, each distinct but connected, and so believable, quite 'real'. We come again and again to Chaucer, to sound with him this awareness of the complexity of consciousness – of conscience – in all its contradiction, the unholy and the holy on pilgrimage inside us, travelling cheek-by-jowl.

What the Parson *really* is, is an honest follower of Christ, who takes the simple Christian message and vivifies it day to day. But that makes him Thomas Arundel's worst nightmare. Because he is a Lollard? No, because he's in the church, one church, as much a Roman as St Paul, who *made* the church, and whose words the Parson quotes as bookmark for his tale.

If Archbishop Arundel had understood the Parson and his tale like this, perhaps he would have recognized it as at once a priceless gift and a mortal, shattering attack.

For the Parson is concerned with choices: what you do is who you are. And what Arundel had done with his (and Henry IV too, for that matter) was to sell his birthright for a mess of pottage – the mitre and the crozier and the crown. The king, it seems, may have understood as much, given the self-recrimination and doubt of his dark last years.

But Arundel? Perhaps not, but then again perhaps he did too. After all, the mighty archbishop and persecutor of the heretics left behind a will identical in phrasing and humility to the sort left by his foes the Lollards. Was he being the consummate politician to the end – covering all his options? Or did he secretly believe, in his heart of hearts, that the Parson and his like were the rightful church – the true believers – even as he smashed them on the anvil of *real politik*?

Although we will never know how Arundel reacted to what we believe to have been Chaucer's last works, it is possible to say that Chaucer created those works in a climate of almost hysterical religious soul-searching that was entirely

Arundel's creation. It is therefore not unreasonable to read them as at least partially addressed to the archbishop. How could they have been anything else in those dangerous times?

In *The Parson's Tale*, Chaucer attempts to reconcile orthodox belief in the efficacy of confession and absolution with the ideals of poverty and purity that characterized the radical clergy of the day. Perhaps he was hoping against hope that this demonstration of reconciliation would help his case.

Perhaps he knew it would not. But what else could he do?

CHAPTER 19

We accuse ...

~

As we warned at the beginning, this is a murder-mystery with no solution. Everything about Chaucer's last moments on earth is uncertain – lost in the limbo of history's missing evidence, where all is speculation.

Even the evidence that Chaucer died on 25 October 1400 is not overwhelming. It has become the 'traditional' death date, and yet another date is possible (in 1402) and this date encourages us to re-open the matter of 'what Chaucer died of'.

It is perfectly possible that Chaucer died suddenly of natural causes – perhaps the plague or 'a surfeit of lampreys', whatever they are and however you have a 'surfeit' of them. Such evidence as we have suggests a sudden death rather than a slow decline, and there is an abundance of circumstantial evidence to indicate that Chaucer's death may have been the result of a criminal act, carried out by the state.

The turbulence and insecurity of King Henry's usurpation triggered a strategy of intimidation '*pour encourager les autres*'. The burnings of Sawtre and Badby are spectacular examples of this policy in practice. Chaucer, in contrast to these men, was a prominent figure in court circles, and it would not have been a good idea to have made his disappearance spectacular. If his disappearance was, indeed, perceived to be necessary by those in power, the means would have had to have been much more discreet.

'*Cui bono?*' applies to the mysterious death of Geoffrey Chaucer. King Henry IV was a nervous man. From the chivalrous hero of his youth he seems to have transformed into a paranoid ruler who trusted no one and nothing – least of all his own insecure grip on the throne. He seems to have been plagued with guilt about his own grab for power. As a result, unpalatable facts were air-brushed out of history. The usurper wanted the record to fit in with his own nervous construction of who he was. What is more, he wanted the poets and writers of his court to support his illegitimate, murderous regime without qualification. Henry wanted full-blown panegyrics, not half-baked, ambiguous 'compliments'.

The chief architect of his coup was England's most powerful churchman, Archbishop of Canterbury Thomas Arundel – a man who was above all a pragmatist. He was a superb politician – the ablest of his time. He was also a man without sentiment or any shred of a genuine spiritual vocation. It was his policy to combine the McCarthyite witch hunt for religious dissidents with the king's search for counter-revolutionaries. Heresy and treason were seamlessly elided in a state policy that entrenched the autocratic power of both usurper and archbishop.

Chaucer's literary output – especially his then current work-in-progress, *The Canterbury Tales,* would have been regarded by Arundel as a subversive and dissident influence on the intellectual life of the society over which the archbishop wanted absolute control.

If Arundel had wanted to suppress *The Canterbury Tales* as he tried to suppress every other bit of writing that challenged the ecclesiastical *status quo*, it seems reasonable to suppose that he would have removed the writer to a 'safe' place, and then disposed of his works – at least as thoroughly as it was possible to do.

Chaucer's biographers have pictured his last days, sitting in his pretty garden in Westminster, drifting into the twilight of a dignified dotage. Perhaps a more likely scenario would be one of the poet starving to death in the archbishop's prison at Saltwood Castle. Or perhaps we should imagine Chaucer meeting a sudden and anonymous end in a darkened back-street, at the hands of a secretly hired assassin. And why not? After all, he'd been seriously mugged on more than one occasion.

Whatever we imagine, these fictional deaths are at least as likely and perhaps *more* likely than the traditional image of his parting from this world, which seeks to divorce Chaucer the man from the political context and dangerous times in which he lived and worked.

If Chaucer were, indeed, the victim of a state-arranged 'disappearance', then we might do worse than point the finger of suspicion at the man who did most to create the climate of fear and intimidation which dominated England during the first decade of the fifteenth century: Thomas Arundel.

> *Mordre wol out; that se we day by day*
> *Thoough it abyde a yeer, or two, or thre.*

Or six hundred years.

THE END

ABBREVIATIONS

A-NTS	Anglo-Norman Text Society
BIHR	Bulletin of the Institute of Historical Research
BJRL	*Bulletin of the John Rylands Library*
BL	British Library
BN	Bibliothèque Nationale
CCR	*Calendar of Close Rolls* (London: HMSO, 1892–)
CFR	*Calendar of Fine Rolls* (London: HMSO, 1911–)
CHMEL	*The Cambridge History of Medieval Literature*, ed. David Wallace (Cambridge: CUP, 1999)
ChR	*Chaucer Review*
CLB	*Calendar of Letter-Books of the City of London*, ed. Reginald R. Sharpe, 50 vols (London: J.C. Francis, 1899–)
CSPM	*Calendar of Select Pleas and Memoranda of the City of London ... AD 1381–1412*, ed. A.H. Thomas (Cambridge: CUP, 1932)
CPR	*Calendar of Patent Rolls* (London: HMSO, 1901–)
CUL	Cambridge University Library
CUP	Cambridge University Press
CWCH	*Calendar of Wills Proved and Enrolled in the Court of Husting, London, 1258–1688*, ed. Reginald R. Sharpe, 2 vols (London: J.C. Francis, 1888–90)
DNB	*Dictionary of National Biography*, ed. Sir Leslie Stephen and Sir Sidney Lee, 63 vols (London: Smith, Elder, 1885–1900)
EETS o.s.	Early English Text Society, original series
EETS e.s.	Early English Text Society, extra series
EETS s.s.	Early English Text Society, supplementary series
EHD	*English Historical Documents*, gen. ed. D.C. Douglas, 10 vols (London: Eyre & Spottiswoode, 1956–77); vol. 4, *1327–1485*, ed. Alec R. Meyers; vol. 5, *1485–1558*, ed. C.H. Williams
EHR	*English Historical Review*
ELH	*ELH: A Journal of English Literary History*

ELJ	*Ecclesiastical Law Journal*
FCS	*Fifteenth Century Studies*
Foedera	Thomas Rymer, *Foedera, Conventiones, Literae, et cujuscunque generis Acta Publica*, 2nd edn, 20 vols (London, 1727–45; reprinted Farnborough: Gregg International, 1967)
HMC	Historical Manuscripts Commission
HMSO	Her Majesty's Stationery Office
Index of Wills, PCC	
	Index of Wills Proved in the Prerogative Court of Canterbury ... and now preserved in the Principal Probate Registry, London, 10 vols, ed. J.C.C. Smith *et al.* (London, 1893–1948; reprinted Nendeln: Kraus, 1968–79)
JEBS	*Journal of the Early Book Society for the Study of Manuscripts and Printing History*
JEGP	*Journal of English and Germanic Philology*
JEH	*Journal of Ecclesiastical History*
JMEMS	*Journal of Medieval and Early Modern Studies*
JMH	*Journal of Medieval History*
JMRS	*Journal of Medieval and Renaissance Studies*
JWCI	*Journal of the Warburg and Courtauld Institutes*
Loeb	Loeb Classical Library
LSE	*Leeds Studies in English*
MAE	*Medium Aevum*
MED	*Middle English Dictionary*, ed. Hans Kurath, S.M. Kuhn, and R.E. Lewis (University of Michigan Press, 1954–2000)
MLN	*Modern Language Notes*
MLQ	*Modern Language Quarterly*
MLR	*Modern Language Review*
MS	*Medieval Studies* (Toronto)
NCMH	*New Cambridge Medieval History*, VI, *c. 1300– c. 1425*, ed. Michael Jones (Cambridge: CUP, 2000)
N&Q	*Notes and Queries*
NLH	*New Literary History*
OUP	Oxford University Press

Papal Letters	*Calendar of Entries in the Papal Registers (Regesta Romanorum Pontificum) relating to Great Britain and Ireland: Papal Letters,* ed.W.H. Bliss, C. Johnson, J.A.Twemlow *et al.*, vols I– (London: HMSO, 1893–)
PBA	*Proceedings of the British Academy*
PCC	Prerogative Court of Canterbury
PL	*Patrologia Latina*, ed. J.-P. Migne
PRO	Public Record Office
PMLA	*Publications of the Modern Language Association of America*
PQ	*Philological Quarterly*
REED	*Records of Early English Drama*
RES	*Review of English Studies*
RHS	Royal Historical Society
Rot. Parl.	*Rotuli Parliamentorum,* ed. J. Strachey, 6 vols (London: House of Lords, 1767–83)
RS	Rerum Britannicarum medii aevi Scriptores, or Chronicles and Memorials of Great Britain and Ireland during the Middle Ages (Rolls Series)
RSTC	*A Short-Title Catalogue of Books Printed in England, Scotland, and Ireland and of English Books Printed Abroad 1475–1640,* ed. A.W. Pollard and G.R. Redgrave, 2nd edn rev. W.A. Jackson *et al.*, 3 vols (Bibliographical Society, 1976–91)
SAC	*Studies in the Age of Chaucer*
SATF	Société des Anciens Textes Français
SHF	Société d'Histoire de France
SR	*Statutes of the Realm*, ed. T.E. Tolmins *et al.*, 11 vols (Dawsons, 1810–28; reprinted 1963)
SN	*Studia Neophilologica*
SP	*Studies in Philology*
TRHS	*Transactions of the Royal Historical Society*
UCPE	*University of California Publications in English*
UTQ	*University of Texas Quarterly*
YES	*Yearbook of English Studies*
YLS	*Yearbook of Langland Studies*

NOTES

INTRODUCTION

1. Our modernization of John Lydgate, *The Flower of Courtesy*, verse 34 – quoted in Brewer 1978b, I, 45.
2. Our modernization of Thomas Hoccleve, *The Regement of Princes*, ed. Furnivall, 179.
3. 'the noble philosophical poete in Englissh ... in witte and in good reson of sentence he passeth al other makers.' *Complete Works*, ed. Skeat, VII, 123.
4. Translation in Brewer 1978, I, 41. Gower, *Confessio Amantis*, ed. Macaulay, III, Bk 8, ll. 2941–7.
5. ... But nathelees, certeyn,
   I kan right now no thrifty tale seyn / That Chaucer, thogh he kan but lewedly / On metres and on rymyng craftily, / Hath seyd hem in swich Englissh as he kan / Of olde tyme, as knoweth many a man; / And if he have noght seyd hem , leve brother, / In o book, he hath seyd hem in another.
   Introduction to The Man of Law's Tale, in Benson 1987, ll. 45–52.
6. 'With bookes of his ornat endyting / That is to al this land enlumynyng.' Hoccleve, *Regement*, ed. Furnivall, ll. 1967–74.
7. See Brewer 1978, I, 63.
8. 'Chaucer is deed that had suche a name/Of fayre makyng ... ' John Lydgate, *The Siege of Thebes*, ed. Erdmann, *Prologue*, ll. 39–40.
9. And in this lond yif ther any be
   In borwe or toun, village or cite
   That konnyng hath his tracis for to swe
   Wher he go brood or be shet in mwe
   To hym I make a direcciounan
   Of this boke to han inspeccioun.
   John Lydgate, *Troy Book*, ed. Bergin, I, Bk. 5, ll. 3531–6.
10. Til that he [Chaucer] cam & thorugh his poetrie
    Gan oure tonge firste to magnifie
    And adourne it with his elloquence
    To whom honour and laude and reuerence
    Thorugh–oute this londe gh(?)oue be & songe
    So that the laurer of oure englische tonge
    Be to hym gh(?)ove for his excellence.
    Lydgate, *Troy Book*, ed. Bergin, I, Bk 3, ll. 4541–7
11. Pearsall 1992, 275; Gardner 1976, 313; Brewer 1978a, 211, 215.
12. In the short poem, 'Lenvoy de Chaucer a Scogan', Chaucer seems to class himself amongst those who are 'hoor and rounde of shap' ('grey and chubby') and calls himself 'olde Grisel' (old Grey horse) but, as Laila Z. Gross remarks (in Benson 1987, 1087), to assume that the poem must be very late, on the grounds that 'hoor' is intended literally, is to ignore the bantering tone of the poem. Similarly, we cannot take too seriously Chaucer conventional use of the topos of 'affected modesty' in 'The Complaint of Venus':
    For elde, that in my spirit dulleth me,
    Hath of endyting al the subtilte
    Wel nygh bereft out of my remembraunce ...
    because he goes on to use it as 'a sly way of calling attention to the technical virtuosity of his poem'. See Benson 1987, 1081.
13. Crow and Olson 1966, 532–3.
14. *Knighton's Chronicle*, trans. Martin, 501.

1. THE COURT THAT CHAUCER LIVED IN

1. Creton, *Metrical History*, 217–41, trans. Webb.
2. Chandos Herald, 135.
3. Barber 1986b, 85.
4. Mathew 1968, 14–15.
5. *Oeuvres Poètiques*, ed. Roy I, 232–3; trans. Gillespie 1997b, 118.
6. Saul 1997, 346.
7. For Richard and chivalry see Gillespie 1997b, 115–38.
8. Barron 2000, 318.
9. See *The Parson's Tale*, ll. 760–65, and 'Former Age' ll. 33 ff. in Benson 1987, 314, 651. See also Schlauch 1945, 152.
10. Dahmus 1966, 20.
11. Barron 2000, 318.
12. Froissart, *Chronicles*, trans. Johnes, II, 573–4.
13. EHD, ed. Myers, IV, 174–5.
14. Saul 1997, 178.
15. Saul 1997, 178 n. 7; 179.
16. Barron 2000, 318.
17. *Knighton's Chronicle*, trans. Martin, 407.
18. McFarlane 1972, 29.
19. McFarlane 1972, 30.
20. Bennett 1992, 9. Walsingham *Historia Anglicana*, ed. Riley, II, 156.
21. Saul 1997, 189.
22. *Westminster Chronicle*, trans. Hector and Harvey, 329.
23. McNiven 1987, 50– 1.
24. Barron 2000, 297.
25. *Westminster Chronicle*, trans. Hector and Harvey, 205.
26. Barron 2000, 302.
27. Barron 2000, 318.
28. *Westminster Chronicle*, trans. Hector and Harvey, 205.
29. Saul 1999a 41.
30. See Mathew 1968, 1–2; Saul 1997, 346–7 (italics added).
31. Mathew 1968, 1.

2. CHAUCER AND RICHARD II

1. Green 1980, 103.
2. Mathew 1968, 16–17.
3. *'le plus rude homme du mon'*, Deschamps, *Oeuvres completes*, ed. Raynaud, VII, 266–93; quoted in Mathew 1968, 30.
4. Mathew 1968, 5.
5. Mathew 1968, 30.
6. 'the erles usage was alwayes, that it was hyghe noone or he arose out of his bedde, and supped ever at mydnight.' Froissart, *Chronicle*, trans. Berners, IV, 136.
7. Froissart, *Chronicle*, trans. Berners, IV, 138.
8. Coleman 1996, 111–12.
9. 'These esquiers of houshold of old be acustumed, wynter and somer, in after nonys and in euenynges, to drawe lordez chambrez within courte, there to kepe honest company aftyr theyre cunynge [understanding], in talking of cronycles of kynges and of other polycyez [*specula principis*], or in pyping, or harpynge, singing, other actez marciablez (*martial*), to help ocupy the court and acompany straungers, tyll the tym require of departing.' *Household of Edward IV*, ed. Myers, 128–9.
10. See Chaytor 1945 (1966 edn), 13–15.
11. Hudson 1978, 26.
12. *Knighton's Chronicle*, trans. Martin , 271.
13. Coleman 1996, 121.
14. Burrow 1982, 47.
15. Coleman 1996, 170.
16. Clanchy 1979, 198.
17. Pearsall 1977, 73.
18. Scattergood 1983, 29–43.
19. Saul 1997, 364. Eberle 1999 has a very useful summary of the available literature on the subject; see 231–2, n. 2.
20. Scattergood 1983, 36.
21. Scattergood 1983, 38–9.
22. Green 1976, 235–59.
23. See *The Book of the Duchess* ll. 1314 ff., in Benson 1987, 329.
24. Gower, *Confessio Amantis*, ed. Macaulay, II, Prol. ll. 24 ff.
25. BL MS Harley 7333
26. Strohm 1992, 69–70.

27. Scattergood 1983, 37.
28. *The Tale of Melibee*, l.1650, in Benson 1987, 234.
29. *Melibee*, ll.1667–71, in Benson 1987, 235.
30. *Melibee*, ll. 1674–6, in Benson 1987, 235.
31. *Melibee*, ll. 1037–41, in Benson 1987, 219.
32. Strohm 1989, 51.
33. 'And preie God save the king, that is lord of this langage, and alle that him feith berith and obeieth, everich in his degre, the more and the lasse. But considre wel that I ne usurpe not to have founden this work of my labour or of myn engyn. I n'am but a lewd compilator of the labour of olde astrologiens, and have it translatid in myn Englissh oonly for thy doctrine. And with this swerd shal I sleen envie.' *Treatise on the Astrolabe*, ll. 56–64, in Benson 1987, 662.
34. Strohm 1989, 39
35. For much of what follows see Green 1980, 112 ff.
36. Our modernization of *Havelock the Dane*, ll. 13–16. ed. Sands, 58.
37. See *Lays of Courtly Love* trans. Terry, 11.
38. See Green 1980, 112.
39. Green 1980, 112.
40. Nicholls 1985, 142.
41. See Justice 1999, 672.
42. See *The Master of Game*, ed. Baillie-Grohman, 3–4; also Pearsall 1992, 181.
43. Salter 1980, 77–8.
44. Saul 1997, 361.
45. Barron 2000, 331; and further Bennett 1992, 13.
46. Bennett 1992, 14.
47. Derek Pearsall 1982 (51) suggests that *Sir Gawain* might have made exactly such an entertainment for Christmas or New Year's; Bennett 1979 (81–2) and 1983 (234–5) records that Richard II spent Christmas of 1398 in Lichfield; and see further Saul 1997, 361.
48. Bennett 1992, 8.
49. Bennett 1999, 189. Saul 1997 reckons Richard's first language was French.
50. Froissart, *Chronicles*, trans. Johnes, II, 577.
51. Creton, *Metrical History,* trans. Webb, 168.
52. Kendrick 1997, 290–1.
53. Wallace 1999, 486. For the importance of the vernacular see Mathew 1968, 3–9.
54. Wogan-Browne 1999, 131.
55. Saul 1997, 360. See also Green 1980, 5.
56. Green 1980, 55.
57. Bennett 1992, 15.
58. Eberle 1999, 248–9.
59. Crow and Olson 1966: *vellectorum camere regis*, 126; *scutiferi*, 100; and *tam de camera quam de diversis officiis in hospicio domini regis*, 105.
60. '*Poete Hault, loënge d'escuîrie*'. See Brewer 1978, I, 40–1.
61. Green 1980, 38.
62. Green 1980, 25.
63. Strohm 1989, 40.
64. Pearsall 1992, 210.
65. Howard 1987, 455.
66. Howard 1987, 456–7.
67. Laila Z. Gross warns that the line 'At my requeste, as three of you or tweyne' appears in only one out of ten known manuscripts; see Benson 1987, 1084.
68. 'the kyngis court to writen lettres or writis … that thyse ocupacions shul be euere menis to make hem grete in the world.' *Wimbledon's Sermon*, ed. Knight, 73, ll. 189–92. See also Owen 1966, 181.
69. Green 1980, 38.
70. Green 1980, 12.
71. Green 1980, 127.
72. This is the lease on the Westminster tenement dated 24 December 1399. See Crow and Olson 1966, 535.
73. 'Daunt in Itaille, Virgile in Rome toun, Petrak in Florence hadde al his plesaunce, And prudent Chaucer in Brutis Albion Lik his desir fond vertuous suffisaunce, Fredam of lordshepe weied in ther ballaunce, Because thei flourede in wisdam and science, Support of princis fond hem ther dispence.' Ed. Bergin, II, 436.
74. Scattergood 1983, 41.
75. Salter 1980, 76.
76. *Legend of Good Women*, Prol. F. ll. 495–7, in Benson 1987, 602.
77. Green 1980, 204.
78. Taylor 1999, 19.
79. Elizabeth Salter 1980, 77, writes that the clientele of the royal courts 'depended very much on the King himself, and … rigid distinctions between political and cultural activities cannot ever have really existed. The dissociation of the upper echelons of the nobility and the royal family from the court

as an administrative body is quite artificial if we are trying to assess what pressures there may have been upon Chaucer in his emergent, as well as his mature, years as King's esquire, royal servant and man of letters.' See also Bennett 1992, 7, 11.

80. Sittingbourne – a small town in Kent 39 miles from London. The Summoner swears to tell two or three tales to 'quit' the Friar before they reach 'Sidyngeborne' – *Canterbury Tales*, III, l. 847, in Benson 1987, 116.

81. Saul 1997, 333–4.

3. THE NATURE OF RICHARD'S RULE

1. 'Unlike his French and Burgundian counterparts, the British king or other magnate as reader was not an official person; his reading was not a public, official act – nor had he thought of commissioning histories that would enshrine his official self, including his reading.' Coleman 1996, 142.

2. McKisack 1959, 490; see also 436–8, 496–8; and further Saul 1997, 432.

3. *Continuatio Eulogii*, 379 in Given-Wilson 1993, 68.

4. We are indebted to a communication from Nigel Saul for much of this discussion. See also: 'The most widely publicized contemporary tradition of Richard is that of the tyrant ...' Jones 1968, 167.

5. *Westminster Chronicle*, trans. Hector and Harvey, 139.

6. *Westminster Chronicle*, trans. Hector and Harvey, 139.

7. *Westminster Chronicle*, trans. Hector and Harvey, 139.

8. 'How this noble king reveres and loves God's Church! How sympathetically and anxiously he exerts himself to champion her liberties and preserve them! Why there is not a bishop so jealous as he is for the rights of the Church, so that on many occasions, but for him and him alone, she might have lost her privileges.' *Westminster Chronicle*, 326–7.

9. *Westminster Chronicle*, lv–lvi, lxiii, lxiv, lxxii–lxiii. Barbara Harvey takes a dim view of Richard's character and ascribes the Monk of Westminster's conversion to Richard's case to the King's deviousness and cunning and the Monk's credulity: see lxxiv–lxxv. For the Tresillian case, see Aston 1967, 346 ff.

10. Nigel Saul diagnoses Richard as suffering from a 'narcissistic' personality disorder. See Saul 1997, 459.

11. Saul 1997, 350–2, 348, 341.

12. Saul 1997, 439.

13. Dante, *De Monarchia* I, xii, trans. Milano, 646.

14. 'For the trouthe of thynges and the profit been rather founden in fewe folk that been wise and ful of resoun than by greet multitude of folk ther every man crieth and clatereth what that hym liketh. Soothly swich multitude is nat honest' (*Melibee*, l. 1068). 'And sith ye woot wel that men shal alwey fynde a gretter nombre of fooles than of wise men, and therfor the conseils that been at congregaciouns and multitudes of folk, there as men take moore reward to the nombre than to the sapience of persones, ye se wel that in swiche conseillynges fooles han the maistrie' (*Melibee*, l. 1257). See Benson 1987, 220, 225.

15. See Eberle 1999, 252.

16. Marsilius of Padua, *Defensor Pacis*, trans. Gewirth , *Dictio* I, *cap. 8, para.* 3. It should be noted, however, that Marsilius was regarded in his own time as slightly dangerous: 'To be a Marsilian was regarded as subversive in a way similar to that which, centuries later, attached to being a Marxist.' Gewirth, xix.

17. Schlauch 1945, 147.

18. Dante, *De Monarchia, Lib.* I, *cap.* 12. See also Schlauch 1945, 142.

19. Saul 1997, 386.

20. Saul 1999, 5.

21. Cambridge MS Corpus Christi College 61, f.1 v.

22. *Legend of Good Women*, F. 239–40, in Benson 1987, 594.

23. Barron 2000, 323.

24. *Chronicle of Adam Usk*, trans. Given-Wilson 1997, 61.

25. *Chronicle of Adam Usk*, 61–3.
26. *Secretum Secretorum*, ed. Manzalaoui, I, 364.
27. Given-Wilson 1999, 119.
28. *Historia Vitae et Regni Ricardi Secundi*, ed. Stow, 121–2. See also Goodman 1999, 80.
29. Coleman 1996, 142.
30. Strohm 1989, 26.
31. Strohm 1989, 32.
32. Strohm 1989, 40.

33. 'From 1367 to 1400, with no large break except for the six years between 1388 and 1394, Chaucer enjoyed one or more annuities at the exchequer ... He was thus for many years a recipient of annuities of a class against which there was complaint in parliament from time to time.' Crow and Olson 1966, 533.
34. Strohm 1989, 38–9.
35. Strohm 1989, 204 n.14.

4 · A TIME OF INTELLECTUAL FERMENT

1. Thoresby, *The Lay Folks' Catechism*, ed. Simmons and Nolloth. See also Clopper 1999, 759; and Watson 1999, 336.
2. *Knighton's Chronicle*, trans. Martin, 243, 303.
3. Letter 88, in *Life of the Church*, ed. D'Arcy, 274.
4. Justice 1999, 666.
5. The papal palace still stands in Avignon, and the false floor to the Treasury is now on public display.
6. See Dahmus 1970, 27–9.
7. Somerset 1998, 5.
8. *Knighton's Chronicle*, trans. Martin, 243–5.
9. *Knighton's Chronicle*, trans. Martin, 295, 301, 303, 309.
10. Gower, *Vox Clamantis* Bk III, ll. 1023–30, trans. Stockton, 139.
11. Barron 2000, 308; and also Strohm 1992, 5.
12. Walsingham, *Historia Anglicana*, ed. Riley, II, 8–13; trans. Dobson 1983, 367.
13. Barron 2000, 305, 308.
14. See Brooks 1985, 258–70 and Dyer 1984, 9–42.
15. Hilton 1973, 225.
16. *Anonimalle Chronicle*, 133–40; trans. Dobson 1983, 127.
17. Saul 1997, 47–9.
18. See Dante, *De monarchia*, trans. Milano, 643–4. (The translation is slightly clarified.)
19. Marsilius of Padua, *Defensor Pacis*, trans. Gewirth, 59.
20. *Chronicon Henrici Knighton*, II, 129–32; trans. Dobson 1983, 135.
21. *Anonimalle Chronicle*; trans. Dobson 1983, 164.

22. Langland, *Piers Plowman*, ed. Kane and Donaldson, B Prol. 103–38 : 'The kynge and the comune . and kynde witte the thridde / Shop lawe and lewte ech man to knowe his owne.'
23. Eberle 1999, 231–53, 250.
24. Philippe de Mézières, *Letter to King Richard II*, trans. Coopland, 54.
25. Marsilius of Padua, *Defensor Pacis*, trans. Gewirth, 80.
26. *Anonimalle Chronicle*; trans. Dobson 1983, 164.
27. See McFarlane 1972, 18.
28. Saul 1997, 52.
29. Gower, *Vox Clamantis*, Bk VI, 560, ed. and trans. Stockton 1962, 232.
30. Watson 1999, 340. See also: Somerset 1998, 24–5.
31. *Political Poems and Songs*, ed. Wright , I, 278.
32. *Chronicle of Adam Usk*, trans. Given-Wilson, 5.
33. *Westminster Chronicle*, trans. Hector and Harvey, 15–17.
34. *Westminster Chronicle*, trans. Hector and Harvey, 19.
35. McKisack 1959, 419.
36. Prescott (forthcoming).
37. *Knighton's Chronicle*, trans. Martin, 297.
38. *Knighton's Chronicle*, trans. Martin, 313.
39. See Dahmus 1970, 10–12.
40. See Saul 1997, 77.
41. See Netter, *Fasciculi Zizaniorum*, 272–4; trans. Dobson 1983, 376–8.
42. See Netter, *Fasciculi Zizaniorum*, 300.
43. See Dahmus 1970, 108.
44. McNiven 1987, 39.

5. THE CHURCH STRIKES BACK

1. Before 1382 'the practical question of the suppression of heresy had hitherto scarcely troubled the English ecclesiastical authorities'; see McNiven 1987, 36.
2. Aston 1993, 299.
3. Watson 1999, 337–8.
4. Somerset 1998, 17.
5. Watson 1999, 339
6. Somerset 1998, 19.
7. See Hudson 1988, 197.
8. Workman 1926, II, 162 ff.
9. Workman 1926, II, 165.
10. See Chaucer's 'Retracciouns' following *The Parson's Tale*, ll. 1080–91, in Benson 1987, 328.
11. Green 1980, 127, 134.
12. Langland, *Piers Plowman*, C–text, ed. Pearsall, vi ll. 61–66. 'Hit by-cometh for clerkus . Crist for to seryen, /And knaues vncrouned . to cart and to worche. /For shold no clerk be crouned [tonsured] . bote yf he ycome were /Of franklens and free men. and of folke yweddede ./ Bondmen and bastardes . and beggers children ,/Thuse by-longeth to labour . and lordes kyn to seruen.' See also Watson 1995, 838.
13. *'que null Neif ou Villeyn mette ses Enfants de cy en avant a Escoles put eux avancer par Clergie, & ce en maintenance & salvation de l'honour de toutz Frankes du Roialme.'* Rot. Parl., iii, 294. See also Orme 1973, 192–3.
14. Saul 1997, 301–2.
15. 'He was the equal of the exalted'; in the Latin: *'elatos suppeditavit'*. This is translated in the Westminster Library information leaflet as 'He lent his aid to those in power'. Philip Lindley 1997 translates it as: 'He overthrew the proud'; see his discussion, 60–83.
16. The phrase is McNiven's 1987, 56.
17. Workman 1926, II, 165.
18. *Westminster Chronicle*, trans. Hector and Harvey, 117.
19. *Knighton's Chronicle*, trans. Martin, 425.
20. Barron 2000, 315.
21. See Justice 1999, 670, and McNiven 1987, 53.
22. *Ego te faciam morte, scilicet turpissima ...* Johannis de Trokelowe, *Chronica et Annales*, ed. Riley, 183.
23. McNiven 1987, 60.
24. McFarlane 1972, 181.
25. McNiven 1987, 57.
26. T. Rymer, *Foedera* (1740 edn.) vol. 3, part 4, 105–6.
27. Weever 1631, 471–2. See also Aston 1984b, 293, n. 42.
28. Thanks to Christine Reynolds, the Assistant Keeper of the Muniments at Westminster Abbey Library, for her help with this. Also thanks to Nigel Saul and to Shane Butler, University of Pennsylvania. All agree that the most commonly used translation is incorrect. See Lindley 1997, 69.
29. For the dating of the lettering we are, once again, indebted to Nigel Saul.

6. WAS RICHARD REALLY UNPOPULAR?

1. McKisack 1959, 498; see also Steel 1941, 41–2, 203–4.
2. 'No one else was responsible ... Richard was the sole author of his misfortune.' Saul 1997, 434.
3. Saul 1997, 438.
4. Gower, *Vox Clamantis*, Bk VI, ll. 1180–90, trans. Stockton 1962, 248–9.
5. Gower, *Vox Clamantis*, Bk VI, ll. 550–60, trans. Stockton 1962, 232.
6. Gower, *Vox Clamantis*, Bk VI, ll. 570–80, trans. Stockton 1962, 233.
7. Fisher 1964, 115.
8. Fisher 1964, 116.
9. Fisher 1964, 118.
10. Fisher 1964, 66–7.
11. Crow and Olson 1966, 531.
12. Stow 1993, 3–29.
13. *'Hic in principio declaret qualiter in anno Regis Ricardi secundi sexto decimo Iohannes Gower presentem libellum composuit et finaliter compleuit, quem strenuissimo domino suo domino Henrico de Lancastria tunc Derbeie Comiti cim omni reuencia spe-*

cialiter destinauit.' Gower, *Confessio Amantis*, Prol. 22 (margin) ed. Macaulay, II, 2. As Nicholson 1984a, 174, notes, 'This note appears only in later copies of the second and third recensions ... [and] the very form of Henry's name ... is enough to indicate that both the colophon and the rubric were written much later than the original presentation to Henry, in all likelihood after he became king.'

14. '*Derbeie Comiti, recolunt quem laude periti,/Vade liber purus, sub eo requiesce futurus.*' Gower, *Confessio Amantis*, Bk VIII, l. 3172ff., ed. Macaulay, III, 478. See also Fisher 1964, 123.

15. Nicholson 1984a, 171.

16. Nicholson 1984a, 174. See further Nicholson 1984b, 123–43 and Nicholson 1987, 130–42.

17. Nicholson 1984a, 171.

18. Fisher 1964, 124.

19. Saul 1997, 437.

20. *Chronicle of Adam of Usk*, trans. Given-Wilson 1993, 91.

21. Given-Wilson 1999, 108.

22. Johannis de Trokelowe, *Chronica et Annales*, ed. Riley, 252; trans. Given-Wilson 1993, 124.

23. Taylor 1999, 23.

24. *Chronicle of Adam of Usk*, trans. Given-Wilson 1993, 63.

25. Martin 1997, 63.

26. *Knighton's Chronicle*, trans. Martin, 531.

27. Simon Aleyn, vicar of Bray, Berkshire, from 1540 to 1588 became a byword for changing his allegiance to suit the times.

28. Martin 1997, 62.

29. *Kirkstall Abbey Chronicles*, ed. Taylor 117; trans. Given-Wilson 1993, 94–6.

30. See Given-Wilson 1993, 4.

31. Galbraith 1932, 12–29.

32. Stow 1984, 68–102.

33. Stow convincingly disposes of Galbraith's argument for a later date by demonstrating that Galbraith was in fact quoting from the printed Rolls series of the *Chronicon Angliae* which was taken not from MS Bodley 316 but MS Harley 3634. See Stow 1984, 79.

34. Bodley 316. See Stow 1984, 82–3.

35. 'In his history written in 1388, Walsingham was not critical of Richard.' Stow 1984, 84.

36. Stow 1984, 84 – quoting *Chronicon Angliae*, 353–4.

37. Stow 1984, 80.

38. Stow 1984, 84.

39. Stow 1984, 71.

40. Gransden 1982, II, 137. She quotes Walsingham's comment '*Vae terrae, cujus rex puer est,*' Richard's perigrinations round the realm and his extortions of monies from abbeys on behalf of his Queen – all from Walsingham, *Historia Anglicana*, ed. Riley, II, 97.

41. See Taylor 1999, 27.

42. See Given-Wilson 1993, 70.

43. Johannis de Trokelowe, '*Annales Ricardi Secundi*', in *Chronica et Annales,* ed. Riley, 199–239; trans. Given-Wilson 1993, 72–3.

44. Given-Wilson 1993, 2, writes: 'There is little contemporary evidence that Richard was encountering widespread opposition to his rule in the mid–1390s. On the contrary, it was his opponents, most notably Gloucester and Arundel, who, having failed to capitalise on their successes in 1387–88, now appear to have become isolated in their antagonism to the king and his new following among the magnates.'

45. Walsingham, *Historia Anglicana*, ed. Riley, II, 103.

46. See Taylor 1999, 26.

47. Walsingham quoted by Given-Wilson 1993, 32.

48. Barron 1990, 142–3.

49. Barron 1968, 10–14.

50. Walsingham quoted by Given-Wilson 1993, 32.

51. One chronicle that is otherwise thoroughly pro-Richard, the *Dieulacres Chronicle*, tells us that by 1399 Richard had provoked popular opprobrium. It says that as a result of the king's demands for blank charters, 'evil rumours began to spread through the whole community because of the harsh bondage to which they were subjecting themselves', and that because of the rumours of extortions practised by his Cheshire bodyguard Richard was 'held in fatal odium by his subjects'. See Given-Wilson 1993, 31–2.

52. See Duls 1975, 139; and further Creton, *Chronicque,* ed. Williams, 151–2.

53. Creton, *Chronicque*, ed. Willliams,

210–11. Jenico survived and became a trusted envoy for Henry.

54. Creton , *Chronicque*, ed. Williams, 144.

55. Creton , *Chronicque*, ed. Williams, 144.

56. Barron 2000, 321–2.

57. See Johannis de Trokelowe, '*Annales Ricardi Secundi*', in *Chronica et Annales*, ed. Riley, 240–52; trans. Given-Wilson 1993, 121.

58. *Brut*, ed. Brie, II, 545.

59. *An English Chronicle of the Reigns of Richard II, Henry IV, Henry V, and Henry VI, written before 1471*, ed. Davies, 39. For discussion, see also Strohm 1996, 116.

60. We omit Froissart's accounts in his *Chroniques* and their continuation the *Chroniques de Monstrelet*, because they are generally regarded as without any historical relevance.

61. Trans. Given-Wilson 1993, 244.

62. Given-Wilson 1993, 30.

63. Given-Wilson 1993, 8.

64. Trans. Given-Wilson 1993, 147.

65. Given-Wilson 1999, 110.

66. Barron 1990, 132.

67. Barron 1990, 132.

68. *Chronicque de la Traison et Mort de Richart Deux Roy Dengleterre*, ed. Willliams, 215.

69. Saul 1997, 422.

70. Saul 1997, 203. For a slightly different assessment see Saul 1999b.

71. McFarlane 1972, 37, 49.

72. *Chronicque de la Traison et Mort de Richart Deux Roy Dengleterre*, ed. Willliams, 150.

73. *Chronicque de la Traison et Mort de Richart Deux Roy Dengleterre*, ed. Willliams, 157–8.

74. Froissart, *Chronicles*, trans. Johnes, II, 666.

75. See Barron 2000, 328.

76. *Chronique du religieux de Saint-Denys* ed. Bellaguet, II, 677; trans. Given-Wilson 1993, 105–6.

7. CHAUCER'S WORLD CHANGES

1. Froissart, *Chronicles*, trans. Johnes, II, 666. See also: McFarlane 1972, 47.

2. *CPR, 1396–1399*, 425.

3. *CFR, 1391–9*, 293. See for discussion Saul 1997, 404.

4. See Barron 2000, 328.

5. *Chronique du Religieux De Saint-Denys*, ed. Bellaguet, xix, 11; quoted in *Chronicque de la Traison et Mort de Richard Deux Roy Dengleterre*, ed. Williams, 157, n.1.

6. *Rot. Parl.* III, 383.

7. *Chronique Du Religieux De Saint-Denys*, ed. Bellaguet, II, 677; trans. Given-Wilson 1993, 105–6.

8. Stubbs 1890, III, 7. See also McFarlane 1972, 9.

9. McFarlane 1972, 37.

10. *Chronique du Religieux de Saint-Denys*, ed. Bellaguet I, 681. McFarlane 1972, 37–8 exaggerates somewhat. He says: 'The French and English agreed that Henry was the outstanding performer of his nation.' Actually Froissart doesn't mention Henry at all at this tournament, and the *Chronique du Religieux de Saint-Denys* merely says that in one particular contest against '*les trois tenants*', Henry, Count of Derby and his followers '*furent reconnus comme les plus braves de tous les assaillants*'.

11. Wylie 1884, IV, 128. *Calendar of State Papers ... Milan*, ed. Hinds, 1. And see further McFarlane 1972, 39.

12. It was also more profitable, since if Henry claimed the throne 'by conquest' all goods and estates fell into his possession.

13. Wylie 1884, I, 83. See Creton, *Metrical History of the Deposition of King Richard II*, trans. Webb, 152–3.

14. Stubbs 1890, III, 7. See also McFarlane 1972, 9.

15. '*Et auxi q'il fuist ordeigne par auctorite de parlement come desuis, que le dit Duke de Hereford, ne viendra en nul manere en la companye de dit Thomas Duk de Norffolk, ne de Thomas d'Arundell, & q'il n'envoiera ne ferra envoier, ne resceivera ne ferra resceivr', par message, n'autrement, ne ne mellera en nul manere ovesque nul de eux; & ceo sur la peigne come desuis.*' *Rot. Parl.*, III, 383; see also Given-Wilson 1993, 90–1.

16. When his father died in 1375 he was left a portion of only 2000 marks. See Creton, *Metrical History of the Deposition of King Richard II*, trans. Webb, 47 n. u.

17. *CPR 1396–1399*, VI, 280.
18. *Diplomatic Correspondence of Richard II*, ed. Perroy, 172.
19. *Literae Cantuariensis*, ed. Sheppard, III, 70–2. See also Aston 1967, 374. For Salutati's letters see: *Epistolario di Coluccio Salutati* ed. Novati, III, 360–3, 497–501, 618–21.
20. *Diplomatic Correspondence of Richard II*, ed. Perroy, 173.
21. *Chronicle of John Hardyng*, ed. Ellis, 349.
22. *Literae Cantuariensis*, ed. Sheppard, III, 70.
23. See Saul 1997, 395–9.
24. Sercambi, *Croniche*, II, 397, as quoted in *Epistolario di Coluccio Salutati*, ed. Novati, III, 361.
25. Aston 1967, 374.
26. Kirby 1987, 53; and see also McNiven 1987, 67.
27. On Richard's assurances that no harm would come to him, Arundel persuaded his brother the Earl to leave the safety of Reigate castle and meet with his king, thus beginning a sequence of events that ended in the execution of the Earl of Arundel.
28. Johannis de Trokelowe, '*Annales Ricardi Secundi*,' in *Chronica et Annales*, ed. Riley, 240–52; trans. Given-Wilson 1993, 115.
29. Given-Wilson 1993, 116, 118.
30. Creton, *Metrical History of the Deposition of King Richard II*, 341–415; trans. Given-Wilson 1993, 48.

31. Creton, *Metrical History of the Deposition of King Richard II*, 341–415; trans. Given-Wilson 1993, 137 .
32. Creton, *Metrical History*, 341–415; trans. Given-Wilson 1993, 141.
33. Creton, *Metrical History of the Deposition of King Richard II*; 341–415; trans. Given-Wilson 1993, 145.
34. Creton, *Metrical History of the Deposition of Richard II*, trans. Given-Wilson 1993, 150.
35. McFarlane 1972, 49.
36. Given-Wilson 1993, 40.
37. To our knowledge, the only writer who supports this reading is the Rev. John Webb, who edited Creton's *Metrical History*. He wrote in 1819 that the fact of Henry's return with Arundel 'proves that Henry had an eye to extremities, when he took for his companion and counsellor one who was so odious to the king'. See Creton, *Metrical History of the Deposition of Richard II*, 50.
38. Creton, *Metrical History of the Deposition of King Richard II*, trans. Webb, 46–55.
39. Creton, *Metrical History of the Deposition of King Richard II*, trans. Webb, 46–55.
40. See Given-Wilson 1993, 136.
41. *Chronicon de Adae de Usk*, ed. Thompson, 174–86; trans. Given-Wilson 1993, 158.
42. Kirby 1970, 53.
43. *Chronicle of Adam of Usk*, ed. and trans. Given-Wilson, 81.
44. Given-Wilson 1993, 112.

8. CHAUCER'S LAST BLOODY YEAR

1. Johannes de Trokelowe, '*Annales Ricardi Secundi*', in *Chronica et Annales*, ed. Riley, 322–32, trans. Given-Wilson 1993, 228.
2. Johannes de Trokelowe, '*Annales Ricardi Secundi*,' in *Chronica et Annales*, ed. Riley, 240–52; trans. Given-Wilson 1993, 119–20.
3. Johannis de Trokelowe, '*Annales Ricardi Secundi*', in *Chronica et Annales*, ed. Riley, 240–52; trans. Given-Wilson 1993, 124.
4. *Historia Vitae et Regni Ricardi Secundi*, ed. Stow, 151–60 quoted in Given-Wilson 1993, 127.
5. *Kirkstall Abbey Chronicles,* ed. Taylor, 121–5; trans. Given-Wilson 1993, 133.
6. See *Dieulacres Chronicles* ed. Clarke and Galbraith, 171.
7. *Kirkstall Abbey Chronicles* , 121–5, trans. Given-Wilson 1993, 134.

8. Given-Wilson 1993, 200.
9. Letter from Archbishop Arundel to the Convent of Canterbury Cathedral, in *Literae Cantuariensis*, ed. Sheppard, III, 73–5; See Given-Wilson 1993, 237; quoting: *Foedera* VII, 124.
10. *Historia Vitae et Regni Ricardi Secundi*, ed. Stow, 164–5, trans. Given-Wilson 1993, 239.
11. Given-Wilson 1993, 228.
12. If it were, the government soon decided they had to restrain this sort of lynch-mob mentality. Adam of Usk records that a decree was issued on 8 February, forbidding attacks on traitors or rebels without the King's permission or proper legal process. See *Chronicle of Adam Usk*, trans. Given-Wilson 1997, 91 and n. 5. For John Cosyn's

involvement see Given-Wilson 1997, 49, n. 74.

13. *Chronicle of Adam of Usk,* trans. Given-Wilson 1997, 31.

14. See *CPR 1388–1392,* 253; and further the discussion in Bellamy 1973, 186.

15. See Richardson 1936, 21–2.

16. Saul 1997, 207.

17. *Chronique de la Traison et Mort de Richart Deux Roy Dengleterre,* ed. Williams, 245–6.

18. *Chronicle of Adam Usk,* trans. Given-Wilson 1997, 89.

19. *Chronicle of Adam Usk,* trans. Given-Wilson 1997, 89.

20. See Wylie 1884, I, 105–6; also Kirby 1970, 88.

21. *Select Cases in the Court of the King's Bench under Richard II, Henry IV and Henry V* ed. Sayles, VII, 124.

22. Bellamy 1973, 181.

23. Barron 1990, 144–5; McNiven 1987, 96.

24. McNiven 1987, 79.

25. Strohm 1996, 63–4.

26. 'During his lyfe whome as it is said god touched and was a lepre er he dyed.' BL MS Cot. Claudius A.viii, f.17. Quoted by Strohm 1996, 116.

27. Strohm 1996, 63, 196.

9. CHAUCER'S ENEMIES GAIN POWER

1. McNiven 1987, 65; Aston 1967, 377. For a sympathetic account of Arundel's career, which sees him as a churchman first and only reluctantly a politician, see Davies 1973, 9–15.

2. *CLB,* ed. Sharpe, I, 115–16.

3. McNiven 1987, 65.

4. Workman 1926, II, 341.

5. Thoresby, *Lay Folks' Mass Book,* ed. Simmons, 107–9.

6. Thoresby, *Lay Folks' Mass Book,* ed. Simmons, 380. For early versions of the Mass see Dolan 1995, 13–24.

7. Workman 1926, II, 39.

8. s.v. 'Eucharist' in *The Catholic Encyclopaedia* on the Internet : 'Finally, Transubstantiation differs from every other substantial conversion in this, that only the substance is converted into another "the accidents remaining the same" just as would be the case if wood were miraculously converted into iron, the substance of the iron remaining hidden under the external appearance of the wood.'

9. McNiven 1987, 25.

10. *DNB.* See also Workman 1926, I, 284.

11. Wyclif, *de Apostasia,* 103,106, 116,119; and see further Workman 1926, II, 38.

12. Wyclif, *Trialogus,* ed. Lechler, 247.

13. Workman 1926, II, 259, actually says the only one was Bottisham. But John Gilbert also had a doctorate in theology.

14. Dahmus 1966, 8.

15. Dahmus 1966, 8.

16. Dahmus 1966, 14–15.

17. *DNB* quotes *Chronicon Angliae,* 258; *Eulogium Historiarum sive Temporis,* ed. Haydon III, 356. For other members of the Blackfriars Council see Workman 1926, II, 258, and Emden 1957, I.

18. See Dahmus 1970, 25.

19. Strohm 1999, 47.

20. *Eulogium Historiarum sive Temporis,* ed. Haydon, III, 407.

21. Kirby 1964, 41.

22. Watson 1995, 830.

23. Kirby 1964, 45.

24. *Knighton's Chronicle,* trans. Martin, 261. McNiven 1987, 71.

25. Wylie 1884, I, 91–2.

26. Wylie 1884, I, 118.

27. Bellamy 1973, 190

28. Jean Creton tells us that he believed that the body displayed as Richard II to prove that the ex-king was dead was, in fact, Richard Maudelyn. 'I think it was Maudelyn, his chaplain, whose face, size, height and build were so exactly similar to the king's that every one firmly believed that it was good King Richard.' See *Metrical History of the Deposition of King Richard II,* trans. Webb, 221. See also Given-Wilson 1993, 244.

29. *Chronicle of Adam of Usk,* trans. Given-Wilson, 249–51.

30. Davies 1973, 18.

31. Kirby 1964, 46.

32. Wylie 1884, I, 51–2.

33. Strohm 1999, 210.

34. *Epistolario di Coluccio Salutati,* ed. Novati, III, 360–3.

35. Thanks to Nigel Saul and John Law of

Swansea University for this information.

36. Trans. McNiven 1987, 76. Johannis de
Trokelowe, *Chronica et Annales,* ed. Riley,
395–6. *'In Italia' inquit, 'ubi gens esse vide-*
tur criminosissima, et Lombardia praecipue,
circa Corpus maximam impendunt reveren-
tiam ... et puto Deus parcere et propitiari illis

pro fide quam ostendun, et reverentia quam
impendunt, Sacramento.'

37. Strohm 1999, 209–10.
38. *Rot Parl,* iii, 415.
39. McNiven 1987, 61.
40. Wylie 1884, I, 37.
41. Wylie 1884, I, 107.

10. CHAUCER IN THE EYE OF THE STORM

1. As both the Monk of Evesham and the
Kirkstall Chronicle bear witness. See above
p. 138.
2. For more about Henry's alteration of the
record, see above p. 165. See also Johannis
de Trokelowe, *Chronica et Annales,* ed.
Riley, 252; trans. Given-Wilson 1993, 124.
3. *Chronicon Angliae,* ed. Thompson, xxiii,
and n.1. The alterations are in BL MS Harley
3634.
4. *Chronicon Angliae,* xxi. See Stow 1984, 81,
and Galbraith 1932, 24. Since the first edition
of this book appeared, an earlier date for the
removal of the *Scandalous Chronicle* has been
suggested. See *The St Albans Chronicle,* I,
1376–94, eds. J. Taylor, W. Childs and
J. Watkiss (Oxford, 2003), lii–lv.
5. Barron 2000, 132–49, and *CLB,* ed.
Sharpe, 450.
6. *EHD,* ed. Myers, IV, 851.
7. Strohm 1998, 54.
8. *Rot. Parl,* III, 459.
9. Baigent and Leigh 1999, 36.
10. *Eulogium Historiarum sive Temporis,* ed.
Haydon, III, 388.
11. McNiven 1987, 94. For Chaucer's contacts
with victims of the Appellants, see Strohm
1989, 27.
12. Crow and Olson 1966, 532. Although his
annuity of 40 marks was renewed, the only
money from it Chaucer actually received
was £5 in June 1400. Henry made Chaucer a
gift of £10 at Michaelmas 1399.
13. Pinet 1927, 50.
14. Strohm 1999, 196.
15. See 'John Gower's early criticism of
Richard', see above, p. 97.
16. For a fuller discussion, see above, p.98 ff.
17. See Gower, trans. Stockton, 289–326.
18. Nicholson 1984a, 171.
19. Chaucer, *Poetical Works,* ed. Bell, III, 417.
20. See Strohm 1992, 92–94.
21. Legge 1953, 18–21.
22. Galbraith 1942, 233–4. Galbraith in turn
simply assumes Henry's was a triple claim.
He quotes the official claim in parliament
and then says it's the same as Chaucer's
claim in the 'Complaint to His Purse': see
234. Since comparison shows they obviously
aren't the same, it's hard to imagine what
Galbraith was thinking.
23. *Rot. Parl.,* III, 422–3.
24. Given-Wilson 1993, 43.
25. *Rot. of Parl.,* III, 423.
26. Johannes de Trokelowe, *Chronica et*
Annales, ed. Riley, 282; trans. Given-Wilson
1993, 186–7.
27. *Rot. Parl.,*III, 423; trans. Given-Wilson
1993, 186. Jean Creton describes the events
as an 'election' but his editor writes: 'Not
only is the business of the day distorted, but
the whole is made to assume the air of an
election.' Creton, *A Metrical History of the*
Deposition of King Richard the Second,
trans. Webb, 200, n. 0.
28. McFarlane 1972, 56–7.
29. 'If the envoy is an original part of the poem,
"Chaucer's Complaint to His Purse" belongs
to the category of "begging poems" ... ;" see
Laila Z. Gross in Benson 1987, 1088.
30. Gower, *Vox Clamantis,* Bk. VI, 1176–8,
trans. Stockton, 248. *Legend of Good*
Women, Prol. F, 1l. 230–1, in Benson
1987, 594.
31. Green 1980, 127.
32. Gower, trans. Stockton, 321.
33. '*A nostre tresgracias, tresexcellent et tresre-*
doubte seigneur le Roy H[enry] *le gracious*
conquerour d'Engleterre'; see *Anglo-*
Norman Letters and Petitions, ed. Legge, 31,
and further discussion in Legge 1953, 18–21.
34. Crow and Olson 1966, 527.
35. Crow and Olson 1966, 532–4.1.
Watson 1995, 830.

11. THE CANTERBURY TALES AS A DEATH WARRANT

1. Watson 1995, 830.
2. Strohm 1998, 51.
3. *EHD*, ed. Myers, IV, 850.
4. Watson 1995, 826.
5. *EHD*, ed. Myers, IV, 857.
6. Watson 1995, 827–8.
7. Watson 1995, 857.
8. Crow and Olson 1966, 506–12.
9. Watson 1995, 858.
10. If peasants all over England asked permission to go on pilgrimage to Canterbury – what would have been remarkable about that? One chronicler mentions the large numbers of pilgrims on the roads at this time, and one of the cryptic rhymes, thought to contain secret instructions, says: 'Make for one head.' Could it mean the Blessed Head of Thomas a Becket (*Caput Beati Thomae*), the focal point of any pilgrimage to Canterbury? Woodruff and Danks 1912, 79–80.
11. This was in 1220, and though the income dipped during the remainder of the thirteenth century, it had risen again by the later fourteenth century. See Finucane 1977, 193.
12. *Papal Letters*, IV (1362–1404), ed. Mills and Twemlow, 432.
13. Coulton 1910, 310–11.
14. Our translation of BL MS Additional 24202; printed by Hudson 1988, 85.
15. Hudson 1988, 86.
16. Mann 1973, 17 ff.
17. For more detail see Kellogg and Haselmayer 1951, 251–77, especially 256.
18. Jusserand 1921, 324.
19. *Memorials of Beverley Minster: Chapter Act Book*, ed. Leach, I, 316–17; reprinted in Kellogg and Haselmayer 1951, 275n. 149.
20. Kellogg and Haselmayer 1951, 259, n.51
21. These relics were still there in a cupboard when Erasmus visited in the sixteenth century. Woodruff and Danks 1912, 276–7.
22. *Knighton's Chronicle*, trans. Martin, 297.
23. Our modernization of Wyclif, *Sermones*, ed. Loserth, II, 164–5; quoted in Workman 1926, II, 17.
24. *English Works of John Wyclif*, ed. Matthew, 154.
25. Kellogg and Haselmayer 1951, 251.
26. Workman 1926, II, 16.
27. *English Works of John Wyclif*, ed. Matthew, 238 (the tract 'Of Servants and Lords').
28. *The Pardoner's Tale*, ll. 919–40 in Benson 1987, 202.
29. *English Works of John Wyclif*, ed. Matthew, 72 (the tract 'Of Prelates') and 266.
30. Kenyon 1981, 120.
31. Kellogg and Haselmayer 1951, 275–6.
32. Kellogg and Haselmayer 1951, 251.
33. Langland, *Piers Plowman*, A-text, ed. Kane, ii, l.46, B-text, ed. Kane and Donaldson, ii, 59, 168–76, iii, l.129, 34; iv, 167, xv, 129–132 xix, 373; 'The Grete Sentence of Curs Expounded,' in *Select English Works of John Wyclif*, ed. Arnold, III, 320. Compare *The Friar's Tale*, ll. 1361, 1310–26 and 1338–74, also the Wycliffite tract 'On the Seven Deadly Sins', in *Select English Works of John Wyclif*, ed. Arnold, III, 166.
34. Hudson 1988, 301.
35. Archbishop FitzRalph for one.
36. In 1323, Pope John XXIII restored to them the ownership of property. See Knowles 1948, 246.
37. Moorman 1968, 350–1.
38. Hudson 1988, 348–49.
39. 'whereas the people who invented friars decreed that the habit should be close-fitting, coarse, and shabby … your present-day friars prefer ample habits, generously cut and smooth of texture, and made from the finest of fabrics. Indeed, they now have elegant and pontifical habits, in which they strut like peacocks through the churches and the city squares …' Boccaccio, *Decameron*, 3rd Day, 7th Story, trans. McWilliam, 243.
40. 'Friar, what do your great hood and your scapular [a garment worn over the shoulders and hanging down to the ankles behind] signify, and your knotted girdle and your ample and wide cloaks that you make of such expensive cloth for yourselves, since meaner and less costly clothes are a greater token of poverty?' Our modernization from *Jack Upland, Friar Daw's Reply and Upland's*

Rejoinder ed. Heyworth, ll. 140 ff.

41. The condemnation came from John of Gaunt's confessor, Richard Maidstone, a Carmelite friar. See Edden 1987, 123. For Ashwardby's Wycliffite affiliations see *DNB*.

42. Wyclif, *English Works of John Wyclif*, ed. Matthew, 12. Another example, from BL MS Cot. Cleopatra B.ii, is as follows: 'Thai [i.e. friars] dele with purses, pynnes, & knyves, / With gyrdles, gloues for wenches & wyues' (See *Historical Poems of the XIVth and XVth Centuries*, ed. Robbins, p. 158, ll. 37–8). In its manuscript, this poem immediately follows the resoundingly Lollard verse '*Heu! quanta desolatio Angliae praestatur*', excerpted above. It further betrays its Lollard affiliation in using the 'CAIM' anagram, which appears often and only in Lollard contexts; see Szittya 1986, 196, and also Aston 1984a, 45–81.

43. 'But hou many euer resseyueden hym, he yaf to hem power to be maad the sones of God,' *John: 12* in *The New Testament in English, according to the version by John Wycliffe ...* ed. Forshall and Madden, rev. edn Skeat, 235.

44. *Jack Upland Friar Daw's Reply and Upland's Rejoinder*, ed. Heyworth, 64, ll. 240–2.

45. *English Works of John Wyclif*, ed. Matthew, 8–9.

46. Boccaccio, *Decameron*, 3rd story, 7th Day, trans. McWilliam, 496.

47. See below, Ch. 13, 'How the Ellesmere MS was censored', p. 255.

48. '*Membra Antichristi reciproce se conculcant*'; *Iohannis Wyclif Opus Evangelicum*, ed. Loserth, 75. See also Fleming 1966, 688–700.

49. *The Summoner's Prologue*, ll.1678–99, in Benson 1987, 128.

50. Chaucer may have got the idea for the 'scurrilous anecdote about the final abode of friars' from a fresco in Pisa of *The Last Judgement* by Francisco Traini, which he could have seen on his journey from Genoa to Florence; see Janette Richardson, in Benson 1987, 876–7, note.

51. Olson 1999, 245.

52. Benson 1987, 129, ll. 1752 and 1757–9.

53. *The Summoner's Tale*, ll. 1765–2155,

Benson 1987, 129–34.

54. Slightly modernized version of *Acts 2* as found in *The Holy Bible Translated by John Wyclif and His Followers*, ed. Forshall and Madden, IV, 510–11. See also Levitan 1971, 236–46. For another interpretation see Kolve 1993, 265–96.

55. Olson 1999, 239–40, 244.

56. See the Monk's description, *General Prologue*, ll.173–88; Benson 1987, 26.

57. Dahmus 1966, 8.

58. *EHD*, ed. Myers, IV, 849.

59. See Johannis de Trokelowe, '*Annales Ricardi Secundi*', in *Chronica et Annales*, ed. Riley, 173, 182. McNiven 1987, 59, however, doubts this account.

60. Workman 1926, II, 28. He quotes *De Officio Regis*; see Pollard and Sayle, eds, 182, 210–11, 275–6, 280–1.

61. On John of Gaunt's position, see Bisson 1998, 81. Gower makes his views clear in his *Mirour de l'Omme*, ed. Macaulay, I, 228, ll. 20245–56. Gaunt had also for a while been the protector of Wyclif.

62. In Uthred of Boldon's treatise *De dotacione ecclesie sponse Christi*; see Durham, MS Cosin A.IV.33, fols 69–99v.

63. *PL* 182, col. 816. The work is the *De moribus et officio episcoporum*. St Bernard of Clairvaux condemns 'proud horses' in his *Apologia ad Guillelmum*, ed. Leclerq, Talbot and Rochais, III, 103, ll. 13–16. On the several meanings of horses as they appear in medieval texts, see especially Kolve 1984, 237–56.

64. *Select English Works of John Wyclif*, ed. Arnold, III, 494–5.

65. Wenzel 1998, 214–16. Compare Bernard of Clairvaux, *Opera*, III, 103, ll. 13–16. The work is the *Apologia ad Guillelmum*, *CCR 1392–96*, 434. See also Hudson 1988, 88–9.

66. Aston 1967, 373, n. 1.

67. Mann 1973, 75.

68. McNiven 1987, 37.

69. Dahmus 1966, 68.

70. Aston 1967, 332. As McNiven 1987, 66, tactfully puts it: Arundel 'did not respond well to overt acts of defiance'.

71. On the orthodoxy of Cambridge compared to Oxford, see Hudson 1988, 92.

72. Mann 1973, 55.

73. Hudson 1988, 391.
74. Hudson 1988, 392.
75. Patricia J. Eberle, Benson 1987, 863, in a note to l. 1173 of the *Man of Law's Epilogue*, derives 'Lollard' 'from the Dutch 'lollaert', 'mumbler (of prayers)', which was applied to members of a lay order of mendicants, regarded as heretics by the clergy.' Wyclif's biographer, Workman 1926, I, 327, says that the Middle English word 'loller', which meant 'a loafer', soon became confused with 'Lollard'. But the 'lolium' deriviation seems more consistent with fourteenth-century perceptions of the word.
76. Netter, *Fasciculi Zizaniorum*, 242; trans. Dahmus 1970, 48: 'Master John Aston ... maintained the opinions of his master Wyclif in a bold manner ... preaching in churches everywhere in the kingdom, he sowed tares with the wheat (*lollium cum tritico seminauit*).'
77. *Knighton's Chronicle*, trans. Martin, 286–7.
78. Matthew 13: 25: 'The kingdom of heaven is like this. A man sowed his field with good seed; but while everyone was asleep his enemy came, sowed darnel (cockle or tares) among the wheat, and made off.' The farmer's men ask to pull the weeds out, but the farmer says no, lest good wheat be harmed. 'Let them grow together and at harvest time I will tell the reapers: "Gather the darnel first, and tie it in bundles for burning" ... ' See also *Knighton's Chronicle*, trans. Martin, 286–7.
79. *Knighton's Chronicle*, trans. Martin, 285.
80. See Watson 1995, 852.
81. See Hudson 1988, 67. Hudson notes, 174, however, that the date, and authorship of John Purvey, are by no means certain.
82. Hudson 1988, 229.
83. Watson 1999, 348. See also Watson 1995, 858.
84. Wallace 1999, 486.

12. WHAT HAPPENED TO CHAUCER'S WORK?

1. Strohm 1998, 196.
2. Bowers 2001, 78. The list of destruction that follows is based on Bowers' catalogue.
3. Sir George Scharf quoted by Hepburn 1986, 13. The two MSS are Cambridge, Corpus Christi College NIS 61, fol. Iv and Oxford, Bodley 581, fol. 9r.
4. Froissart, *Chronicles*, trans. Johnes, II, 577.
5. See Saul 1997, 343.
6. Wilkins 1983, 189.
7. Johannis de Trokelowe, '*Annales Ricardi Secundi*', in *Chronica et Annales*, ed. Riley, 326.
8. *Works of Sir John Clanvowe*, ed. Scattergood, 14.
9. Bowers 2001, 190.
10. A.I. Doyle, Reader in Bibliography, University of Durham, in a private communication.
11. Benson 1987, xxvii.
12. Fisher 1964, 303 ff.; *Piers Plowman*: MS Laud Misc. 581 and TCD MS 212.
13. Edwards and Pearsall 1989, 258
14. Scott 1997, 119; 106.
15. Stubbs 2000.
16. Fisher 1992, 1168–80; reprinted in Pinti 1999, 84, 89.
17. Owen 1991, 4; see also Hanna 1996, 140–55, and Pearsall 1997, 35.
18. Hanna 1996, 154.
19. Hanna, 1996, 123, 124.
20. See Kendrick 1997, 285. The manuscript is: BN, MS fr. 1584.
21. Kendrick 1997, 285–8.
22. See *MED*, s.v. 'compilen': 'to compose or write chronicles or stories'; s.v. 'compilatour': 'a plagiarist or compiler'.
23. See *Text of the Canterbury Tales, Studied on the Basis of All Known Manuscripts*, ed. Manly and Rickert, XI, 30–1.
24. Benson 1981, 80–1.
25. And hadde a wyf that heeld for contenance A shoppe, and swyved for hir sustenance. *The Cook's Tale*, ll. 4421–2, Benson 1987, 86.
26. Stubbs 2000.
27. Stubbs 2000.
28. Stubbs 2000.
29. Scott 1997, 87–120.
30. Doyle and Parkes 1979, xxvi.
31. Lydgate, *Troy Book*, Bk. II, l. 4703; in Bergin, I, 279.
32. Edwards and Pearsall 1989, 261.
33. See Chapter 14.

13. HOW THE ELLESMERE MS WAS CENSORED

1. Jones 1980, 13.
2. Jacques de Hemricourt, *Traité des Guerres d'Awans et de Waroux*, in *Oeuvres*, ed. Borsman, Bayot and Poncelet, III, 40. Jean le Bel, *Chronique*, I, 126–7.
3. Jones 2001, 205–36.
4. Temple-Leader 1889, 295.
5. Temple-Leader 1889, 308. See also *CSPM,*

ed. Thomas, 309.
6. Temple-Leader 1889, 309.
7. Emmerson 1997, 156.
8. Emmerson 1997, 149.
9. *MED*, s.v. 'harp'.
10. Mann 1973, 44–5.
11. *EHD*, ed. Myers, IV, 856.

14. CHAUCER AS A POLITICAL ICON

1. We are following Brewer 1978, I, 39–70.
2. 'The Flower of Courtesy' is a rather endearing homage to Chaucer's *Parliament of Fowls*. It was first assigned an author by Stow in 1561, where he entitles it 'The Flour of Curtesie, made by Iohn Lidgate'. Skeat, *Works of Geoffrey Chaucer*, VII, xlv, writes: 'Probably Stowe had seen it attributed to him in some MS, and made a note of it; but I know of no MS. copy now extant.' In other words, there is no real evidence it is by Lydgate, other than stylistics (see Pearsall 1970, 97). As for the dating, this is derived from the lines:

    Chaucer is deed, that hadde such a name
    Of fair making, that [was], withoute wene,
    Fairest in our tonge, as the laurer grene.
                        'Flour of Curtesye', ll. 236–68
    Skeat reads this passage as indicating that Chaucer's death was a recent event, but in fact it is quite obvious that the lines are perfectly neutral about when the death took place. Skeat also says that 'Schick refers it to Lydgate's Early period' but he offers no other evidence about the date.
3. Strohm 1989, 43.
4. *Works of Geoffrey Chaucer*, ed. Skeat, VII, 237.
5. McFarlane 1972, 104–5, 114–15.
6. *Brut,* ed. Brie, II, 545.
7. McFarlane 1972, 105, 121–2.
8. McFarlane 1972, 103.
9. McFarlane 1972, 106.
10. Henry Scogan, 'A Moral Balade', in *Chaucerian and Other Pieces*, ed. Skeat , 239.
11. McNiven 1987, 138. See for the quotation

Johannis de Trokelowe, in *Chronica et Annales,* ed. Riley 247.
12. For Thomas Chaucer's career see Roskell, Clark and Rawcliffe 1992, ii, 524–32. See also *Works of Geoffrey Chaucer* ed. Skeat, I, 84.
13. See Strohm 1999, 644.
14. For Lewis John's life see Roskell, Clark and Rawcliffe 1992, iii, 494–8
15. *CLB*, ed. Sharpe, I, 114.
16. Roskell 1981–3, III, 164.
17. *Rot. Parl.* IV, 37–8, 44–5.
18. *CLB*, ed. Sharpe, I, 126.
19. McFarlane 1972, 108.
20. Lawton 1987, 777.
21. Strohm 1998, 181.
22. Lawton, 1987, 777.
23. The best manuscript of the poem has a note claiming that Lydgate wrote it 'at the excitacion and styrryng of our worshipfull prince, kyng Harry the fifthe … ' But scholars disagree. Pearsall 1970, 286, points out that 'there is no internal reference, such as Lydgate invariably makes in a major poem, to [Henry's] patronage … Henry V may have suggested a *Life* but not lived to see it. It is impossible, in any case, to date the poem accurately. Schick suggests 1409–11, the modern editors 1421–2, and Norton-Smith after 1434.'
24. As usual, the dates are difficult to work out, and so therefore is the length of the acquaintance. There is a letter from the prince (in French, printed by Pearsall 1970, 29–30) supporting Lydgate's Oxford studies written *c.* 1406–8; but Pearsall warns 'That the prince knew Lydgate personally at this stage is

unlikely, and is not suggested by the letter …
' (30); however, see Norton-Smith 1966, 195,
who believes that Lydgate and the prince
knew each other at Oxford while the prince
was a resident at Queen's College in 1398.

25. In medieval political theory, the king was
universally acknowledged as having 'two
bodies', inseparably intertwined. One was
his own, of mortal flesh; the other was the
kingdom, his 'body politick'. What blotted
the one blighted the other. See Kantorowicz
1957. In his last years, Henry IV became
increasingly convinced that his wasting condition was God's punishment for his execution of Richard.

26. See Edwards and Pearsall 1989, 257–78;
and Mitchell 1968, 112–15.

27. Stubbs 2000.

28. For example, he wrote the title over the
first folio.

29. Stubbs 2000.
See also Doyle and Parkes 1979, xliii, xlvi.

30. Stubbs 2000.
See also Doyle and Parkes 1979, xliii–xliv.

15. CHAUCER'S FINAL DAYS

1. See Fisher 1964, 64ff. and Langland, *Piers
Plowman*, B-text, ed. Kane and Donaldson,
vi, ll. 97–106.

2. Crow and Olson 1966, 548.

3. See *CWCH*, ed. Sharpe.

4. For an account of Lambeth wills, see Smith
1918; see further *Index of Wills*, PCC, I
(1383–1558), ed. J.C.C. Smith (1893).

5. Crow and Olson 1966, 289.

6. From a private communication, quoted
with the owner's kind permission.

7. McFarlane 1972, 208.

8. Pearsall 1994, 404–5.

9. Pearsall 1997, 36.

10. Crow and Olson 1966, 532–3.

11. In September, 1390 Chaucer was attacked
on the road, wounded and robbed by a gang
of thieves who were later caught and convicted in a public trial which many of
Hoccleve's readers probably remembered.
It's uncertain whether he was robbed once or
three times – if the latter, the robberies all
happened within three days, and two on the
same day. See Crow and Olson 1966,
477–89. On Hoccleve's friendship with
Chaucer, see *The Regement of Princes*, ll.
1867 ff., and 2077–9. Not everyone agrees
about how close Hoccleve may have been to
Chaucer: see Mitchell 1968, 118.

12. Somerset 1998 makes plain how 'extracler-
gial' writers converted Latin terms into
English in express opposition to clerical
orthodoxy – and the dangers involved.

13. On the Pierian Spring – a fountain in
Greece, fabled to inspire all who drank from
it – see Brewer 1978b, I, 79.

14. For a translation of the full text of
Surigone's epitaph see Brewer 1978b, I, 79.
Crow and Olson 1966, 549, state categorically
that Caxton had both the tablet and the pillar erected over Chaucer's burial place. But
the grounds for this seem somewhat dubious:
it is unlikely that Caxton would have put up
a pillar – which, rather, was presumably an
existing part of the abbey. The tablet of verses was simply attached to the pillar. The only
record we have of Surigone's text is in
Caxton's printing of Chaucer's translation of
Boethius. Caxton writes: 'the body and
corps lieth buried in thabbay of Westmestre
beside london to fore the chapele of seynte
benet. by whos sepulture is wreton on a table
hongyng on a pylere his Epitaphye maad by
a poete laureat. whereof the copye foloweth
&c'. Then follows the text of Surigone's epitaph, at the end of which Caxton writes: 'It
was the eager wish of your admirer William
Caxton that you should live, illustrious poet
Chaucer. For not only has he printed your
works but he has also ordered this eulogy of
you to be here.' See Blake 1969, 164–6, 178.
It seems to us that this last sentence could
equally mean that Caxton has ordered the
epitaph to be put in the book.

15. Stowe, *Survey of London*, ed. Kingsford, I,
410.

16. Dart 1723, I, 83.

17. Hellman 1998, 16.

18. Crow and Olson 1966, 548.

19. Honeybourne 1932, 316–33. On rentals,

see Rosser 1989, 155.

20. Seton-Watson 1924, 184.
21. *Rot. Parl.*, III, 503–4.
22. Baker 1990, 11, quoting: *A Relation of the Island of England about the Year 1500* (Camden Society. 1847), 34–5
23. Workman 1926, I, 316 ff.
24. MacMichael 1971, 9–14.
25. *Westminster Chronicle*, trans. Hector and Harvey, 337.
26. Aston 1967, 346–7
27. Baker 1990, 11.
28. Crow and Olson 1966, 536.
29. Kirby 1970, 86.
30. Wylie 1884, I, 92.
31. During the whole of Henry's reign, the work on the nave practically ceased, and only began again with the accession of his son. Westlake 1923, I, 138. Of course, Henry's dislike of the abbey may have dated from the plotting

against him, but it is equally possible that he already recognized the abbey as a Ricardian stronghold before he came to power.

32. Aston 1967, 348, 353–4.
33. Gardner 1977, 309.
34. Crow and Olson 1966, 539.
35. *CPR 1396–69*, 43.
36. Crow and Olson 1966, 539.
37. Crow and Olson 1966, 540. Roskell, Clark and Rawcliffe, ii, 524–32.
38. McNiven 1987, 192. For the text of the Lollard Disendowment Bill see *EHD*, ed. Myers, IV, 668–9 and Hudson 1988, 135–6.
39. Hudson 1988, 198 ff.
40. *DNB*
41. 'De uno tenemento cum gardino infra sanctuarium.' Crow and Olson , 538.
42. 'nulle manere de Novellerie en cest parlement;' see Roskell 1983, III, 163.
43. Strohm 1996, 114–15.

16. DID CHAUCER REALLY DIE IN 1400?

1. For a full description of the manuscript and what is known about its history, see Yeager 1984a.
2. See Thomas Berthelet, in Spurgeon 1925, I, 78. Pearsall 1995 seems to believe there was an inscription, including the 25 October 1400 date of death; however, as he notes (53, and n. 13), floor burials in the transepts were very near the bottom of the honorific hierarchy of burial sites in the Abbey, and 'of those buried under the floor many had no inscriptions; no floor-slabs with inscriptions survive from before 1617.'
3. Brigham's original inscription says 'Galfridus Chaucer conditur hoc tumulo', and Bale 1557 says Brigham claimed to have moved Chaucer's remains (*Illustrium maioris Brytannie Scriptorum*, 718) but Bale later rejected Brigham's dating, and it is likely he was merely quoting his friend, without additional evidence.
4. For the little that is recorded of Brigham, see especially Alsop 1981, 49–67; and further Guy 1988, 238–43.
5. Dart 1723, I, ii.86.
6. Yeager 1984a, 273–6. On Brigham's friendship with Bale, see Alsop 1981, 49–67.
7. Leland, 'Inter haec Chaucerus ad canos

devenit, sensitque ipsam senectutem morbum esse; Vismonasterii in australi insula basilicae, D. Petro sacrae, sepultus'; *Commentarii*, 425.

8. I.e., *Illustrium Maioris Britanniae Scriptorm Summarium* and *Scriptorium Illustrium Maioris Britanniae Catalogus*.
9. Yeager 1984a, 274.
10. *Works of Geoffrey Chaucer*, ed. Skeat, VII, 232.
11. Yeager 1984a, 274 and n. 49.
12. John Foxe, *Acts and Monuments of Martyrs* (London, 1684), II, 42, cols A–C.
13. Crow and Olson 1966, 547–8.
14. Workman 1926, ii, 136.
15. Foxe 1570, II, 42, cols A–C.
16. On the role of the *ex officio* Coroner, see Hunnisett 1961.
17. *Workes of our Antient and lerned English Poet Geffrey Chaucer*, ed. Speght, preface (unpaginated), 'His Friends'.
18. *DNB*
19. Crow and Olson 1966, 289–93.
20. For definitions of these terms, see Crow and Olson, 1966, 390–1.
21. Crow and Olson 1966, 579–80.
22. Martin M. Crow and Virginia E. Leland, in Benson 1987, xxiv.

23. Garbaty 1987, 102.

24. Beidler and Decker 1989, 236–50; Beidler 1991, 286–95. In a forthcoming article, Beidler also proposes 'Heile of Beersele' as a source for *The Miller's Tale*.

25. BL MS Additional 5141 has never been officially dated. From the style, it would *seem* to be sixteenth century – though if a copy, then of fifteenth-century origin. One of the portraits found in Hoccleve's *The Regement of Princes* has been suggested as a model (see, for example, Spielmann 1900), but there are a great many differences. The fact is, nobody knows where Add. 5141 came from, who painted it, or when.

26. BL MS Cot. Otho A.XVIII.

27. Pearsall 1984, 75.

28. The date 1402 on the portrait side of BL MS Add. 5141 does not appear to be in the same handwriting as the *vita* on the back – and the ink is quite different. (This the opinion of the very kind Dr Alixe Bovey of the British Library, who courteously re-examined the portrait.) Also, the use of Arabic numerals, rather than Roman, which were customary in medieval manuscripts, suggests that the date was inscribed in the sixteenth century, when Arabics became more common. However, Arabic numerals had been in use since the twelfth century in Italy and elsewhere – though primarily in scientific or mathematical texts. Interestingly, the *Equatorie of the Planetis*, just such a scientific treatise possibly written by Chaucer himself – there is some dispute about who wrote it, but not about the fact that the manuscript (Cambridge University MS Peterhouse College 75.I, 71v–78v) containing it is late fourteenth century and produced in England – uses Arabic numerals consistently, viz, 'the hole diametre shole contene 72 large enches'. See Schmidt 1993.

29. Yeager 1984b, 135–64.

30. For example *The Plowman's Tale* and *Jack Upland*.

31. *Anelida and Arcite*, l. 18 in Benson 1987, 376.

32. Godfrey 1921, 36; quoted by Pearsall 1995, 55.

33. Pearsall 1995, 70.

34. Pearsall 1995, 67.

17. DID CHAUCER REPENT?

1. Crow and Olson 1966, 547; trans. Pearsall 1992, 275.

2. See Wallace 1999, xxii. Less worldly predecessors would include figures like the thirteenth-century Archbishop Peckham. See above p. 185.

3. For the best account see Dahmus 1966, 93 ff.

4. Netter, *Fasciculi Zizaniorum*, 336.

5. *Knighton's Chronicle*, trans. Martin, 263.

6. Workman 1926, II, 272.

7. Dahmus 1966, 142.

8. Workman 1926, II, 136, 337.

9. Dahmus 1966, 145–6.

10. *Knighton's Chronicle*, trans. Martin, 535.

11. Hudson 1988, 160.

12. McNiven 1987, 89. For full text of Purvey's recantation in Latin see: Netter, *Fasciculi Zizaniorum*, 400–07.

13. *Eulogium Historiarum sive Temporis*, ed. Haydon III, 388.

14. Strohm 1998, 54.

15. Hudson 1988, 158.

16. Walsingham, *Historia Anglicana*, ed. Riley, II, 253.

17. Sayce 1971, 229–41.

18. Sayce 1971, 229–41. For a review of the literature on the *Retractions* see: Gordon 1961, 81–96.

19. Coleman 1996, 152.

20. *Parson's Tale (Retractions)*, l. 1081 in Benson 1987, 328.

21. *Parson's Tale (Retractions)*, ll. 1184–5 in Benson 1987, 328.

22. Preface to the Genealogy of the Gentile Gods' in *Boccaccio on Poetry*, trans. Osgood, 62, 69–70.

23. Looten 1931, 243; quoted in Gordon 1961, 89.

24. 'what euere thingis ben writun, tho ben writun to oure techynge', *Rom. 15*: 4, in *The Holy Bible Translated by John Wyclif and His Followers*, ed. Forshall and Madden, IV, 333.

25. *MED*, s.v., 'revoken'.

26. *A Latin Dictionary*, rev. Lewis and Short.

27. *OED*, s.v. 'retract', sb. *Obs.*: 'He wryte also a Book of retraction in whych he correcteth hys owne errours.' Also s.v. 'retractation'.

28. Augustine of Hippo, *Retractationum Libri Duo*, Pro. 2; trans. Brown 1969, 429.

29. For the fullest discussion of the vocabulary see Sayce 1971, 230–48.
30. Trans. Brown 1969, 431.
31. Hammond 1933, 514–16.
32. Pearsall 1992, 332, n. 5.
33. To quote the anonymous Renaissance biographer of BL MS Add. 5141 – Yeager 1984a, 263.
34. See Siegfried Wenzel in Benson 1987 (*The Riverside Chaucer*), 965.
35. Deschamps, *Oeuvres Complete*, ed. Reynaud, I, 2.
36. Calin 1974, 16.
37. Calin 1974, 75.
38. Calin 1974, 87.
39. William Calin, in private correspondence.
40. *EHD*, ed. Myers, IV, 174–5.
41. Gower, *Cronica Tripertita*, Bk. I, 61–100, trans. Stockton 1962, 292–3.
42. *Mum and the Sothsegger,* ed. Day and Steele.

18. CHAUCER AND ARCHBISHOP ARUNDEL

1. Even David Wright omits it on the grounds that it is 'unlikley to interest the general reader'. See *The Canterbury Tales*, 463.
2. For the French original see *Complete Works*, ed. Skeat I, 261–71.
3. See Benson 1987, 1076.
4. This case is made eloquently by the various contributors in Benson and Robertson 1990; see there especially Georgianna 1990.
5. There have been a few exceptions – prominently those assembled by Benson and Robertson 1990 (see n. 697); but see also Mann 1995, who articulates the issue; and, more sympathetically, Kolve 1997. Tables may be turning again with the turn of the century: see the reassessment of Quinn 2001, 169–41.
6. 'An ABC,' ll. 47, 6, 16; in Benson 1987, 638, 637.
7. The arguments for the date of *An ABC* are presented by Laila Z. Gross, in Benson 1987, 1076. For dating of ' Former Age', 'Venus' and 'Bukton', see Gross, in Benson 1987, 1081, 1083 and 1087, respectively.
8. See Crampton 1990; Phillips 1993, 1–19; Stevenson 1996, 27–42.
9. See *MED*, s.v. 'errour'. For a comparison of the two poems see Phillips 1993, 1–19.
10. Guillaume de Deguilleville, *The Pilgrimage of the Life of Man*, trans. John Lydgate, ed. Furnival, 505–18. For a prose translation see *The Pilgrimage of the Lyfe of the Manhode* ed. Henry, I, 149.
11. Kienzle 1991, 291–308. See also Szövérffy 1987, 223–32.
12. Compare the French source: 'Quar quant aucun se desvoie, / A ce que tost se ravoie, / De ta pitié li fais convoy.' See *Le Pèlerinage de Vie Humaine de Guillaume de Deguilleville*, ed. Stürzinger, 342.
13. *1 Tim.*: 4, 7. *New English Bible* trans.
14. *Selections from English Wycliffite Writings*, ed. Hudson, 75.
15. Especially, perhaps, if Arundel were reading *The Riverside Chaucer*, where we are told that 'spille his kynde' means 'spill his semen' – a definition of 'kynde' that seems to elude the *MED*, and which gives for a very puzzling twist to a passage that reads: if 'man or womman spille his kynde inwith that place'. Even in the Middle Ages they didn't think that women produced semen.
16. *The Parson's Tale*, X 780 ff.; see Benson 1987, 315.
17. Aston 1984b, 207.
18. Walsingham, *Historia Anglicana*, ed. Riley, II, 216.
19. *Selections from English Wycliffite Writings* ed. Hudson, 27–8.
20. Netter, *Fasciculi Zizaniorum*, 402.
21. ' … right so sholde he humble his body outward to the preest, that sit in Goddes place. For which in no mannere, sith that Crist is sovereyn, and the preest meene and mediatour bitwixe Crist and the synnere, and the synner is the last by way of resoun, thanne sholde nat the synnere sitte as heighe as his confessour, but knele biforn hym or at his fet, but if maladie distourbe it.' *The Parson's Tale*, X, 988–90, in Benson 1987, 323–4.
22. The confession box was introduced in the sixteenth century by St Charles Borromeo (1538–84) specifically to avoid such practices. See Dolan 1983, 488–9.
23. *The Parson's Tale*, X, 894. 'Preestes been aungels, as by the dignitee of hir mysterye' in Benson 1987, 319.
24. *The Parson's Tale*, X, 890–92, in Benson 1987, 319.

25. *EHD* IV, ed. Myers, 849.
26. Pearsall 1992, 269.
27. 'Another sin that appertains to lechery comes in sleeping, and this sin comes often to those that are maidens, and also to those that are corrupt; and this sin is named in four manners. Sometime of languishing of the body, for the humours are too rank and too abundant in the body of a man; sometimes of infirmity, for the feebleness of the retentive strength, as physic makes mention. Sometime it comes from a surfeit of food and drink; and sometimes it comes from wicked thoughts that are enclosed in a man's mind when he goes to sleep, which may not be without sin; on account of which men must keep themselves wisely, or else may men sin full grievously.' Our modernization of *The Parson's Tale*, X 911–13, in Benson 1987, 320.
28. Blake 1997, 112.
29. Vaughan 1999, 45, and further Owen 1994, 239–49.
30. *The Parson's Tale*, X, 939 in Benson 1987, 321. See Patterson 1978, 351–3.
31. Siegfried Wenzel, in Benson 1987, 956.
32. For *The Legend of Good Women* see above p. 34. The *House of Fame* is unfinished. However, some critics (e.g. Brusendorff 1925, 156) argue that the ending has simply been lost: see John M. Fyler, in Benson, 1987, 990. Of course there is no knowing who the 'man of great authority' might be, but if, as has been also suggested, it were meant to be John of Gaunt, and if it were of 'dubious credit to the person celebrated' it could well be that the ending was deliberately 'lost' upon the usurpation of Henry IV.
33. Stubbs 2000.
34. Strohm 1996, 51.

BIBLIOGRAPHY

PRIMARY SOURCES

Anglo-Norman Letters and Petitions, ed. M. Dominca Legge (Oxford: Blackwell for A-NTS, 1941)

'*Annales Ricardi Secundi*', Johannis de Trokelowe *et anon.*, in *Chronica et Annales*, 199–239 ed. Henry Thomas Riley, RS (London: HMSO, 1866)

The Anonimalle Chronicle: 1333–1381, ed. V.H. Galbraith (London/Manchester: Longmans, Green/University of Manchester Press, 1927)

Augustine of Hippo, *S. Aurelii Augustini Hipponensis Episcopi Retractationum Libri Duo*, in *Opera Omnia Augustini Hipponensis*, PL 32 ('*Retractations*')

Bale, John, *Illustrium maioris Britannie scriptorum, hoc est Anglie, Cambrie, ac Scotiae, summarium* (Wesel and Ipswich, 1548)

_____, *Index Britanniae scriptorum: John Bale's Index of British and Other Writers*, ed. R.L. Poole and Mary Bateson; reprinted with introduction by Caroline Brett and James P. Carley, (1902; reprinted Cambridge: D.S. Brewer, 1990)

_____, *Scriptorium illustrium maioris Brytannie, quam nunc Angliam et Scotiam uovan: Catalogus,* facsimile edn, 2 vols, (Basle: 1557; 2nd edn. 1559; reprinted Westmead: Gregg International, 1971)

Bernard of Clairvaux, *Opera Sancti Bernardi*, ed. J. Leclerq, C.H. Talbot and H.M. Rochais, 8 vols (Rome: Editiones Cistercienses, 1957–74)

Boccaccio, Giovanni, *The Decameron*, trans. G.H. McWilliam (Harmondsworth: Penguin, 1972; reprinted 1995)

_____, *Boccaccio on Poetry, Being the Preface and the Fourteenth and Fifteenth Books of Boccaccio's 'Genealogia deorum gentilium'*, ed. and trans. C.G. Osgood (Princeton, NJ: Princeton University Press, 1930; reprinted 1956)

The Brut, ed. F.W.D. Brie, 2 vols, EETS o.s. 131, 136 (London: Kegan Paul, Trench & Trubner, 1906, 1908; reprinted 2000)

Calendar of State Papers and Manuscripts, existing in the archives and collections of Milan, ed. A.B. Hinds, PRO (London: HMSO, 1912)

Chandos Herald, The, *The Life of the Black Prince by the Herald of Sir John Chandos*, ed. M.K. Pope and E.C. Lodge (Oxford: Clarendon, 1910)

Chaucer, Geoffrey, *The Workes of our Ancient and lerned English Poet Geffrey Chaucer*, ed. Thomas Speght (London: 1598)

_____, *The Poetical Works of Geoffrey Chaucer*, ed. R. Bell, 4 vols (London: G. Bell & Sons, 1878–80)

_____, *The Complete Works of Geoffrey Chaucer*, ed. W.W. Skeat, 7 vols (Oxford: Clarendon Press, 1894–9)

_____, *Chaucerian and Other Pieces ... A Supplement to the Complete Works of*

Geoffrey Chaucer, ed. W.W. Skeat (Oxford; Clarendon Press, 1898)

_____, *The Text of the Canterbury Tales, Studied on the Basis of All Known Manuscripts*, ed. J.M. Manly and Edith Rickert, 8 vols (Chicago: University of Chicago Press, 1940)

_____, *The Canterbury Tales*, ed. Derek Pearsall (London: Allen & Unwin, 1985)

_____, *The Canterbury Tales*, trans. David Wright (Oxford: OUP, 1985)

_____, *The Riverside Chaucer*, 3rd edn., gen. ed. Larry D. Benson (Boston: Houghton Mifflin, 1987)

_____, *The Canterbury Tales: A Facsimile and Transcription of the Hengwrt Manuscript with variants from the Ellesmere Manuscript*, ed. Paul G. Ruggiers, with introductions by D.C. Baker, and A.I. Doyle and M.B. Parkes (Norman, OK: University of Oklahoma Press, 1979)

_____, *The Hengwrt Chaucer Digital Facsimile* CD-ROM produced by The Canterbury Tales Project (Scholarly Digital Editions, 2000), unpaginated, De Montfort University, Leicester

Caxton, William, *Caxton's Own Prose*, ed. N.F. Blake (London: Deutsch, 1975)

Christine de Pisan, *Oeuvres Poetiques de Christine de Pisan*, ed. M. Roy, 3 vols (Paris: 1886–96)

The Chronicle of Adam of Usk 1377–1421, ed. and trans. Chris Given-Wilson (Oxford: OUP, 1997)

The Chronicle of John Hardyng, ed. Henry Ellis (London: Rivington, 1812)

An English Chronicle of the Reigns of Richard II, Henry IV, Henry V, and Henry VI, written before the year 1471, ed. J.S. Davies (London: RHS, 1855)

Chronique du Religieux de Saint-Denys 1380–1422, ed. M.L. Bellaguet, 3 vols (Paris: Crapelet, 1839–52; reprinted 1994)

Chronicon de Adae de Usk AD 1377–1421, ed. E.M. Thompson, 2nd edn. (London: Frowde, 1904)

Chronicon Angliae auctore monacho quodam Sancti Albani, ed. E.M. Thompson, *RS* (London: HMSO, 1874)

Chronicon Henrici Knighton, ed. J.R. Lumby, 2 vols, *RS* (London: HMSO, 1889–95)

Clanvowe, Sir John, *The Works of Sir John Clanvowe*, ed. V.J. Scattergood (Cambridge: D.S. Brewer, 1965; reprinted 1975)

Creton, Jean, *Chronicque de la Traison et Mort de Richard Deux Roy Dengleterre*, ed. B. Williams (London: English Historical Society, 1846; reprinted 1964)

_____, *A Translation of a French Metrical History of the Deposition of King Richard II, Written by a Contemporary*, ed. and trans. John Webb (London: Society of Antiquaries, 1823); *Archaeologia* 20 (1819)

Dante Alighieri, *De monarchia*, in *The Selected Works of Dante*, ed. and trans. Paolo Milano (London: Chatto & Windus, 1972)

Dart, John, *Westmonasterium, or the Histories and Antiquities of the Abbey Church of St Peters, Westminster*, 2 vols (London: C. Bowles, 1723)

Deguilleville, Guillaume de, *Le Pèlerinage de Vie Humaine de Guillaume de Deguilleville*, ed. J.J. Stürzinger (London: Nelson & Sons, 1893)

_____, *The Pilgrimage of Human Life*, trans. Eugene Clasby (New York: Garland, 1992)

Deschamps, Eustache, *Oeuvres complètes*, ed. Auguste H.E. Queux de Sainte-Hilaire and Gaston Raynaud, 11 vols (Paris: SATF, 1878–1903)

The Dieulacres Chronicles, ed. M.V. Clarke and V.H. Galbraith, 'The deposition of Richard II', *BJRL* 14 (1930): 125–81

The Diplomatic Correspondence of Richard II, ed. E. Perroy, Camden Society 3rd series, 48 (London: RHS, 1933)

English Wycliffite Sermons, ed. Anne Hudson (Oxford: OUP, 1983)

Eulogium Historiarum sive Temporis, ed. F.S. Haydon, *RS* (London: Longman, Brown, Green Longmans & Roberts, 1858–63)

Froissart, Jean, *Oeuvres*, ed. Baron Kervyn de Lettenhove, 27 vols (Brussels, 1867–77)

_____, *Chroniques*, ed. Simeon Luce, Gaston Raynaud, Leon Mirot, 12 vols in 14 (Paris: SHF, 1869–1931)

_____, *The Chronicles of Froissart*, trans. Thomas Johnes (London: 1803–05; rev. 1901)

_____, *The Chronicle of Froissart*, trans. Sir John Bourchier, Lord Berners, ed. W.P Ker, 6 vols (London: D. Nutt, 1901–3)

Gesta Abbatum Monasterii Sancti Albani, ed. H.T. Riley, 3 vols, *RS* (London: HMSO, 1867–9)

Gower, John, *The Complete Works of John Gower*, ed. G.C. Macaulay, 4 vols (Oxford: Clarendon Press, 1899–1902)

_____, *The Major Latin Works of John Gower: The Voice of One Crying and The Tripartite Chronicle*, trans. Eric W. Stockton (Seattle: University of Washington Press, 1962)

_____, *The English Works of John Gower*, ed. G.C. Macaulay, 2 vols, EETS 81–82 (1900–01; reprinted Oxford: OUP, 1979)

Havelok the Dane, in *Middle English Verse Romances*, ed. Donald B. Sands (New York: Holt, Rhinehart & Winston, 1966), 55–129

Historia Vitae et Regni Ricardi Secundi, ed. G.B. Stow (Philadelphia, PA: University of Pennsylvania Press, 1977)

Historical Poems of the XIVth and XVth Centuries, ed. Rossell H. Robbins (New York: Columbia University Press, 1959)

Hoccleve, Thomas, *Hoccleve's Works, Vol. III, 'The Regement of Princes'*, ed. Frederick J. Furnivall, EETS e.s. 72 (London: Kegan Paul, Trench & Trubner, 1897)

_____, *The Regiment of Princes*, ed. Charles R. Blyth, TEAMS Series (Kalamazoo, MI: Medieval Institute Publications, 1999)

_____, *Hoccleve's Works: The Minor Poems*, ed. Frederick J. Furnivall and Israel Gollancz; rev. Jerome Mitchell and A.I. Doyle, EETS e.s. 61, 73 (London: 1892, 1925 [for 1897]; reprinted as one volume, London: OUP, 1970)

_____, *Thomas Hoccleve's Complaint and Dialogue*, ed. J.A. Burrow, EETS o.s. 313 (Oxford: OUP, 1999)

The Household of Edward IV: The Black Book and the Ordinance of 1478, ed. A.R. Myers (Manchester: Manchester University Press, 1959)

Jack Upland, Friar Daw's Reply and Upland's Rejoinder, ed. P.L. Heyworth (Oxford: Clarendon Press, 1968)

Jacques de Hemricourt, *Oeuvres de Jacques de Hemricourt*, ed. C. de Borsman, A. Bayot and E. Poncelet, 3 vols (Brussels: Kiessling & Imbreghts, 1910–31)

Jean le Bel, *Chronique de Jean le Bel*, SHF, 2 vols (Paris: Renouard, 1904–5)

Johannis de Trokelowe *et anon.*, *Chronica et Annales*, ed. H.T. Riley, *RS* (London: HMSO, 1866)

The Kirkstall Abbey Chronicles, ed. J. Taylor, Thoresby Society 42 (Leeds, 1952)

Knighton, Henry, *Chronicon Henrici Knighton vel Cnitthon: Monachi Leycestrensis*, ed. Joseph Rawson Lumby, 2 vols (London: Eyre & Spottiswoode, 1895)

_____, *Knighton's Chronicle, 1337–1396*, ed. and trans. G.H. Martin (Oxford: Clarendon

Press, 1995)

Langland, William, *Piers Plowman: The A Version*, ed. George Kane (London: University of London, Athlone Press, 1960)

_____, *Piers Plowman: The B Version. Will's Vision of Piers Plowman, Do-Well, Do-Better and Do-Best*, ed. George Kane and E. Talbot Donaldson (London: University of London, Athlone Press, 1975)

_____, *Piers Plowman by William Langland: An Edition of the C-Text*, ed. Derek Pearsall (London: Edward Arnold, 1978)

_____, *William Langland, Piers Plowman: The Z Version*, ed. A.G. Rigg and Charlotte Brewer (Toronto: Pontifical Institute of Medieval Studies, 1983)

Lays of Courtly Love, ed. and trans. Patricia A. Terry (New York: Anchor Books, 1963)

Leland, John, *Commentarii de scriptoribus britannicis*, 2 vols (Anthony Hall, 1709) *The Life of the Church*, ed. M.C. D'Arcy (London: Sheed & Ward, 1932)

Literae Cantuarienses, ed. J.B. Sheppard, 3 vols, *RS* (London: HMSO, 1889)

Lydgate, John, *Danse Macabre*, ed. Florence Warren, EETS o.s. 181 (London: OUP, 1931)

_____, *The Fall of Princes*, ed. Harry Bergen, 4 vols, EETS e.s. 121–4 (London: OUP, 1924–7)

_____, *The Life of Our Lady*, ed. Joseph A. Lauritis, Ralph A. Klinefelter and Vernon F. Gallagher (Pittsburgh, PA: Duquesne University Press, 1961)

_____, *Minor Poems*, ed. Henry Noble McCracken, 2 vols, EETS o.s. 192 (London: Humphrey Milford for OUP, 1934)

_____, *The Pilgrimage of the Life of Man*, ed. F.J. Furnivall, EETS e.s. 83 (London: Kegan Paul, Trench & Trubner, 1899–1904)

_____, *Troy Book*, ed. Henry Bergen, 3 vols, EETS e.s.97, 103, 106 (London: Kegan Paul, Trench & Trubner, and Frowde for OUP, 1906–10)

_____, and Benedict Burgh, *Secrees of Old Philisoffres*, ed. Robert Steele, EETS e.s. 66 (London: Kegan Paul, Trench & Trubner, 1894)

_____, *Lydgate's Siege of Thebes*, ed. Axel Erdmann (vol. I) and Axel Erdmann and Eilert Ekwall (vol. II), 2 vols, EETS e.s. 108, 125 (London: OUP; Humphrey Milford for OUP, 1911, 1930)

_____, *John Lydgate, Poems*, ed. John Norton-Smith (Oxford: Clarendon Press, 1966)

Marsilius of Padua, *Defensor Pacis*, trans. Alan Gewirth (Toronto: University of Toronto Press, 1980)

The Master of Game, ed. W.A. and F. Baillie-Grohman (London: Chatto & Windus, 1919)

Memorials of Beverley Minster: Chapter Act Book, ed. A.F. Leach 2 vols, Surtees Society 98, 108 (London: Andrews, 1898–1903)

Mum and the Sothsegger, ed. Mabel Day and R. Steele, EETS o.s. 199 (London: Humphrey Milford for OUP, 1936; reprinted 1971)

Netter, Thomas, *Fasciculi Zizaniorum*, ed. W.W. Shirley, *RS* (London: HMSO, 1858)

Philippe de Mezieres, *Letter to King Richard II*, trans. G.W. Coopland (Liverpool: Liverpool University Press, 1975)

The Pilgrimage of the Lyf of the Manhode, ed. A. Henry, 2 vols EETS o.s. 288, 292 (London: OUP, 1985, 1988)

Political Poems and Songs relating to English History, composed during the period from the Accession of Edw. III to that of Ric. III, ed. Thomas Wright, 2 vols, *RS* 14 (London: HMSO, 1859–61)

Salutati, Coluccio, *Epistolario di Coluccio Salutati*, ed. F. Novati, 4 vols (Rome: Istituto storico italiano: 1891–1911)

Scogan, Henry, 'A Moral Ballade', in *Chaucerian and Other Pieces ... A Supplement to the Complete Works of Geoffrey Chaucer*, ed. W.W. Skeat (Oxford: Clarendon Press, 1898; reprinted 1963)

Secretum Secretorum: Nine English Versions, ed. M.A. Manzalaoui, I [text], EETS o.s. 276 (London: OUP, 1977)

Three Prose Versions of the Secreta Secretorum, ed. Robert Steele, EETS e.s. 74 (London: Kegan Paul, Trench & Trubner, 1898)

Select Cases in the Court of the King's Bench under Richard II, Henry IV and Henry V, ed. G.O. Sayles, Selden Society 7 (London, 1971)

Selections from English Wycliffite Writings, ed. Anne Hudson (Cambridge: CUP, 1978)

Sercambi, Giovanni, *Le Croniche*, ed. Salvatore Bongi, 3 vols (Rome: Istituto storico italiano, 1892; reprinted Turin, 1969)

Stow, John, *A Survey of London, Reprinted from the Text of 1603*, ed. C. L. Kingsford, 2 vols (Oxford: Clarendon Press, 1908; reprinted 1973)

Thoresby, John, *The Lay Folks' Catechism*, ed. T.F. Simmons and H.E. Nolloth, EETS o.s. 118 (London: Kegan Paul, Trench & Trubner, 1901)

_____, *The Lay Folks' Mass Book*, ed. T.F. Simmons, EETS o.s. 71 (Oxford: OUP, 1879; reprinted 1968)

Walsingham, Thomas, *Chronica Monasterii S. Albani. Thomae Walsingham quondam Monachi S. Albani, Historia Anglicana*, Vol. I, *AD 1272–1381*; Vol. II, *1381–1422*, ed. Henry Thomas Riley, *RS* (London: Longman, Green, Longman, Roberts and Green, 1863–4)

The Westminster Chronicle, 1381–1394, ed. and trans. L.C. Hector and B.F. Harvey (Oxford: OUP, 1982)

Wimbledon's Sermon, 'Redde rationem vilicationis tue' , ed. I.K. Knight (Pittsburgh, PA: Duquesne University Press, 1967)

Wyclif, John, *The English Works of John Wyclif*, ed. F.D. Matthew, EETS o.s. 74 (London: Trubner, 1902; reprinted 1973)

_____, *Select English Works of John Wyclif*, ed. Thomas Arnold, 3 vols (Oxford: Clarendon, 1867–71)

_____, *The Holy Bible, Translated by John Wyclif and His Followers,* ed. J. Forshall and F. Madden, 4 vols (Oxford: OUP, 1850)

_____, *Iohannis Wyclif, tractatus de Apostasia*, ed. M.H. Dziewicki (London: Trubner, 1889)

_____, *De Officio Regis*, ed. A.W. Pollard and C. Sayle (London: Trubner, 1887)

_____, *Opus Evangelium*, ed. J. Loserth, 4 vols in 2 (London: Trubner, 1895–6)

_____, *Sermones*, ed. J. Loserth, 4 vols (London: Trubner, 1887)

_____, *Trialogus*, ed. G. Lechler (Oxford: Clarendon Press, 1869)

_____, *De veritate sacrae scripturae*, ed. Rudolf Buddensieg, 3 vols (London: Trubner, 1905–7)

SECONDARY SOURCES

Alford 1995. *From Page to Performance: Essays in Early English Drama, In Memory of Arnold Williams*, ed. John A. Alford (East Lansing, MI: Colleagues Press)

Alsop 1981. James Alsop, 'Nicholas Brigham (*d.* 1558), scholar, antiquary and crown servant', *Sixteenth-Century Journal* 12, 49–67

Aston 1967. Margaret Aston, *Thomas Arundel* (Oxford: Clarendon Press)

_____ 1984a. '"Caim's Castles": poverty, politics and disendowment', in Dobson 1984, 45–81

_____ 1984b. *Lollards and Reformers: Images and Literacy in Late Medieval England* (London: Hambledon Press)

_____ 1993 'Wyclif and the Vernacular', in *Faith and Fire: Popular and Unpopular Religion 1350–1600* (London: Hambledon Press)

Baigent and Leigh 1999. M. Baigent and R. Leigh, *The Inquisition* (New York: Viking)

Baker 1990. J.H. Baker, 'The English law of sanctuary', *ELJ* 2, 8–13

Barber 1986a. *Life and Campaigns of the Black Prince*, ed. Richard Barber (Woodbridge, Suffolk: Boydell & Brewer)

_____ 1986b. Richard Barber, 'The Chandos Herald: Life of the Black Prince', in Barber 1986b, 84–139

Barron 1968. Caroline M. Barron, 'The tyranny of Richard II,' *BIHR*, 10–14

_____ 1990. 'The deposition of Richard II', in Taylor and Childs 1990, 132–49

_____ 2000. 'The reign of Richard II', *NCMH*, 297–333

Beidler 1991. 'Chaucer's *Reeve's Tale* and its Flemish analogue', *ChR* 26, 286–95

Beidler and Decker 1989. Peter G. Beidler and Therese Decker, '*Lippijn*: A Middle-Dutch source for the *Merchant's Tale?*', *ChR* 23, 236–50

Bellamy 1973. John G. Bellamy, *Crime and Public Order in England in the Later Middle Ages* (London: Routledge & Kegan Paul)

Bennett 1979. Michael J. Bennett, '*Sir Gawain and the Green Knight* and the literary achievement of the north-west Midlands: the historical background', *JMH* 5, 63–88

_____ 1983. *Community, Class and Careerism: Cheshire and Lancashire Society in the Age of 'Sir Gawain and the Green Knight'* (Cambridge: CUP)

_____ 1992. 'The court of Richard II and the promotion of literature', in Hanawalt 1992, 3–20.

_____ 1999. 'Richard II and the wider realm', in Goodman and Gillespie 1999, 187–204

Benson 1981. Larry D. Benson, 'The Order of *The Canterbury Tales*', *SAC* 3, 77–120

Benson and Robertson 1990. *Chaucer's Religious Tales*, ed. C. David Benson and Elizabeth Robertson (Cambridge: D.S. Brewer)

Bisson 1998. L.M. Bisson, *Chaucer and the Late Medieval World* (Basingstoke and London: Macmillan)

Bitot 1996. '*Divers Toyes Mengled': Essays on Medieval and Renaissance Culture in Honor of Andre Lascombes*, ed. Michel Bitot, Roberta Mullini and Peter Happe (Tours: Publication de l'Université François Rabelais)

Blake 1969. Norman F. Blake, *Caxton and His World* (London: Language Library)

_____ 1997. 'Geoffrey Chaucer and the manuscripts of *The Canterbury Tales*', *JEBS*, 1, 96–112

Bowers 1992. John M. Bowers, 'Piers Plowman and the police: notes toward the history of the Wycliffite Langland', *YLS* 6, 1–50

_____ 2001. *The Politics of Pearl: Court Poetry in the Age of Richard II* (Cambridge: CUP)

Brewer 1978a. Derek Brewer, *Chaucer and His World* (London: Eyre Methuen)

_____ 1978b. *Chaucer, The Critical Heritage*, 2 vols (London: Routledge and Kegan Paul, 1978; reprinted 1995), Vol I, *1385–1837*

Bronson 1940. Bertrand H. Bronson, 'Chaucer's art in relation to his audience', in *Five Studies in Literature*, *UCPE* 8, 1–53

Brooks 1985. N. Brooks, 'The organisation and achievement of the peasants of Kent and Essex in 1381', in Mayr-Harting and Moore 1985, 258–70

Brown 1969. Peter Brown, *Augustine of Hippo: A Biography* (Berkeley and Los Angeles: University of California Press)

Brusendorff 1925. Aage Brusendorff, *The Chaucer Tradition* (London: OUP)

Burrow, J.A. 1982. *Medieval Writers and Their Work: Middle English Literature and Its Background, 1100–1500* (Oxford: OUP)

Calin 1974. William Calin, *A Poet at the Fountain: Essays on the Narrative Verse of Guillaume de Machaut* (Lexington: University of Kentucky Press)

Chaytor 1945. H.J. Chaytor, *From Script to Print: An Introduction to Medieval Vernacular Literature* (Cambridge: CUP, reprinted 1966)

Clanchy 1979. M.T. Clanchy, *From Memory to Written Record: England 1066–1307* (Cambridge, MA: Harvard University)

Clopper 1999. Lawrence Clopper, 'From Ungodly *ludi* to Sacred Play', in ,Wallace 1999, 739–66

Coleman 1996. Joyce Coleman, *Public Reading and the Reading Public in Late Medieval England and France* (Cambridge: CUP)

Coulton 1910. G.G. Coulton, *Life in the Middle Ages* (Cambridge: CUP)

Crampton 1990. Georgia Ronan Crampton, 'Chaucer's singular prayer', *MAE* 59, 191–213

Crow and Olson 1966. Martin M. Crow and Claire C. Olson, eds. *Chaucer Life-Records. From materials compiled by John M. Manly and Edith Rickert, with the assistance of Lilian J. Redstone and others* (Oxford: Clarendon Press)

Dahmus 1966. Joseph H. Dahmus, *William Courtenay, Archbishop of Canterbury 1381–1396* (Philadelphia, PA: University of Pennsylvania Press)

——— 1970. *The Prosecution of John Wyclif* (New Haven, CT: Yale University Press)

Davies 1973. R.G. Davies, 'Thomas Arundel as Archbishop of Canterbury 1396–1414', *JEH* 14, 9–15.

Dobson 1983. *The Peasants' Revolt of 1381*, ed. R.B. Dobson, 2nd edn. (London: Macmillan)

——— 1984. *The Church, Politics and Patronage in the Fifteenth Century*, ed. R.B. Dobson (Gloucester: Alan Sutton; New York: St Martin's Press)

Dolan 1983. T.P. Dolan, 'Administering shrift in *Piers Plowman*, *N&Q* 30, 488–9

——— 1995. 'The Mass as performance text', in Alford 1995, 13–24

Doyle and Parkes 1978. *Medieval Scribes, Manuscripts and Libraries: Essays Presented to N.R. Ker*, ed. A.I. Doyle and Malcolm Parkes (London: Scolar)

——— 1979. 'A Paleographic Introduction', in *The Canterbury Tales: A Facsimile*, ed. Ruggiers, xxi, xliv–xlvii

Duls 1975. Louisa D. Duls, *Richard II in the Early Chronicles* (The Hague: Mouton)

Dyer 1984. C. Dyer, 'The social and economic background to the rural revolt of 1381', in Hilton and Aston 1984, 9–42.

Eberle 1999. Patricia J. Eberle, 'Richard II and the arts', in Goodman and Gillespie 1999, 231–53

Edden 1987. V. Edden, 'The debate between Richard Maidstone and the Lollard Ashwardby (*c.* 1390)', *Carmelus* 34, 123

Edwards and Pearsall 1989. 'The manuscripts of the major English poetic texts', in Griffiths and Pearsall 1989, 257–78

Emden 1970. A.B. Emden, *Biographical Register of the University of Oxford to AD 1500*, 3 vols (Oxford: OUP, 1957, 1959; reprinted 1970)

Emmerson 1997. Richard K. Emmerson, 'Text and image in the Ellesmere portraits of the tale-tellers', in Stevens and Woodward 1997, 143–70

Finucane 1977. Ronald C. Finucane, *Miracles and Pilgrims: Popular Beliefs in Medieval England* (London: Dent)

Fisher 1964. John H. Fisher, *John Gower, Moral Philosopher and Friend of Chaucer* (New York: New York University Press)

_____ 1992. 'A language policy for Lancastrian England', *PMLA* 107, 1168–80; reprinted in Pinti 1999, 81–99

Fleming 1966. John V. Fleming, 'The antifraternalism of the *Summoner's Tale*', *JEGP* 65, 688–700

Foxe 1570. John Foxe, *The Actes and Monuments of the Christian Martyrs*, 4th edn., ed. Josiah Pratt, 8 vols (London: Religious Tract Society, 1877)

Galbraith 1932. V.H. Galbraith, 'Thomas Walsingham and the *Saint Albans Chronicle, 1272–1422*', *Speculum* 47, 12–29

_____ 1942. 'A New Life of Richard II', *History*, new series 26, 223–9, reprinted in V.H. Galbraith, *Kings and Chroniclers: Essays in English Medieval History* (London: Hambledon Press, 1982).

Garbaty 1987. Thomas J. Garbaty, 'Chaucer, the Customs and the Hainault connection', *SAC* Proceedings 2, 95–102

Gardner 1976. John C. Gardner, *The Life and Times of Chaucer* (New York: Knopf)

_____ 1977. *The Poetry of Chaucer* (Carbondale and Edwardsville, IL: Southern Illinois University Press, 1977)

Georgianna 1990. Linda Georgianna, 'The Protestant Chaucer', in Benson and Robertson 1990, 55–69

Gillespie 1997a. *The Age of Richard II*, ed. James L. Gillespie (London: Stroud)

_____ 1997b. 'Richard II: chivalry and kingship', in Gillespie 1997a, 115–38

Given-Wilson 1986. Chris Given-Wilson, *The Royal Household and the King's Affinity: Service, Politics and Finance in England 1360–1413* (New Haven, CT: Yale University Press)

_____ 1987. *The English Nobility in the Late Middle Ages: The Fourteenth-Century Political Community* (London: Routledge & Kegan Paul)

_____ 1993. (ed. and trans.) *Chronicles of the Revolution 1397–1400* (Manchester: Manchester University Press)

_____ 1999. 'Richard II and the Higher Nobility', in Goodman and Gillespie 1999, 107–28.

Godfrey 1921. Walter H. Godfrey, *The Parish of Chelsea, Part III: The Old Church, Chelsea, London County Council, Survey of London*, 7 (London: Country Life)

Goodman and Gillespie 1999. *Richard II: The Art of Kingship*, ed. Anthony Goodman and James Gillespie (Oxford: OUP)

Goodman 1999. Anthony Goodman, 'Richard II's Councils', in Goodman and Gillespie 1999, 59–82

Gordon 1961. J.D. Gordon, 'Chaucer's retraction: a review of opinion', in Leach 1961, 81–96

Gordon, Monas and Elam 1997. *The Regal Image of Richard II and the Wilton Diptych*, ed. Dillian Gordon, Lisa Monas and Caroline Elam (Coventry: Harvey Miller)

Gransden 1982. Antonia Gransden, *Historical Writing in England*, 2 vols (London: Routledge & Kegan Paul, 1974–82)

Green 1976. Richard Firth Green, 'King Richard's Books Revisited', *The Library* 31, 235–9

_____ 1980. *Poets and Princepleasers: Literature and the English Court in the Late Middle Ages* (Toronto: University of Toronto Press)

Griffiths and Pearsall 1989. *Book Production and Publishing in Britain 1375–1475*, ed. Jeremy Griffiths and Derek Pearsall (Cambridge: D.S. Brewer)

Guy 1988. John A. Guy, *Tudor England* (Oxford: OUP)

Hammond 1933. Eleanor Hammond, 'Chaucer's 'Book of the Twenty-five Ladies', *MLN* 48, 514–16.

Hanawalt 1992. *Chaucer's England: Literature in Historical Context*, ed. Barbara Hanawalt (Minneapolis, MN: University of Minnesota Press)

Hanna 1996. Ralph Hanna III, *Pursuing History: Middle English Manuscripts and Their Texts* (Palo Alto, CA: Stanford University Press)

Hellman 1998. Hal Hellman, *Great Feuds in Science* (New York: Wiley)

Hepburn 1986. F. Hepburn, *Portraits of the Later Plantagenets* (Woodbridge, Suffolk: Boydell & Brewer)

Hilton 1973. Rodney H. Hilton, *Bondmen Made Free: Medieval Peasant Movements and the English Rising of 1381* (London: Temple Smith)

Hilton and Aston 1984. *The English Rising of 1381*, ed. Rodney H. Hilton and Thomas H. Aston (Cambridge: CUP)

Honeybourne 1932. M.B. Honeybourne, 'The sanctuary boundaries and environs of Westminster Abbey and the College of St. Martin-Le-Grand', *Transactions of the British Archaeological Association*, new series 38, 316–33.

Howard 1976. Donald R. Howard, *The Idea of the Canterbury Tales* (Berkeley and Los Angeles: University of California Press)

———— 1987. *Chaucer and the Medieval World* (London: Weidenfeld & Nicholson)

Hudson 1978. Anne Hudson, *English Wycliffite Writings* (Cambridge: CUP)

———— 1988. Anne Hudson, *The Premature Reformation* (Oxford: OUP)

Hunnisett 1961. R.F. Hunnisett, *The Medieval Coroner* (Cambridge: CUP)

Jones 1968. R.H. Jones, *The Royal Policy of Richard II: Absolutism in the Later Middle Ages* (Oxford: Blackwell)

Jones 1980. Terry Jones, *Chaucer's Knight: The Portrait of a Medieval Mercenary* (London: Weidenfield & Nicholson; rev. ed. 1984; new rev. ed. London: Methuen, 1994)

———— 2001. 'The image of Chaucer's Knight', in Yeager and Morse 2001, 205–36.

Jusserand 1921. J.J. Jusserand, *English Wayfaring Life in the Middle Ages (XIVth Century)*, trans. L.T. Smith (London: Unwin)

Justice 1999. Steven Justice, 'Lollardy', in Wallace 1999, 662–89

Kantorowicz 1957. Ernst Kantorowicz, *The King's Two Bodies: A Study in Medieval Political Theology* (Princeton, NJ: Princeton University Press)

Kellogg and Haselmeyer 1951. A.L. Kellogg and L.A. Haselmeyer, 'Chaucer's satire of the Pardoner', *PMLA* 66, 251–77

Kendrick 1997. Laura Kendrick, 'The *Canterbury Tales* in the Context of Contemporary Vernacular Translations and Compilations', in Stevens and Woodward 1997, 281–306

Kenyon 1981. J.P. Kenyon, *A Dictionary of British History* (London: Secker & Warburg)

Kienzle 1991. B. Kienzle, 'Mary speaks against heresy: an unedited sermon of Helinand for the Purification, Paris BN ms. lat. 14591', *Sacris Erduri* 32, 291–308

Kirby 1964 J.L. Kirby, 'Councils and councillors of Henry IV', *TRHS*, 5th series, 14, 35–65

———— 1970. *Henry IV of England* (London: Constable)

Knowles 1948. D. Knowles, *The Religious Orders in England* (Cambridge, 1948).

Kolve 1984. V.A. Kolve, *Chaucer and the Imagery of Narrative: The First Five Canterbury Tales* (Palo Alto, CA: Stanford University Press)

———— 1993. 'Chaucer's Wheel of False Religion', in Taylor 1993, 265–96

———— 1997. 'God-denying fools and the medieval "religion of love"', *SAC* 19, 3–59

A Latin Dictionary, rev. C.T. Lewis and C. Short (Oxford: OUP, 1879; reprinted 1969)

Lawton 1982. *Middle English Alliterative Poetry and Its Literary Background*, ed. David Lawton (Cambridge: D.S. Brewer)

———— 1987. 'Dulness and the fifteenth century', *ELH* 54, 761–99

Leach 1961. *Studies in Medieval Literature in Honor of Professor A.C. Baugh*, ed. MacEdward Leach (Philadelphia: University of Pennsylvania Press)

Legge 1953. M. Dominica Legge, 'The gracious conqueror', *MLN* 68, 18–21

Levitan 1971. Alan Levitan, 'The parody of Pentecost in Chaucer's *Summoner's Tale*', *UTQ* 40, 236–46

Lindley 1997. Philip Lindley, 'Absolutism and regal image in Ricardian sculpture', in Gordon, Monas and Elam 1997, 60–83.

Looten 1931. Le Chanoine Looten, *Chaucer, ses modèles, ses sources, sa religion* (Lille: Facultés catholiques)

MacMichael 1971. N.H. MacMichael, 'Sanctuary at Westminster', *Westminster Abbey Occasional Papers* 27, 9–14

McFarlane 1972. K.B. McFarlane, *Lancastrian Kings and Lollard Knights* (Oxford: Clarendon Press)

McKisack 1959. May McKisack, *The Fourteenth Century 1307–1399* (Oxford: Clarendon Press)

McNiven 1987. Peter McNiven, *Heresy and Politics in the Reign of Henry IV* (Woodbridge, Suffolk: Boydell & Brewer)

Manly 1926. John Matthews Manly, *Some New Light on Chaucer* (1926; New York: Peter Smith, 1952)

Mann 1973. Jill Mann, *Chaucer and Medieval Estates Satire* (Cambridge: CUP)

———— 1995. 'Chaucer and Atheism', *SAC* 17, 5–19

Martin 1997. G.H. Martin, 'Narrative sources for the reign of Richard II', in Gillespie 1997a, 51–70

Mathew 1968. Gervase Mathew, *The Court of Richard II* (London: Murray)

Mayr-Harting and Moore 1985. *Studies in Medieval History Presented to R.H.C. Davis*, ed. H. Mayr-Harting and R.I. Moore (London: Hambledon Press)

Mitchell 1968. Jerome Mitchell, *Thomas Hoccleve: A Study in Early Fifteenth-Century English Poetic* (Urbana, IL: University of Illinois Press)

Minnis, Morse and Turville-Petre 1997. *Essays on Ricardian Literature Presented to John Burrow*, ed. A.J. Minnis, Charlotte C. Morse and Thorlac Turville-Petre (Oxford: OUP)

Moorman 1968. J. Moorman, *A History of the Franciscan Order from Its Origins to the Year 1517* (Oxford: OUP)

Myers 1959. *The Household of Edward IV: The Black Book and the Ordinance of 1478*, ed. A. R. Myers (Manchester: Manchester University Press)

Nicholls 1985. J.W. Nicholls, *The Matter of Courtesy: A Study of Medieval Courtesy Books and the Gawain-Poet* (Woodbridge, Suffolk: Boydell & Brewer)

Nicholson 1984a. Peter Nicholson, 'The dedications of Gower's *Confessio Amantis*', *Mediaevalia* 10, 159–80.

———— 1984b. 'Gower's revisions in the *Confessio Amantis*', *ChR* 19, 123–43

———— 1987 'Poet and scribe in the manuscripts of Gower's *Confessio Amantis*', in Pearsall 1987, 130–42

Olson 1999. Glending Olson, 'The end of the *Summoner's Tale* and the uses of Pentecost', *SAC* 21, 209–45

Orme 1973. Nicholas Orme, *English Schools in the Middle Ages* (London: Methuen)

Owen 1991. Charles A. Owen, Jr, *The Manuscripts of the Canterbury Tales* (Cambridge: D.S. Brewer)

———1994. 'What the manuscripts tell us about the "Parson's Tale"', *MAE* 63, 239–49.

Owen 1966. N.H. Owen, 'Thomas Wimbledon's sermon', *MS* 28, 176–97

Patterson 1978. Lee Patterson, 'The *Parson's Tale* and the quitting of the *Canterbury Tales*', *Traditio* 34, 331–80

Pearsall 1970. Derek Pearsall, *John Lydgate* (London: Routledge & Kegan Paul)

——— 1977a. *Old and Middle English Poetry* (London: Routledge & Kegan Paul)

——— 1977b. 'The Troilus frontispiece and Chaucer's audience', *YES* 7, 68–74

——— 1982. 'The alliterative revival: origins and social background', in Lawton 1982, 34–53

——— 1984. 'Thomas Speght (ca. 1550–?),' in Ruggiers 1984, 171–92

——— 1987 (ed.) *Manuscripts and Texts: Editorial Problems in Later Middle English Literature*

——— 1992. *The Life of Geoffrey Chaucer: A Critical Biography* (Oxford: Blackwell)

——— 1994. 'Hoccleve's *Regement of Princes*: The poetics of royal self-representation', *Speculum* 69, 386–410

——— 1995. 'Chaucer's tomb: the politics of reburial', *Medium Aevum* 64, 51–73

——— 1997. 'Pre-empting closure in the The *Canterbury Tales*: old endings, new beginnings', in Minnis, Morse and Turville-Petre 1997, 23–38

Pinet 1927. Marie-Joseph Pinet, *Christine de Pisan* (Paris: Champion)

Pinti 1998. *Writing after Chaucer: Essential Readings in Chaucer and the Fifteenth Century*, ed. Daniel J. Pinti (New York and London: Garland)

Phillips 1993. Helen Phillips, 'Chaucer and Deguilleville: The *ABC* in context', *MAE* 62, 1–19

Prescott (forthcoming). Andrew Prescott, 'The hand of God: reactions to the Peasants' Revolt of 1381', in *Proceedings of the Harlaxton Conference for 2000*, ed. N.J. Morgan (Woodbridge, Suffolk: Boydell, for Harlaxton College, British Campus of the University of Evansville)

Quinn 2001. William A. Quinn, 'Chaucer's problematic *Prière*: An *ABC* as artifact and critical issue', *SAC* 23, 109–41

Richardson 1936. H.R. Richardson, 'Heresy and lay power under Richard II', *EHR* 201, 1–28

Roskell 1965. J.S. Roskell, *The Commons and Their Speakers in English Parliament 1376–1523* (New York: Barnes & Noble)

——— 1981–3. *Parliament and Politics in Late Medieval England*, 3 vols (London: Hambledon Press)

Roskell, Clark and Rawcliffe 1992. *History of Parliament: The House of Commons, 1386–1421*. ed. J.S.Roskell, L.Clark and C.Rawcliffe, 4 vols (London: Stroud).

Rosser 1989. G. Rosser, *Medieval Westminster 1200–1540* (Oxford: OUP)

Ruggiers 1979. *The Canterbury Tales: A Facsimile and Transcription of the Hengwrt Manuscript with Variants from the Ellesmere Manuscript*, ed. Paul G. Ruggiers, with introductions by D.C. Baker, and A.I. Doyle and M.B. Parkes (Norman, OK: University of Oklahoma Press, 1979)

——— 1984. *Editing Chaucer: The Great Tradition*, ed. Paul G. Ruggiers (Norman, OK: University of Oklahoma Press)

Salter 1980. Elizabeth Salter, 'Chaucer and internationalism', *SAC* 2, 71–9

Saul 1997. Nigel Saul, *Richard II* (New Haven, CT: Yale University Press)

——— 1998. *Richard II and Chivalric Kingship*, Inaugural Lecture at Royal Holloway,

University of London, 24 November 1998 (London: Royal Holloway)

_____ 1999a. 'The kingship of Richard II', in Goodman and Gillespie 1999, 37–58

_____ 1999b. 'Richard II: author of his own downfall', *History Today* 49 (9), 36–41 Sayce 1971. Olive Sayce, 'Chaucer's 'Retractions': The conclusion of the *Canterbury Tales* and its place in literary tradition', *MAE* 40, 229–41

Scattergood 1983. V.J. Scattergood, 'Literary culture at the court of Richard II', in Scattergood and Sherborne 1983, 29–43.

Scattergood and Sherborne 1983. *English Court Culture in the Later Middle Ages*, ed. V.J. Scattergood and J.W. Sherborne (London: Duckworth)

Schlauch 1945. Margaret Schlauch, 'Chaucer's doctrine of kings and tyrants', *Speculum* 20, 133–56

Schmidt 1993. A.V.C. Schmidt, *The Ownership of the Equitorie of the Planetis* (Woodbridge, Suffolk: Boydell & Brewer)

Scott 1997. Kathleen L. Scott, 'An hours and psalter by two Ellesmere illuminators', in Stevens and Woodward 1997, 87–120

Seton-Watson 1924. R.W. Seton-Watson, 'The destruction of sanctuary', in *Tudor Studies Presented … to Albert Frederick Pollard*, ed. R.W. Seton-Watson (London: Longmans, Green)

Smith 1918. J. Challenor Smith, 'A calendar of Lambeth wills', *The Genealogist*, new series 34, 53–126

Somerset 1998. Fiona Somerset, *Clerical Discourse and Lay Audience in Late Medieval England* (Cambridge: CUP)

Spielmann 1900. M.H. Spielmann, *The Portraits of Geoffrey Chaucer*, Chaucer Memorial Lectures (London: Chaucer Society)

Spurgeon 1925. Caroline F.E. Spurgeon, *Five Hundred Years of Chaucer Criticism and Allusion 1357–1900*, 2nd edn, 3 vols (Cambridge: CUP)

Steel 1941. Anthony Steel, *Richard II* (Cambridge: CUP)

Stevens and Woodward 1997. *The Ellesmere Chaucer: Essays in Interpretation*, ed. Martin Stevens and Daniel Woodward (San Marino, CA: Huntington Library)

Stevenson 1996. Kay Gilligan Stevenson, 'Medieval rereading and rewriting: the context of Chaucer's "ABC"', in Bitot 1996, 27–42

Stow 1984. George B. Stow, 'Richard II in Walsingham's Chronicles', *Speculum* 59, 68–102

_____ 1993. 'Richard II in Gower's *Confessio Amantis*: some historical perspectives', *Mediaevalia* 16, 3–29

Strohm 1989. Paul Strohm, *Social Chaucer* (Cambridge, MA: Harvard University Press)

_____ 1992. *Hochon's Arrow: The Social Imagination of Fourteenth–Century Texts* (Princeton, NJ: Princeton University Press)

_____ 1996. *England's Empty Throne: Usurpation and the Language of Legitimation 1399–1422* (New Haven, CT: Yale University Press)

_____ 1999. 'Hoccleve, Lydgate and the Lancastrian court', in Wallace 1999, 640–61

Stubbs 1890. William Stubbs, *The Constitutional History of England in Its Origin and Development*, 3 vols (Oxford: Clarendon Press, 1874–8; 4th edn. 1890)

Stubbs 2000. Estelle Stubbs, 'Observations', in *The Hengwrt Chaucer Digital Facsimile*, CD-ROM, edited by Estelle Stubbs (Scholarly Digital Editions, Leicester)

Szittya 1986. Penn R. Szittya, *The Anti-Fraternal Tradition in Medieval Literature* (Princeton, NJ: Princeton University Press)

Szövérffy 1987. J. Szövérffy, 'Maria und die Heretiker: ein Zisterzienserhymnus zum Albigenser-krieg', *Analecta Cisterciansia* 43, 223–32

Taylor 1999. John Taylor, 'Richard II and the Chronicles', in Goodman and Gillespie 1999, 15–35

Taylor and Childs 1990. *Politics and Crisis in Fourteenth-Century England*, ed. John Taylor and Wendy Childs (Wolfeboro Falls, NH: Sutton)

Taylor 1993. *The Centre and Its Compass: Studies in Medieval Literature in Honor of Professor John Leyerle*, ed. R.A. Taylor (Kalamazoo, MI: Medieval Institute Publications)

Temple-Leader 1889. J. Temple-Leader and Giuseppe Marcotti, *Sir John Hawkwood (L'Acuto): The Story of a Condotierre*, trans. Leader Scott (London: Unwin)

Vaughan 1999. Míceál F. Vaughan, 'Creating comfortable boundaries: scribes, editors and "The invention of the *Parson's Tale*"', in *Rewriting Chaucer: Culture, Authority and the Idea of the Authentic Text, 1400–1602*, ed. Thomas A. Prendergast and Barbara Kline (Columbus, OH: Ohio State University Press, 1999), 45–90

Wallace 1992. David Wallace, 'Chaucer and the absent city', in Hanawalt 1992, 59–90

_____ 1997. *Chaucerian Polity: Absolutist Lineages and Associational Forms in England and Italy* (Palo Alto, CA: Stanford University Press)

_____ 1999. *The Cambridge History of Medieval English Literature*, ed. David Wallace (Cambridge: CUP)

Watson 1995. Nicholas Watson, 'Censorship and cultural change in late medieval England: vernacular theology, the Oxford translation debate and Arundel's constitutions of 1409', *Speculum* 70, 822–64

_____ 1999. 'The politics of Middle English writing', in Wogan-Brown *et al.* 1999, 331–52

Weever 1631. John Weever, *Ancient Funerall Monuments within the vnited Monarchie of Great Britaine, Ireland* [etc.] (London)

Wenzel 1998. Siegfried Wenzel, 'Robert Lychlade's Oxford sermon of 1395', *Traditio* 53, 203–30

Westlake 1923. H.F. Westlake, *Westminster Abbey: The Church, Convent, Cathedral and College of St Peter, Westminster*, 2 vols (London: Allan)

Wilkins 1983. Nigel Wilkins, 'Music and poetry at court: England and France in the late Middle Ages', in Scattergood and Sherborne 1983, 183–204

Wogan-Brown, Watson, Taylor and Evans 1999. *The Idea of the Vernacular: An Anthology of Middle English Literary Theory, 1280–1520*, ed. J. Wogan-Brown, N. Watson, A. Taylor and R. Evans (Exeter: University of Exeter Press)

Woodruff and Danks 1912. *Memorials of the Cathedral and Priory of Christ in Canterbury*, ed. C.E. Woodruff and W. Danks (London: Chapman & Hall)

Workman, H.B. 1926. *John Wyclif*, 2 vols (Oxford: OUP)

Wylie 1884. J.H. Wylie, *History of England under Henry the Fourth*, 4 vols (London: Longman, Green, 1884–98)

Yeager 1984a. R.F. Yeager, 'British Library Additional MS. 5141: an unnoticed Chaucer *Vita*?', *JMRS* 14, 261–81

_____ 1984b. 'Literary theory at the close of the Middle Ages: William Caxton and William Thynne', *SAC* 6, 135–64

_____ 1990. *John Gower's Poetic: The Search for a New Arion*, Publications of the John Gower Society, 2 (Cambridge: D.S. Brewer)

Yeager and Morse 2001. *Speaking Images: Essays in Honor of V.A. Kolve*, ed. R.F. Yeager and Charlotte C. Morse (Asheville, NC: Pegasus Press)

INDEX

PICTURE ACKNOWLEDGEMENTS

The authors and publisher would like to thank the following for their kind permission to reproduce the images in this book.

Picture Research: Emily Hedges

KEY

BL British Library, London
BAL Bridgeman Art Library, London
HL Huntington Library, San Marino, California

Title Page BL (Harl. 4866 f. 88); **9** BL (Roy. 20 b. VI. f. 1v.); **11** Private Collection; **12** BL (Cotton Nero. D. VII. f. 110); **13** BL (Cotton Nero. D. VII. f. 109); **16** BL (Harl. 4380 f. 89 Min.); **17** BL (MS. Roy. 14 E. IV. f. 244v.); **18** BL (Harl. 4425 f. 14v.); **19** The Art Archive/Bodleian Library, Oxford (MS. 264); **20** BAL/Bibliothèque Nationale de France; **22** Private Collection; **23** Ministero Beni e Att. Culturali – Florence, Galleria degli Uffizi © 1990, Photo Scala, Florence; **25** National Portrait Gallery, London; **32** BAL/Musée Condé, Chantilly, France (MS. 65/1284 f. 4v.); **36** BL (Harl. 4380 23vi. Min.); **39** National Portrait Gallery, London; **41** Angelo Hornak Library, London; **46** Mary Evans Picture Library; **47** Leeds Castle, Kent; **49** Bibliothèque Nationale de France (Fr. 2813 f. 3v.); **50** BAL/Duomo, Florence, Italy; **52** BAL/Corpus Christi College, Cambridge; **55** HL (EL 26 C. 9 f. 72r. detail); **58** BL (Roy. 20 C. VII. f. 134v.); **60** BL (Roy. 10 A. XIII. f. 2v.); **62** Private Collection; **63** Corbis/Bob Battersby/Eye Ubiquitous; **64** Terry Jones; **68** BL (Roy. 18 E. I. f. 165v.); **72** BL (Roy. 20 B. VI. f. 2); **79** Terry Jones; **86** Private Collection; **88** BAL/Private Collection; **92** Private Collection; **95** Corbis/Angelo Hornak; **96** BAL/Westminster Abbey, London, UK; **97** © Southwark Cathedral/Andrew Yale; **106** Corbis/Niall MacLeod; **111** BL (Harl. 1319 f. 5 detail); **115** BL (Harl. 4380 f. 141 Min.); **119** BL (Harl. 1319 f. 57); **121** Private Collection; **123** Private Collection; **125** Corbis/Vanni Archive; **129** Michael Holford; **130** BL (Harl. 1319 f. 37v.); **133** BL (Harl. 1319 f. 12); **137** Bibliothèque Nationale de France (Fr. 2646 f. 323v.); **140** Angelo Hornak Library, London; **142** The BAL/Bibliothèque Nationale de France (Fr. 2643 f. 11); **147** The Art Archive/Bodleian Library, Oxford (MS Laud misc. 165 f. 5r.); **149** BAL/Musée Condé, Chantilly, France; (MS. 76/1362 f. 3v.); **157** © Topham/Woodmansterne; **158** BL (Roy. 18 E. II. 416v. Min.); **161** BL (MS Yates-Thompson Codex 36. F. 182 r.); **166** BL (Roy. 13 E. IX. f. 5); **167** Private Collection; **168** Private Collection; **171** © Southwark Cathedral/Andrew Yale; **179** Terry Jones; **185** Bologna, Museo Civico © 1990, Photo, Scala, Florence; **186** HL (EL 26 C. 9 f. 1r.); **188** BAL/British Library, London, UK; **191** HL (EL 26 C. 9 f. 138r. detail); **195** Michael Holford; **201** HL

(EL 26 C 9 f. 81r. detail); **204** HL (EL 26 C 9 f. 76v. detail); **208** BL (Harl. 2799 f. 185v. Min.); **211** BAL/Lauros/Giraudon; **213** Private Collection; **215** Private Collection; **217** HL (EL 26 C 9 f. 88r. detail); **218** Corbis/Chris Andrews; **219** HL (EL 26 C 9 f. 206v. detail); **224** Corbis/John Heseltine; **228** BAL/Corpus Christi College, Cambridge; **230** BL (Harl. 4431 f. 4 Min.); **232** HL (EL 26 C 9 f. 153v. detail); **233** National Library of Wales (Peniarth MS 392D f. 2r.); **234** HL (EL 26 C 9 f. 153v.); **238** HL (EL 26 C 9 f. 50v. detail); **239** © Southwark Cathedral/Andrew Yale; **241** National Library of Wales (Peniarth MS 392D f. 57v.); **244** BL (Toy. 18. D II. f. 148 detail); **246** Terry Jones; **247** HL (EL 26 C 9 f. 10r. detail); **248 top** BL (Roy. C VII. f. 133 Min.); **248 bottom** The Huntington Library, San Marino, California (EL 26 C 9 f. 10 r. microscope detail); **249 top** HL (EL 26 C. 9 f. 10 r. detail); **249 bottom** BAL/Duomo, Florence, Italy; **250** State Archives, Lucca; **251 top and detail below centre** HL (EL 26 C 9 f. 10r. detail); **251 centre and detail bottom** BAL/Duomo, Florence, Italy; **252** HL (EL 26 C. 9 f. 10r. detail); **253** HL (EL 26 C 9 f. 169r. detail); **254** HL (EL 26 C 9 f. 169r. microscope detail); **255** Private Collection; **256** HL (EL 26 C 9 f. 169r.); **258** BL (Harl. 4866 f. 88); **261** Private Collection; **262** National Portrait Gallery, London; **267** BL (Arundel 38 f. 37 Min.); **273** BL (Harl. 4866 f. 88); **275** National Library of Wales (Peniarth MS 392D f. 212v.); **276** HL (EL 26 C 9 f. 153v.); **280** BAL/Lambeth Palace, London, UK (MS. 279 ff. 5v.); **282** BAL/British Library, London, UK; **287** Private Collection (from The Journal of the British Archaeological Association no. 38 [1932]); **288** Bibliothèque Nationale de France (Fr. 2645 f. 238v.); **290** Mary Evans Picture Library; **296** BL (MS. Add. 5141); **299** Private Collection; **303** Private Collection; **305** Corbis/Jason Hawkes; **311** ML Design ; **315** Terry Jones; **322** Corbis/Patrick Ward; **324** BL (MS. Roy. 20 C VII. f. 48 Min.); **329** BL (Add. 34294 f. 199v.); **331** BAL/Roger-Violet, Paris; **332** Private Collection; **333** BAL/Leeds Museums and Galleries (Lotherton Hall) UK; **337** BL (Harl. 1319 f. 12); **338** Sonia Halliday; **340** Bibliothèque Nationale de France; photo: akg-images/ VISOARS; **342** BAL/Archivo di Stato, Siena, Italy; **344** HL (EL 26 C 9 f. 206v. detail); **346** BL (MS. Add. 39843 f. 29); **353** BL (MS. Roy. 10 E IV. f. 187).